INA Dixon   ARTST.
          VNC Spring 208

Knocking on Labor's Door

Justice, Power, and Politics

COEDITORS
Heather Ann Thompson
Rhonda Y. Williams

EDITORIAL ADVISORY BOARD
Peniel E. Joseph
Matthew D. Lassiter
Daryl Maeda
Barbara Ransby
Vicki L. Ruiz
Marc Stein

The Justice, Power, and Politics series publishes new works in history that explore the myriad struggles for justice, battles for power, and shifts in politics that have shaped the United States over time. Through the lenses of justice, power, and politics, the series seeks to broaden scholarly debates about America's past as well as to inform public discussions about its future.

More information on the series, including a complete list of books published, is available at http://justicepowerandpolitics.com/.

Knocking on Labor's Door

Union Organizing in the 1970s and
the Roots of a New Economic Divide

· ·

LANE WINDHAM

The University of North Carolina Press   Chapel Hill

This book was published with the assistance of the Authors Fund of the University of North Carolina Press.

Set in Charis by Westchester Publishing Services

Manufactured in the United States of America

The University of North Carolina Press has been a member
of the Green Press Initiative since 2003.

Library of Congress Cataloging-in-Publication Data
Names: Windham, Lane, author.
Title: Knocking on labor's door : union organizing in the 1970s and the
    roots of a new economic divide / Lane Windham.
Other titles: Justice, power, and politics.
Description: Chapel Hill : University of North Carolina Press, [2017] | Series:
    Justice, power, and politics | Includes bibliographical references and index.
Identifiers: LCCN 2016059292| ISBN 9781469632070 (cloth : alk. paper) |
    ISBN 9781469632087 (ebook)
Subjects: LCSH: Labor unions—United States—History—20th century. |
    Industrial organization—United States—History—20th century. | Labor
    movement—United States—History—20th century. | Labor laws and
    legislation—United States—History—20th century. | Labor—United
    States—History.
Classification: LCC HD8072.5 .W56 2017 | DDC 331.89/12097309047—dc23
    LC record available at https://lccn.loc.gov/2016059292

Jacket illustration: Lillian Lightbourne, a welder and member of Ironworkers
Local #201 working in a fabrication shop in Washington, D.C., in 1979.
Photograph by Martha Tabor, © University of Maryland (courtesy of Martha
Tabor Collection, University of Maryland Libraries, http://hdl.handle.net/
1903.1/35149).

An earlier version of Chapter 4 originally appeared as "Signing Up in the
Shipyard: Organizing Newport News and Reinterpreting the 1970s," *Labor:
Studies in Working-Class History of the Americas* 10, no. 2 (2013): 31–53.

To all who organize for justice

Contents

Figures, Illustrations, and Table

Table

Abbreviations Used in the Text

ACTWU	Amalgamated Clothing and Textile Workers Union
AFA	Association of Flight Attendants
AFL-CIO	American Federation of Labor and Congress of Industrial Organizations
AFSCME	American Federation of State, County, and Municipal Employees
ATMI	American Textile Manufacturers Institute
CBTU	Coalition of Black Trade Unionists
CLUW	Coalition of Labor Union Women
CUAIR	Construction Users Anti-Inflation Roundtable
DRUM	Dodge Revolutionary Union Movement
EEOC	Equal Employment Opportunity Commission
FFACT	Fiber, Fabric, and Apparel Coalition for Trade
GCIU	Graphic Communications International Union
GE	General Electric
GM	General Motors
HERE	Hotel Employees and Restaurant Employees
IAM	International Association of Machinists
IBEW	International Brotherhood of Electrical Workers
ILGWU	International Ladies' Garment Workers' Union
IUE	International Union of Electrical, Radio, and Machine Workers
LLRG	Labor Law Reform Group
MFA	Multi-Fiber Arrangement
NAACP	National Association for the Advancement of Colored People
NAM	National Association of Manufacturers
NEA	National Education Association

NLRA	National Labor Relations Act
NLRB	National Labor Relations Board
OCAW	Oil, Chemical, and Atomic Workers
PSA	Peninsula Shipbuilders Association
RCIA	Retail Clerks International Association
RCIU	Retail Clerks International Union
SEIU	Service Employees International Union
TWUA	Textile Workers Union of America
UAW	United Auto Workers
UFCW	United Food and Commercial Workers
UFW	United Farm Workers
UMW	United Mine Workers
UNITE	Union of Needletrades, Industrial and Textile Employees
USWA	United Steelworkers of America

Knocking on Labor's Door

Introduction

One sweltering July morning in 1976, Jan Hooks, a thirty-one-year old Southern white woman trained as a secretary, crushed a hard hat over her head of unruly curls. The 1970s offered fresh promise for America's working class, and Hooks wanted in. Growing up in the 1950s, she had watched her father leave each morning for his job at the Newport News Shipbuilding and Dry Dock Company in Virginia. Yet she had never really considered that she might follow in his footsteps. By 1973, things had changed. That year the nation's largest private shipbuilder for the navy started recruiting women for production jobs, keeping in step with the federal government's new affirmative action guidelines. Hooks's twin sister, Ann Warren, was among the first women hired. Separated from her husband, Hooks was raising two girls alone, and she knew office work would never pay as much as her sister's blue-collar shipyard job. That's how Hooks soon found herself hauling a toolbox down into the mouth of a nuclear-powered guided-missile cruiser and embarking on her new shipwright career.[1]

Her first assigned task was to clean metal scraps with a three-inch brush in the ship's deep recesses, alongside another woman. "And I was shaking, tired, scared to death. . . . We sat there until I smoked my cigarette and drank a Pepsi and got myself calmed down." Within a few weeks she began training as a crane operator, and held great pride in her eventual rise to a job that allowed her to drive the 150-ton, eight-story-tall giants with a pocket-size remote control.[2]

Yet Hooks did not just want any job when she crawled down into that ship's hold; she wanted a really good job. Though her shipwright position paid better than most jobs available to women, Newport News shipyard workers remained among the lowest-paid shipbuilders in the nation and their pensions were paltry. They began to organize a new union with the United Steelworkers of America (USWA). One crisp and cold January morning in 1978, Hooks served as an official observer for a National Labor Relations Board (NLRB) election at the shipyard involving nineteen thousand workers. Hooks ticked off the welders', riggers', and mechanics' names from her polling station by the number 11 dry dock, offering a friendly nod and

Newport News Shipbuilding workers eagerly await news of their NLRB election results (1978). USWA Collection, Communications Department Records. Reproduced with the permission of the Historical Collections and Labor Archives, Special Collections Library, the Pennsylvania State University Libraries.

a smile to those she recognized. Theirs was the largest single workplace union election ever held in the South, and it would be the largest NLRB election held at a single worksite in the nation in the 1970s.[3]

After the workers had finished casting their ballots, Hooks joined the crowd at the union hall that evening waiting for the results of the vote count. "We walked the floor, we listened to the radio, we prayed, we cried. When we finally got the notice—yes, we had won it—it was like 'Are you telling me the truth?' We couldn't believe it. I mean, not only did we win the election, we beat the heck out of them."[4]

Hooks and her coworkers joined a wave of millions of workers who attempted to organize unions in the private sector during this pivotal decade, including throughout the South. Leading these drives were men of color, women of all backgrounds, and young baby boomers just entering the workforce. Long excluded from the nation's best jobs and many unions, such working people had won new access through the 1964 Civil Rights Act.

They readily combined old working-class tools—like unions and labor la·
with newer legislative victories from the civil and women's rights mo
ments in order to shore up their prospects in a changing economy.[5]

Their experience reminds us that the 1970s were far from the "last days of
the working class," as asserted by one historian.[6] Rather, these were the first
days of a reshaped and newly energized American working class. Women
and people of color had long been members of the working class through
their paid employment, families, and communities; what was new in the
1970s was their entrance into the sorts of well-paid, secure jobs set at the
heart of the nation's economy. Once they got the coveted jobs, they pushed
to unionize. When employers thwarted these organizing attempts, they
blocked workers' access to collective bargaining, a key economic equalizer.[7]

This is not the typical tale that historians spin about the 1970s, a decade
they often paint as one of working-class backlash and defeat. Private-sector
organizing declined in the 1970s, so their oft-told story goes, when bureaucratic unions stopped reaching out to workers and workers turned
away from unions. As evidence, labor scholars often point to union density,
meaning the percentage of the workforce with a union, or to the number of
workers actually winning union elections; both figures turned downward
in these years. Too often, they use declining union membership as a sim-
plistic proxy for measuring working-class motivation and mobilization; this
erases the magnitude and breadth of the organizing efforts that a transformed working class waged in the crucial years of the 1970s.[8]

Yet what if we look at the numbers in a new way that allows us to get at
workers' own hopes and aspirations? Rather than relying on union victory
rates or membership levels, this book focuses on the workers who tried to
form unions, whether they won or not. It looks at the number of workers
who went through the NLRB election process each year, those the NLRB
calls "eligible voters" in representation elections. A closer look reveals that
roughly five million such private-sector workers—or about half a million
each year—lined up to vote in NLRB elections in the 1970s. From this vantage point, we can see that there was no decline in labor organizing in this
decade. In fact, quite the opposite was true. Workers kept voting in union
elections at generally the same pace as during the 1950s and 1960s, the heyday of American labor; when we also factor in the nearly three million
workers who swelled public-sector unions' ranks in the 1970s, then it is clear
that this decade was one of tremendous organizing efforts.[9]

What did decline, however, was workers' ability to win those union
elections. Working people confronted an enormous increase in employer

FIGURE I.1 Eligible voters in NLRB elections (RC) (1949–1999)

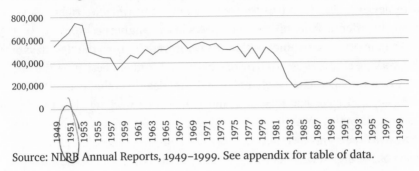

Source: NLRB Annual Reports, 1949–1999. See appendix for table of data.

resistance to union organizing in that decade; from 1970 to 1980, the number of charges of employer unfair labor practices more than doubled, as did the tally of illegal firings. Though workers fought to form unions, increasingly they lost their elections. While workers won roughly 80 percent of the union elections in the 1940s, by the late 1970s they won fewer than half.[10]

Nevertheless, working men and women did not give up. The absolute number of private-sector workers eligible to vote in union elections remained more or less consistent at about half a million a year from the mid-1950s to the early 1980s (figure I.1). Workers kept trying to win unions in the same numbers, despite the massive increase in employer resistance in the 1970s. The proportion of the entire workforce coming to NLRB elections continued a slow slide as the workforce grew, yet the precipitous drop off in organizing efforts did not happen until the early 1980s (figure A.1). To this day, the number of workers voting in union elections has never rebounded to anywhere near the robust level of the 1970s.[11]

Manufacturing workers struggled to form unions in the 1970s, as did bank tellers, hospital workers, university clericals, nurses, flight attendants, wait staff, and athletes. Even security guards who worked for Pinkerton, the notorious strike-breaking firm, successfully won a union in this decade. Though NLRB statistics do not indicate the race or gender of the voters in union elections, I used a host of sources to unearth the complexity of the workforce going to the union voting booth in the 1970s. Polling, oral history interviews, news accounts, union records, and even the papers of corporate, antiunion attorneys reveal that many of the workers who wanted to form unions were young, female, or black—exactly the sort of new workforce that had gained unprecedented access to the nation's better working-class jobs following advances achieved by the civil and women's rights movements. The South plays a key role here; African Americans led many of the region's union organizing efforts after migrating back to Southern states and when entering jobs that had long been closed to them, such as in textiles.[12]

Over the decades since Hooks first entered a ship's hold, working people's economic prospects have dimmed—not only in the United States but also across developed nations. Today many workers face a new economic precariousness, laboring all hours of the day, juggling part-time jobs, and barely scraping by on low wages and paltry benefits. The gap between the wealthy and poor has become a chasm.[13] Though union organizing remained vigorous, the "long 1970s" did indeed prove to be an economic turning point that set the stage for working people's present crisis.[14]

In 1968, labor was still strong, even as global competition began to deepen, and liberal social movements were potent enough to shape the administration of President Richard Nixon. Real incomes had roughly doubled since the 1940s, income inequality was low by historical standards, and employer-provided health care and pensions were common, especially among union members. In 1973, a full 24 percent of workers in the United States were members of a union. Yet America's corporations had recently begun to face their first substantial global competition since before World War II, and their rate of profit growth was slowing. After a global oil crisis and the end of a fixed currency system shocked the economy, a 1975 recession rocked the nation when unemployment and inflation soared.[15]

Yet this was no cyclical crisis. It was the birth of a new economic divide. For decades, wages had risen along with productivity, but starting in the 1970s they were decoupled. Never again would production and nonsupervisory workers take home as large a weekly paycheck in real dollars as they had in 1972. By the early 1980s, working people's share of the nation's total income started to decline; this was something that many economists thought would never happen. When the economy rebounded in the late 1980s and 1990s, those with high incomes prospered, but America's working men and women never fully shared in the recovery.[16]

In part, key structural shifts drove this new economic divide. A global market strung together by innovative technologies compelled workers from all across the world to compete for jobs. Well-paid jobs in America's manufacturing sector lost ground to far worse jobs in retail and service. Finance pushed aside industry as the economy's core. U.S. workers' shrinking access to labor unions, however, also fed the nation's growing inequality because fewer workers benefitted from collective bargaining's equalizing effects. Scholars have clearly demonstrated that unions boost wages, bolster benefits, and even improve long-term outcomes for union members' children. Yet the percentage of private-sector workers in unions fell from about a quarter in 1973 to a mere 14 percent by 1986. By 2016, only a paltry 6.4 percent were union members, a nadir not seen in the United States since 1900. This precipitous decline in union density meant that the American working class had far less power to counter neoliberal policies and to maintain broadly shared prosperity in the face of globalization and other structural changes. After all, in the mid-twentieth century, collective bargaining had lifted the prospects of even workers without a union, as many competing employers matched union wages and benefits. The loss in union density and in workers' bargaining power since 1973 accounts for between one-fifth and one-third of early twenty-first-century economic inequality.[17]

Why did unions decline? Many historians and journalists place the blame squarely on bureaucratic unions, which they portray as inept and complacent, and a working class that they believe lost interest in organized labor. They point to American Federation of Labor and Congress of Industrial Organizations (AFL-CIO) president George Meany's response when a reporter asked him in 1972 why AFL-CIO membership was sinking as a percentage of the workforce: "I don't know. I don't care. . . . Why should we worry about organizing groups of people who do not appear to want to be organized? . . . The organized fellow is the fellow that counts." Yet few have dug underneath this leader's utterly tone-deaf statement to see that the very next year was the historical peak in the number of union elections, and that the entire decade was one of huge contestation around organizing.[18] Labor's pro-war stance on the Vietnam War profoundly disappointed New Left scholars who wrote from a deep-seated suspicion of organized labor.[19] A new generation of intellectuals then asserted that labor had become so bureaucratized and weak by the 1970s that unions were no longer organizing.[20] Even textbooks now perpetuate this myth. "Most unions became agents acting on behalf of their dues paying members on a shrunken field of combat. With but a few exceptions (Teamsters, ILGWU, SEIU), no great organizing drives were undertaken by major national unions or the AFL-CIO itself for decades," claims one such classroom text. This framing undergirds Jefferson Cowie's much-acclaimed *Stayin' Alive*, in which he mistakenly asserts that by the mid-1970s the "record-breaking strikes . . . and vibrant organizing drives that had once promised a new day for workers were reduced to a trickle." In this story, the old institutions of labor hold less relevance and power: the individual rights consciousness that grew out of the civil rights movement proves stronger than the New Deal collectivity that had once built up unions.[21]

documentary

The white, male working class often plays a central role in this narrative of 1970s working-class decline. Vicious riots against school busing seize center stage, as do the highly visible male construction workers who beat up Vietnam War protesters. Union members reportedly resented their own unions and refused to follow their lead. This account of the 1970s working class is not wholly wrong. After all, working people faced quite a shock when the economy transformed so abruptly. They expected growth to continue, and when they collided with the reality of the economic crisis many members of the working class were, in the words of one writer, "mad as hell." This was especially true of some white, working-class men who saw their economic prospects rapidly dimming, and found in racial and gender progress a ready scapegoat.[22]

Yet this focus on a hard-hatted "silent majority" is far too narrow to capture the decade's full working-class promise. The story changes dramatically if we broaden the gaze of labor history beyond the white, blue-collar men who already had unions in the 1970s and include the millions who were outside labor's ranks, seeking to get in. Doing so quickly complicates common narratives for labor's decline and reveals that, in fact, many workers were actively organizing unions throughout the 1970s and that many of these would-be unionists were men and women of color and white women who often combined labor and civil rights law to win economic power. Members of the reformulated working class did more than unionize, of course; they were active in welfare reform groups, prison reform, neighborhood and civic groups, strikes, and union democracy movements. Scholars have long noted that a diverse group of workers swept into public-sector unions in this decade. Yet the private sector remained key; 82 percent of the nation's workers in the mid-1970s were still in the private sector.[23] A focus on the wave of private-sector union organizing allows us to get at the heart of working people's demand for full economic inclusion and reveals the decade's surprising transformative possibilities. Who were these union activists and what happened to their efforts? What did they think they would gain by forming unions? If workers were still actively forming unions in the 1970s, how does that change our understanding of the shaping of late twentieth-century capitalism?

In addressing these questions, *Knocking on Labor's Door* benefits enormously from the work of labor historians who find a conjuncture, rather than a disconnect, between the civil rights, women's rights, and labor movements. They highlight, for instance, the women who used the Civil Rights Act to fight their way into construction jobs, and the white, female flight attendants who filed Equal Employment Opportunity Commission charges about routinely getting fired at age thirty-five. This book sharpens the focus on private-sector NLRB organizing; we will see that auto and shipyard workers, women in department stores and offices, Southern textile operatives, and hospital workers all joined the ranks of those workers who built on ideas from rights movements to exercise collective labor power in the 1970s.[24]

When we shine the historical spotlight on the working people who tried to form unions in the 1970s, it becomes clear that it is not enough to blame lousy labor leaders or an individualistic working-class culture for labor's decline. In fact, employer resistance to organizing was a far more effective culprit, coupled with U.S. policies and laws that encouraged and enabled this employer behavior. But why did employers decide to fight union organizing with such a vengeance in the 1970s? After all, while U.S. employers had never embraced unions, especially in the South, labor and management had found a kind of tenuous balance in the mid-twentieth century that only tilted dramatically back in the employers' direction by the final quarter of the century.[25]

Employers had a huge incentive to resist union organizing because of the particular role collective bargaining played within the U.S. employment-centric social welfare system. This system had solidified after World War II when, even as European governments bolstered their state-based social welfare provisions through universal health care and pension plans, the United States expanded its more privatized system. U.S. law did not require employers to provide these benefits, however. Rather, unions negotiated with employers for much of citizens' social welfare through collective bargaining.[26]

Employers were shocked to face increased global competition in the 1970s and a decreased rate of profit, and saw a very real incentive to get out from under the weight of their social welfare obligations. After all, if workers won a union, employers would most likely be on the hook not only for higher wages but also for better retirement, health benefits, and perhaps even supplemental unemployment compensation. A global economy meant far less bargaining power for workers, and employers pressed their advantage. They squeezed unionized workers and increasingly resisted new unionizing, breaking labor law more frequently by firing and threatening union supporters. They did not stop there, but also hired more temporary workers, contracted out labor, and offshored jobs. Scholars may have missed the potency of the emerging working class, but employers did not. They were keenly aware that America's working class was transforming and mobilizing in a bevy of viable union organizing drives. We will see how employers turned to a new breed of management consultants who rang alarms bells about, and profited from, the activism of America's diversifying working class.[27]

When workers knocked on labor's door, did unions answer? Did union leaders do enough to reach out to the reshaped working class of the 1970s? Their record was mixed. Racism and sexism were still very real in unions in the 1970s, and at times workers had to pry their doors open using civil rights charges. Even as many women and people of color reached out to labor, unions were slow to diversify, and the pace of change at the leadership level was glacial.[28] Yet a broad range of workers signed up to join unions, and unions helped them organize and file for elections. Unions' slow record on diversity should not obscure workers' propensity to organize in these pivotal years. In fact, women and people of color often set the pace for union organizing efforts, encouraging many white men also to sign cards and vote yes, including in the South.

Unearthing the robust level of labor organizing in the 1970s allows us to more clearly see that U.S. working-class activism mirrored that of workers around the world. Unions swelled throughout much of the globe in the 1970s as working people struggled against an incipient neoliberalism; of twenty-three developed nations, eighteen saw their union movements grow. It was a decade of major labor unrest in Latin America, and the shrinkage of manufacturing drove workers into the streets in Italy's "hot autumn" of 1969 and England's "winter of discontent" in 1978–79. These massive strikes bookended a decade of turmoil in Europe. Some experts have pointed to declining union density rates in the United States and have concluded that the nation's working class had become somehow different, more complacent and compliant by the 1970s. Yet a metamorphosed American working class did, in fact, join this worldwide uprising in the 1970s, and NLRB elections were one of their chosen platforms.[29]

The first part of this book offers a national-level study of this union organizing wave. Chapter 1 describes how union organizing developed as the gateway through which workers had to enter before they could fully access the most secure tier of the nation's employer-centered social welfare regime—collective bargaining—and how labor law increasingly narrowed that entryway. In chapter 2, we meet many of the people who led the nation's new unionizing push: the baby boomers, women, African American workers, immigrants, and Southerners. Chapter 3 reveals how mainstream corporations tried to weaken labor law in the late 1960s and then sharply stepped up workplace resistance to union organizing.

Part 2 looks to stories from a variety of industries to show how these forces coalesced at a ground level. Chapter 4 takes us to the Newport News shipyard, where the gains of the civil and women's rights movements clearly fed the union's fire. But perhaps Newport News was an outlier? After all, navy ships by law had to be built in the United States, so these shipyard workers were arguably less affected by a globalizing economy and so perhaps felt free to organize. Chapter 5 explores this question by examining two union elections among workers in another Southern industrial setting—textile production at Cannon Mills in Kannapolis, North Carolina—and puts their organizing efforts in dialogue with trade policy. Yet Newport News and Cannon Mills were both industrial-sector employers, and much of the job market in the 1970s shifted into service and retail. We will see in chapters 6 and 7 that workers actively unionized in these sectors as well. Five thousand retail workers successfully formed a union at Woodward & Lothrop department store in Washington, D.C., and Boston's clerical workers organized for workplace power outside the increasingly fraught collective bargaining system. These stories remind us that while a global economy and the rise of traditionally nonunion sectors were certainly key factors in labor's decline, we should be wary of the idea that capitalism's latest shifts inherently precluded working-class power. After all, no natural law says that retail and service jobs must be bad jobs, that global interconnectedness must mean class disparity, or that broad economic prosperity is doomed to be unattainable today.

"I think more unions, more working people, are going to get together, statewide, nationwide. We know what we want, we want a fair shake," asserted Peggy Carpenter in 1981, not long after she and her coworkers won a union at the Newport News shipyard. Carpenter, of course, was wrong: U.S. workers did not organize at unprecedented levels in the 1980s. This book's conclusion focuses on the period from 1981 to 1985, when unions pulled back from NLRB organizing in the face of recession, continued resistance from employers, and the further weakening of labor law under the Ronald Reagan administration. In 1982 union organizing plummeted. Half as many workers voted in union elections that year as in 1979.[30] To this day, the number of workers voting in NLRB elections has not risen anywhere near that of the 1970s, when millions in a newly transformed workforce picked NLRB elections as their class weapon of choice. Carpenter's hope and optimism, however, remind us that even as President Reagan took office, workers had reason to believe that they could win greater power at the workplace and in government. This study asks readers to dwell in that moment when U.S.

unions were still relatively strong, and when labor's decline seemed far less certain. After all, there were more union members in the United States in 1979, twenty-one million, than at any other point in the nation's history.[31]

Unions today remain an effective economic booster for those who can access them. In 2014, union members earned 15 percent more per hour than did workers without a union, even after controlling for levels of education, occupation, and other factors. The union wage premium was even higher for African American and Hispanic workers. Union members also remain more likely to have good health coverage and defined-benefit pensions. Union members have long enjoyed better wages and benefits; what has changed is that far fewer members of today's diverse working class remain privy to that union advantage.[32]

When we fully appreciate the economic-leveling potential of union organizing efforts in the 1970s, then we see the impacts of employers' resistance and weak labor law as all the more calamitous. America's working people were finally poised to lay claim to an inclusive and broadly shared economic prosperity, one that had been promised by the New Deal but only started to bear fruit by the late 1960s after years of protest by social movements. When workers rushed to exercise their full economic citizenship and form unions, they encountered deep structural barriers, the contours of which are only becoming clear with more historical distance. Employers in the United States had a large incentive to fight unions because unions forced employers to provide citizens with the fullest social welfare benefits the country had to offer. Federal policy continues to embrace this firm-based social welfare model, yet it still has neither strengthened collective bargaining nor created other, newer tools that would force employers to provide the levels of job security, good wages, and guaranteed pensions that workers once won through collective bargaining. Any twenty-first-century attempt to build power for working people will have to confront the fact that when U.S. policy allowed—and even encouraged—employers to narrow workers' access to collective bargaining, it helped weaken the entire social safety net.[33]

When Jan Hooks plunged into the darkened depths of that guided-missile cruiser on her first sweltering morning in the shipyard, she believed that she was seizing a bright economic future. Like millions of other workers, once she got the job from which she had long been excluded, she sought to win higher wages, good benefits, and control over the terms of her work by forming a union. While Hooks won her election, millions of workers could not; it turned out that NLRB elections had become increasingly weak tools

Jan Hooks embraces a coworker after their union victory (1978). USWA Collection, Communications Department Records. Reproduced with the permission of the Historical Collections and Labor Archives, Special Collections Library, the Pennsylvania State University Libraries.

with which to shape one's economic fate. The fact that U.S. labor law was too weak to uphold workers' right to form unions set the terms on which all working people would face a globalizing and deindustrializing economy, and helped lay the foundation for a more precarious and unequal economy by the century's end. We will never know whether the transformed working class's union organizing could have had a greater impact. We cannot say for certain whether a swell in unions' ranks might have tempered U.S. neoliberal policies or tilted the political field in the working class's favor. What is clear is that when America's working people faced a new capitalistic structure in the 1970s, far too few had full access to unions and collective bargaining, and so they faced those fundamental shifts on much weaker footing. What follows is the story of the working women and men who—like Hooks—stood on the threshold of that change and fought to make the nation's new economy work in their favor by knocking on labor's door.

Part I

1 The Dilemma of the Narrow Door

In 1979, Barbara Cash and her coworkers faced a predicament. Cash made her living unpacking boxes for the Woodward & Lothrop department store warehouse in Washington, D.C., expertly tagging clothes as she hung them on rack after rack. A small and powerfully built African American woman, she had followed her cousin into the job at age seventeen and began loading crates for the freight elevators. By 1979 she was a thirty-year-old mother of two. Though Cash had health insurance and a retirement plan through her husband's job, many who worked alongside her were not so fortunate; they could not afford the company's health care and pension plans. Inflation was rampant, and nearly 70 percent of the workers had family incomes below what the federal government determined they needed just to get by. While top management had a carefully calibrated contract, including generous stock options and huge severance packages should they be laid off, Woodward & Lothrop's rank-and-file workers had no such guarantee of economic security.[1]

Though workers had an independent union—the Union of Woodward & Lothrop Employees—it was a weak holdover from a company union whose sole founding purpose had been to dodge the more radical and assertive Congress of Industrial Organizations (CIO) in 1938. "With a union you get a raise every year . . . with the independent union you got whatever they thought you should have, it wasn't no set thing," remembered Cash. She and many of her coworkers took pride in working for the city's renowned department store, but their low wages and benefits signaled that their employer undervalued their work. They knew very well that in America's market-centric society, respect and pay were interlinked. They were ready to make a change. That's why Cash and her 5,300 coworkers began to organize a new union in 1979.[2]

First they collected union cards; Cash signed hers at a big meeting at a New York Avenue hotel. Then they filed for a union election with the U.S. government. They endured a twelve-week contested campaign and then finally won the vote count, which legally obligated Woodward & Lothrop to bargain with them. After four months of contentious negotiations, the workers won an 8 percent annual wage increase, more affordable health care and retirement programs, and protection from arbitrary dismissal.[3] They'd wanted more economic security, and it took organizing a union to get it.

Cash's story illustrates the central role that firm-level collective bargaining played in the U.S. social welfare "regime," the multilayered framework of policies and public and private institutions that a nation uses to manage citizens' social risk. If Cash had been born in another country—in France or Germany, for instance—she would not have had to vote in a union election in order to receive robust medical, retirement, and income maintenance provisions. In fact, most of her social protections would not have been determined by her employer at all. Rather, by virtue of citizenship alone, Cash would have received health care coverage and an ample pension, her wages would have been subjected to higher levels of government intervention, and her nation's laws would have guaranteed her far more job protection. In most European nations, collective bargaining covered far fewer social welfare issues than in the United States, and it was also industry wide, rather than firm by firm. In the United States, however, most citizens in the post–World War II era received social welfare provisions through their individual employers or a family member's employer, a system one scholar labels a "public-private welfare state." The government offered only a thin safety net, much of which also depended on employment, including a minimum wage and Social Security provisions that benefited mainly retirees. So how did the nation ensure that its individual corporations continued to step up and fulfill their social welfare role? The government provided some carrots, like tax breaks for employer-provided health care. It also relied on a big stick: firm-level collective bargaining through labor unions.[4]

Though at first glance collective bargaining—negotiations over wages, benefits, and working conditions—seems to have been a private affair between a labor union and an employer, the government's role was central. Employers did not bargain collectively out of goodwill. They did so because they were required by federal law to negotiate with employees who voted for a union. Collective bargaining, in the mid-twentieth century, enabled unions to set higher wage and benefits standards not only for union members but also for much of the industrial economy, because employers routinely followed the lead of the unionized industrial giants. Collective bargaining thus undergirded the most robust and secure tier of the nation's social welfare regime. "Organized labor wasn't simply a minor bit player in the 'golden age' of welfare capitalism in the United States," notes sociologist Jake Rosenfeld. "It was *the* core equalizing institution." In the United States, unions made sure that rising productivity translated into rising wages and thus did the work of economic redistribution that the state undertook in many European countries in the post–World War II period.[5]

Scholars tend to treat collective bargaining as static and monolithic, but from a worker's perspective it was quite fluid. Workers routinely dropped out of its reach when they or a family member lost a job. Like Barbara Cash, they sometimes swapped a weak union for a strong one. Those who were not union members, meanwhile, had three ways to enter collective bargaining's influence: they could organize a union, get a job in a unionized facility, or get a job with an employer that matched unionized wage and benefit levels. In each case, someone—somewhere, at some point in time—had to organize a union. Union organizing thus held a very specific and heretofore understudied place within the U.S. public-private welfare regime. It was the narrow door through which America's working men and women had to enter before they could benefit from collective bargaining's leavening effects and before they could harness the state's full redistributive power.[6]

How U.S. Workers Won and Lost the Right to Organize a Union

Many private-sector workers in the United States first gained a permanent right to organize unions with the 1935 National Labor Relations Act (NLRA), or Wagner Act. This New Deal legislation grew out of Progressive Era experiments with government support for collective bargaining. Congress mandated that workers had the "full freedom of association" and protected their right to "designation of representatives of their own choosing, for purposes of negotiating the terms and conditions of their employment." Under the Wagner Act, if the government certified that the workers had a union, then the company was obligated to enter into collective bargaining. Not only that, but the act made it the "policy of the United States" to protect this right. The law did not cover everyone equally, however. The NLRA excluded many jobs that women and people of color tended to hold, like housekeeping and farming. The Wagner Act's reach was thus limited from its inception.[7]

In its early years, the law's enforcement agency, the NLRB, required employers to remain neutral on the issue of a union. In the first five years after the Wagner Act's passage, the NLRB even certified workers' unions without an election in about a quarter of cases if workers could prove through a petition, strike list, or show of membership cards that a majority supported the union. The employer was not supposed to weigh in on the election process because, according to the NLRB, an "employer cannot express his opinion in a vacuum. Behind what he says lies the full weight of his economic position, based upon this control over the livelihood of his employees."[8]

Within only a few years the tide would begin to turn in employers' direction. When the NLRB came under fire from conservative members of Congress in 1939, it began to change policy and generally required elections. In 1941 the Supreme Court decided employers could weigh in during those elections as long as they were not "coercive." One management journal fully appreciated the significance of the chance to electioneer, calling it "a bargaining tool par excellence for industry," and lamented that so few employers actually used that tool. Nevertheless, before and during the war, the board's enforcement remained vigorous and employers' resistance remained relatively in check. U.S. workers still routinely could form unions and won more than three-quarters of union elections in the 1940s, though they had less success and ran into more employer resistance in the South. Unionization efforts soared to all-time highs during World War II, when more than a million workers each year voted in union elections. Yet conservative lawmakers and employers never truly gave up, pushing legislation to weaken the NLRB in the 1940 Smith Act, for instance.[9]

The 1947 Taft-Hartley Act was a game changer. A Republican-dominated Congress successfully pushed the legislation through, overriding a presidential veto. Taft-Hartley constituted a major revision to the Wagner Act and dramatically weakened unions on many fronts. Among other provisions, the law made it harder for workers to form unions and enter into collective bargaining. It required an election for certification, unless the company waived that right, and codified employers' right to campaign speech. The act also allowed states to ban the union shop, a provision requiring workers to join the union within thirty days of being hired. Labor had developed union shops as a solution to the free rider problem in which workers could benefit from a contract without supporting the union that negotiated it. The Taft-Hartley Act opened the door to increased employer influence on union elections by reinserting employers squarely into the election process, and so marked a turning point in workers' freedom to organize. Most employers, however, did not make full use of their new prerogatives to resist union organizing until the 1970s, in the face of increasing global competition.[10]

In a fateful twist, at the same historical moment that workers' access to unions became more limited, unions began to matter even more to workers; unions took on a far greater responsibility for negotiating citizens' economic security. During World War II, many unions had begun to accept employer-provided benefits in lieu of wage increases, which were restricted by the National War Labor Board. Yet, after the war, it was not clear whether the country would increase or decrease the government's role in providing citizens' social welfare. Many unions demanded a more robust state presence and pushed for, though failed to pass, universal health coverage in the Wagner-Murray-Dingell Bill, full employment legislation that would guarantee all workers a job, and even legislation that would link wages to prices.[11] Unions shifted tactics as it became clear that their legislative attempts to build a cradle-to-grave social safety net were failing against potent resistance from conservative lawmakers. United Mine Workers (UMW) president John Lewis first demanded a company-funded, union-based health and welfare provision in the 1945–46 round of bargaining, and United Auto Workers (UAW) president Walter Reuther also began to prioritize health care in 1946. Union leaders also turned to negotiating health and retirement plans as a way to incentivize membership after Taft-Hartley allowed many workers to opt out. They hoped that workers would see union-negotiated benefits as a new reason to join up.[12]

Companies and conservative lawmakers resisted unions' efforts to increase their role in negotiating the nation's social welfare. They did not want workers to have a say in employer-provided benefits, arguing that benefits were not issues that should be subject to government-mandated collective bargaining. After all, employers had traditionally only offered health care and retirement policies to a few select managers. They understood that such benefits were the new shop-level battle, and they wanted to drive unions further away from their members. Historian Jennifer Klein describes how employers successfully pushed Taft-Hartley's sponsors to outlaw the kinds of union-run benefit plans with which the movement had been experimenting. Instead, the law only permitted union welfare trust funds if administered jointly with employers, what would become known as "Taft-Hartley" plans. Employers won this class battle at the congressional level with the passage of the Taft-Hartley Act. But then the judicial and executive branches legitimated labor's ability to bargain over health and pension benefits. The 1948 *Inland Steel* NLRB decision opened the door for unions to bargain on health care and retirement plans, and a 1949 Harry S. Truman fact-finding board on a major steel strike ordered the company to bargain on issues of benefits.[13]

The next several years were contentious ones as employers and workers struggled over the developing employer-provided social safety net. Fifty-five percent of the strikes in 1949 and 70 percent in the first half of 1950 were over health and welfare issues.[14] The end result was that collective bargaining became a centerpiece of the nation's social welfare regime. By 1954, three-quarters of union members were covered by a health plan or pension through collective bargaining, up from one-eighth in 1948. At first, these gains were limited to union members, but over the ensuing decades the benefits spread. A mere 16 percent of workers had regular medical coverage in 1950, but nearly 70 percent did twenty-five years later. Only 19 percent of private U.S. workers had a pension plan in 1945. By 1960, that number rose to 40 percent. "Taft-Hartley" plans, meanwhile, developed into collectively bargained, multiemployer health and welfare funds covering millions of workers, especially in the building and construction trades. Unions continued to lift workers' wages, too. By the time Barbara Cash formed her union in 1979, workers with a union earned 16 percent more per hour than those without a union. Workers also used their unions to increase their control over their work lives, building a system of workplace jurisprudence that allowed them to make sure the most senior workers were promoted first, and to legally appeal supervisors' unfair penalties or dismissals.[15]

Collective bargaining impacted even workers without unions as employers in major industries matched unionized gains. Ninety-six percent of manufacturing employers, for instance, reported in 1979 that they set wage rates according to industry-wide surveys, a practice that allowed union-negotiated rates to drive up standards. One business school professor studied twenty-six nonunion companies over thirty years and found that they followed organized companies in setting wages and benefit rates up through the early 1980s.[16]

Not only did collective bargaining set the standards for America's paychecks, but part of its broad economic impact rested on management's fear of union organizing. Companies matched union wages and benefits in order to thwart workers' unionization efforts, a trend that deepened in the 1970s. One management consultant urged all employers to follow "union-free standards" and give workers "competitive wages and benefits equal to (or preferably better than) that of both union and non-union competitors." One 1970 study of employers facing unionization drives revealed that 92 percent changed their employment policies during the time of the campaign, including 52 percent who gave their workers raises and 23 percent who raised benefits. When some workers within a big firm had a union and others did not, many firms adopted the unionized rates in order to contain unions. "You get the same benefits—union or non-union," one General Electric (GE) executive assured a group of workers who were about to vote on whether to form a union in Bangor, Maine, in 1978.[17]

The threat posed by new union organizing even bolstered the power of long-standing collective bargaining relationships. The textile workers' union—in an industry that was only 10 percent unionized in the South— proactively used the specter of Southern unionization to raise textile workers' pay, including in unionized Northern shops. For over twenty years, the union engaged in what it called "Southern wage agitation drives" in which each year it would pick dozens of nonunion plants to target for mass leafleting before going to the bargaining table for unionized workers. "Good things don't just happen," urged one such leaflet, with a tear-off union card at the bottom. Sometimes these leaflets did generate organizing leads, but mostly they were a strategy to force management's hand in collective bargaining, remembered the union's former research director Keir Jorgensen.[18]

Collective bargaining did not lift everyone, however. The U.S. social welfare regime developed as a stratified system, with the highest tier reserved for the white men most likely to hold the unionized, industrial jobs at its core. Men of color and women of all backgrounds had long labored in jobs that not only paid less and offered less security than the sorts of jobs that were more available to white men, but were often not even covered by New Deal social security programs, such as old-age pensions, minimum wage laws, and basic labor law. Southern congressmen held particular power in the shaping of the New Deal; they helped ensure that the 1935 Social Security Act, the 1938 Fair Labor Standards Act, and the NLRA would maintain the region's racial hierarchies. As a result, more than half of the nation's African American workers were effectively excluded from the Wagner Act because they worked in agriculture and domestic service.[19] Yet collective bargaining's limits were not just a matter of law but one of de facto injustice as well. Many employers refused to hire women and people of color for the good industrial jobs most likely to be covered by or influenced by collective bargaining, and many unions supported management in this decision. Though African American workers had long been part of many unions, some unions continued to exclude black workers from their ranks and many had segregated locals in the South.[20]

By the mid-1960s, however, after pressure from the civil rights movement, the most secure tier of the U.S. employer-based welfare regime was finally opening up to people like Cash, an African American woman. Title VII of the Civil Rights Act of 1964 prohibited employment discrimination on the grounds of race, sex, color, religion, or national origin, arguably making it the single biggest challenge to employers' workplace power since the passage of the Wagner Act. The Civil Rights Act resolved some of the New Deal's contradictions and lowered the barriers to workforce entry. These new employment standards would also be available to new immigrants entering the country after the passage of the 1965 Hart-Celler Act, a law that loosened certain restrictions on immigration. The transformation of the New Deal's employment limitations was not complete—domestic service and agricultural jobs were still excluded from the Wagner Act, for example. Yet, by the 1970s, white male privilege at work had been dealt a heavy blow, and the wave of young baby boomers just entering the workforce found a changed landscape. Whole groups of people had permanent opportunities open to them that simply had not been available to their parents, whether that meant young black workers pouring into Southern industry or women building careers. As these groups entered the workforce in new ways, they demanded full access to the coveted, highest-paying jobs and quickly turned to organizing unions. By the late 1970s, they had created a sea change in union membership; nearly one in four black women who worked in the private sector was a union member, as were more than a third of black men. The tide was turning fast, but it turned out that prospects were darkening on the horizon ahead.[21]

Entering through a Narrow Door

Cash got her job at Woodward & Lothrop in 1966, just as the company began hiring more than a few token black workers. Cash was part of a younger, more diverse workforce that was very keen on pushing out the old, company-influenced union and organizing its own new union in order to improve workers' jobs. Yet by the time Cash and her coworkers formed a union with the United Food and Commercial Workers (UFCW) in 1979, they found that union organizing in the United States had become a very onerous process. It would not be enough for a majority of them to sign union cards, as was the case in much of Canada, or to simply declare their interest in a union, as in Sweden. They had no guaranteed legal right to a union in every workplace, as was the case in Germany.[22] Rather, Cash and the Woodward & Lothrop workers would first have to prove to the government that at least 30 percent of them wanted a union—usually by signing union cards. Then they would have to endure what was typically an eight- to twelve-week campaign period in which employers campaigned against the union, routinely pulling employees off their jobs and forcing them to listen to antiunion propaganda. Their employer could even prohibit them from speaking in these meetings. The union, meanwhile, would be barred from entering the workplace. By the time of Cash's union election, 30 percent of employers facing a union campaign fired at least one worker.[23] Yet such employers did not incur large fines or penalties if caught—they simply had to rehire the worker, pay the lost wages, and hang a sign in the break room stating they had broken the law. Only if half of the workers were still willing to vote for a union after this fraught campaign would the NLRB mandate that the employer sit down and negotiate a worksite-specific collective bargaining agreement that would finally provide job security and better wages and benefits. This dysfunctional union election process became the only mechanism by which many U.S. workers like Cash could access their nation's fullest social welfare system.

How had it gotten so difficult to organize a union by the late 1970s? Over the decades after Taft-Hartley's passage, the NLRB fluctuated in how it interpreted organizing law (often depending on which political party held the White House), but the general thrust was that the NLRB steadily ceded its role as referee. Employers then pressed that advantage, starting in the 1970s.[24] Consider, for instance, the issue of whether employers could force their workers to attend company meetings against the union, often known as "captive audience" meetings. The original Wagner Act's neutrality rule barred such meetings and, in fact, the board explicitly prohibited such meetings in 1946. The board reversed position in 1948, citing Taft-Hartley as the reason, and allowed employers to force workers to attend meetings against the union. The Truman NLRB ruled that unions had the right to reply if employers held such meetings in the 1951 *Bonwit Teller* case, but then in 1953 the Dwight D. Eisenhower board stripped unions of that same right in the *Livingston Shirt Corporation* case. A series of decisions in the late 1960s further determined that employers could prohibit workers from discreetly leaving the room during such meetings and at the same time could refuse to let union supporters join the meeting.[25] By the mid-1970s, the end result was that employers could legally cherry-pick the workers who were undecided about the union, force them to attend coercive meetings against the union, and never be required to allow the union equal say. When textile worker Cynthia Hanes spoke up in favor of a union during such a mandatory meeting at Cannon Mills in 1985, the boss threw her out: "I wanted to go to a meeting so when they started telling their lies, I could embarrass them. . . . That's why they didn't want me in there."[26] This was a far cry from the neutrality required by the original Wagner Act. The number of employers requiring such meetings increased by a third in the thirty years between 1968 and the late 1990s, by which time 92 percent of employers held them.[27]

Employers also gained more freedom to threaten to shut down if the workers voted in a union. At first, the NLRB seemed to support workers on this issue; it softened Taft-Hartley's impact soon after its passage in the *General Shoe* decision in 1948, requiring that union elections must take place in "laboratory conditions" free from such coercion. Even if an employer did not expressly violate the law, if it created a coercive atmosphere, the election could be considered invalid. Nevertheless, in the early 1950s the NLRB decided that an employer was within legal bounds when it predicted it would have to close to meet unions' wage demands. The board changed that rule in 1962, deciding that such predictions of company closure were actually threats.[28] In the 1970s the board reversed policy yet again, making such threats legal as long as the company did not threaten to close solely because of the union. By the 1990s, half of all employers facing workers' organizing campaigns threatened to shut down if the workers formed a union.[29]

Organizing a union also became more difficult because, in the 1970s, a new breed of management consultants began to teach employers exactly how to threaten their workers and press their legal advantages. "The employer's greater opportunity to communicate with its employees, the virtually complete access to the minds of the voters during working hours, and the control management could exert over employees gave the employer a considerable advantage over his union counterparts," asserted Alfred DeMaria, one of the most well-known antiunion consultants of the decade.[30] Employers began to break the law far more frequently, and state penalties were scant. Unfair labor practice charges increased sevenfold between 1950 and 1980 to over thirty thousand a year. Though technically unions could commit unfair labor practices too, for example, by making threats, the NLRB found that employers were at fault in 82 percent of the cases with merit. But even when the NLRB faulted the employer for threatening or harassing workers, little came of it. Antiunion consultant Fred R. Long of West Coast Industrial Relations Associates, for instance, was captured on tape in 1976 telling a room of clients, "What happens if you violate the law? The probability is you will never get caught. If you do get caught, the worst thing that can happen to you is you get a second election and the employer wins 96 percent of those second elections."[31]

Organizing was far less fraught in the public sector. When public-sector workers tried to form unions, they were usually successful in doing so, even during the 1970s and 1980s when private-sector workers faced such heavy employer resistance. Public-sector employers rarely fought their efforts with the same vehemence. Federal government workers first won the right to collective bargaining in 1962 when President John F. Kennedy issued Executive Order 10988, covering two million federal workers. State- and city-level public-sector workers won the right to form unions over the course of the 1960s and early 1970s when many states passed new laws allowing public workers to collectively bargain. By 1975, public workers could legally collectively bargain in thirty-six states. Whereas in the mid-1950s virtually no public-sector workers had unions, by the mid-1980s over 40 percent of public-sector workers were covered by a collective bargaining agreement, compared to 14 percent in the private sector. Public-sector union organizing maintained its momentum into the 1970s as an average of four hundred thousand government workers flocked to unions each year, including many women and people of color. Teachers, firefighters, public office workers, and sanitation workers all organized and successfully won the right to enter into the collective bargaining relationship, even as their counterparts in the private sector found their unionization wave broken apart by unchecked employer resistance.[32]

Once employers manipulated weak labor law and made it more difficult for workers to walk through labor's door, unions were hard-pressed to fulfill their obligations as chief negotiators for the nation's social welfare. They sunk increasingly scarce resources into negotiating and servicing the collective bargaining agreements that redistributed the nation's corporate wealth, but too often they found they had to do so at the expense of fresh organizing. Union leaders were thus stymied by the prospect of administering parts of the employer-based welfare regime and simultaneously expanding its limits. "There is a strong tendency, given the many frustrations of organizing and servicing demands for staff time, to slip away from organizing," the AFL-CIO's organizing director Alan Kistler wrote to its president Lane Kirkland in 1980.[33] Union leaders felt the pressures of the competing demands. "Some unions, including our own, have shifted from organizing to bargaining and servicing," said Ken Brown, president of the Graphic Communications International Union (GCIU) in a 1984 top-level AFL-CIO strategy session in which leaders wrestled with how to handle plummeting union membership. "By the very regularity of contract, bargaining is regularly thrust upon us; we have to do that." By the mid-1980s, unions had pulled back on union organizing efforts through the NLRB and were bringing half as many workers to the union voting booth as in the 1970s.[34]

Alan Kistler (center), director of AFL-CIO Department of Organization and Field Services, talks with reporters (1977). *AFL-CIO News*, February 5, 1977. Courtesy of Special Collections and University Archives, University of Maryland Libraries. © 2017 University of Maryland.

In short, the context in which Barbara Cash signed her union card mattered deeply. Even as unions took on an increased role in pushing for citizens' health care, pensions, and economic security after World War II, labor law allowed employers to limit workers' ability to enter unions. Employers in the United States bore an outsize role in social welfare provision, and they had a higher incentive to resist workers' union organizing efforts than did employers in nations where the state provided more social welfare. This was especially the case once they faced increased global competition in the 1970s. Therein lay the crux of Cash's dilemma; in order to attain full social welfare in the U.S. system, she needed a union, but it had become devilishly difficult to organize one. In the end, this contradictory situation shortened the reach of that liberalizing economic and political project scholars have called the "New Deal Order."[35]

Yet, back in the spring of 1979 at the Woodward & Lothrop warehouse on M Street, this downward trajectory was by no means apparent. There, supervisors faced a tidal wave of union support from workers like Cash who understood that if you wanted economic security and social welfare guarantees in the United States, a union contract was still your best bet. The supervisors banned workers from signing union cards on the warehouse floor—something that they were within their legal rights to do. A group of women workers outmaneuvered their male bosses by turning the ladies' restroom into a union safe house where they could sign cards. When they ran out of union cards, they called out to organizers for more through the chicken wire that covered the bathroom windows. The organizers rolled up the cards and shoved them through the chicken wire holes, and the women poked them back out once signed. "They were giggling and laughing, and I know supervisors knew what was happening but there wasn't anything they could do . . . they couldn't very well go busting into the ladies' room," remembered union organizer John Brown. In signing up for the union, Cash and her coworkers energetically joined the ranks of millions of workers in this decade who made a full claim to their nation's particular form of economic security. It is their story to which we now turn.[36]

2 Millions Go Knocking

. . . .

Henry Davison left his hometown of Monroe, Louisiana, in 1965 because, as a young black man, "I couldn't find a job. . . . People in Monroe wanted to pay you two dollars an hour, but when you'd go out to buy a car it would cost the same as up North." Davison found work in Chicago at a Ford assembly plant and only returned home to Monroe in the mid-1970s to raise his family. He landed a job at General Motors' (GM) new Guide Lamp plant in 1976, at a wage that was still lower than that of workers up north: "It began to gnaw on me some—a few of us began to talk about how it wasn't right that we were being discriminated against."[1]

In late 1976 Davison and his coworkers began to organize with the UAW and voted 323–280 in favor of the union. When they negotiated their first union contract in 1977, they won far more economic and social welfare security, such as pay raises up to eighty-six dollars a week and the same vision and dental plans enjoyed by GM workers who had long had a UAW contract. "I walked into that plant today and felt like my job was secure for the first time since I started working for GM," said Davison the day he first clocked in under the new agreement.[2]

Historians have overlooked people like Davison. Their history of 1970s decline leaves little place for a black man who returned to the South and successfully unionized his auto plant.[3] Yet Davison was far from alone in his desire to form a union, improve his job, and elevate his family's economic standing; he was part of the unheralded wave of nearly five million private-sector workers who voted in NLRB elections and pushed to form unions in the 1970s. Working men and women passed out union cards in the nations' factories, stores, restaurants, and hotels. Flight attendants rallied to demand unions, secretaries wrote manifestos, professional football players voted for a union, and hospital workers embraced with gusto their new legal right to organize. Employees of the Midwest Stock Exchange unionized, as did bicycle couriers and bank employees in Washington, D.C. Auto workers at Volkswagen in Westmoreland, Pennsylvania, the nation's first foreign car assembly transplant, went union in 1978. When 450 mostly young employees of the Yosemite Park and Curry Company said they wanted a union in 1976, NLRB agents rode on horseback to their remote camps with

Henry Davison with his wife, Ernistine Davison, and their four children. *Solidarity*, 1977. © United Auto Workers.

collapsible ballot boxes strapped to the horses' sides. The workers voted in a union two to one.[4]

Who were these workers who tried so hard to organize unions in the 1970s, and what did they want? Many were part of a transformed and newly diversified working class. Men of color and women of all backgrounds gained new access to positions in the U.S. workforce by the 1970s, benefiting from the new laws and workplace expectations won by the civil and women's rights movements. Members of these groups had long been an integral part of the working class through their families and communities, even when they were not wage earners.[5] Yet in the 1970s millions of women entered the paid workforce for the first time, and people of color had new means to reach the sorts of jobs at the nation's economic core from which they had been excluded. Immigrant workers, especially in urban areas like Los Angeles and New York, also found new entry to the job market after the Immigration and Nationality Act of 1965 changed the nation's course on immigration. As these workers stepped into their newly won jobs, they fought to make these good jobs even better, seeking unions to elevate pay, improve working conditions, and win greater levels of respect. Many were Sunbelt workers whose unionizing efforts increased dramatically in the 1970s. These Southern efforts were buoyed by workers like Davison who were among the two million African Americans who began a reverse migration to the Southern states after 1970; many carried with them union experience gained up north. Many of these unionizing activists were young baby boomers who had come of age in a period of protest, and they were ready to push for their rights. They assumed the U.S. economy would continue to grow and prosper as it had for decades; they wanted to share in the economic feast. Thus, when recession and economic turmoil seemed to threaten their path to economic security, they used new understandings about their rights to take on their employers in numerous venues, including collectively through union organizing campaigns.[6]

Private-sector union organizing efforts were not the only battlefield for a reconfigured working class. Strikes, campaigns for union democracy, and public-sector union organizing were also key. The strike wave of the early 1970s was unlike any the nation had seen since 1946. In 1970 alone, one in six of the nation's union members went on strike, such as in the huge illegal walkout among 150,000 postal workers that included many people of color.[7] Though there were fewer strikes by the end of the 1970s than at the high-water mark ten years earlier, workers kept walking out in impressive numbers right up until the decade's close. Miners struck for 110 days in late 1977 and early 1978, forcing President Jimmy Carter to invoke the Taft-Hartley Act to get them back to work. There were eleven strikes in 1979 that involved ten thousand workers or more, including over two hundred thousand truckers represented by the Teamsters, thirty-four thousand UAW-members at International Harvester, and forty-seven thousand workers at United Airlines. Seventy-five thousand independent-owner truckers parked their rigs when they struck that summer, leaving vegetables to rot across the nation. A comparison to later years puts the breadth of even the late-1970s strike activity into sharp relief. In 1979, workers in large workplaces idled the nation for more than 20,000 manpower days, a number that would plummet to a mere 7,000 by 1985 and to a paltry 740 by 2015.[8]

The late 1960s and 1970s also witnessed huge movements aimed at making unions more democratic and inclusive. Young rank-and-file members pushed the boundaries of their unions' bureaucracies. Union members in the Teamsters, the UMW, and the UAW all formed internal democracy organizations and women banded together to form the Coalition of Labor Union Women (CLUW). Black trade unionists disillusioned with the union movement's slow progress on racial inclusion formed a range of groups from the Coalition of Black Trade Unionists (CBTU) to the Dodge Revolutionary Union Movement (DRUM). Ed Sadlowski made a failed bid for the presidency of the steelworkers' union, running on a platform of more militancy and racial diversity through the Steelworkers Fight Back organization.[9]

Organizing in the public sector soared in the 1970s, driven especially by the women and people of color who were increasingly likely to hold the nation's teaching, sanitation, hospital, and government office jobs. Union membership among public workers first took off in the 1960s after these workers won the right to form unions, and these gains continued in full force throughout the 1970s. Public-sector union membership grew by more than 2.7 million between 1973 and 1979, reaching nearly 6 million by the close of the decade. The American Federation of State, County, and Municipal Employees (AFSCME) alone topped a million workers by 1984, and over a third of that membership growth happened after 1973. Public school teachers were particularly interested in forming unions; over the 1970s, the National Education Association (NEA) grew by nearly one hundred thousand members a year.[10]

The same energy that pulsed through these strikes, internal union reform efforts, and public-sector organizing flowed through unionizing efforts in the private sector. The AFL-CIO's organizing department urged its leadership to build on this momentum, arguing in 1971 that after the "civil rights revolution of the 60's . . . blacks and Mexican Americans . . . see the relationship of progress toward first-class citizenship to their organizational activity with respect to job rights and economic progress." The civil and women's rights movements had changed the way working-class people, including some white men, understood their relationship to their employers. If the long-standing mores surrounding race and gender at work could crumble, then why should working people put up with disrespect, low pay, and shoddy benefits on the job? The new rights consciousness from these movements fed the union fires and inspired millions of private-sector workers to try to organize for increased labor rights on the job.[11]

Young Baby Boomers and Unions

By 1976 nearly half the nation's workforce was under the age of thirty-five. Scholars and journalists often portray baby boomers as individualistic and disillusioned in the 1970s, and far less likely than their parents or grandparents to turn to the collectivity of unions.[12] Yet polling shows that young workers were, in fact, more open to unions than were older workers. Forty-five percent of blue-collar workers under twenty-five said they would vote yes in a union election, nearly double the 28 percent of over-fifty-fives who would vote yes, according to a study funded by the Department of Labor in 1977. Gallup polling showed that a higher percentage of people under thirty approved of unions than did the general public in 1981.[13] Local surveys of working people facing unionization drives confirm that young people were the most interested in organizing. Workers under the age of thirty-five at the Woodward & Lothrop department store, for example, were nearly twice as likely as were older workers to support a union.[14]

Young workers' interest in organizing unions was part of their wider discontent and new sense of rights, both at work and in society at large. That dissatisfaction drove the well-publicized 1972 strike among young insurgents at the Chevy Vega plant in Lordstown, Ohio, a cross-race rebellion in which workers sought to seize back control over their lives on the production line. Yet young workers also pushed the boundaries in ways that did not make headlines, such as by calling in sick, quitting, and doing poor work. At one Ford plant, the quit rate hit 25 percent in 1972. New expectations about their rights shaped this younger generation's work experience. Alton Glass, for instance, followed his father into the Newport News shipyard. His father was the son of sharecroppers and spent most of his life in the segregated South. As a young black man of the 1970s, Glass felt more free than did his father to engage in activism and to take on racism in the yard: "Where my Dad would tell me to shut up . . . I wouldn't shut up. And my supervisors, who were older and white, would expect me to shut up. And I wouldn't." Glass later went on to serve as president of his local union.[15]

Boomers' experiences with the Vietnam War shaped their union organizing. A number of middle-class, antiwar activists from the New Left developed into labor activists, often getting manufacturing jobs with the intent of organizing them, or serving as union organizers among health care and clerical workers.[16] Meanwhile, Vietnam veterans often led unionizing efforts when they returned to the workforce. Upon returning from Vietnam, Jacob Little helped organize a union at the Eagle and Phenix mill in Columbus, Georgia, in 1979. As a young black man who had grown up in the segregated South, he built his unionizing efforts on the confidence he gained from supervising white soldiers. "The employer has to realize that he owns the plant, but he doesn't own the employees," asserted Bernard Mings, a Vietnam veteran fired for trying to form a union at Ingersoll-Rand in Campbellsville, Kentucky, in 1976.[17]

Employers were well aware that their young workforces were pushing back with a new intensity, and they worried about the impact of young workers' newfound freedoms. "They want—and, indeed demand—relevant and significant jobs from the beginning of their career. If such jobs are not assigned to them they are very inclined to leave the company and look elsewhere," complained one executive of Union Carbide Corporation. In a book entitled *Maintaining Nonunion Status*, antiunion consultants warned that employers must deal with young workers' changing attitudes in order to combat unions. "Those of you who deal with younger workers often hear: 'This job is boring. This job is dull. Why do we have to do this?'" The consultants urged employers to open up paths to job advancement in order to avoid unions.[18]

An influx of young black workers sometimes tipped the scales toward the union as these workers organized at new levels, especially in the South. Consider the case of Marion Crawford and Monroe Auto Equipment Company in Hartwell, Georgia, an auto parts transplant from Michigan. Crawford remembered that while he was in high school, this company's nearly all-white workforce hung Walter Reuther in effigy, beat union organizers, and held a mock funeral for the UAW after voting it down.[19] Their mock grave marker read,

Less [sic] we forget, Here Lies UAW,
Born in Greed, Died in Defeat,
July 23, 1964.[20]

Crawford applied for a job at Monroe Auto Equipment after his high school graduation, but management told him they only hired black workers as janitors, and they did not need any janitors. Instead, Crawford entered the army and served in Korea.[21]

The passage of the 1964 Civil Rights Act would shake up Southern workplaces like Monroe Auto Equipment and force employers to diversify their workforces. The company began to hire black workers for a variety of positions in 1966, and later that year a cross-race coalition of union supporters narrowly prevailed in a second election. They did so despite the fact that the company hired as its consultant John Tate, the man who pioneered a new breed of union busters and who would later serve as the architect of Wal-Mart's antiunion citadel.[22]

By the time Crawford returned from the army and landed a job at Monroe Auto Equipment in January 1968, the company was refusing to negotiate with the workers who won their union in 1966, and the company and union were deep in the midst of what turned out to be a fifteen-year battle. Crawford remembered that the company's new hires, many of whom were young and black, were key to the union's continued support: "Most of the younger people just wanted to have a fair shot. . . . Young people were shifted around, moved around, got all the dirty jobs . . . and young people were interested in benefits." Though African American workers were a minority in the plant, they were a majority of the union supporters. Like Crawford, most grew up in the South and had no direct experience with unions, but many of them learned about the benefits of union contracts from relatives who had moved north, in part to escape the South's racially unjust workplaces.[23]

In 1973, the workers still did not have a union contract. The NLRB ordered the company to bargain, but sixteen months later the workers still could not get the company to move on issues as simple as a grievance procedure. "We strongly urge you to continue this fight," Crawford and two other leaders wrote to UAW vice president Irving Bluestone in 1975. "To lose now would set back [the] labor movement in the small towns of the South for many years."[24] Meanwhile, a former Piggy Wiggly grocery store consultant showed up in Crawford's town of Hartwell and suddenly began a campaign for an "independent" union, the kind of tactic typically masterminded by Tate. The independent union gathered enough cards to trigger an election in 1976, and the company beat both unions.[25]

Yet Crawford and his coworkers didn't give up. The UAW successfully persuaded the NLRB to overturn that election, arguing that it should not count after the company broke labor law. When a conglomerate bought the plant, the new owners finally agreed to negotiate a contract in 1978. The workers won free health insurance, better pay, and a grievance procedure, which Crawford, by then a thirty-three-year-old electrician, called the "top accomplishment." Young workers like Sammy Lewis, a white, twenty-nine-year-old toolmaker, helped buoy the win: "One man, he ain't got a chance: it takes sticking together." Yet as soon as the first contract was up in 1981, an independent union again triggered an election and the company won. "They had their representatives campaigning against the union. . . . They told people the company would shut down if the union remained," remembered Crawford. Though the workers had lost their UAW union, the benefits of the single, three-year contract continued to influence company policy for years to come, especially around such issues as health insurance and job safety. Crawford worked there for forty-two years, and retired in 2010 as an electrical engineering technician. Yet he never again had a chance to be a union member.[26]

I Should Be Screaming It from the Rafters

Women powered the new wave of unionization attempts. Their rate of work-force participation jumped nearly 9 percentage points in the 1970s and grew nearly twice as fast as over the previous two decades. The year 1978 marked the first time that a majority of U.S. women worked for wages. A whopping twelve million more women were in the labor force by the end of the decade than at its beginning, and increasingly they were mothers of small children.[27] For many women, holding a job was a necessity given the economic downturns of the 1970s; when families hit hard economic times, they reacted by sending women into the workplace. This was a new situation for many white females but a very familiar one for black women, whose workforce participation had long outstripped that of white women.[28]

As women entered the workforce, many brought with them new ideas about their rights. After all, the feminist movement was in full swing by the early 1970s and had an immediate and potent impact on women's economic lives. No longer could employers place want ads for separate men's and women's jobs; the Supreme Court outlawed such ads in 1973. Long denied credit in their own names, women won an equal right to credit cards and mortgages with the Equal Credit Opportunity Act in 1974.[29] The rising sense of hope and possibility fed women's efforts to build new unions and other workplace-based organizations. According to Karen Nussbaum, a founder of the women office workers' group 9to5, "In the early 1970s . . . an insurgent consciousness propelled a wide cross section of women to reconsider their role in life, be open to collective action, and challenge their employers. They believed change was possible."[30]

Women were, in fact, more open to unions than men. In 1977 polling, 46 percent of blue-collar women told pollsters they would join a union tomorrow if given the chance, compared to only 35 percent of blue-collar men.[31] One AFL-CIO survey on NLRB elections showed that when women made up less than half the workforce, the election win rate was 33 percent, but in units of at least three-quarters women, the win rate jumped to 57 percent.[32] In all, nearly three million women joined unions' ranks between 1960 and 1980, a figure that includes newly organized workers and women hired into already unionized workplaces. The influx of organizing women helped equalize unions' gender balance. In 1960, only 18 percent of all union members were women; that figure jumped to 34 percent by 1984.[33]

Two-thirds of the women pouring into the private-sector workforce in the 1970s worked in the service, retail, and financial sectors—jobs in which unions had made few inroads. More than seven million women worked in retail, for instance, and three million in the finance, insurance, and real estate sector. Though the term "finance" invokes images of men in suits on Wall Street, in fact this industry was 58 percent female by 1979 and included the women working in banks and insurance companies. Banking alone was 70 percent female. A full ten million women worked in the service sector by 1979. The number employed in health services, such as nursing facilities and hospitals, soared by 1.6 million over the decade. Over 1.2 million women worked in "business services," a sector that included the "temporary help" and "employment agencies" that burgeoned in this decade. Temp industry employment doubled over the course of the 1970s, including in jobs far afield from the office typewriter.[34]

Union membership in banks, retail, and the service sector had long lagged behind that in manufacturing, but working people in these sectors were increasingly turning to unions. Though the NLRB does not break out voters by gender, we can cross-reference the industries in which women's employment was growing with those where workers were triggering union elections. A quarter of NLRB voters in the 1970s worked in the service, retail, or financial sectors, nearly double the percentage of the late 1960s, as shown in figure 2.1. In the service sector alone, the number of workers coming to union elections in 1980 was six times greater than the number in 1965. Organizing efforts in these female-intensive sectors were clearly growing.[35]

Clerical workers were the locus of energy for the women's unionization movement of the 1970s in the way that garment workers had been at the turn of the twentieth century.[36] More women worked as secretaries, as bookkeepers, and in other sorts of clerical jobs than in any other job category. While women had long worked as office workers, they were now more likely to see their place in the workforce as a permanent one and to be the sole supporters for their families. Many women who worked as secretaries sought to redefine their jobs as professional and essential, defying the stereotype of office wives who got the coffee and pampered their male bosses. They led the way not only in forming unions but also by founding more than a dozen workplace-based and women-centered organizations for secretaries in the 1970s. Such women workers and activists founded Women Employed, for instance, in 1973 as an organization to represent nonmanagerial women office workers in Chicago. Women Employed used public hearings and worksite confrontations to win major back pay suits and force employers to develop comprehensive affirmative action plans. A similar group for office workers formed in New York City in 1974 under the banner of Women

FIGURE 2.1 NLRB eligible voters by sector (1965–1985)

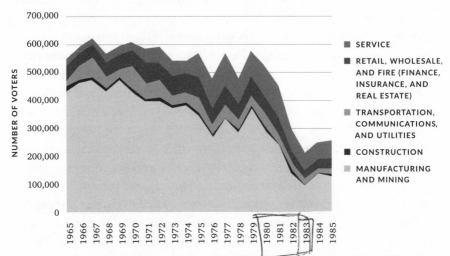

Source: NLRB Annual Reports, 1965–1985, table 16. Eligible voters in RC, RM, and RD elections.

Office Workers. In Boston, clerical workers created 9to5 in 1973. They sought out the national union that would give them the most autonomy and in 1975 created Local 925 of the Service Employees International Union (SEIU) as a companion organization. This later grew into SEIU District 925, a union devoted to organizing office workers nationwide.[37]

Not all secretaries rode the women's movement's momentum. "We do not feel we're subservient or put down," asserted Margaret Dillon, president of the National Secretaries Association—a group that argued for secretaries to maintain their separate female sphere within the business world.[38] Yet many who drove the decade's unionization wave shared the attitude of one clerical at Boston University: "I work my tail off, I produce work for all kinds of professors," Barbara Rahke remembered. "I am getting paid nothing, and . . . I should be screaming it from the rafters."[39]

In fact, such private universities became hotbeds for clerical unionizing in the 1970s after the NLRB folded colleges into its jurisdiction in 1970. By the end of the 1980s, some 70 percent of these campaigns resulted in union representation. Many women who staffed offices in higher education were no longer satisfied with the slight elevation in prestige that came with their jobs. Clerical workers at Columbia, Boston University, Brandeis, the University of Chicago, the University of Southern California, New York University, Seton Hall, and Vassar were among those who initiated successful unionization drives at private-sector universities in the 1970s. Office staff at other universities, such as Tufts and Howard, found their efforts defeated by employer resistance from these esteemed universities.[40] A "union can guarantee *absolutely nothing* . . . employees could end up with less than they have presently," asserted Virginia Tierney, Boston University director of personnel, in 1978 as part of a rather typical university antiunion effort that emphasized strikes and dues. Yale hired the notorious union buster Seyfarth, Shaw, Fairweather and Geraldson to try to stop its clerical workers from unionizing in the early 1980s, the same firm that fought the Newport News shipyard workers. Nevertheless, university office workers found a greater level of success than did many corporate clerical workers, in part because they had the support of some faculty and staff unions, and because they were able to leverage community outrage to soften the administrations' stances.[41]

Bank workers' experiences were more typical of what happened when private-sector office workers tried to unionize. "We got smashed over and over," Karen Nussbaum recalled of SEIU District 925's efforts to organize in banks and insurance. "These businesses had not traditionally been unionized, and they were damned if they were going to be the first ones in the new wave. We never had an easy election."[42] Over a million women worked in banks by the late 1970s, and many turned to unions to increase exceptionally low wages; one Department of Labor study in Chicago found women's wages in banks were 59 percent of those of men. Women who worked in banks also hoped to gain some control as increased automation degraded their labor.[43]

The most well-known group of would-be unionists formed the Willmar Bank Employees Association in 1977 and went on a fifteen-month unsuccessful strike to win union recognition. The women took a stand against low wages and protested promotions that favored men with less seniority. These bank tellers were featured in the documentary *The Willmar 8*, produced by Mary Beth Yarrow, who was herself from Willmar, Minnesota. They even garnered a *60 Minutes* feature.[44]

Yet this high-profile effort was only part of a larger push for unions among women bank workers nationwide. This endeavor involved at least six different unions, and turned out to be a Sisyphean task as the banks rolled back nearly all their efforts.[45] Workers at Seattle First National Bank, for instance, won their first collective bargaining agreement in 1968 after having had a small, independent labor organization for thirty years. When the 4,700 workers could not force the company to sign another contract in 1978, they interviewed a range of unions, and then affiliated with the Retail Clerks International Union (RCIU). Yet even an AFL-CIO national boycott could not force the company (then called Seafirst) to sign a contract, a struggle that became even more difficult when the bank merged into the Bank of America in 1982. Though the union continued to push into the 1990s, the tellers never got another contract. The tellers who unionized with the UFCW Local 876 at Wyandotte Savings Bank in Michigan in 1979 likewise failed to bring home a contract. The First National State Bank of New Jersey managed to repel a unionization attempt in 1977 by using the NLRB to force the workers to organize at all twenty-one branches at once. Bank workers, such as the six hundred workers at National Bank of Washington, D.C., and those at a few banks in Chicago, won some victories but by 1980 only thirty banks out of fifteen thousand were unionized.[46]

Bank executives largely succeeded in rebuffing these efforts, but even so they were spooked by women workers' unionization attempts. They flocked to antiunion seminars, for instance, and crowded to get a glimpse of the opposition at a screening of *The Willmar 8* at the American Bankers Association annual meeting.[47] Women bank workers met greater success when they organized outside the increasingly weakened and vulnerable NLRB process. The 9to5 association in Boston was able to get the Department of the Treasury's help in opening up job opportunities at the New England Merchants Bank, for example, as well as get two other local banks to sign affirmative action agreements.[48]

Flight attendants, 95 percent of whom were women, also built unions, fighting to turn what were widely seen as temporary jobs for young, unmarried women into permanent, secure positions. They wrested their union out from under the pilots' union in 1974 to form the Association of Flight Attendants (AFA). Marching with signs reading "Storks Fly, Why Can't Mothers?," they demanded an end to company policies that barred pregnant flight attendants. They used picketing, Equal Employment Opportunity Commission (EEOC) charges, and union contracts to beat back company weight requirements for attendants. Mass protests followed when Ozark Airlines, for instance, suspended a five-foot-eight-inch-tall woman for being 4 pounds over the maximum weight of 137 pounds. Beyond their push for job security, they also fought for respect. When the airlines escalated their use of stewardess' sexuality in order to sell seats—such as in Continental's ad campaign "We Really Move Our Tails for You"—the brand-new union objected. Under their own headline, "Move your tails for somebody else," the women complained to the company, the Civil Aeronautics Board, the EEOC, and the public.[49] Flight attendants' interest in unions was so strong that they continued to organize and vote in union elections throughout the 1970s, despite the fact that all major carriers except Delta were already unionized. Many flight attendants still viewed the AFA as under the pilots' union's thumb, and flight attendants at National, Northwest, and Continental, for instance, all voted to join new unions. They also organized outside unions' ranks, such as in the Stewardesses for Women's Rights association.[50]

Despite many women's burning interest in unions, labor was inconsistent at best in its efforts to reach them. On one hand, as early as 1971, the AFL-CIO's organizing department reported to its top leadership body, the Executive Council, that women were interested in unions and though "untouched by the phenomenon of collective bargaining for many years suddenly felt the press of economic stagnation and decided that it was 'their turn.' "[51] Yet some leaders were slow to change their views on women workers, and unions included women at the staff and leadership levels at a snail's pace. Up until months before his death in early 1980, AFL-CIO president George Meany remained unsure about women's interest in unions: "Many women, forced into the job market by the pressures of inflation, are grateful to be working at all. Thus, there is initial resistance to a union."[52] Unions dragged their feet on hiring women as organizers. As late as 1986, only 9 percent of organizers were female according to an AFL-CIO survey, though their win rate was 61 percent compared to 41 percent for male organizers. In 1983, the UAW had only one woman working as a full-time organizer in the entire South.[53] Jackie Ruff got fired when she tried to organize the newspaper where she worked in 1974. She asked the graphic arts union for a job, and the male staffer told her, "Oh no, we would never have women organizing the union." Not to be deterred, she later served as executive director of the SEIU District 925.[54]

The women who wanted to unionize in the 1970s were joining organizations in which women members themselves were struggling with deep-seated sexism. After the passage of the 1964 Civil Rights Act, 2,500 women filed gender discrimination charges with the EEOC in the first year alone, and hundreds of them named their unions as defendants. International Union of Electrical, Radio, and Machine Workers (IUE) lawyer Winn Newman told the EEOC that women members faced substantial harassment from male members when they tried to win equal access to jobs, including "slashing the tires of women, gun shots in their homes." Newman helped the women in his union root out gender discrimination by using their contracts as tools to force employers to end sexist practices and, when that did not work, filing union-led charges with the EEOC.[55] When women unionists founded CLUW in 1974, it was the nation's first cross-union coalition for women. CLUW successfully pushed the AFL-CIO to support the Equal Rights Amendment, and included childcare facilities and expanded maternity leave as some of its first goals. The women's movement had hit home for labor. "As long as the organizing of women was external to the labor movement, those guys didn't care," remembered Judith Berek, a union organizer who attended the founding convention of CLUW. "Once it became internal, they had to care."[56]

Women continued to knock on labor's door, and unions increasingly responded by making them the focus of organizing efforts. For instance, an AFL-CIO survey of California union elections in the mid-1960s reveals that only a quarter of the voters in fifteen recent elections were female. By the early 1980s, 69 percent of the NLRB elections in a survey of 225 elections involved units with a majority of women, and 32 percent involved units that were more than 85 percent female. Nurses, waitresses, bank tellers, legal secretaries, textile workers, and cashiers were all among the millions of women who voted in NLRB elections in this decade.[57]

African Americans Led the Way

Black women and men often led the decade's organizing drives, regularly inspiring other workers to join them. African American workers were the most likely group to turn to union organizing in the 1970s, in both the public and the private sectors. A full 70 percent of blue-collar people of color in 1977 polling said they would vote for a union.[58] One AFL-CIO study shows that they did just that. At workplaces where at least three-quarters of the workers were people of color, the NLRB election win rate was 65 percent, compared to a win rate of a mere 38 percent among workforces where minority workers made up less than a quarter.[59]

It had not always been apparent that African American workers would be the nation's staunchest union supporters. In 1935, a tiny fraction of African Americans were union members. Yet African Americans became increasingly likely to hold jobs eligible for unionization—those outside agriculture and domestic service—following World War II. They nearly doubled their numbers in industrial jobs during the war, and a half a million joined CIO unions during World War II. By 1960, a fifth of workers in the auto industry, for example, were African American. Following the Civil Rights Act, black workers rapidly organized new unions and found increasing success in securing already-unionized jobs.[60]

Black workers' new unionizing wave transformed the labor movement. By 1971, one out of every three new union members was black.[61] Black workers' union membership rates rapidly rose above those of white workers in the private sector. In 1973, a full 44 percent of black men in the private sector were union members. Black women's rate of union membership peaked in 1979 when nearly one in four in the private sector was a member of a union; by the decade's close, black women's unionization rate outstripped that of white women by two to one. Though black workers' union density slid in later years alongside overall union membership, black workers today remain the most likely group to be private-sector union members.[62]

Yet, in order to organize in the 1970s, black workers first had to force many unions to open their doors. Some unions had long excluded black workers from their ranks, and many of even the most progressive CIO unions had segregated locals in the South into the 1940s and 1950s. Herbert Hill, the NAACP's labor director, found that as late as 1958 three national unions had constitutional provisions barring African Americans, while ten others had segregated locals. Even when national unions tried to force change, white union members at the local and state levels often resisted racial equality within their unions.[63]

The Civil Rights Act finally outlawed such racial discrimination. Black workers used the EEOC as a tool to force open unions throughout the 1970s, and the number of Title VII lawsuits against unions rose dramatically. AFL-CIO records show, for instance, that 1,600 charges of discrimination were filed against unions in 1973, and, by 1978, the EEOC still had a couple thousand such cases open. The number of cases decided against unions rose 20 percent between 1977 and 1980.[64] Even as union membership became more diverse, union leaders and staff were often reluctant to accept black members as leaders. "There was huge resistance on the part of the older white leadership," remembered Bruce Raynor, a young textile union staffer in the 1970s who later served as the clothing and textile union's president. "The staff was almost totally white, in many cases fairly conservative on the race issue. . . . That's the way the union looked."[65]

Some unions were more accessible than others to African American workers. Frederick Simmons, for instance, saw family members in Saint Louis and Detroit win leadership positions in the UAW in the 1960s and was shocked to find that opportunities in the building trades were not the same for him as a black man by the mid-1970s in Seattle. He entered an electrician apprenticeship program where he helped organize a one-day protest when other construction workers objected to women and people of color on the job. After spending several years without seeing any other people of color on job sites, he organized an Electrical Workers Minority Caucus within International Brotherhood of Electrical Workers (IBEW) Local 46 to build a community of support, and later became president of his local union in 1996.[66] Todd Hawkins, an African American ironworker in Seattle, remembered apprenticing with a white, racist journeyman who refused to teach him the trade or even share the blueprints: "You're walking around about to bust all day because you can't be insubordinate to your journeyperson."[67] Nevertheless, black workers saw some of their largest gains during this period in the building trades. For example, African American workers were a miniscule one-tenth of 1 percent of the Asbestos Workers union members in 1968, but made up 10 percent of the membership by 1983. African American workers in Hawkins' Iron Workers rose from 5 to 12 percent of the membership during the same period.[68]

African American workers turned to unions in part because unions meant better pay and benefits. The median black family's income was still 58 percent of that of whites in 1970.[69] Unions raised black workers' wages—in 1978, a black male worker with a union made 25 percent more per hour than those without a union on the job, a higher union differential than the 19 percent for white men.[70] A union contract also offered some insurance against discrimination on the job. It cemented wage increases and offered a clear progression for job promotions, one that allowed for a legally enforceable grievance procedure if a white supervisor picked favorites. "Some white women are given clean and easy jobs while black women with more seniority are given dirty jobs," said Brenda Robinson, an African American woman who helped form a union at the Newport News shipyard. "The Steelworkers . . . stands for equal treatment."[71]

Many black workers saw no contradiction between the individual legal gains of the civil rights movement and the collectivity of the labor movement; from their perspective, the movements simply offered different tools with which to forge a better life within a racially stratified capitalistic economy. In fact, many workers used their union contract to shore up gains made through the civil rights movement. Edward Coppedge, for example, remembered why he and his coworkers turned to the steelworkers at Newport News despite the fact that many black workers had already won better jobs through one of the nation's first EEOC consent degrees. "Number one is promotion and wages. We had a department down there that had black folks that hadn't had a raise in years and couldn't get one. . . . They really didn't move on civil rights until the Steelworkers got there. . . . They knew that the union was behind you."[72]

Unions were an especially strong leveler for African American women, who had long suffered double discrimination in the workforce. For decades, they found themselves mainly restricted to jobs in the domestic and agricultural sectors that were not covered by federal labor law. In 1940, 60 percent of black women worked as domestic servants. During World War II, six hundred thousand African American females got good industrial jobs, but following the war they were less likely to retain those jobs than were black men.[73] After the civil and women's rights movements, black women began to gain new entry to a wider range of jobs, including those eligible for unionization. By 1979, nearly a third of black women worked as clericals, though they remained overrepresented in the lower-paying office jobs, frequently working as file clerks and mail handlers. About one in six worked as operatives in manufacturing, topping the percentage of employed white women who worked in factories. African American women also signed on as hospital workers, nurses, and sales clerks, all areas that saw heavy union organizing activity in the 1970s. Black women were far less likely than were white women to rise to highly paid, professional jobs; white women were more than twice as likely to be managers, for instance.[74]

When African American women found themselves concentrated in blue- and pink-collar jobs, they turned to unions to help give them a needed lift on the job. Black women who were union members earned 16 percent more per hour in 1978 than those who did not have a union.[75] Unions also helped them narrow racial pay inequities. Though white women had long earned more than black women, by 1980 the overall wage gap by race for women in the private sector had narrowed to just under 4 percent. Then this wage gap between white and black women more than doubled in the 1980s and 1990s, in part due to the decline in unions. One expert estimates that had private-sector unions remained at their 1979 levels into the early 2000s, the wage gap between black and white women would have been about 30 percent lower.[76] "As a black woman, I know that the best hope for a decent standard of living for both women and blacks is effective trade union representation," Coretta Scott King, civil rights leader and widow of Dr. Martin Luther King Jr., told a union convention in 1979. "I know that, without union representation, a woman is likely to be viewed by her employer as little more than a source of low wage labor."[77]

Black workers, especially women, led much of the nationwide push in hospital unionization. Black workers' ranks among hospital professional staff grew quickly; by the early 1980s they made up a sixth of licensed practical nurses, for instance, and a fifth of dieticians. While hospital workers had been organizing since the late 1950s and were quick to strike for recognition, more than one and a half million worked for private, nonprofit hospitals. Federal law barred these hospital workers from holding union elections until the NLRB changed its policy in 1974.[78] Nurses, licensed practical nurses, aides, dieticians, data operators, food service workers, and nursing home staff all drove through a massive effort at unionization as soon as they could do so. Health care workers filed two hundred petitions for elections in the first month after the NLRB's decision through at least a dozen unions. One union active in hospital organizing, District 1199, developed what it called a "union power—soul power" organizing model, which built squarely on the civil rights struggle.[79]

African American women who labored as domestic workers also demanded new workplace rights in the 1970s, organizing as they rode Southern city buses to work or gathered in Northern skyscraper laundry rooms. They launched new groups, like the Household Technicians of America and the Domestic Workers of America, which were not unions in the traditional sense but organizations that worked to transform and professionalize domestic workers' relationships with their household employers. They fought for and won a revision to the Fair Labor Standards Act in 1974 for a minimum wage, and in 1976 won the right to unemployment insurance.[80]

In fact, African Americans were organizing so actively in the 1970s that it seemed they might be the vanguard that would finally split open the nonunion South. Southern textiles, for instance, had long been a difficult industry for unions to organize. The CIO's Operation Dixie, the 1946 effort to organize the South, floundered among white textile workers who were wary of uniting with the small number of blacks who held these jobs. Even as late as 1963, less than 5 percent of textile workers were black. Yet this industry saw a major shift following the 1964 Civil Rights Act, and by 1980 African Americans made up more than a quarter of textile workers.[81]

Black workers became the core of renewed efforts by the textile workers' union to organize in the 1970s, including at the J. P. Stevens plant in Roanoke Rapids, North Carolina. The J. P. Stevens campaign is perhaps the single most well-known private-sector union organizing campaign of the decade because the union's consumer boycott of this linens manufacturer gained broad support, and because the campaign was immortalized in *Norma Rae*, the 1979 blockbuster movie. The movie is based on the struggles of a real-life, white textile union activist, Crystal Lee Sutton. Yet, to capture the true dynamics of this campaign, the movie's heroine should have been African American. After all, black workers turned the tide in Roanoke Rapids. The textile union had first launched the J. P. Stevens campaign back in 1963, and all but gave up in the face of what one Fifth Circuit judge called in 1969 the company's "massive multi-state campaign to prevent unionization of its southern plants."[82] Yet the influx of black workers into the Roanoke Rapids facility opened up possibilities for organizing that had once seemed closed. In five years alone, from 1970 to 1975, the black workforce in the plant increased from 19 to 37 percent, and these workers brought with them tremendous interest in unionizing.[83]

Racial divisions, however, remained potent. Many white J. P. Stevens workers were reluctant to support what they thought of as a black union, and such divisions were key to J. P. Stevens's antiunion campaign. Management frequently sent letters to all workers—white and black alike—on the eve of a union election that read, "We would at this point like to say a special word to our black employees. . . . It is among you that the Union supporters are making their most intense drive—that you are being insistently told . . . that by going into the Union in mass, you can dominate it and control it in this Plant . . . as you may see fit."[84] The company's "special word" to black workers thus linked the union to black workers' increased power, and played on many white workers' fears that a union would further erode their racial privilege. Nevertheless, worker support across races buoyed a union win at J. P. Stevens in August 1974. It took another six years, and one of the nation's first union-led "corporate campaigns," to wring a contract from the company. Racially based employer tactics were not limited to textiles: "The hospital always tried to make the union seem like a racial issue, like it was blacks causing the trouble," remembered Shirley Williams, a nursing assistant at the Tuomey hospital in Sumter, South Carolina. The interracial group overcame this tactic and won their union in 1980.[85]

The rights consciousness that grew from the civil rights movement sometimes served as a newly made tool for the entire new working class, available even to white men. As black workers moved deeper into Southern industries in the 1970s, their new assertiveness about their rights, born out of the civil rights movement, spilled over into private-sector unionizing efforts and helped white workers find new backbone for organizing. "The confrontations and civil rights progress of the black people has had an impact on white textile workers," explained the Textile Workers Union of America (TWUA) organizing director to his union's president in 1970. "The entry of blacks into textile plants and the manner in which blacks stand up for their rights has made the docile textile workers sit up and take notice."[86] White Southern workers had never been solidly antiunion, and by the 1970s black workers' unionizing spirit offered a new energy, especially to young whites. Workers under the age of thirty and black workers, for instance, were the most pro-union groups among Cannon Mills workers in the notoriously antiunion company town of Kannapolis, North Carolina. There, even 44 percent of young white workers self-identified as pro-union in the mid-1970s.[87] Tim Honeycutt was one such white Cannon Mills worker. He fought "race wars" with black students when his high school desegregated, but found that his racial prejudice weakened when he worked with black workers in the mill and joined them in unionization efforts at Cannon Mills. "We're after equal rights and freedom," he later asserted, anchoring his explanation for his unionization impetus in rights-based language.[88] At Duke University Hospital, a 1974 walkout among black female clericals inspired white workers to action, though the 1976 unionization effort with AFSCME ultimately failed. "I don't mind saying the blacks showed the way and I admire them for it. I don't think we could have taken the lead on our own," said one white skilled-trade hospital worker who helped push unsuccessfully for a union.[89] Black workers' propensity to unionize offered real growth potential to labor in the 1970s; it promised to help the movement bridge or, at least, leapfrog over persistent racial divisions in the working class.

Sunbelt Workers Organized

Industry followed the pull of air conditioning, highways, military contracts, low union density, and cheap taxes to the South and Sunbelt states in the 1960s and 1970s. The South led all American regions in economic growth as employment in manufacturing expanded faster than in any other part of the nation in the 1960s and 1970s. Sunbelt states' share of employment grew by 10 points between 1967 and 1983, the same number by which "Snowbelt" states' share dropped.[90] Employers looked to the South and West as bastions of antiunionism, a trait marketed by regional boosters who sought to lure Northern industrial jobs to their towns. "What are nice companies . . . doing in a place like this?" asked Greenville, South Carolina, Chamber of Commerce recruitment ads marketing "a positive labor climate" and a "reasonable tax structure." That "positive" labor climate included laws prohibiting union security agreements in nearly all Southern states. In fact, unionization rates in Southern states remained exceptionally low—South Carolina, for instance, had the lowest rate at 7.8 percent in 1980, compared to New York's near 40 percent union density.[91]

Low unionization rates and antilabor attitudes among regional elites have masked the intensity of Sunbelt workers' unionization efforts. The result is that, as much as is known about industries' move to the Sunbelt in these years, far less is known about the broad unionization efforts among workers. In fact, NLRB reports show that Sunbelt workers intensified their efforts to form unions in the 1970s. Forty-four percent of the people eligible to vote in NLRB elections in the 1970s, for instance, were in Southern and Sunbelt states, up from 38 percent in the 1960s (figure 2.2). The percentage of voters in the Sunbelt dropped to 41 percent in the 1980s.[92] Despite their antiunion reputation, many Southerners increasingly wanted unions. Blue-collar Southerners who were not already union members were more likely than those in any other region of the country to report they would vote for a union in 1977.[93] Among them, of course, were many African American and female workers.

The Deep South posed the most formidable challenge to national unions based geographically and culturally in the North. Nevertheless, the 1970s seemed a moment of promise when unions might finally open new vistas, even where they had suffered defeat so many times before. Consider, for instance, the UAW's reaction to what it labeled the GM "Southern strategy." GM had some presence in the South following World War II and operated unionized facilities in Atlanta and Arlington, Texas. It accelerated its move south in the 1970s and built most of its new assembly and parts plants there, opening nine new plants south of the Mason-Dixon line between 1972 and 1978.[94] When workers at these GM plants tried to organize a union with the UAW in Clinton, Mississippi, and Fitzgerald, Georgia, in 1974 and 1975, the company responded with antiunion leaflets, meetings, and threats. However, the UAW still had great power within GM at that time as it represented 95 percent of the company's 390,000 U.S. hourly workers. The UAW used a series of "mini-strikes" to force GM to agree to a neutrality agreement in 1976 national contract negotiations.[95]

This neutrality agreement buoyed Henry Davison's unionizing efforts at GM's Guide Lamp plant in Monroe, Louisiana, after he returned to the South. At first, Davison and his coworkers faced tremendous company resistance,

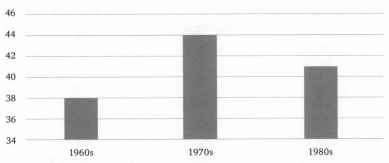

FIGURE 2.2 Percentage of total NLRB eligible voters in the South/
Sunbelt states by decade (1960–1989)

Source: NLRB Annual Reports, 1960–1989, table 15 (1960–1971) and table 15A
(1972–1989).

and the company attempted to screen out pro-union workers in the hiring and training process. Once the workers petitioned for an election in
1976, GM held what it termed "commander call" meetings each Monday,
mandatory-attendance meetings in which the plant manager urged the
workers not to vote for a union. Local boosters fought the union as well.
"Give Yourself a Christmas Present—Vote No on Dec 22," read roadside signs
put up by the Louisiana Association of Business and Industry, a group that
had spearheaded a successful "right-to-work" drive in that state. Yet GM
signed the neutrality agreement just weeks before the scheduled union vote
in Monroe, and local management was forced to back off their antiunion
stance. Absent vicious company threats, Davison and his coworkers were
able to win their union and access the kind of robust level of economic
security that had long eluded Southern workers. It was a point well understood by Betty Crosser, a twenty-four-year-old machine operator who cited
"mostly the security" as her reason for voting yes. "I'm single—I may never
get married—and I have to support myself. I have to think about my future,
my retirement."[96]

In the end, the UAW was able to curtail much of GM's Southern strategy
and help workers win unions in many of the new Southern plants, but not
without a major fight. Local management often ignored the company's
official neutrality policy. "I heard that one guy was talking about it and that
he got fired, so I don't want to know anything about it," asserted one woman
about a failed union drive in Saginaw, Alabama. The UAW also struggled
to prove its worth to Southern workers accustomed to lower pay. Many
workers shared the sentiments of one Alabama GM electrician who noted

that his twelve-dollars-an-hour wages far outstripped local rates: "I take what they give me and gladly spend it, but we are overpaid."[97] When GM built a major assembly plant in Oklahoma City, the union worried that the softness of the neutrality agreement would hurt its chances there. It turned out that the Oklahoma City vote was scheduled a mere two days after the start of 1979 GM-UAW negotiations, and the UAW threw down the gauntlet. President Doug Fraser went through the ritual handshake to open the meeting but then walked out of negotiations, refusing to return until GM agreed to send top officials to Oklahoma City to investigate charges that managers had handed out antiunion T-shirts and leaflets. The gamble worked, and Oklahoma City workers voted 1,479 to 658 for the union. Workers at GM plants followed suit in Shreveport, Louisiana, in 1979 and Decatur, Alabama, in 1982, for example, and the company agreed to recognize the union after a majority of workers signed cards in Alabama, Mississippi, and Georgia.[98]

Though the UAW rolled back GM's attempt to outrun the union in the South, the UAW was slower to meet other Southern workers' broad demands for organizing. While two-thirds of workers' organizing requests came from Sunbelt states, the UAW had no full-time black organizers assigned to the region in 1983 and few Southerners. Internal organizing reports show that they were doing far more organizing in the Midwest and Michigan than in the South throughout the decade, and the union did not even start a concerted Southern drive (beyond the GM effort) until 1977.[99]

Unions tried a number of joint projects to organize in the South and Sunbelt, including in Florida's "space belt" and a community-focused effort among furniture workers in Tupelo, Mississippi. The AFL-CIO's Houston, Texas, effort in the early 1980s received lots of fanfare, yet saw few gains.[100] The most successful of these cross-union efforts was the AFL-CIO's Los Angeles, Orange Counties Organizing Committee, which began in the 1960s but remained labor's most substantive joint organizing project into the early 1980s. When Teamsters president Jimmy Hoffa first heard about the project, he claimed it would "not organize 50 people . . . it's all propaganda and hot air." In fact, this shared organizing campaign organized nearly half a million workers over twenty years.[101]

The project was Walter Reuther's brain child, growing out of his 1961 push to force the newly minted AFL-CIO to make good on its promise of deepened organizing efforts. "Do we have the will, the good sense and the unity of purpose needed to create a practical organizational mechanism?" asked Reuther in his proposal to the AFL-CIO for a "comprehensive, cooperative, coordinated organizational drive." Reuther had his eyes on burgeoning job growth in Southern California, and pushed the AFL-CIO to begin a combined project through the newly formed organizing committee.[102] The project launched in 1963 and originally included fifty-seven unions. The level of coordination was impressive, as unions had long jealously guarded their jurisdictions. Each union submitted to the AFL-CIO a list of its current locals in the two county areas, and a list of potential organizing targets divided into five sectors. Each union agreed to contribute money and organizers according to their size. The original staff budget was $230,000 a year, half of which the AFL-CIO paid, including for a director. The unions in each sector then sat down and hashed out the acceptable organizing targets. Unless the group agreed to the target, the unions would not organize there. Unions would sometimes agree to petition jointly, or to confer with one another, but they would not oppose one another.[103]

Reuther's brainchild paid off, and even helped halt the city's union density slide for a few years in the mid-1960s. A core of about thirty-five unions stuck with the project. They met each quarter, working out approved targets. Many of the elections were in traditional manufacturing, like the UAW at Cadillac Gauge, the USWA at Harvey Aluminum, and the IUE at Packard-Bell's television plant. Others were in newer industries, like the International Association of Machinists (IAM) win at Scientific Data Systems or the Oil, Chemical, and Atomic Workers International Union (OCAW) wins at Shell Chemical Division and Biosciences Laboratory, the largest privately owned clinical lab in the world. The project served not only to coordinate organizing but also to spur it, for organizers routinely had to go sit next to their peers from other unions and talk about the state of their campaigns. By 1978, the project had organized 358,000 workers, 217,000 of whom came through NLRB elections. By 1984, they had organized nearly half a million of these Sunbelt workers.[104]

Sí Se Puede! 是的, 我们可以![105]

The Civil Rights Act was not the only legislation that shook up America's workplaces; the 1965 Immigration and Nationality Act, often known as the Hart-Celler Act, also helped to recast America's working class by allowing workforce entry by millions of previously excluded immigrants. The new law changed the national origins quotas that had been in place since 1924 and that effectively excluded most Asians and Africans. The new U.S. immigration system still had quotas, but these allowed immigration from all countries and focused more on immigrants' skills and family relationships with citizens.[106] Hart-Celler was only implemented in 1968 and, by the early 1970s, the United States was still only 4.7 percent foreign-born, the lowest rate since before the 1840s. Then roughly ten million immigrants entered the country between 1970 and 1990.[107] By the close of the twentieth century, the nation's foreign-born population had nearly doubled compared to its 1970 level, and these immigrant workers spurred a number of union organizing drives, including among janitors, poultry and meatpacking workers, and construction workers nationwide. During the 1970s and early 1980s, however, when immigration was just starting to grow, immigrant workers' union organizing efforts were concentrated in urban centers like Los Angeles and New York, where the first new wave of immigrants tended to settle.[108]

Los Angeles immigrant workers turned to unions to help try to mediate their work experiences in auto plants, garment factories, restaurants, and furniture manufacturers, even though many were undocumented. More undocumented workers headed to Los Angeles than to any other city—up to a third lived there by 1985. Many labor leaders, journalists, and scholars deemed undocumented workers to be unorganizable: "The millions of workers who are in this country illegally seldom join unions . . . because they fear deportation and the return of poverty in their homeland," wrote *Los Angeles Times* labor reporter Harry Bernstein.[109] In fact, many did successfully organize, like the two hundred Mexican and Central American immigrants at Camagua Mattress Company, a water bed manufacturer in Los Angeles, who won an NLRB election in 1985 and launched a boycott to force their company to sign a first contract.[110]

Yet, like native workers, Los Angeles's immigrant workers often ran into a wall of increased employer opposition when they tried to unionize. The majority of High Tide Swimwear workers in Los Angeles who struck for a union in 1975 were undocumented workers. They lost their NLRB election after the company fired and replaced forty-six of the pro-union strikers.[111] When undocumented workers at Vogue Coach Company, a Los Angeles manufacturer of recreational vehicles, formed a union and won a contract with the UAW in 1978, the company retaliated by triggering a raid by the Immigration and Naturalization Service that swept up ninety workers a few days before the contract was signed. Two years later, when the majority Hispanic workforce struck for eighteen weeks for higher wages and more time off, one of their contract demands was that the company stop using these sorts of raids to intimidate workers. Raids, or even the threats of such raids, became increasingly common employer tactics. When workers at Rowe Furniture Company in Los Angeles formed a union in 1978, an immigration raid detained eighteen of the thirty new union members. When the mostly Japanese and Latino workforce at Horikawa Japanese restaurant in Los Angeles's Little Tokyo tried to form a union with Local 11 of the Hotel Employees and Restaurant Employees Union (HERE) in 1980, the NLRB found that the company had illegally threatened the workers with deportation.[112]

New York was also a center for immigrant union organizing, especially among the new Chinese immigrants in the Chinatown garment shops.[113] Katie Quan worked in these shops in the 1970s, and went on to become a union organizer and leader in the 1980s. She remembered that the new Chinese immigrants getting jobs in New York's sewing shops looked to the International Ladies' Garment Workers' Union (ILGWU) to shore up security. "Local 23–25 used to have new membership meetings with 75 to 100 workers per week joining the union. . . . The first thing they wanted to do after getting off the plane . . . was to join the union so that their benefits would start right away." Unlike employers in much of the rest of the country in the 1970s, the Chinese-run sewing shops often did not resist the union because the union steered contracts to unionized shops.[114] The union was slow to change its practices to fully incorporate these new members, long continuing to hold union meetings in English, for instance, despite the fact that so many members only spoke Chinese. Nevertheless, when Chinese contractors reacted to increased foreign competition by trying to avoid signing union contracts in 1982, twenty thousand garment workers took to the streets of New York City in a march that was reminiscent of the Uprising of 1909—though this time the workers were not Eastern European but Chinese. The workers won their strike and forced the shops to sign the standard union agreement.[115] Many Chinese restaurant workers also organized, often affiliating with Local 69 of HERE. Some even founded their own community-based labor organization, the Chinese Staff and Workers' Association. When waiters at the upscale Silver Palace struck rather than share more tips with management, they forced the company to meet their demands and recognize their organization in 1981. Another effort at Hunan Garden failed in the face of employer resistance.[116]

Hispanic workers, both those born in the United States and immigrants, often had pro-union sentiments. Throughout the 1970s, Hispanic workers were more likely to be union members than others in the general population. Polling showed that a majority of Latino workers said they would choose to vote for a union.[117] For example, three thousand Texas garment workers at the Farah Manufacturing Company, mostly native Chicanas, used a strike and consumer boycott to force their employer to recognize their union in 1974.[118] Though workers on the cutting floor had voted for a union in 1970, the company refused to sign a contract. By 1972 workers were fed up with low wages, arbitrary treatment, and frequent firings and were no longer content to wait for the NLRB process. One union organizer watched from a nearby café in shock as hundreds of workers poured out of the San Antonio plant: "It was a feeling of pure panic. . . . The workers took it out of our hands."[119] Workers at the El Paso facility walked out a week later, joining what would become a nearly two-year strike. The company patrolled the plant gates with dogs and local police arrested strikers, many in the middle of the night, prompting an NLRB judge to call the company "lawless . . . trampling on the rights of employees as if there were no law, no board and no Ten Commandments." The union's consumer boycott crippled Farah's operations and the company admitted that it was largely responsible for a dramatic drop in the value of company stock.[120] The boycott and strike brought the company to the bargaining table, and the workers won a contract that included wage increases of up to $0.80 an hour over the life of the three-year contract—a significant increase over their $1.70 an hour pay—as well as company-paid insurance and maternity benefits.[121]

The organizing struggles of the United Farm Workers (UFW) among California's grape and vegetable workers were the most well-known and celebrated efforts among Hispanic and Filipino workers. The NLRA had excluded farmworkers, so in the 1960s the UFW tried to persuade other union members, like truckers, to refuse to ship wine made from nonunionized grapes. After employers got an injunction to force the union to end this secondary boycott, the UFW turned instead to a successful boycott of table grapes; seventeen million people refused to eat or buy grapes between 1966 and 1972, according to one Department of Agriculture study. California's farmworkers won the right to legally form unions in 1975 under the California Agricultural Labor Relations Act, effectively tearing down the "wall that agribusiness had built in the 1930s to keep the New Deal out of their fields and orchards," according to historian Frank Bardacke. The workers exercised their new right with gusto. In the first thirty days of the Agricultural Labor Relations Board's existence, twenty-five thousand farmworkers voted in 178 elections, often choosing between the UFW and the Teamsters. By the late 1970s, the UFW had about fifty thousand members

at the height of its strength, though it would end the 1980s much diminished.[122]

While many immigrants nationwide showed interest in joining unions,
many union leaders and members remained hostile to them. The AFL-CIO
officially opposed amnesties for undocumented immigrants until it reversed
its policy in 2000, finally supporting a path to citizenship.[123] The federation's long-standing policy supporting tight immigration controls reflected
the fact that many of its member unions saw immigrants as competitors for
jobs. "The biggest issue we have to contend with is the illegal alien," said
Gale Van Hoy, executive secretary of the Houston Building Trades Council,
in 1983, explaining the failure of a much-hailed joint unionization effort in
Houston. "If they're illegal, they shouldn't be in our union, and we shouldn't
be bothering with them." Yet many unions did open their doors and actively
organize immigrant workers in the 1970s and early 1980s, including the
ILGWU in sewing shops in Los Angeles and New York, District 1199 and SEIU
in hospitals and nursing homes, HERE in hotels and restaurants, and
AFSCME among Head Start and government service workers. "Any worker . . .
regardless of where he's from, has the same rights as any U.S. citizen to become a member of a union," asserted Houston Organizing Project organizer
Demetrio Lucio.[124]

Promise Denied

Growth in union membership in the United States has historically come in
spurts, shooting up quickly in the early 1880s, during World War I, and after
the passage of the Wagner Act.[125] America was poised to see another such
spurt in union growth in the 1970s as a transformed working class rose to
lead new organizing attempts. Women, people of color, and young baby
boomers pushed en masse for full economic security through unions, attempting to organize in record numbers in banks and universities, in auto
parts plants and sewing shops, in urban metropolises and small towns
throughout the South. They fought for unions even as they endured the
structural shift to retail and service jobs driven by the global economy. If
the new working class was going to take jobs as nurse's aides, cashiers, and
data processors, then they would struggle to make these jobs into good,
union jobs. In the end, however, this promise of a new surge in union membership growth never blossomed. Though these workers' efforts did lead to
union growth in the public sector, the workers were far less likely to win

Millions Go Knoc

their private-sector union elections than were working people in previous generations. Far too few of the members of this reconfigured working class were ever able to form unions because they faced a new and solid wall of resistance from employers and because the federal government did not step up to enforce their unionizing rights.[126]

Employers were well aware of the power of America's new and emerging working class. They mobilized in new ways, first attacking the law undergirding union organizing in the late 1960s, then breaking that law with unprecedented frequency, constructing an entire antiunion industry throughout the 1970s. "The interventions of those consultants into the organizing and collective bargaining fields represents a far more comprehensive threat than they have presented to particular organizing campaigns or the particular bargaining relationship," AFL-CIO director Alan Kistler told a group of labor leaders in 1983.[127] Employers sought to both weaken the legal regime refereeing union organizing and make a science out of fighting workplace organizing. We turn now to a study of this U.S. employer assault on union organizing in the 1970s—the battle plan, the armaments, and the warriors themselves.

3 Employers Close the Door

Union busting was a hot controversy in the early 1980s, and Phil Donahue, king of the television talk show, featured a prominent antiunion consultant on his new late-night series. "No, Mr. Donahue, we don't bust unions," avowed Herbert G. Melnick of Modern Management Methods. "Our firm is a company that helps employers and employees understand one another." Donahue turned his microphone to Patty Everett, a nurse's aide at a Connecticut hospital where Melnick's firm had recently orchestrated a union defeat. Everett described the supervisor who would "intimidate me with questions, attack my ego" in mandatory, closed-door meetings. Donahue then cued up a Modern Management Methods film that taught supervisors how to defeat unions; he pointed out that workers now lost more union elections than they won. "Union membership and power is eroding and many companies are . . . hiring law firms and management consultants to come in and help stop the union," declared Donahue, urging viewers to call in at 1-800-MIDNIGHT to jump into the fray.[1]

Though union busting aroused sufficient vitriol in 1983 to land Melnick in the television hot seat, companies already had been ramping up their resistance to union organizing for nearly two decades. As global competition increased in the 1960s and 1970s, U.S. employers had begun to think that labor costs were bleeding them dry. To compete, they sought to cut costs on a number of levels, including by quashing a powerful, growing movement of new union organizing. It was a battle they waged in two stages. First, a number of the leaders of the nation's largest corporations—such as those at GE, Ford, and U.S. Steel—began in late 1965 an effort to roll back the laws protecting workers' organizing and bargaining rights through a new alliance, the Labor Law Reform Group (LLRG). After they failed in their efforts to change the law, employers began to increasingly bend and break the law in the 1970s. While there had long been antiunion employers and firms, employers now developed and honed a new set of techniques to fight union organizing, promulgated through business schools and the vastly expanded "union-avoidance" industry. New management consultants bred fear among managers about the nation's diversifying workforce and often used black and female workers' organizing activism to gin up business. By the time of the late 1970s battle around labor law reform legislation under the Jimmy Carter administration, employers no longer sought to change the law. Rather, they used a new level of political activism to defend an emerging status quo that offered companies tremendous latitude to resist workers' union organizing.

Why Employers Mobilized

In the mid-1960s, more than three-quarters of manufacturing plants were covered by collective bargaining agreements, and labor represented one of the strongest, most united lobbying forces in Washington. Collective bargaining agreements helped to redistribute the nation's wealth and set the wage and benefit standards for much of the nation's industrialized core.[2] Labor's heyday coincided with an era of national economic strength. Though some industries, like textiles and steel, had weakened in the 1950s, most industries rode a growing economy in the two decades after World War II. The tide started to turn, however, between 1965 and 1973 when the rate of profit for private business fell by 29 percent. Among manufacturers, it fell by more than 40 percent. Nations that had been flattened by the war, like Germany and Japan, were now back on their feet and ready to compete. Many employers were alarmed when the nation imported more merchandise than it exported starting in 1971, the first time since 1893.[3]

The United States then faced quick external economic shocks, such as the oil crisis and the end of the fixed-currency world system put in place following World War II. The 1974–75 recession was the worst the nation had seen in the postwar era; inflation reached an eye-popping 11 percent in 1974, and unemployment peaked at 9 percent in May 1975.[4] Inflation was particularly worrisome to employers and conservative politicians, who were quick to blame wages for the high prices and slow growth that economists called stagflation. "Inflation is the universal enemy of 100 percent of our people," asserted President Gerald Ford, explaining why he prioritized it over unemployment policy. Blaming labor became many elites' default position. "For Organized Labor, What Replaces 'More'?" asked *New York Times* labor reporter A. H. Raskin in his 1975 Labor Day column that excoriated some unions' paid leaders as "pork choppers" who demanded cost-of-living increases in members' contracts, at any cost.[5]

Manufacturers especially struggled as advances in shipping and distribution began to allow companies all over the globe to compete. A new breed of giant container ships, for instance, increased cargo capacity fivefold over the 1970s and brought competitors to newly expanded U.S. ports. The rat of corporate profit remained tepid throughout the decade because, in the fac of this new globalization, many businesses, especially manufacturers, could not easily pass off higher costs to consumers. The profitability slowdown did not bottom out until the early 1980s, and it influenced business' decisions throughout the decade.[6]

Meanwhile, during the 1970s and early 1980s, the locus of economic power began to shift away from manufacturing toward finance. Ironically, unions' own success in pushing for increased pensions helped swell the stock markets, giving new power to institutional investors and financial analysts. "Shareholder value," or elevated stock price, began to matter more than long-term workforce development and research. A new generation of financiers gained control of many of the nation's corporations through leveraged buyouts and treated them as bundles of tradable assets. Concerned about the low profit rate, corporate boards increasingly tied executive pay to stock prices by the 1980s, richly rewarding CEOs for short-term market gains.[7]

Large businesses reacted in a number of ways to win more power and flexibility within the new demands of this globally and financially directed capitalism. Labor costs, in this context, were something that managers could more easily control and squeeze than the intangible forces of the global marketplace. In order to cut costs and boost profits, companies began to build a model of employment in which they could avoid providing security and social welfare for employees. They hired far more temporary and part-time workers, for instance, and began to subcontract out work that had once been done by employees, ultimately helping to build what one scholar terms the "fissured workplace." They pushed down labor standards and wages, retreated from health care and retirement coverage, and created more precarious jobs with little long-term security or promise.[8]

Business also became far more politically active than ever before. By the late 1970s, a conservative business movement developed a broad and influential class resistance to state regulation and effectively helped reverse the tide of liberal expansion that held such sway through the 1960s. New corporate lobbying offices, political action committees (PACs), think tanks, and public relations firms served as the architectural framework for business leaders' conservative political activism. The Chamber of Commerce increased its membership fourfold in the decade and dramatically boosted its lobbying efforts. In 1971, only 175 business firms had registered lobbyists; by 1979, that number had jumped to 650. In the early 1970s, labor PACs contributed more to campaigns than business PACs did, but by the end of the decade business spending far outstripped that of labor.[9]

Employers also reacted to the new economic paradigm by increasing their resistance to union power and to workers' union organizing efforts. In earlier decades, employers had been split on whether to oppose labor or to attempt to compromise, with many major unionized companies eschewing the antilabor vehemence of groups like the National Association of Manufacturers (NAM). Auto and steel, for instance, operated within essentially oligopolistic markets and the large majority of workers were union members. Such large manufacturing companies found that unions tamped down wage competition, so they had a heavy incentive to find common ground with labor.[10] Yet this incentive changed in "an era of a cost price squeeze," remembered Douglas Soutar, a vice president of the American Smelting and Refining Corporation who went on to cofound the Business Roundtable in 1972, an organization that served as a center for business' conservative political activism. "People began looking for ways to economize and found out that . . . they had given it away in the contract."[11]

Like Soutar, many employers placed the blame for their new woes squarely on labor. "Unions are too big and too strong," asserted NAM in 1967. Top NAM executives warned that "the excessive—and constantly growing—power of the trade union movement has acquired a position of dominance over American industry."[12] The 1969–70 GE strike by thirteen unions seemed to confirm the executives' worst fears. Though GE management had long been able to play its unions off one another in bargaining, this time 150,000 workers struck nationwide for a hundred days. The GE strikers won higher wages, better retirement, and no-cost health insurance.[13] GE also faced formidable activism among its unorganized workers who triggered 437 separate elections at GE facilities from 1961 to 1982; the elections covered thirty-five states, including many in the South.[14]

Manufacturing employers in particular desperately wanted to free themselves of the wage and benefit pressures they perceived as vampires on their profit rates. And so they attacked labor, the entity responsible for securing wages and benefits from employers within the U.S. social welfare regime. After all, American corporations had to compete against companies in countries in which many of the social welfare costs were covered by the government rather than by employers.[15] The change in employer attitudes to unions was not monolithic, and many unionized companies continued their pluralistic rhetoric, at least. The vice president of BFGoodrich asserted in 1978 that his company was "fully comfortable in maintaining its extensive . . . union relationships." Yet even the most unionized companies were shifting attitudes. BFGoodrich's executive, for example, made this olive branch statement within a speech entitled "Learning to Live without the Union," in which he lamented that "too many of us in the business community have in the past looked to large unions to insulate us from wage competition."[16]

Executives faced a new wave of union organizing just as they hit the new era of global competition. Even as many maintained the bargaining relationship with their workers who were already union members, major manufacturers sought to limit the number of workers who could access collective bargaining and tried to keep many workers from ever forming unions in the first place.

Stage One: Employers Try to Change the Law

Long before union busting made its Phil Donahue debut in 1983, employers began laying the groundwork for a new approach to labor. First, a number of large employers tried to change the rules of the game in order to limit labor's influence and union organizing's reach. In 1965, Douglas Soutar teamed up with his good friend Virgil Day, vice president of GE and chair of the U.S. Chamber of Commerce's Labor Relations Committee, to organize a handpicked group of high-level executives to address what they understood as outsize union power. The group first called itself the "nothing committee," a reference to its attempt to remain confidential. It would later be known as the Labor Law Reform Group, or sometimes the Labor Law Study Group.[17] Soutar and Day soon recruited the well-connected Fred Atkinson of R. H. Macy and met with a group of three legal experts they dubbed the "the troika."[18] The group brought in nine other "thought leaders" from major corporations to form a steering committee, many of whom had long been at the heart of the nation's unionized labor-management system, including Ford, AT&T, U.S. Steel, and Union Carbide.[19] The LLRG thus represented a move by large unionized corporations to challenge labor—not just by moving factories to the less unionized South but by pooling resources to mount a frontal assault on the laws protecting workers' basic rights.[20]

The LLRG's formation was certainly not the first time U.S. businesses had coordinated efforts against labor. For example, businesses united in the early twentieth century's open shop drive to break workers' strikes and organizing efforts. A formidable alliance of businesses in the 1930s influenced the impact of the New Deal on America's workplaces.[21] Employers contested workers' shop floor power at the nation's unionized workplaces throughout the 1940s and 1950s and battled with unions for the public's hearts and minds. Nevertheless, the level of deliberate business coordination in the LLRG was a startling enough change in the 1960s that one *Los Angeles Times* journalist labelled it "the first time the nation's major corporations . . . have joined forces in a single operation."[22]

The high-level group of executives commissioned the troika to do a study of exactly which parts of labor law should be changed to their benefit. By 1967 the resulting report was circulating among members of Congress.[23] The report started by decrying "certification of unions without secret ballot elections." This was a reference to the John F. Kennedy and Lyndon B. Johnson NLRBs' renewed willingness to recognize a union without an election if the company violated the workers' rights during the election period. The study lamented the NLRB's increased willingness to rule as impermissible much of what employers often said during election campaigns, such as threats about plant closings if the workers chose a union. The LLRG claimed the NLRB was "muzzling employers who would tell their employees of disadvantages inherent in unionization." They were appalled when the NLRB ordered the textile giant J. P. Stevens not only to hold a new election in its plants after it was found to have massively violated its workers' rights, but also to read the finding aloud and mail the decision to its employees. The group also deplored the NLRB's decision to allow smaller subunits of workers to vote on unionization. This was especially important to unions who were trying to organize in the service and retail sectors and found it difficult to win elections among workers spread over multiple facilities.[24]

The study went through existing labor law, proposing changes, line by line, that would meet the employers' needs. The group outlined twenty-three proposed amendments that would, among other remedies, require secret-ballot elections for certification, strengthen employer "free speech," insist on "meaningful" bargaining units, and "prevent improper remedies" for employer unfair labor practices during representation campaigns. Its final solution was to abolish the NLRB jurisdiction entirely in unfair labor practice cases, and instead either turn that function over to the judiciary or create a new "United States Labor Court" with judges appointed for twenty-year terms. The executives thus sought not only to change the rules of the game but to abolish the labor law referee altogether.[25]

The next step was to try to change public opinion, softening the way for congressional acceptance of their labor law reforms. For this, they hired an executive director, formed a "public information committee," and deployed the Hill & Knowlton public relations firm.[26] That firm pushed the group's ideas on labor law reform in memos to newspaper editors, a national circuit of speeches, and packages for women's clubs and even helped *Reader's Digest* gather and research material for a special investigative report.[27] Hill & Knowlton had a fair amount of success getting traction for its campaign, especially with the opinion pages of the smaller newspapers. The Bridgeville, Pennsylvania, paper, for instance, featured a cartoon version of the NLRB knocking over Justice, depicted as a young woman holding scales. Virtually identical editorials critical of the board appeared in the *Macomb Daily* (Michigan), *Northern Virginia Sun* (Arlington), and the *Richmond Independent* (California) in 1968.[28]

The LLRG aimed to win its changes after the 1968 elections, but the group's hopes were dashed. The Congress remained Democratic, and even though Republican Richard Nixon won the presidency, he did so by a narrow margin that forced him to court union support throughout his first term. One LLRG leader remembered that the group intended to introduce the reforms through Nixon's new labor secretary, but "when we went looking for George Shultz right after the inauguration, he was down at Bal Harbour chatting it up with Meany."[29] The group did find legislators to introduce bills on many of its recommendations, such as requiring secret-ballot elections and banning workers from picketing for union recognition, but these bills got little traction.[30] "Since the Labor Law Reform Group was established, we have not had a Congress receptive to labor law changes," wrote the NAM's executive committee in 1971, noting that a Nixon administration representative told them that while "the administration is receptive to labor law reform . . . don't count on it too much."[31]

Nevertheless, the LLRG continued to expand its membership to more than forty corporate members and opened an office in Washington in 1971.[32] The LLRG soon merged with two other employer groups to form the Business Roundtable in 1972. The other groups included a small group of politically active executives known as the March Group—founded by Alcoa and GE executives—and another employer organization, the Construction Users Anti-Inflation Roundtable (CUAIR). A broad coalition of large businesses had established CUAIR in 1969 to limit unions' ability to force higher wages and benefits on the construction of their facilities and stores. The Business Roundtable was the first business lobby to limit membership to top CEOs of Fortune 500 groups, and it soon had enormous political clout. "No organization can hire the talent we can put together," said the chair of Alcoa. "It would be impossible." Douglas Soutar and GE's Virgil Day were both instrumental in pushing for the merger and shaping the Business Roundtable's direction, and it included many of the same companies that were part of the LLRG.[33]

Through the Business Roundtable, these business leaders joined the burgeoning conservative political activity among corporations in the 1970s. The Business Roundtable expanded its attacks beyond unions and the NLRB to other government regulations and agencies, killing the campaign for a consumer protection agency, for instance, and weighing in on issues as diverse as Social Security, the EEOC, and the Arab oil boycott.[34] Yet labor law remained a key concern. The LLRG essentially became the Business Roundtable's Labor-Management Committee, whose stated objectives included publicizing the Labor Law Reform Study and implementing as much of it as possible through "legislation, changed administration and litigation."[35]

Overall, the large corporations' attempt to rewrite labor law in the late 1960s and early 1970s was not as effective as they had hoped because unions still had such strong political sway. Yet, over the next decade, many of the LLRG's wish list items would come true. The law itself would not change much, but the context for union organizing changed dramatically. The NLRB, for instance, steadily made it easier for employers to resist union organizing. Soon after Nixon's appointment, Soutar worked with Shultz to find a candidate who would lead the NLRB in the direction sought by the LLRG. They tapped Edward Miller, a Chicago management-side lawyer and member of the LLRG's blue ribbon committee. He was appointed over the objections of labor, which dubbed him a "corporation lawyer."[36] The Miller-led NLRB under Nixon quickly began "putting more obstacles in the path of union negotiators and organizers," according to the *Wall Street Journal*.[37] It allowed employers to tell organizing workers that signing union cards would be "fatal" and cause "turmoil," that if they chose a union they could lose what they had because bargaining "starts from scratch" and "everything is up for negotiation." The board decided that employers legally could predict that they would have to close up shop due to financial difficulties if the workers voted yes.[38] The Miller board also was far less willing to order a company to bargain with a union without an election when the company broke the law. For instance, even after an employer physically assaulted two union organizers at the Green Briar Nursing Home, the Miller board felt there was no "lingering impact" that would affect workers' decision whether to vote for a union.[39] The John Fanning board under the Carter administration did little to reverse the trend of weakening labor law, registering only as what one historian of the NLRB terms "a blip on long-term policy" that would persist and deepen under the Donald Dotson board in the Ronald Reagan years.[40]

Stage Two: Employers Bend and Break the Law

When they couldn't change the law, employers began to focus on breaking and circumventing it. They increased their ground-level efforts against workers' organizing efforts, and their tactics grew increasingly sophisticated and effective. By 1977, unionizing workers began to lose more than half of their elections for the first time since the Wagner Act's inception.[41]

While many employers had long resisted unionization, three new developments emerged in the 1970s concerning employer resistance to organizing at the workplace. First, employers became more willing to break the labor law governing new union formation. Second, resistance to union organizing spread deep within the nation's core industries as even unionized and manufacturing employers increasingly fought workers' new organizing efforts. Third, a large antiunion consultant industry proliferated. These antiunion firms, often in partnership with the nation's business schools, promulgated a new pedagogy that linked remaining "union-free" to good management. They taught large numbers of managers to stretch, and even overstep, the limits of the law, a development that essentially changed the terms of union elections. The new union-busting industry both encouraged and profited from employers' fears about the new wave of women and people of color who pushed for unions.[42]

Increased lawbreaking was the first of the three big developments in employer behavior in the 1970s. More employers became willing to violate the law at the workplace, resulting in a surge in unfair labor practice charges against companies. According to labor law, employers could not fire or threaten workers for supporting the union, for instance, nor could they spy on workers, threaten to shut down if the workers voted in a union, or promise workers more money or perks if they rejected a union. The NLRB considered such acts "unfair labor practices" or ULPs.[43] Unfair labor charges against employers soared exponentially during the 1970s. Though the number of workers who tried to form unions remained steady at about half a million a year, those workers faced far more employer lawbreaking. All ULP charges against employers rose sevenfold between 1950 and 1980, and the number of the most severe type of charges—those dealing with discrimination or unfair dismissal for union support—rose nearly sixfold. Figure 3.1 shows the steep rise in all charges against employers, called

FIGURE 3.1 Unfair labor practices (ULP) charges against employers (1950–1990)

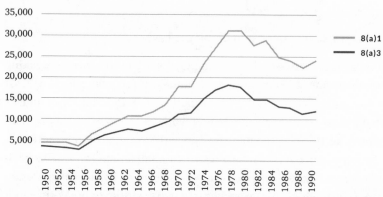

Source: NLRB Annual Reports, 1950–1990, table 3 (1950), table 2 (1951–1990).

8(a)1 charges, and the ones dealing with discrimination for union support and firing, called 8(a)3 charges.[44]

These were not empty charges. In fact, the number of workers to whom the NLRB awarded employer back pay in 1980 was nearly seven times greater than in 1950.[45] Not all unfair labor practices tracked by the NLRB were filed during organizing cases. For instance, unions also filed ULP charges when employers violated union members' rights on the job. Nevertheless, the numbers clearly paint a picture of employers' increased willingness to break the law. Indeed, by 1980 the NLRB found more employers guilty of firing workers for union activity than ever before.[46]

Yet the penalties for labor law violations were too weak to hold back the assault. Typically, if the NLRB found that an employer illegally fired a union supporter during an organizing campaign, that company would simply have to rehire the worker, pay the worker the wages owed, and post a sign in the break room explaining that it broke the law. If the employer violated labor law multiple times during a campaign, then the NLRB could order a new election, though this would do little to negate the original threats' effects. Very occasionally, the NLRB would order the company to begin bargaining without a new election. There were no large fines, no employer went to jail, and the costs for breaking labor law were negligible. In fact, the efficacy of labor law in the midcentury decades rested less on the NLRB's punitive power than on mainstream employers' grudging compliance.[47]

The second major development was that many more mainstream industrial companies became willing to resist unionization efforts, including in union-dense geographic areas. No longer was union busting a Southern and small-firm phenomenon, as Fortune 500 firms with long-standing bargaining relationships ramped up their resistance to union organizing at the workplace. By the end of the decade, even large manufacturers skirted the law, delayed at every step, and increasingly spoke out against new union organizing, even when some of their workers were already covered by collective bargaining agreements. "It requires a certain nerve for those companies whose names you see in the batting order of big hitters in the bargaining game to try to keep plants unorganized," a vice president of BF-Goodrich told an industrial relations convention in 1978. "Management is more sophisticated and bolder . . . and the times 'they are a-changing.' "[48] Companies attending one 1979 seminar by Charles Hughes, a prominent antiunion consultant, included such blue chip companies as Rockwell International, Honeywell, BFGoodrich, Bechtel, and Celanese.[49]

Union-busting tactics moved squarely into the industrial sector, the area where unions had traditionally been the strongest and that had long formed the core of the nation's economy. A sectoral analysis of ULPs from 1950 to 1980 reveals that workers trying to form unions in the industrial sector in the 1970s actually became more likely to face employer lawbreaking than in those sectors that were historically less unionized, such as retail and service. In the 1950s and 1960s, the ratio of ULPs filed against employers to the number of election petitions in the industrial, service, and retail sectors remained fairly low and remained similar across sectors. In the 1970s, however, when all workers faced far more employer lawbreaking, industrial-sector workers bore an even greater share of the employer resistance. By the end of the decade, the ratio of the number of ULPs filed against employers to the number of election petitions in the industrial sector had actually outstripped the ratio in both service and retail, though hospital workers and retail clerks certainly saw their share of resistance, too (figure 3.2).[50]

The third development in employers' resistance to union organizing in the 1970s was their increased use of antiunion management consultants and lawyers who, in turn, helped shift the paradigm of acceptable employer behavior. Through an avalanche of seminars, trainings, books, and speeches, these new "management consultants" helped make mainstream a level of antiunionism that had once been extreme in the midcentury labor-management arrangement. "Any management that gets a union deserves it—and they get the kind they deserve," was the mantra of one sought-after consultant.[51] These hired guns helped entrench the concept that managers

FIGURE 3.2 Ratio of ULPs (CA) filed against employers to petitions filed for union certification (RC) by sector (1950–1980)

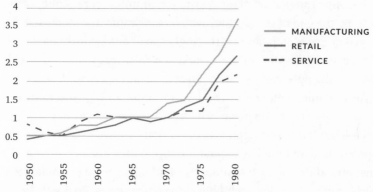

Source: NLRB Annual Reports, 1950–1980, table 5.

could and should avoid unions in all arenas, and they educated managers about the low costs of skirting the law.

The antiunion labor consultants of the 1970s had roots in earlier decades. Firms like Sears and Kodak built on the human resources movement of the 1940s and used behavioral and psychological research to undercut unionizing efforts.[52] The architect of Sears's antiunion fortress, Nathan Shefferman, worked for the original NLRB, and in 1939 formed the nation's first antiunion firm, Labor Research Associates, in Chicago. His staffers went on to found the leading firms of the 1970s union-buster movement, including John Sheridan and Associates and the firm that would become known as Modern Management Methods, or Three M.[53] Earle K. Shawe, a lawyer and consultant whom one government official in 1981 called "the consummate pro . . . the consummate gunslinger," also worked in the 1930s for the NLRB, where he served as the lawyer who forced Bethlehem Steel to bargain with its workers. He then founded a management-side law firm in Baltimore following the passage of Taft-Hartley. There he filed the nation's first unfair labor practice against a union in 1948 and began a career helping employers fight unions.[54] John Tate, the architect of Wal-Mart's antiunion policy starting in the 1970s, got his start in 1956 organizing three hundred firms into the Midwest Employers Council.[55]

Yet management resistance to unions in the earlier decades was neither as widespread nor as accepted as it would be by the 1970s and 1980s. While there were just a handful of antiunion firms at the beginning of the 1970s, by decade's end there were hundreds. One management firm founder told

a congressional hearing in 1979 that his industry grew tenfold over the preceding decade. The AFL-CIO estimated that by 1979 a full 70 percent of all campaigns involved some sort of management consultant or outside legal counsel.[56] For example, Melnick's firm, Modern Management Methods, made a name for itself by taking advantage of the private-sector wave of union organizing, first fighting hospital unionorganizing efforts, and then moving on to help universities, banks, and insurance companies fight their workers' unionization efforts. It specialized in teaching supervisors to attack the union, even as it worked hard to stay out of the spotlight.[57] A number of other management-side law firms grew rapidly in the 1970s in order to capture the growing demand for legal advice on how to avoid unions. Louis Jackson cofounded the firm Jackson and Lewis, for instance, in 1958 after he left the employ of Nathan Shefferman, and the firm expanded quickly in the 1970s by fighting unions at hospitals and nursing homes. Seyfarth Shaw, the law firm that fought unionization efforts at Newport News and Yale University, quadrupled in size in the last five years of the 1970s.[58]

Key to employers' turn toward antiunion consultants in the 1970s was the wave of worker organizing efforts, especially by women and people of color. The reshaped working class wanted a union, and no one knew that better than the employers themselves. One antiunion management consultant warned, "Danger: a union can muster a most potent campaign when it can take advantage of a 'racial' or 'sexist' theme."[59] Management consultants simultaneously stoked employers' fears and instructed them on how to beat back their diversified workforces' collective efforts. For instance, the AFL-CIO reported that antiunion consultant Woodruff Imberman told a Wake Forest University management seminar in 1979, "Blacks tend to be more prone to unionization than whites . . . you have to follow the EEOC laws and . . . there is no reason for you to be heroes about this . . . and fill up the workforce with Blacks. If you can keep them at a minimum, you are better off." An infiltrator in the meeting reported that Imberman went on to urge clients to hire Cubans but "stay the hell away from" Puerto Ricans, noting that they all counted as Hispanic for EEOC diversity purposes. When the *Wall Street Journal* asked Imberman to confirm the infiltrator's report, Imberman conceded that "he advised them to hire only as many blacks as legally necessary."[60]

In *Confessions of a Union Buster*, Martin Jay Levitt spelled out how his employer, Three M, capitalized on the wave of organizing in the health care industry that was driven by many women and people of color. According to Levitt, Three M developed tactics in that industry to "awaken within the mostly white supervisor corps a hatred of blacks . . . contempt for women, mistrust of the poor." When training supervisors to fight the health care union Local 1199, for instance, Levitt and his colleagues often showed the union's own film about a Charleston, South Carolina, hospital campaign with a majority black workforce. "We particularly like a scene in which a very fat, very dark female face fills the screen, and the woman says in a thick, southern drawl, 'Jes' gimme eleven nahhhnty-nahhn.' . . . We didn't say much when we showed the film. We didn't have to . . . we tapped the fears that resided in the hearts of our listeners."[61] Consultants profited by feeding employers' fears about their diverse workforces. For example, Robert Kai Whiting of Dallas-based Whiting & Associates offered to teach attendees at his upcoming management seminar how to do a "Union Vulnerability Audit," which included determining if they were at risk because of "a substantial percentage of blacks, Hispanics or females in your workplace."[62]

Consultants were especially shrill about women's increased organizing and its link to women's newfound rights consciousness. Martin Payson, a partner at Jackson and Lewis, warned that the "most significant trend in labor-management relations today is the union drive to organize female office workers. . . . The new organizing effort has coincided with awakening recognition by women of their rights, and with the passage of laws protecting those rights."[63] Many rang alarm bells for the mostly male management class about the implications of the gender shifts within union organizing. "Organizing is up in office-clerical, in the professions," warned one consultant. "The hottest area now is health care. If you stepped off a curb in San Francisco and got hit by a beer truck, there's a good possibility that the nurse at the hospital would be a Teamster."[64] While employers once thought that women were less likely to unionize, consultants taught them that attitudes had shifted. "All indications are that women are now more inclined to vote union than men," warned one consultant. "This is entirely consistent with the women's movement, by whatever name."[65]

Union busters not only capitalized on rising demand but also profited from the new equal employment regulations. The creation of the EEOC in the Civil Rights Act of 1964 and its later expansions helped spur employers to adopt affirmative action. Starting in 1970, the Department of Labor required all firms with federal contracts worth $500,000 to have affirmative action plans. Then through the Equal Employment Opportunity (EEO) Act in 1972, Congress extended protection to government employees and gave the EEOC the power to sue in federal court.[66] Employers were now forced to deal with a host of new rules on the job. Consultants and management-side lawyers stood ready to assist, offering one-stop shopping for managing the newly diversified workforce. Shawe, for instance, had helped employers fight unions since the late 1940s, but by the 1970s he expanded his services to include updating clients on the latest EEO trends, such as comparable pay. When one major insurance company faced both a unionorganizing drive and a major class-action lawsuit, his firm provided training for the managers on both how to "take extra precaution to assure fairness" and how to be vigilant about spotting union activity.[67] The *Advanced Management Reporter*—a newsletter "helping companies *stay* union free"—featured a regular "EEO corner."[68]

Business schools and professors worked in tandem with antiunion consultants to help shift management's values on unions. By the 1970s, U.S. business managers were far more likely to have gone to business school than in previous decades and were far more likely to do so than managers in other industrialized nations.[69] Business schools in the 1970s began to teach students that unions were an unnecessary expense on the cost-and-balance sheet, tutoring them in how to avoid unionization. William E. Fulmer spent fifteen years at the Harvard Business School and then served in the administration at George Mason University and other business schools. In a series of Harvard Business School case studies dating from 1975 to 1981, he purported to explore union organizing in "an analytical and unbiased manner." Yet, in a discussion of employers' "tactical decisions" concerning ULPs, he taught that since the NLRB response to employer unfair labor practices was so lengthy and the penalties "quite mild," "it is quite possible for management to effectively destroy an organizing effort or, at the very least, signal to employees the relative ineffectiveness of the union in dealing with management."[70] John G. Kilgour, a management professor who joined the faculty of California State University in 1972, asserted that his 1981 book, *Preventative Labor Relations*, was an "objective study." Yet this step-by-step union-avoidance manual offered a blueprint in how to open up and remain nonunion. It imparted that "it is foolhardy to build a new facility where the probability of encountering serious union attention is higher than necessary," and then built a "Union Risk Index," which rated each state by the probability that its workers would try and succeed to form a union. Kilgour even suggested capital flight: "For the sake of completeness, we should note that another way of avoiding unions altogether is to leave the country."[71]

Business schools taught managers that they needed outside consultants to deal with unionization. Fulmer authored one Harvard Business School case study that told the story of a new personnel manager whose major rookie mistake was not hiring an outside labor attorney to help fight a successful unionization effort.[72] The business school academy thus helped shift what it meant to be a "good manager" in relation to unions. "In all but the most unusual circumstances it is almost negligent for a company to allow unionization to happen," asserted Kilgour. "When one surveys all the things a nonunion employer can do to stay that way . . . the employer would almost have to try to get itself organized to end up with a union."[73] Universities themselves began to host the myriad of antiunion seminars made available by union consultants. The University of Delaware, Denver University, the University of San Francisco, the University of Alabama, Clemson, and Wake Forest University were among the schools hosting such seminars in the late 1970s, and, according to the AFL-CIO, one consultant boasted of having taught at thirty universities.[74]

Antiunion consultants and lawyers did far more than fight union organizing efforts already under way. Much of their work involved instructing clients in how to avoid unions completely, often by opening nonunion facilities, hiring people who were the least likely to unionize, and being perfectly clear that the company philosophy was a nonunion one. They thus both tapped into management's growing desire to avoid unions and helped normalize antiunion management practices. The consultant Charles Hughes, who held a doctorate in management psychology, trained over twenty-seven thousand managers and supervisors how to "remain union-free" between 1974 and 1984. "No labor union has ever captured a group of employees without the full cooperation and encouragement of managers who create the need for unionization," advised Hughes.[75] Stephen Cabot, a Philadelphia lawyer, helped firms decide where to locate in order to remain nonunion, sometimes even identifying specific areas of cities where workers were the least likely to unionize. By 1983, nearly half of firms identified remaining union-free as their most pressing labor relations goal.[76]

Much of the antiunion consultants' work, however, came after workers already showed interest in a union. Once employers realized that their workforces were signing union cards, they often called in consultants to usher them through the union campaigns, step by step, in order to defeat the workers' organizing efforts. They made good use of the predictable patterns in an NLRB election process. First, at least 30 percent of workers had to sign union cards or petitions showing an interest in a union, and then they petitioned the NLRB to hold an election. The union and company worked out the "bargaining unit," or the specifics of who could vote, and about ten to twelve weeks later the NLRB agents came to the workplace to hold a union election. Meanwhile, the company was free to talk with workers as much as they wanted during the work day, on work time, and the union representatives were prohibited from entering the property.[77]

Consultants first advised employers how to discourage card signing. "The name of the game is to prevent the election and chill the union off," Alfred DeMaria, a popular consultant in the mid- to late 1970s, told the *Wall Street Journal*. "Those cards are vile and they're dangerous." DeMaria advised employers how to legally dissuade workers from signing a union card. "The Board has approved some surprisingly strong employer statements," he assured. "One employer was lawful when it told its workers, 'Don't sign any cards; they can be fatal to business.'"[78] Once the workers successfully signed enough cards to file a petition with the NLRB for an election, consultants taught employers to delay each step of the NLRB process as long as possible. For instance, consultants urged employers to demand a protracted NLRB hearing to determine which workers got to vote. "Always go to hearing. . . .

I have yet to see a situation where time worked against the employers in an election," urged Fred Long in an executive meeting captured on tape by a union infiltrator in 1975, a transcript of which surfaced in a 1979 congressional hearing. "Suffice it to say, you have at least 500 issues. So you litigate those issues. . . . You could come up with them for almost a year, as we did in one case."[79] Consultants advised employers to never agree to what the NLRB called a "consent" election, in which both parties agree that the NLRB regional director can arbitrate disputes, but instead advised them to insist on a "stipulation" for certification, which sent disputes to the national NLRB. In 1962 the more cumbersome stipulated certifications made up only 27 percent of cases, but by 1977 they made up a full 70 percent.[80] Such delays cost organizing workers dearly. One study found that each month of delay between the filing of the petition and the election decreased the workers' chance of winning their union election by 2.5 percent.[81]

Consultants also instructed employers how to manipulate the loopholes in the NLRB process in order to seed the voting group with as many "no" votes as possible. "Hire five of your relatives on a regularly scheduled part-time basis. . . . You have 60 days to hire even a hell of a lot of people if you need to," urged Long in the closed-door executive session. DeMaria's public advice was more measured in his book entitled *How Management Wins Union Organizing Campaigns*: "Employers should note that under existing NLRB rules a limited amount of 'stacking' a payroll is permitted."[82]

Consultants developed elaborate systems for training frontline supervisors how to track and sway union sentiments among workers. They knew that supervisors often came from the rank and file and their loyalties could lie with the union. Therefore, consultants advised employers to make clear that supervisors' jobs were on the line. "Employers are entitled to the undivided loyalty of their supervisors and have the full right under the law to discharge supervisors who are not loyal," advised DeMaria.[83] Shawe's firm, Shawe & Rosenthal, met with supervisors at Hecht's at least once a week during a 1981 union campaign and advised supervisors how to pressure workers within the law: "Ask Associates to think about the hard feelings which are always created when a strike occurs . . . bad feelings and sometimes violence."[84] Consultants often relied on supervisors to track the sentiments of employees during the campaign. One "highly confidential management document" taught supervisors at Cannon Mills in 1982 how to rate each worker in their department from the strongest for the company to the weakest, and to profile employees by race, sex, and age.[85] "The front line supervisor is the best possible communicator in a campaign," advised

Melnick. Companies like Melnick's often spent weeks at the worksite, training supervisors and offering advice, though rarely appearing before the workforce. Staying behind the scenes helped them sidestep the requirement to file a report under the Labor and Management Disclosure Act of 1959, a law that only required reports on direct dealings with workers. Unions submitted seventy-one thousand reports in 1983 disclosing salaries and budgets, for instance, but only 198 labor consultants or their employers filed such reports.[86]

Consultants and lawyers taught companies how to threaten unionizing workers with loss of benefits and strikes while skirting the legal prohibitions on such threats. They provided employers with letters, speeches, and backgrounders that made clear to workers that the company would not really have to offer anything new if the workers won the right to collective bargaining. "The Hotel does not have to agree to a single thing the union proposes so long as we bargain in good faith," asserted one Shawe & Rosenthal fact sheet created for the Boardwalk Regency Hotel in Atlantic City. "All the union can do, if the Company does not agree to its demands, is call the employees out on strike."[87] In fact, most consultants and employers were quick to alarm workers about potential strikes. "Tell employees that the law permits the hiring of a permanent replacement for anyone who engages in an economic strike," urged Brandeis University to its supervisors in 1976 when librarians tried to unionize.[88]

Employers learned how to legally threaten workers with plant closure if they voted in a union, a threat that held enormous sway in the climate of capital flight by the late 1970s and early 1980s. DeMaria suggested a sample letter carefully calibrated to legally threaten workers with job loss: "If excessive wage demands add a lot to our already existing losses it could force us to close. . . . We won't close just because a union is voted in. . . . Only if union demands . . . cause substantial additional losses would we be forced to consider the business as unprofitable. You're free to vote as you please. But vote smart."[89] It was the sort of bending of the law exemplified by one plant manager at a GE facility in Goldsboro, North Carolina, facing a union drive in 1978. "Cleveland Welds . . . was represented by the IUE, as were a number of other plants that have closed, including Cleveland Lamp plant, Oakland Lamp plant. . . . Don't mistake me. I'm not saying we will automatically lose our business if the Union wins the election. But it's clear that unions . . . can, and they do, hurt people's job security."[90]

If the workers did manage to win a campaign, employers routinely delayed or avoided actually signing a collective bargaining agreement—the very relationship that the entire election process was designed to facilitate. One

L-CIO survey found that among workers who won elections, only ⸻ percent ever actually got a union contract.[91] If all else failed, consultants taught employers the ins and outs of how their workers could decertify a union already in place. "If a company loses a representation election . . . a decertification election may be viewed as the next step in the long-run program of remaining nonunion," instructed Professor John Kilgour.[92] Decertification elections had once been rare, but then the numbers of such elections doubled between 1972 and 1982.[93] Shawe lauded the turn toward "de-unionization," and instructed companies how employees could prompt a decertification election. For instance, after the spice giant McCormick acquired an Indianapolis firm where the workers had recently unionized, Shawe's firm issued a memo walking the company through processes for de-unionizing before an anticipated move to South Bend, where it could try to operate nonunion.[94]

The employer campaigns against unionization in the 1970s were remarkably potent. They effectively unraveled the same federal rules governing organizing that the LLRG had once sought to rewrite. U.S. workers still had the right to organize on paper, but by the end of the decade they were losing it in practice as they faced defeat in more than half of the elections that they themselves had triggered. The AFL-CIO's assistant organizing director told Congress in 1984, "I've been involved in organizing off and on . . . since 1967 and can assert categorically that the state of the art in employer resistance to employees' organizing efforts has achieved a level of sophistication and effectiveness far exceeding that of the late '60s and early '70s."[95] Doreen Lavasseur, a union organizer who helped university and clerical workers organize throughout the decade, recalled the ground-level impact of the employer campaign on workers: "I would just watch these people go from feeling strong and like we need to do something to feeling like totally terrified to do anything, and paralyzed."[96] The rise in employer lawbreaking, the spread of employer antiunion campaigns deep into the nation's core industries, and the tutorials of union consultants coalesced to undermine the potency of U.S. labor law by the decade's end.

The Labor Law Reform Act

In the face of increased employer resistance to organizing, the labor movement sought to strengthen the laws that guaranteed workers' rights to form unions through the Labor Law Reform Act in 1977 and 1978. Employers had once been the ones who wanted legal changes, but they had since perfected the art of manipulating weak labor law. They defended the status quo by the late 1970s, leveraging organized business's new political activism to block labor's attempt to shore up workers' organizing rights.

Labor's wish list was long for the new Carter administration. In addition to labor law reform, the AFL-CIO's 1977 legislative priorities included a three-dollar-per-hour hike in the minimum wage, a thirty-five-hour workweek, and universal coverage of all workers under the Fair Labor Standards Act.[97] Unions first tried to shore up their power through a common situs picketing bill that would have legalized strikes of different construction unions on a common worksite. The legislation had already passed Congress in 1975, but President Ford vetoed it under enormous pressure from contractors. When the bill again went before Congress in 1977, a coalition of more than a hundred business organizations, including the Business Roundtable, used intense grassroots lobbying and a public media campaign to squarely defeat the bill.[98]

Organized labor had been caught flat-footed by the effectiveness of organized business's campaign. Nevertheless, unions pressed forward to try to pass a larger revision of labor law that would address the organizing crisis. Labor originally set its sights much higher than the rather modest labor law changes that ended up going before the House and Senate as the Labor Law Reform Act. Labor wanted to change the cumbersome, two-step certification process required by U.S. labor law under which workers first must sign cards to trigger a union election and then wait months to vote. Unions proposed a "card check" provision under which unions would be automatically certified as the bargaining representative once a majority of workers signed up to be members, as was the case in many parts of Canada. Unions sought to repeal section 14(b) of the Taft-Hartley Act, the provision allowing states to prohibit a union shop. Finally, unions wanted a provision that would require a business that bought a unionized facility to honor the union contract.[99]

The Carter administration refused to include all three of these more major changes, instead meeting with labor leaders and working out a compromise that Stuart Eizenstat, domestic policy chief, labeled a "much more modest set of reforms . . . because they (unions) *very much* want Administration backing for their bill."[100] President Jimmy Carter offered the reforms as his own labor law reform bill to Congress on July 18, 1977, rejecting a suggestion by some staff members to simply issue a message of support.[101] The bill's major provisions included holding elections more quickly (within fifteen to twenty-five days) after workers petitioned for an election, allowing union representatives equal access inside the workplace when employers held antiunion meetings, paying workers double back pay when they were illegally fired for forming a union, prohibiting repeat labor law violators from getting federal contracts, and increasing the number of NLRB members to seven in order to expedite board processes.[102]

In addition to meeting with labor leaders, the Carter administration met repeatedly with the Business Roundtable, the Chamber of Commerce, and NAM in the process of writing the bill. The administration thought that while the fight would be a tough one, they had extinguished much of the business opposition's fire. "Because we involved the business community and because they achieved a number of compromises, their reaction has been vastly muted . . . and will therefore be less vociferous," Eizenstat assured President Carter just after the bill went to Congress.[103] Labor, too, believed that it could convince many employers with major collective bargaining relationships to eschew a fight, telling reporters they expected as many as twenty-five companies to back the bill.[104]

In fact, the Business Roundtable was at first split on whether to oppose the bill. A number of leaders of major, unionized firms—like Thomas A. Murphy of GM and Reginald Jones of GE—had at first argued that the bill was not worth jeopardizing peaceful labor relations. After all, the roundtable had successfully lobbied to exclude from the House bill the provisions dealing with card check, repeal of Taft-Hartley's 14(b), and contract continuity. The final bill was thus already more palatable to many of them.[105] Yet many members of the Business Roundtable staunchly opposed the reform legislation and instead argued for maintaining the existing law. A large block of the roundtable's policy committee pushed to join NAM and the chamber in opposing the bill. Nonunion, retail firms like Sears, Roebuck opposed the bill, and so did some unionized firms like Bethlehem Steel, Firestone, and Goodyear. Fresh union organizing was central to their concerns. They worried the law would make it "most difficult to maintain as nonunion such groups as engineers, technicians, branch banks, or retail units, etc.," according to one Firestone executive.[106] Labor leaders and the Carter administration proved woefully mistaken in believing they could win the support of major corporations for the bill. In the end, the Business Roundtable policy committee voted squarely to oppose the House bill, joining a broad coalition of American business—including NAM, the chamber, the National Federation of Independent Business, and other small business groups—to defend the broken status quo.[107]

Corporate leaders who had once sought to reshape labor law now defended it, because it was now so weak. "Speaking for American industry, the NAM strongly supports the existing law," asserted NAM chair and vice chair of U.S. Steel R. Heath Larry in 1977.[108] Such a statement was quite a reversal from a man who had tried to roll back labor law as one of the original steering committee members for the LLRG.[109] Heath now defended the current law, which "guarantees to workers the opportunity to determine whether or not they want union representation," and labeled the reform bill as "largely a bag of free organizing tools for unions." The employers did back Republican John Erlenborn of Illinois's "Employee Bill of Rights Act of 1977," which would have made it easier for employers to trigger elections and prohibited employers from bargaining before an election, but it was a weak effort compared to the LLRG's attempt and it went nowhere.[110] Instead, the employers put the bulk of their energy into defending a labor law that now served their purposes.

Employer groups mobilized as a united front, putting into action the lobbying power, relationships, and structures they had forged over the last decade. NAM and the Associated Builders and Contractors helped found a coalition of employer groups called the National Action Committee for Labor Law Reform in June 1977 to spearhead opposition. The Chamber of Commerce whipped up fear against the bill among those members: "If we lose the 'big one,' we accept all the demands made by the unions over the last 25 years. And that is a *horrendous* prospect." NAM armed its members with kits containing sample letters to lawmakers, model letters to stockholders and suppliers, and a tutorial on communicating with the media. Firestone's chairman, for example, sent a letter to shareholders warning that the bill "grants inordinate organizational and protective power to unions," and asked them to contact their members of Congress.[111]

The bill passed the House on October 6, 1977, after a two-day debate with strong support, 257 to 163, with thirty-six Republicans supporting the bill.[112] When it passed through the Senate Human Relations Subcommittee in January, Utah senator Orrin Hatch immediately vowed a filibuster.[113] The AFL-CIO wanted the president to prioritize the Senate bill for the 1978 congressional session, but Carter chose to lead with the Panama Canal treaty, giving business even more time to mobilize. Small-business opposition to the bill turned out to be crucial for swinging senators' support, and the NAM and chamber worked alongside the Small Business Legislative Council, recently founded in 1976, to put a small-business face on the entire business movement's campaign. "The biggest threat is not to large companies," the chamber argued in its member newsletter. "The real danger here is to small business." The group helped mobilize five thousand small-business representatives for a rally, a maneuver that was unusual enough to catch the White House's attention.[114]

Labor also put up a strong fight, mounting what AFL-CIO president George Meany called "one of the most massive campaigns we've ever waged in our history."[115] The unions brought in scores of victims of labor law abuse to lobby Congress, for instance, and mobilized support from a wide coalition including the NAACP, the National Organization for Women, the National Urban League, and the United States Conference of Catholic Bishops. The AFL-CIO established a special Task Force on Labor Law Reform and publicized horror stories from across the nation of workers who had been discharged, threatened, and bribed and then forced to wait years for the NLRB process. Nearly 150 Newport News Shipbuilding workers were among those cheered for at a massive USWA rally for labor law reform in Washington.[116]

When the bill came to the Senate floor in mid-May 1978, it faced a nineteen-day filibuster. The bill's supporters tried five times to secure the sixty votes needed to shut down debate but encountered a formidable floor manager in Hatch, who kept support tight. The Democratic supporters scrambled to find support among Southern Democrats such as Lawton Chiles (Florida), Russell Long (Louisiana), and Dale Bumpers (Arkansas).[117] Labor Secretary Ray Marshall remembered that Vice President Walter Mondale managed to hold Democrat John Sparkman of Alabama incommunicado and brought him to the Senate in his car, only to see Sparkman vote against it. The bill died after the sixth cloture vote on June 22, 1978.[118]

Labor had known that the battle would be difficult, but it was shocked by the vehemence and coordination of the business attack. "I am frankly puzzled by the campaign against this bill," wrote Meany during the Senate debate.[119] The AFL-CIO's first-ever full-page *Wall Street Journal* ad reflected the group's sentiments in early May, just before debate began on the Senate floor. In an "Open Letter to American Business," Meany asked business, "Why? What is your motivation? . . . Where is the moral basis for your attacks? Is not the real intent of this attack the destruction of the uniquely American system of collective bargaining? . . . Do you want to destroy American trade unionism?"[120] Many labor leaders felt deeply betrayed by the businesses they had considered partners in labor management. Days before the final cloture vote, the new UAW president Douglas Fraser resigned from the president's Labor-Management Group, where he had served alongside leaders such as GE's Reginald Jones, charging that the "ugly multimillion dollar campaign against labor law reform" was indicative of "a one-sided class war" that broke "and discarded the fragile, unwritten compact" between labor and business.[121]

Closing the Door to Economic Security

The employer resistance to union organizing reminds us that while globalization and technological change certainly did impact union membership in the final third of the twentieth century, the steep decline of union density in the United States was not a natural process. Unions did not just melt away. Rather, when employers faced a new upsurge of global competition, they increased their resistance to unions as one key component of a multipronged effort to rewrite the nation's workplace rules. Employers desperately sought to get out from under the weight of private social welfare costs and wage obligations, and so sought to limit the numbers of workers who could enter into collective bargaining. Large corporations first tried to roll back the laws protecting workers' organizing rights in the late 1960s. When they were unsuccessful in doing so through Congress, they increased their workplace-level fight in the 1970s, violating the law at record levels and making new use of antiunion consultants. When labor and their allies then tried to restrengthen the rules governing organizing in 1977–78, large and small businesses mobilized to block this legislative change. Having shut the door on workers' organizing efforts, they fought to keep it closed.

Employers launched their assault on labor to counter a real and potent organizing threat: a reshaped working class that offered new promise to the flagging union movement in the 1970s. Employers believed that they needed to deflect this surge in union organizing in order to check workers' demands for higher wage and benefits standards and to gain more control in a rapidly changing economy. They had even more than union organizing in their sights; they sought the unilateral power to set the terms for the nation's workplaces under a globalized and financialized capitalism. We turn now to the ground level, to the people of color, young people, women, and Southerners who actively led the organizing campaigns that provoked such a potent backlash. Their stories reveal how new ideas about workplace rights flowed from the civil and women's rights movements, and uncover how employers' growing resistance to organizing played out against the background of globalization and the rise of the service and retail sectors.

Part II

4   Signing Up in the Shipyard

Edward Coppedge was admittedly a bit "naïve and reckless" when he left his family's hard-scrabble tobacco and cotton farm in Castalia, North Carolina, in the late 1950s, but he also had a stubborn and persuasive style that would serve him well. He traveled 150 miles and a galaxy away to the Newport News, Virginia, shipyard because the only local options for young African American men like him were in dangerous sawmills and seasonal tobacco sheds. It took months to talk his way into the shipyard, and once inside he was relegated to cleaning ships, mostly alongside other black men. After nearly a year of "going every day and asking for a transfer," he finally secured a coveted spot as a welder, a job more commonly held by whites.[1]

Yet far too many African Americans remained stuck in the dirty, low-paying jobs at the shipyard. It took several lawsuits under Title VII of the 1964 Civil Rights Act to challenge the status quo, and even then, racial inequities persisted. By the late 1970s, Coppedge helped lead his coworkers in a USWA union organizing effort. African American men like Coppedge joined with newly hired women like Jan Hooks and a fresh generation of workers from all backgrounds to overthrow a company-controlled union that had been in place for nearly forty years. When Tenneco—the conglomerate that had owned the Newport News Shipbuilding and Dry Dock Company for ten years—followed the 1970s corporate pattern of hiring antiworker consultants and dragging its feet in court, the workers did not wait for the law to slowly churn out justice. They struck for eighty-two days in order to force the navy contractor to recognize their union, braving guardsmen with dogs sent by the governor of Virginia to harass the picket lines. Coppedge would go on to serve as one of the USWA Local 8888's first presidents, and he would help build a union that remained active on civil and women's rights issues for decades.

There is no question that blue-collar workers lost power in the 1970s, when employers reacted to a globalizing economy by upending the rules that had governed postwar labor relations. But no one told Coppedge and his coworkers that their role in the drama of the 1970s American working class was supposed to be a tragic one. These workers and their organization proved potent and capable in the face of rising corporate power. Rather than

Edward Coppedge helped coworkers organize a USWA union and later served as Local 8888's president. USWA Collection, Communications Department Records. Reproduced with the permission of the Historical Collections and Labor Archives, Special Collections Library, the Pennsylvania State University Libraries.

giving in to a burgeoning right-wing, grassroots conservatism, these activists increased their demands on the state by using its mechanisms to organize private-sector unions. The civil rights movements of the 1960s and 1970s did not derail these workers' unions but instead greased the wheels of victory as workers learned to use civil rights tools and the union in tandem.

Newport News workers had one additional advantage not available to most other industrial workers in the 1970s: by law their product had to be built in the United States. Their story thus allows us to see working-class agency in action in the 1970s in a context not so determined by unfettered globalization and its resulting structural barriers. Can a labor triumph help us better understand a period known for working-class defeat? As we examine the push and pull that characterized the tumultuous 1970s, what happens if we shine the historical spotlight on working people who actually won?[2]

Newport News Shipbuilding and the Union Stopper

If you visited Newport News in 1978, there was no missing the shipyard. The dry docks sprawled for two miles along the James River as cranes towered over the town like skyscrapers, emblazoned with the Tenneco name. The shipyard was founded in 1886 as the Chesapeake Dry Dock & Construction Company and won its first navy contract in 1893. Tenneco, one of the world's largest diversified companies, bought the struggling shipyard in 1968 and sunk $100 million into the operation. Five years later, the shipyard had a billion dollars in backlogged orders, and by 1978 the shipyard was the largest employer in the state. More than a third of the money circulating in the entire Tidewater local economy came from the company. It was a major navy contractor that built and refurbished navy aircraft carriers and nuclear submarines, and it also did private work. Nevertheless, the company experienced the same kind of profit squeeze that faced so many employers by the end of the decade: in 1978, the year of the union election, it made just $14 million in earnings, half its 1975 earnings. The new president, retired Navy admiral Ralph W. Cousins, knew that he needed to turn those reduced profits around.[3]

The company had a long and intertwined relationship with the Peninsula Shipbuilders Association (PSA), a union at the shipyard. The company first established an employee representation plan (ERP) in 1927 at a time when many companies set up their own such unions as a welfare capitalism tactic designed to contain workers' labor activism. Employer representatives served alongside employee representatives (paid by the company) on the joint committees that governed the ERP. The shipyard's workforce was about a fifth African American in the 1930s, and the white and black workforces each had their own ERP representatives.[4] One of the purposes of the NLRB, as established by the Wagner Act in 1935, was to force employers to recognize workers' own democratic organizations over such company unions. In fact, in one of the first NLRB cases to come before the Supreme Court, the court ruled in 1939 that Newport News' ERP was company directed and ordered the company to disestablish it. The ERP jettisoned its company-paid representatives and, within a month of the court's decision, regrouped as a union—the PSA—and soon bargained with the company for a new contract.[5] Like the ERP, the PSA had a number of black delegates and leaders. The CIO's Industrial Union of Marine and Shipbuilding Workers of America wanted to represent the workers, but it chose not to challenge the validity of this new company union, instead trying to beat it at the ballot box. It was a bad choice. The PSA won a 1944 NLRB election over the CIO, and the PSA became one of the nation's largest independent unions.[6]

Despite the PSA's claim to independence, the company's hand remained very visible in its affairs. In fact, Robert Moore—a former PSA delegate in the 1960s and 1970s and later a supporter of the USWA—said that it was not really a union but rather a "union stopper" that the company encouraged to keep a more effective union out. The PSA did have a process for worker grievances, though it almost never took those grievances to an outside arbitrator—a right that is fundamental to most unions' practices. The PSA constitution had no provisions for general meetings with workers. Workers in various departments could vote on their delegates, who in turn would attend the only available union meetings and make all the decisions about leadership, finances, and bargaining. It was a democracy in name only, for few workers were even members of the PSA. At the time of the USWA election, only about a third of the workers in the yard were PSA members. The PSA never even held a convention until the USWA organizing drive began.[7]

During its fifty years in the Newport News shipyard, the PSA beat back four attempts by outside unions to represent the workers: by the CIO in 1944, the International Brotherhood of Boilermakers in the 1950s, and the IAM in the 1960s and early 1970s.[8] The company had a vested interest in keeping the PSA as the workers' representative. For instance, the company's president sent a letter to all workers in 1972 urging them not to sign IAM union cards: "If you haven't signed one of these cards, I hope you won't . . . so far as I'm concerned, there already is a bargaining agent—the Peninsula Shipbuilders Association."[9]

The PSA was a legacy holdover from corporate welfare tactics of the 1920s and 1930s, and by the 1970s most companies eschewed such company unionism, recognizing that such employee groups often paved the way for stronger unions. In fact, independent unions had long served as a kind of bridge for workers' more radical unionization efforts, and the PSA proved to be no exception. Though the PSA and USWA battled for the right to represent the Newport News workers, it is likely that the PSA's presence ultimately facilitated the USWA local. After all, the PSA provided these Southern workers with a familiarity with unions that they were unlikely to get elsewhere, and created a strong leadership cadre who understood how the unionizing system worked and longed for better. Coppedge, for instance, served as a PSA delegate for many years before he helped found the USWA local because he believed that some union was better than no union. Yet he was appalled by the PSA's relationship with the company: "The independent union was controlled and owned by the company. . . . You basically [got] what they wanted to give you." Nearly all the original USWA activists had some experience within the PSA organization.[10]

Civil Rights at the Shipyard

The civil rights movement catapulted issues of racial inequality to the center of the nation's public sphere. It emboldened many black workers, inspiring a new "rights consciousness" that both propelled them to file equal rights charges and energized their union impulse. Though many scholars find a dichotomous relationship between civil and labor rights, the Newport News story reveals that the struggle for these rights was often deeply interwoven at the workplace level. At every step of the way, the yard's black workers used whatever tool seemed most potent in order to ensure economic security and equality. Eventually, when the federal government's civil rights remedy seemed both intermittent and limited, a number of them turned to the USWA to help secure long-lasting change. It was no coincidence that after various unions tried four times to overthrow the PSA, the group of Newport News workers who finally succeeded included more African Americans and women. For these workers, the USWA was a tool they could use to both shore up their newfound civil rights and win economic security.[11]

In the summer of 1965 a group of African American employees, working with the NAACP, filed a suit against the shipyard under Title VII of the 1964 Civil Rights Act. They charged that their employer denied promotions on account of race and did not allow black workers into the higher-paying jobs. Many yard facilities, such as water fountains and restrooms, were still segregated at this time. The company had a long history of hiring a multiracial workforce. African Americans, however, held the lowest-paying jobs and had little access to high-skilled jobs, for example, as electricians or first-class mechanics.[12] The EEOC found reasonable cause in its investigation of racial discrimination. In 1966 the shipyard signed what turned out to be a landmark conciliation agreement, and it did so under government threats to withhold its navy contracts. The Newport News agreement was the most far-reaching of the more than a hundred agreements the EEOC signed in

1966; it mandated equal pay for equal work, more promotions for black workers, and equal access to apprentice school slots. EEOC chair Franklin D. Roosevelt Jr. termed it "a model of comprehensive affirmative action." The agreement was controversial. Far-right Republican Paul Fannin denounced the settlement from the Senate floor and the NAM accused the EEOC of overstepping its mandate.[13]

At first, a clear-cut tension did seem to distinguish civil rights remedies from labor rights at Newport News. The PSA promptly protested the EEOC decision, charging that the agreement between the company and the government violated its labor contract.[14] But then the story muddied. Thirty-one black members of the PSA disagreed with their organization and filed their own report, arguing for the PSA to help the EEOC implement the agreement. "Any steps that the union takes in disagreement of [sic] the agreement between the Equal Employment Opportunity Commission and the company would be detrimental to the union," they insisted.[15] In fact, their instinct was right on target; it turned out that government action on civil rights was only sporadic without a worker institution pushing for its implementation. A year after the conciliation agreement, the EEOC reduced the scope of its ongoing review of the company's practices, deciding that the agreement "was satisfactorily concluded," despite the fact that there were seventy-six charges of discrimination pending.[16]

Black workers continued to press for change, especially in the transportation department. African Americans made up the majority of workers in this department but continued to hold the worst, lowest-paying jobs—driving trucks and processing scrap—despite the conciliation agreement. The company even paid them less than operators of mobile equipment in other, mostly white departments.[17] Tensions remained high in this department where, in 1967, workers walked out in support of two coworkers disciplined for refusing to work overtime to meet production quotas for the Vietnam War. The transportation workers' walkout sparked a broader wildcat strike among white and black workers, who rioted for two nights when they thought the company tried to bring in strikebreakers.[18] Then, in 1969, thirteen black workers in the transportation department signed on to a class-action lawsuit against the company charging that the EEOC's conciliation agreement left a majority of black workers still stuck in low-paying jobs and without access to apprenticeships. At first, the PSA was not a party to the suit, and the shipyard argued that the union's contract should be a bar to proceeding. The PSA agreed to join the workers' suit, however, after a judge required the union's participation in order to proceed. The

PSA was no doubt inspired by its own black leadership who had so vocally supported EEOC action in 1966 and by its own members' militancy in the 1967 wildcat. The suit spurred the federal government to tighten affirmative action standards at the yard, holding up $700 million in new contracts until the shipbuilder agreed to sign a new conciliation agreement in 1970, which put a heavier emphasis on recruitment, training, and promotion.[19]

Though the original suits were all focused on racial discrimination, the shipyard also began a major push to hire more women in 1973. The company had not retained the women who, for a brief time, built ships at the yard during World War II, and it was not until the early 1970s that the company routinely hired women into production jobs and the first woman graduated from the company's Apprentice School (first established in 1919). The company's decision to increase its hiring of women came on the heels of the deepening potency of the EEOC's equity campaign on issues of gender. Congress had given the EEOC the power to sue in federal court in 1972, and it promptly did so on behalf of women. For example, in January 1973 the EEOC won a $15 million back pay suit for thirteen thousand women workers at AT&T. In light of this new emphasis on gender discrimination, the shipyard took action, presumably choosing to do so rather than put its federal contracts at risk by being out of step with government expectations on civil rights.[20]

USWA Organizing Drive Kicks Off

Yet such changes were still not fast enough for Coppedge and three other African American men: Oscar Pretlow, Ellis Cofield, and W. T. Hayes. Though all had been PSA members and leaders over the years, by the mid-1970s they were weary of company unionism and the PSA's inaction on racial equality. Despite the government's intervention, they felt that white supervisors freely used their power to promote white workers over blacks and they saw few options for recourse. "We went out and filed and followed up on discrimination in trying to get the shipyard to live by the Civil Rights Act, but we didn't have anybody backing us. . . . To say we are going to go out there and take on the company on civil rights, the PSA was not the union. They wouldn't do it," remembered Coppedge.[21] The group of four men secretly reached out to the USWA in October 1976 to explore having the union represent the yard workers. They chose the USWA because that union was already working with the shipyard's 1,200 ship designers who had pulled out of the PSA a few years earlier.[22] They arranged a meeting with Elmer

SWA director of organizing, who originally thought the campaign
ost an impossible project." He insisted that the USWA would not
campaign until the men had a volunteer organizing committee of
red workers. The men, meanwhile, balked when the USWA only
_____ two white staffers to the campaign, Jack Hower and John Kitch-
ens. "If you want the union in here, black people are going to be the people
that lead the parade," Coppedge told Chatak, who then assigned a black
organizer, Roosevelt Robinson.[23]

The activists and organizers began to form an organizing committee that
slowly expanded over the next months, reaching out to likely supporters and
building its strength behind the scenes. The yard was about half black and
half white by the late 1970s, and black workers were far more likely than
white workers to support the USWA, a pattern that surveys showed was typical across the nation.[24] Organizers were careful to build a mixed-race
leadership group, which meant spending extra time developing white leaders, a task the organizers often accomplished at a Moose lodge and local
bars. By the end of July 1977, the USWA had built the required committee
of five hundred yard workers, a group that was ready to spearhead an effort
to oust the PSA. One steamy August morning, they began passing out USWA
authorization cards at the nineteen gates the workers used to enter the
yard. The workers' union campaign was now out in the open and moving
quickly.[25]

Many Newport News workers saw a new union as a doorway to increased
economic security. "Job security, income security plus health security equals
FAMILY security," read one USWA mailer. Key issues included wages that
were less than the national shipyard average and poor retirement benefits.
The PSA had signed a retirement agreement in 1969 that counted people's
service only from that year forward. People who had already put in forty
years stood to earn as little as forty dollars a month on retirement under
this system. Many people were particularly upset that Tenneco had cut a
paid twenty-minute lunch break period; they saw this as emblematic of a
larger lack of respect from the conglomerate. Yet not everyone was for the
USWA, and the PSA enjoyed significant support. "About two years ago, I de-
served a raise and wanted to go back on day shift, but I was told I couldn't
have either," explained Twanna C. Lewis, an African American worker, who
said that the PSA helped her with both issues. S. F. McMillan supported the
PSA because they had helped him out with some attendance issues, and
helped him finance his truck. Yet for many Newport News workers, a new
union essentially would mean a chance to force their company to offer them

higher wages, better benefits, and more security—essentially, a more secure tier of the U.S. social welfare regime.[26]

Organizing Newport News posed an incredible logistical challenge. The workers would have to file cards with the government signed by more than 30 percent of the workforce, or more than six thousand workers; only then would the NLRB schedule an election. Shipyard workers lived in communities scattered all over the Chesapeake region. Many commuted from as far as fifty miles away on buses or in carpools. Workers began to gather union cards any way they could—at the gates at six o'clock in the morning, in people's homes, even in the vans that brought workers to the shipyard from as far away as North Carolina. "We would sneak behind the toolbox racks, behind the machinery," to get the cards signed, remembered Jan Hooks. "Sneaky. In the bathrooms. Lord, some of the conversations we had in the bathrooms. That's where we did a lot of our organizing."[27] The USWA organizers began to branch out far from the shipyard and held meetings with groups of workers where they lived, in local recreation centers, in churches, and in hotel conference rooms. The campaign was heavily dependent on its large volunteer committee rather than on the small USWA staff. "Nobody knew those guys," said Coppedge of the USWA organizers, "so every meeting they held we went and introduced them. . . . We had meetings everywhere, all over, every night of the week."[28]

The USWA organizers found strong support among an interracial group of women, who made up more than 10 percent of the workforce. Many women took the job because it was the best opportunity around, even though the going was rough. "It wasn't my intent to go down in the shipyard and get dirty and crawl through tanks, but that's where the money was and I had a child so that's what I did," remembered Peggy Carpenter, who pointed out that many of the women were single mothers like her. Breaking the gender barrier was not easy. Hooks went to the PSA about a promised pay raise but "I couldn't get anybody to represent me because they still resented the women. . . . 'You are taking a man's job,' that type of stuff." Hooks attended a meeting the USWA organizers called just for the women, and she began to organize others to join, helping to develop a core cadre of the organizing committee. The women found they had tremendous momentum after jumping the yard's gender hurdles, and their courage inspired some men to join the effort. "A lot of them moved because of the women standing up in the union . . . they followed us along," recalled Carpenter.[29]

At each shift change, PSA members gathered outside the gates to counter the USWA supporters who collected union cards. Wearing special PSA decals emblazoned on their white helmets, they would challenge and taunt the USWA activists, who often wore their union ball caps. The USWA supporters gathered enough signatures to file for an NLRB election in December 1977. The thousands of union cards were so heavy that the string binding them cut and bloodied the union organizer's hands as he carried them to the NLRB office to file for election. The NLRB set the date of the election for January 31, 1978.[30]

The Campaign Hits High Gear

As soon as the USWA emerged as a threat, Tenneco turned to the PSA to serve as its frontline defense. "The stalking horse for them was the independent [union]. . . . That was the way they chose to do it," remembered Carl Frankel, the USWA attorney. The head of personnel at Newport News, D. T. Savas, told workers at the first-ever PSA convention that "the Steelworkers are out to 'raid' the PSA. . . . Reject the Steelworkers; don't be coaxed or pressured into signing a Steelworkers card."[31] After the company fired one USWA supporter for circulating a letter critical of the PSA, an NLRB judge found that the company had broken the law and that its attitudes "disclose[d] a desire on its part to shore up the fortunes of a labor organization with whom it had achieved a comfortable relationship and whose status was being challenged by a potential rival." The NLRB also found that PSA representatives threatened workers that they would be fired if they continued to support the USWA, and otherwise coerced USWA supporters.[32] The company gave the PSA tremendous latitude in its campaign efforts. Carpenter remembered not being allowed to speak up when PSA supporters met with her work group: "I recall saying, 'Well, you had a chance to speak, let me speak.' And that was a no-no." Robert Moore was still a PSA delegate at this point, and he voted for the PSA in the election. He had free rein to walk the yard with his PSA buttons, armband, and decals on his hard hat. After one of the frequent PSA campaign meetings with the company, Moore recalled that the PSA "gave us all a little piece of paper . . . with what you'd lose [with the union] that type of stuff. When you walked around and someone asked you a question you just more or less read it off to them."[33]

Though the shipyard leaned on the PSA to wage much of the fight against the union, Tenneco also pulled workers into closed-door meetings to talk against the union. Danny Keefer remembered that supervisors would hold meetings "and they would be letting you know that if you go that way instead of keeping the PSA, things are going to be different here. Not to your best interest." Tenneco's campaign was orchestrated by Seyfarth, Shaw, Fairweather & Geraldson, one of the largest management-side law firms in the nation. Seyfarth Shaw joined the surge of growth among antiunion consultants and firms in 1970s, representing the lettuce growers (in their efforts to fight the United Farmworkers) and the *Washington Post* (in a bitter pressmen's strike). The firm was notorious for pioneering the tactic of forcing a strike in order to weaken or decertify a union.[34]

African American leaders in the town split over the unionization issue, perhaps reflecting larger class tensions in Newport News' sizeable black community. Carpenter remembered that much of the support in the black community for the PSA and company came from the middle class: "You've got to take into consideration probably they never worked in the plant and a lot of their people could have been management. They are not going to buck them." Milton Reid, for example, the professional editor and publisher of the local African American newspaper, adamantly opposed the USWA effort. A week before the vote, he published a full-page editorial urging a vote for the PSA and predicting that affirmative action might one day negate the need for a union at all: "With the way affirmative action has taken place since 1971, and with the benefits being received by the work force, there might just come the day when the management will out union the necessity for any union."[35] Yet racial uplift and strong unions were still squarely linked in many local black leaders' minds. Though the local black Hampton Roads Ministers Alliance supported the PSA in the election, a number of its members publicly denounced the group's decision. Rev. W. Henry Maxwell, a local Baptist minister and former local NAACP president, led the black clergy's efforts for the steelworkers' union in the weeks before the vote. He later accused the shipyard of "flagrantly denying the will and decision of the blue-collar workers of the shipyard" when it did not honor their choice on unionization.[36]

The USWA scheduled a massive rally four days before the vote. When the Reverend Martin Luther King Sr. surprised the PSA and company by agreeing to speak, publisher and editor Reid called his friend to urge him to rethink. King subsequently announced that he was canceling his appearance, and the USWA immediately dispatched a group of supporters and leaders to Atlanta to meet with him. He nevertheless bowed out, allegedly because of ill health, and sent his aide, who urged a vote for the USWA. More than 2,500 workers came together at that rally in the Hampton Coliseum two days before the vote. Harold Ford Sr., a two-term African American congressman from Tennessee, referenced the controversy over King's absence in his speech and hinted at a generational difference within the civil rights movement. He said he wanted Tenneco "to know Dr. King is 78 and I'm 32 and those threats won't work."[37]

Election Day was cold and clear. The voting started at five thirty in the morning on January 31, 1978, and ended at six o'clock in the evening. A total of 17,210 workers voted, first lining up at fifteen polling places and then voting in booths before dropping their ballots in boxes. Sixty-five NLRB staff people oversaw the massive election, joined by official observers from the company, PSA, and the USWA, including Jan Hooks.[38] As voting wrapped up, the PSA held an early victory party at its new headquarters, complete with a dance band and catered food. The USWA supporters anxiously gathered at the steamfitters' union hall. At ten o'clock that evening, the television news announced that the PSA was ahead 55 to 45 percent in the vote count. Spirits sunk. At about midnight, a local photographer rushed into the union hall and asked why the mood was so glum. He announced that the USWA supporters had just won, 9,093 to 7,548. Workers hoisted him to their shoulders and rushed him to the microphone, where he made the official announcement as the room erupted in hugs and tears. At noon the next day, the USWA supporters hosted a victory march in the yard to celebrate their new union.[39]

Within five days of the January election, the company and PSA filed nearly identical objections to the election, arguing that the NLRB officials mishandled it. In May, the regional director of the NLRB recommended that the union be certified and that the objections be dismissed. Tenneco and the PSA demanded a review by the full NLRB in Washington, D.C., which then also recommended certifying the USWA union. "It is obvious that the election was not error free," wrote the three-member panel. "However, in our judgment the free choice of these workers was not thwarted." The panel members pointed out that the magnitude of such a sizeable election caused logistical problems, but those were not sufficient to jeopardize the election.[40] Tenneco followed by appealing the decision to the Fourth Circuit Court of Appeals. Newport News Shipbuilding's president, Ralph Cousins, put a high-road spin on the company's decision to drag out the process: "We, unlike the NLRB, cannot accept election misconduct and irregularities in free elections. . . . The principle of conducting unbiased elections is too precious to our nation and its democratic process to be casually put aside."[41]

The USWA supporters, meanwhile, began to build their union even as their case wound its way through the courts. They held their first election of officers in late August 1978 and elected an interracial group of eleven

Oscar Pretlow (left) and Ellis Cofield (right), two of the four original activists for the USWA union, celebrating their union election victory (1978). USWA Collection, Communications Department Records. Reproduced with the permission of the Historical Collections and Labor Archives, Special Collections Library, the Pennsylvania State University Libraries.

leaders from a field of sixty candidates. "Even though the company didn't recognize us we elected our officers. We set up and got ready to meet with the company," remembered Carpenter, the local's new financial secretary. In mid-November, they held another massive union meeting at the Hampton Coliseum in which 7,500 workers stood together and were officially sworn in as members of Local 8888 of the USWA.[42]

Strike!

Tenneco knew that it could buy time by appealing the NLRB's decision to the Fourth Circuit. Even NLRB officials admitted their process could take years. Nearly a year had gone by since they had voted for their union, and the steelworkers' supporters grew impatient with the glacial pace of the nation's labor law. Newport News workers had a decision to make. Should they let their case lumber through the courts? Or did they have the strength to walk out? They would make their decision at the end of a year marked by massive strikes throughout the country. During 1978, nearly thirty-five thousand coal workers had struck in March, more than three hundred thousand railroad workers had walked out in July, and fifty-five thousand grocery clerks in Southern California started their strike in August.[43]

"We won count-wise, we had won every court case," remembered Hooks. "You get to the point where you have had all you are going to take and the hell with them. The only thing that a working person has to withhold is their work." More than 7,500 workers gathered in December 1978 and voted to authorize a strike at any time. At that rally, U.S. under secretary of labor Robert Brown called the Tenneco situation "a classic case for labor law reform" and promised the Labor Department would do what it could to bring labor peace. Meanwhile, U.S. labor secretary Ray Marshall asked the union and company to meet in his offices to discuss the issues at hand. Forty-three newly elected bargaining committee members traveled to Washington for the meeting, but the company refused to participate. "A meeting with the Secretary of Labor will not resolve the legal questions surrounding our objections," argued Newport News' vice president for corporate relations. "Since our differences are in litigation, we see no purpose in attending your meeting." The company "obviously felt they had a strong hand to play in court. . . . They knew the longer the strike lasted the weaker the union's position would become," remembered Marshall.[44]

The workers began their strike on January 31, 1979, one year to the day after they voted for their union. They carefully organized the picket lines with twenty-one stations within a two-and-a-half-mile radius and used CB radios to communicate. The governor of Virginia sent in over a hundred state troopers to monitor the picket lines and bolster the city police. The company, meanwhile, armed security guards with .38 pistols, mounted a water cannon on the gates, and gave its guards SWAT team training.[45]

The second day of the strike became chaotic. State and local police moved in on the pickets with police dogs, one of which attacked Betty Johnson, a USWA picketer. At one gate there were twenty state and local police in riot gear with four dogs to control seventy-five pickets. When the police refused to allow the picket line to cross the plant's driveway at the Sixty-Eighth Street gate, Wayne Crosby, Local 8888's first president, put on a placard and boldly walked across the drive. He was promptly arrested for violating the state's right-to-work law. Meanwhile, one picketer used a knife to threaten workers crossing the picket line until another picketer told him to stop. One man drove through the line in his car with a motorcycle helmet on his head.

Another calmly strolled through with his hands in his pockets. More arrests followed in the next few weeks. Strikers began scattering jack rocks (welded-together nails) around the shipyard gates to flatten the tires of workers attempting to go to work. Strikers also used speedboats to set up a floating picket outside the James River docks in order to deter deliveries, dubbing themselves the "Steelworker Navy."[46]

The workforce, community, and even families were split over the strike. "Out of my whole family, I was the only one who didn't cross the picket line," recalled Rickie Pike, whose father and uncle were among those who crossed. "I was very much the outcast of the family." Pike's daughter was born during the strike and, because of the tension in the family, his relatives did not visit the hospital to welcome the new baby. Those dead set against the strike, including the local newspaper editorial board, emphasized its economic impact. Tenneco "saved our economy on the Peninsula and created over 10,000 new jobs . . . and now all of a sudden people say they are no good," argued one worker in a letter to the editor. Yet, another striker's letter protested the police's actions against picketers, and made clear that he understood the strike as a working-class struggle: "The officials responsible for this are poor people haters. They want to see the poor working people walked on by Tenneco or any other big company." The USWA held a massive march of support on March 2, bringing in union members and other supporters from around the country. More than four thousand people marched through the streets of Newport News, chanting, "Eighty-eight! Close the gate!"[47]

In the early weeks of the strike, Local 8888 was able to squeeze Tenneco. Though the company claimed that 60 percent of the workforce was reporting to work by mid-February, a local newspaper reported that the figure was closer to 20 percent. The USWA began sending weekly benefits to the striking workers. The union got the power company to grant extensions on workers' electric bills and made similar arrangements with local banks, finance companies, and landlords. The workers set up free childcare services so parents of young children could more easily join the picket lines.[48]

Nevertheless, as the strike wore on into weeks and then months, it became much more difficult for the members of Local 8888 to hold the line. The company advertised for workers to replace strikers, hiring one thousand by April and dubbing them "permanent replacements."[49] The union claimed that the company illegally interrogated and harassed workers and offered them financial incentives to cross the line. The company settled the case by posting an NLRB notice, though it refused to admit fault. By mid-April, even the union acknowledged that half the workers were reporting to work, while the company put the figure at three-quarters.[50]

The USWA, meanwhile, was under myriad pressures to end the strike. Secretary of Labor Marshall had been against the strike from the start, urging USWA president Lloyd McBride to wait to strike until the company's appeal was heard by the Fourth Circuit. The strike was expensive since the USWA headquarters not only provided strike benefits—as much as $3 million—but also funded a massive support system. For instance, the legal assistance was larger than anything the USWA had undertaken in twenty years, and at least fourteen lawyers were working nearly full time on various aspects of the case. By the end of March, two months into the strike, McBride admitted that it had been a "tactical blunder" to paint the strike as a major breakthrough. He began to put pressure on the USWA district director, Bruce Thrasher, and the local staff running the effort to end the strike.[51] On April 13, six thousand workers once again packed the Hampton Coliseum and, after a hot debate, voted to suspend the strike in a week and to wait out the board process. Yet many strikers did not want to return. These dissidents won one concession: they demanded that the company not call their offer to return to work "unconditional." The company agreed, and workers were scheduled to return to work on April 23, 1979.[52]

Bloody Monday

Though the union officially ended its picket line on Sunday night, and workers were scheduled to return to work a week later, many strikers turned out at the gates on Monday morning, April 16. They were angry they had lost and did not want to go back to work. In a kind of wildcat action, workers began marching through the town, throwing rocks and breaking windows. "They did some damage. Rocks, bottles, anything we could get, we busted windows and everything. But we never touched anybody. We never hurt anybody," remembered Hooks, who contrasted the strikers' property damage to the personal violence they suffered at the hands of the police.[53]

A crowd of strikers locked arms and sang "We Shall Not Be Moved" while blocking a number of workers attempting to go to work. The city and state police responded with a massive show of force, gathering on Washington Avenue in full riot gear. They looked like a wall of black armor to one young striker.[54] Hooks stood in front of a local store, watching the police form a phalanx with their batons ahead of them and rush up Washington Avenue

USWA striker George Furge and Newport News police on April 16, 1979. Photograph by Bruce Colwell, courtesy *Virginian-Pilot*. Historical Collections and Labor Archives, Special Collections Library, the Pennsylvania State University Libraries.

through the masses of strikers. "They started running, they started hitting, shoving, pushing. . . . They shoved me, started beating me across the back and kidneys with a baton, there was three of them." The police beat and arrested strikers and bystanders indiscriminately. Four police, including the deputy chief, beat one lone striker with batons as another dozen officers and police dogs surrounded them.[55] Other police knocked one local reporter to the ground. They rushed the union hall, forcing one striker through the front plate-glass window. The officers caught Bill Bowser, an elected local union leader, at the foot of the stairs, where they beat him and broke his leg as he lay unconscious on the floor. Cynthia Boyd-Williams was inside the union hall working on the financial books, and she watched in astonishment as union members began throwing furniture down the stairwell to make a blockade.[56] The deputy chief of police reportedly told officers on duty to "make sure you add charges of breach of the peace and resisting arrest on everyone who went to the hospital to cover our asses."[57]

What later became known as "Bloody Monday" did not turn the tide, however. A week later, the strikers went back to work as planned and suspended their eighty-two-day strike. Hooks remembered, "I cried every step of the way."[58]

Squeezing through Labor's Door

If the workers' strike had taken place a decade later, the story of their union likely would have ended there. Though the labor movement had lost its 1978 effort to strengthen labor law, in 1979 the NLRB still had a Democratic majority appointed under Jimmy Carter and, unlike the Ronald Reagan and George H. W. Bush boards, did give real weight to its mission to protect workers' freedom to form unions. Even though the wheels of justice were frustratingly slow and employers mucked up the gears at every chance, the workers still had a chance to win in the courts.[59]

During the strike, the Fourth Circuit Court of Appeals judge had decided that at least one of the company's and PSA's charges had possible merit. The Fourth Circuit sent the case back to the NLRB and ordered it to hold a hearing into whether the election could have been fraudulent. The new NLRB hearing began in mid-March, and it revolved around the allegation that the NLRB officers' conduct left open the possibility that there could have been chain voting. This is an election fraud scheme in which voters bring blank ballots outside the voting area to be marked by a campaigner, and the ballots are returned secretly via another voter. Though no one ever testified that such chain voting took place, the shipyard brought in witnesses who testified that they had seen blank and torn ballots floating around the polling places. The hearings spanned three weeks and included about ninety witnesses. On May 2, the NLRB's administrative law judge dismissed the charges of fraud and upheld the workers' victory. The company appealed the decision to the Fourth Circuit Court of Appeals, which heard oral arguments before considering the case yet again.[60]

Meanwhile, the Newport News workers continued building their union. They were not deterred by the endless court delays nor by the defeat of labor law reform. They expanded their organizing committee to 900 members, and 530 workers served as temporary stewards who wore buttons in the yard. The workers also held new officer elections, and thousands voted in the elections using special balloting machines. They elected Coppedge president of Local 8888 and chose a majority of African Americans to serve as the local's elected leadership.[61]

Finally, on October 11, 1979, the Fourth Circuit Court of Appeals upheld the NLRB's decision that the Newport News workers had fairly chosen the USWA as their bargaining representatives. The company had faced continual pressure behind the scenes from the Department of Labor. "They depended on government contracts and the government was not favorable to them," remembered Marshall. "That was what, I think, finally caused them to cave in." The company chose not to appeal any further. It had taken twenty-one months and four legal rulings, but Coppedge, Hooks, and their coworkers had finally squeezed through labor's door and won their USWA collective bargaining rights. That night three thousand people packed the Hampton Coliseum yet again as the organizing team and lawyers received a standing ovation.[62]

Contract negotiations began in early November 1979 at the local Holiday Inn. Key issues included pensions, guaranteed raises, and health and safety. The union members elected twenty-six workers to the bargaining committee, and among their ranks were three of the four men who had first reached out to the USWA.[63] The workers' union and the company reached an agreement that they signed on March 31 with a big yellow pen in front of an audience of television cameras and reporters. "We went from one of the lowest paid shipbuilders in the industry to the highest-paid, and better benefits," said Coppedge. Pay rates for a first-class mechanic, for instance, X
went up from $6.90 to $9.15 during the three-year contract, and by 1985 were up to $11.50.[64] The workers had long been frustrated by the ability of supervisors to determine when they moved up the wage scales. The USWA contract ensured that wage progress was based instead on years served, thus cementing a level of economic security that had eluded workers after the EEOC's conciliation agreements. Now everyone could get the raises if they worked there long enough. The next agreement in 1983 lifted wages and benefits even higher, strengthening the pension plan and eliminating the hospitalization co-pay, for example.[65]

The members of Local 8888 used their new union contract as a base to build an organization that fought for a progressive agenda and nurtured a culture of activism. The PSA had not involved workers in decisions about politics; in fact, the PSA actually endorsed the Republican John Dalton for governor of Virginia in 1977 despite the fact that he was a strong supporter of the state's right-to-work laws. In their new USWA local, workers who were part of an active political action committee quizzed dozens of candidates before issuing an endorsement. They lobbied at the state capitol for improved laws on unemployment compensation and sat on statewide committees on

ining. Hooks, for instance, traveled with the local union to Washing-
numerous rallies and actively registered coworkers to vote.[66]

The new local beat back a decertification attempt by the PSA in 1983, solidly trumping the independent union by a vote of 13,591 to 2,535.[67] Democracy remained alive and well in the new union, which itself became the
terrain for progressive action. For example, Local 8888 initially had only
men in the top positions, including as trustee, a top leadership office in the
local union. "That just gave me all the drive and determination in the world
because we just left a union that wouldn't let us do what we felt like we
wanted to do. I wasn't going to have that," recalled Boyd-Williams. She
threw her hat in the ring in 1983 and was elected the first woman trustee.[68]

The new USWA Local 8888 activists continued to weave together civil
and labor rights, using their collective labor institution as a base from which
to monitor and even expand the rights of African Americans and women at
the shipyard. For instance, the union was a plaintiff in a key Supreme Court
test case expanding legal coverage for pregnancy. When the shipyard insisted on offering only $500 in maternity benefits to workers' wives, while
giving full benefits for other spousal medical issues, a male employee filed
a complaint with the EEOC under the Pregnancy Discrimination Act of 1978.
He argued his wife should get full benefits. The union soon followed up with
its own charge on behalf of six other male union members whose spouses
wanted full maternity coverage. The combined charges led to a historic 1983
Supreme Court decision in which the court used the new pregnancy discrimination law to overrule its earlier decision that pregnancy could be treated
as a special case in employment issues. The court now required employers
who paid medical expenses for employees' spouses to offer everyone equal
coverage, including for maternity costs, and the case set an important pre-
cedent for ending discrimination against pregnancy. In many ways Local
8888 became an organization of the "long civil rights movement," one that
fought for economic gains even as it pursued an agenda of civil equality and
justice.[69]

Local 8888 also became part of a wider organizing tradition. The local's
leaders joined in union campaigns, reaching out to workers throughout the
South who did not already have a union. For example, Rickie Pike later vol-
unteered as an organizer on a campaign among US Airways workers in
Charlotte, as did Hooks, who also helped Smithfield packing workers win a
union with the UFCW. Such a commitment to organizing allows us to in-
terrogate scholars' assertions that under the post–World War II social com-

pact, workers became satisfied with their share of the pie and did not reach out to expand the benefits more broadly. In fact, after winning their own union, the USWA Local 8888 leaders worked to expand the social compact beyond their base by trying to usher more workers through labor's doors.[70]

The Newport News shipyard workers' victory reveals the breadth of working people's resistance in the 1970s. Their organizing drive was the largest NLRB election in the 1970s, the largest ever in the South, and the largest in the history of the USWA.[71] However, Newport News was no outlier. Workers were challenging employers all across the nation until the end of the 1970s, demanding a more equitable distribution of wealth and a real shot at long-term security.

Yet if Newport News workers found success when they went knocking on labor's door, why did so many others fail? Workers had routinely won more than 70 percent of union elections in the 1950s, but by the end of the 1970s, they were winning only 48 percent. This was largely because corporations fought back, breaking labor law at an entirely new level. Industrial employers even became more likely than those in other sectors to break labor law and to capitalize on workers' job insecurities, threatening to move overseas if workers unionized. Meanwhile, the federal government did not prioritize national or global policy that would support domestic industry and encourage corporations to keep jobs in the United States.[72] Yet Hooks and her coworkers had special leverage not available to other industrial workers. Newport News was the only navy yard that could build and refurbish nuclear aircraft carriers, and navy ships, by law, had to be built in the United States. While Newport News workers faced fierce employer resistance as they organized and struck, these workers were less subject to competitive forces from the changing global economy than other U.S. workers. They had more room in which to fight back. The events at Newport News allow us to see what might have happened if the nation had developed a coherent industrial and trade policy that anchored jobs in the United States, undercutting employers' threats to move shop.

We turn now to a group of Southern industrial workers whose story is similar to that of the Newport News workers but who received no such protection from the storms of globalization. The Cannon Mills textile mill workers in Kannapolis, North Carolina, also built on momentum from the civil rights movement to create a new union, finding new energy among the young, African American workers who won access to textile jobs through the Civil Rights Act. Unlike Newport News shipyard workers, who made a product protected from foreign trade, Cannon Mills workers saw their employer use the new insecurities driven by globalization as an antiunion device. By the late 1970s and early 1980s, the Cannon Mills workers' defeat became far more typical than the Newport News workers' union organizing success.

5 Out of the Southern Frying Pan, into the Global Fire

No one was more surprised than the union when Cannon Mills textile workers very nearly voted for it in a 1974 NLRB election. Just one union organizer, Robert Freeman, had launched the campaign to organize the company's sixteen thousand workers with the TWUA. It was the first such union election ever held at the antiunion behemoth in Kannapolis, North Carolina, and the largest election ever held in the U.S. textile industry. African American workers were at the forefront of this surprising labor groundswell. Textile employers had long refused to hire black men for any but the most dusty and dirty textile jobs, and they had declined to hire black women altogether. When African American workers at Cannon Mills finally gained full access to textile jobs and unions under Title VII of the Civil Rights Act, they went on to support a union in order to shore up their newfound economic security with a collective bargaining agreement. Analysts predicted that as more African Americans and young workers entered the South's textile mills, they would bring unions in with them. It therefore came as a shock in 1985—after an even more diversified Cannon workforce again asked the government to hold a union election—when the company soundly defeated the union by a clear margin of two to one.[1]

What accounted for the downturn in Cannon Mills workers' support for the union between 1974 and 1985, especially after so many had predicted the union's eventual success? Grappling with this question allows us to test the usual narratives about U.S. labor's steep decline in the late twentieth century by highlighting increased employer resistance to union organizing. The Cannon Mills case makes clear that unions were still actively organizing, many Southern textile workers did want unions, and the civil rights movement boosted—rather than weakened—their collective organizing momentum. At Cannon Mills, in fact, a newly diversified workforce had nearly organized itself out of the Southern frying pan of paternalism and racism in 1974, buoyed by gains from the civil rights movement. Then, in the 1985 NLRB election, workers found themselves hurled into the global fire by Cannon's threats that a union would make their jobs even more vulnerable to imports.

The Cannon Mills case complicates the idea that globalization was a neutral, inevitable force undermining workers' unions. Instead, it illustrates how U.S. manufacturers used globalization as a weapon against a reshaped working class as it tried to organize unions. The Cannon Mills case also reveals a previously unseen path by which the retail sector overtook manufacturing in a globalizing economy. Cannon Mills made these threats to its workers even as the company successfully lobbied alongside the textile union for import limits as a part of a long-standing joint labor-management alliance. When such companies resisted the efforts of textile workers to form unions, they weakened their own partner in their campaign against the ascendant retail industry's push for free trade policies.[2]

A Big Deal for Kannapolis

In 1974, textile manufacturing was not only the South's largest industry; it was an essential national industry, too. One in eight U.S. manufacturing workers was either a textile or apparel worker, an employment level on par with auto or steel. Though textile employment in the United States began to weaken in the 1950s, the industry enjoyed a revival by the late 1960s, in part because of Vietnam War–era government contracts. In the decade before 1974, the number of textile mill employees rose 14 percent to over a million workers. The industry then faced tremendous global pressures. Its workforce shrunk by 27 percent between 1974 and 1985, the years of the Cannon elections, hemorrhaging nearly three hundred thousand jobs as imports soared. Over the ensuing decades, globalization and technological change roiled the industry not only in the United States but around the world.[3]

Yet, in the early 1970s, Cannon Mills was still going strong, producing half the nation's towels and a fifth of its sheets. The Cannon family founded the textile mill town, Kannapolis, just north of Charlotte, North Carolina, in 1907. It remained a true company town, incorporating only in 1984. Cannon Mills literally owned the land that sat under the churches, schools, post office, and courts, and owned many of the workers' homes, lined up in rows and nearly all painted white. The Kannapolis complex was one of seventeen Cannon manufacturing plants in the Carolinas and, at 5.9 million square feet, it was larger than the Pentagon. Though Charles Cannon died in 1971, workers still felt his paternalistic influence by the time of the union drive in 1974. Cannon Mills paid the Kannapolis workers' water bills, heavily subsidized their electricity, and even footed half the bill for the local police department.[4]

Workers tried to form a union at Cannon Mills multiple times, their periodic efforts spanning nearly the entire twentieth century. In 1921, six thousand Cannon workers struck and Charles Cannon broke their union, firing and evicting union supporters. In the 1934 general textile strike, Cannon used local police to close all the roads and turned back five hundred "flying squadron" picketers who toured from mill town to mill town.[5] Workers formed a union in one small Cannon mill in Thomasville, North Carolina, during World War II—Amazon Mills—but Cannon Mills officials forced a seventeen-month strike in 1947 and then, according to the union, refused to hire anyone with "one drop of union blood." The ten union organizers sent to Kannapolis as part of Operation Dixie, the 1946 CIO effort to organize the South, never got any traction.[6] An even larger and more promising joint TWUA/AFL-CIO effort from 1956 to 1958 included fifteen staffers, a weekly radio program, and a union publication called the *Cannon Uniter*. Though at least 5,000 workers out of 18,500 signed union cards, Cannon knocked the wind out of the effort with a hefty pay raise.[7] Time and time again, workers tried to form unions, but they quickly found out exactly where Cannon stood. "Mr. Charlie was not subtle about it," remembered a Charlotte businessman. "He'd walk up to a man and call him by his first name and he'd say, 'I knew ya daddy boy, I'd sho hate to see you go.'"[8]

Yet Cannon Mills was changing by the 1970s, and one of the biggest transformations was racial. For decades, white workers had staffed most of the South's textile mills. Cannon Mills, like many textile companies, began to hire more black workers following President John F. Kennedy's 1961 Executive Order No. 10925, which mandated affirmative action to ensure equal racial opportunity within federal contractors. Cannon Mills first began hiring black women in production jobs in 1962 and escalated its hiring after the Civil Rights Act of 1964.[9] "It was a big deal for Kannapolis women to start working in the mills, because the only jobs black women had then was working in white women's homes, babysitting or house cleaning," remembered Janet Patterson, who started at Cannon in 1965 as one of the company's first African Americans to hem fitted sheets.[10] In 1967 the EEOC held a series of high-profile, public meetings designed to force textile executives to change their ways and to signal to black workers that they had an ally in the federal government.[11]

Civil rights legislation also prompted changes within the TWUA, whose record on race was mixed. When black workers were part of the TWUA in the South before the mid-1960s, they often were part of segregated locals, and even into the early 1970s African American union members found that many of the union's white-led locals were reluctant to use their grievance procedures to take on issues of racial discrimination on the job.[12] When the TWUA tried to organize Cannon in the 1950s, it held meetings for white workers at the Concord Hotel and meetings for black workers at the Masonic Lodge rather than choosing a location where everyone would be welcome. At a national level, the TWUA was more progressive on racial issues than its Southern locals, passing a resolution denouncing the White Citizens Councils, for instance. Yet it found that Southern white textile workers' opposition to integration spilled over into organizing campaigns. One young white Cannon worker threw a leaflet in a union organizer's face in 1957, saying, "I have no use for unions. A lot of us can't see any sense in giving them money when they stand for mixing the races and we don't."[13] Civil rights legislation, however, changed the terms on which Southern textile organizing campaigns would be waged. By the 1970s, black workers held many more textile jobs at Cannon, and the TWUA organizers reached out to them as strong union supporters.

Daisy Crawford—a young black woman in her twenties—was watching these changes carefully. Over her years working at Cannon Mills, Crawford used every tool in her toolbox to push for change, blending civil rights and labor tactics in order to win greater economic security. After entering a low-level job at Cannon in 1966, she agitated for and eventually won the right to train as a weaver. She soon discovered that Cannon Mills would not rent its company-owned mill houses to black single mothers like her, only to those who were white. In response, Crawford went straight to the top. Her letter to President Lyndon B. Johnson informed him of the housing discrimination at Cannon. That letter went first to the Housing and Urban Development Department, then to the Department of Justice, and finally triggered an FBI investigation. The U.S. government filed suit against Cannon Mills in 1969, alleging discrimination in both employment and hiring. In the resulting 1971 consent decree, Cannon agreed to hire and promote more black workers and take "affirmative steps" in housing.[14] Yet Cannon Mills was slow to change its ways, and although by 1971 more than three thousand of the mills' sixteen thousand workers were black—a higher percentage of African Americans than in the local population—they remained stuck in the poorest jobs. A quarter of Cannon's black workers were in the lowest-paying blue-collar jobs, compared to only 5 percent of whites. In 1974 the company still had ninety-four job classifications that were all white. "My job consists of sweeping and opening waste machines," said one black woman, noting that her job used to be done by black men. "I have been working on this job for three years and have never seen a white woman doing this work."[15]

Like many of the Newport News workers, Crawford and other black workers at Cannon tried to accelerate the pace of change by exercising civil and labor rights remedies in tandem. Even as they pushed for increased access to the mill's full range of jobs, they also supported unionizing. African American workers at Cannon Mills were twice as likely as white workers to back the union. Their union support often grew out of a new sense of rights and possibilities that was rooted in the civil rights movement. Cannon "had to put us in," one African American woman told a reporter, explaining her decision to vote yes in the upcoming election. "I'm not going to forget that," she concluded.[16] Crawford testified in the federal government's suit against Cannon Mills, and she joined fifteen other black coworkers in filing their own class-action suit against Cannon Mills in 1970 with help from the NAACP Legal Defense Fund. The suit that resulted, *Hicks v. Cannon Mills,* was one of the largest of its type in the South. Crawford was also a union activist, stepping up as one of the TWUA's most outspoken supporters in 1974 and serving as one of the union's observers in the NLRB election. Cannon Mills fired Crawford in 1975 after she slapped an antiunion loom fixer who had groped her breasts and called her a racial epithet. The loom fixer only got a five-day suspension. Crawford used every lever for justice available to her, filing both an EEOC charge of racial discrimination and an NLRB charge. The NLRB found that her unfair dismissal charge had no merit, but the EEOC found in her favor and held Cannon in contempt of its 1971 conciliation agreement. In this case, the government proved to be more active on civil than labor rights, but Crawford herself was active on both.[17]

The 1974 Union Election

Textile mills were still booming in early 1974, and the industry needed workers. TWUA union organizer Robert Freeman could feel that tight labor market in his bones the way some people feel the weather in an arthritic knee, for it meant workers would be more willing to challenge the company. Freeman was just the man to help them do it.[18]

Freeman was the son of a Cannon worker and had grown up in the mill's shadow. He worked briefly at Cannon in high school before becoming a union organizer. At fifty-one, his lifelong mission was to organize the mill.[19] Described by TWUA staffers as both a "rugged individualist" and a personable optimist, Freeman was continually at odds with TWUA leadership. A large man with a big voice, he roamed the South finding interest among workers, and then ran union organizing campaigns single-handedly, often without even getting permission from his supervisors. "He was recognized as a lone wolf among his colleagues," recalled TWUA researcher Keir Jorgensen. "But they couldn't argue with his success in . . . generating a campaign."[20] Freeman's organizing efforts were driven by a heavily class-based philosophy rooted in his Kannapolis experience. "We have been degraded all our lives by the cotton mill owners. . . . If we complained . . . we were referred to as 'trouble makers' . . . who wanted to be uppity people," read one of his letters to Cannon workers.[21] He believed the entire Southern power structure was tilted against textile workers, and that in order to effectively challenge this structure, workers must build their own union without a lot of hand holding. "We will never organize the South with organizers," he told one AFL-CIO official. "As a matter of fact, we are destroying ourselves with organizers. We overstaff our campaigns."[22]

Freeman begged for the right to unionize the workers at Cannon Mills, arguing that the time was ripe. Though his superiors were skeptical, they decided there was little harm in letting him have a go of it since it often took two or three tries to organize massive industrial mills. Freeman launched the campaign in October 1973 and began holding periodic meetings and passing out lengthy, newspaper-style leaflets at the mill gate. A core group of about two hundred workers solicited union cards within the facility and a surprising number of workers sent them back in the attached self-mailer.[23]

Raises, benefits, and promotions topped the list of issues most important to Cannon Mills workers, according to a survey commissioned by the union. Some workers were incensed when Cannon claimed that its wages, averaging just over three dollars an hour, were high for industry standards. They argued in anonymous letters to management that benefits were middling at best. For instance, Cannon implemented a retirement system in 1964, but a thirty-five-year employee would only take home thirty-five dollars a month, in part because there was no credit for service prior to 1964.[24] Workers fully understood that Cannon had a lock on their social welfare, and some turned to unions to force the company to turn the key. Many felt overworked and wanted to control the pace of their job. "You can't take time to get a deep breath," complained one weaver. "You have to keep at the job continuously."[25]

Polling showed that black and young workers were especially keen on a union. African American union support was roughly double that of whites.

Meanwhile, a full 44 percent of white workers under the age of thirty supported the union, citing promotions and pay as their reasons. "The young people wasn't hard, I could sign the young people, but the older people, they were just, 'oh no!'" remembered Delores Gambrell, a white union supporter who was in her twenties at the time.[26] African American workers were especially interested in winning a right to job promotions and were concerned about layoff policy, since they remained the most likely workers to hold the lower-tier positions and thus to be the first laid off. Despite the conciliation agreement, there was no one policing the day-to-day reality of race discrimination in the plant, and white supervisors routinely played favorites. Leonard Chapman was an African American union supporter who recalled, "The supervisors were terrible on a black man. He could hardly breathe without them getting all over him for any little thing. . . . They wanted to show their dominancy over you."[27] Young women, too, brought a new sense of rights consciousness to their experience at Cannon Mills. "A woman don't have a chance. Women don't get to be supervisors, or even any promotions," complained one such worker.[28]

Antiunionism was strongest among the white workers over the age of fifty, especially white women. Historian Nancy MacLean describes how many white women in the nation's Southern textile mills took a resigned approach to black women's employment in the years after the Civil Rights Act, eschewing public protest for tightening social boundaries elsewhere. Many older white Cannon workers' opposition to the union likely represented this sort of quiet discomfort with progress toward racial equality. They viewed the union as an organization for black workers, not for them. Longtime Cannon worker Estelle Spry showed such uneasiness, for instance, in her letter to Cannon supervisors explaining why she planned to vote no for the union even though she was unhappy with the company's pension: "They sure do the older people dirty that is in retiring age. That is discrimination. I think that is what they call it. The Blacks is the one that will get Cannon Mills in Union."[29]

By August 1974, 6,510 of the 16,000 workers had signed union cards, and Freeman was able to petition the NLRB to hold its first-ever union election at Cannon Mills. The NLRB held the pre-election conference at the one neutral site it could find, the Gem movie theater, and set the date of the election for November 20, 1974.[30] Freeman agreed with the TWUA leadership that Cannon workers were likely to lose; he predicted at the time of filing that they would get 40 percent of the vote. Yet he argued that the union must first educate the workers in order to lay the groundwork for a future victory. In order to equip Cannon workers with the tools needed to really wrest back power, he believed, they needed a larger world view that put their company-owned town in perspective. When Freeman targeted the Kannapolis police department, for example, reporters found that Cannon had indeed reimbursed the county sheriff's office for half of the town's police staff and that a Cannon vice president received a carbon copy of the daily arrest sheet from the police station.[31]

Freeman needed every arrow in his quiver because, though Charles Cannon had recently died, antiunionism at Cannon Mills headquarters was still very much alive. Top management laid out the company philosophy for frontline supervisors: "It is our intention to oppose the Union without swerving or change. . . . For all of you in supervision there can be no middle ground . . . no neutral position." Workers were forced to watch a videotaped antiunion message from the company's president. Huge plywood boards sprang up across the mill, covered with literature against the union, including photos of machine guns on the roof in the textile uprisings in 1934, and newspaper articles from the 1921 strike. "They had enough of [sic] plywood for bulletin boards to build another plant up there," marveled union supporter L. C. Wright.[32] Management worked hard to paint the union as an outsider, despite the fact that Freeman was from Kannapolis. One cartoon featured a fat union boss in an elaborate New York City office, surrounded by money bags, saying, "Sho' is Green in the South." One training manual told supervisors what they could and could not say. "I don't trust those fellows at all. They are a bunch of thugs, gangsters, Socialists and Communists and the truth is not in any of them," was on the permissible list.[33] The larger Kannapolis community lent a hand in supporting the company's efforts, and the company invited the sheriff, mayor, local doctors, and postmaster to a meeting against the union. The president of the local bank assured Cannon executives that many business leaders had talked with Cannon employees on a "one-to-one basis in support of management in the upcoming election."[34]

Notably absent from both the company and the union's rhetoric, however, was any discussion of global competition or imports. Leaflets and company literature in 1974 urged workers to consider dues, fines, strikes, assessments, and the union's stance as outsiders. Cannon and its supporters did assert that the union would hurt its competitive stance, but the context was a domestic one. Workers were more fearful that they would lose their individual jobs if they supported a union in 1974 than that the plant would close. Job insecurity because of imports only grew later on, in the late 1970s and early 1980s, at Cannon Mills.

Voting began at 7:00 A.M. as the third shift got off work. Workers voted in thirty-one polling places, overseen by a phalanx of two dozen NLRB staffers, 136 union observers, and a nearly equal number of company observers. A full 97 percent of the workers cast a ballot that day before polls closed at 9:00 P.M. It took the NLRB staffers over two hours to hand count the ballots at the district court house. Glenna Chambers, Cannon worker and company supporter, rang a victory bell at 11:27 P.M. as the NLRB officials announced that Cannon had defeated the TWUA, 8,473 to 6,801.[35]

Cannon officials and industrialists across the South breathed a collective sigh of relief. In the aftermath of the union's defeat, business leaders from around the South proved that class consciousness was still alive and well. "We are well aware of the fact you carried the ball for all of us," wrote one CEO of a Southern yarn company to Cannon's top executive. J. P. Stevens officials commiserated: "As you know, we have been through a lot of this sort of thing and it is not pleasant." Telegrams and letters poured in from R. J. Reynolds Tobacco, Belk's, Coca-Cola, Elon College, Fieldcrest Mills, Rich's Department Store, and many more.[36] What elites found most notable about the election was just how close the workers came to overcoming the historic obstacles to unionization in Southern textiles. "Cannon Won, but TWUA Displayed Strength," read one *Charlotte Observer* headline, and the paper editorialized that the close vote was "a signal to the industry." Many credited the diversifying workforce with turning the union tide. "As you get more younger workers, more women and more blacks into textiles, there will be more union victories," asserted one textile analyst. "I think there will be a union at Cannon."[37]

Lobbying on Trade: An Uneasy Partnership

Even as workers at Cannon Mills came close to winning an election in one of the most traditionally antiunion corners of the nation in 1974, the textile industry began to feel the impact of global competition at a deeper level. Though the industry had enjoyed a recent upsurge and employed over a million workers, 1973 marked a peak in textile jobs that would never again be matched. U.S. textile and apparel workers became among the first workers to feel the full brunt of late twentieth-century globalization as the industry rapidly shed jobs. Forty years later, there would be little more than one hundred thousand U.S. textile jobs.[38]

Though technological advances impacted the industry's demise, the way in which globalization played out in U.S. textiles was not a natural process.

Rather, the industry's rapid hollowing out reflected a political struggle between those who sought to protect domestic jobs and industry and those who fought regulated trade. Though free traders ultimately triumphed, in the 1970s U.S. textile workers and their companies were powerful political actors who still possessed remarkable sway in their joint lobbying efforts.[39] Even as Cannon Mills and the union battled at the workplace level, they joined hands in potent joint labor-management lobbying efforts that helped shape the nation's policy decisions on trade. Such joint endeavors were important levers of power for the textile union, which had never represented a large portion of its industry, unlike unions in auto or steel.

The textile labor-management partnership on trade had deep roots. Charles Cannon was a leader in the American Cotton Manufacturers Institute when the John F. Kennedy administration asked representatives of industry and labor to join in a tripartite Management-Labor Textile Advisory Committee in 1961.[40] Industry and union representatives sat side by side and sought to shape the administration's textile policy on imports and quotas. They successfully fought together for passage of the Multi-Fiber Arrangement (MFA) of 1974, an agreement by fifty textile- and apparel-producing nations to build a complex system of quotas that governed the industry, under four variations, until it was phased out by 2005. Under the MFA, nations negotiated with one another to determine just how many wool coats, polyester blouses, and yards of cotton fabric, for example, could come out of any one nation into another. No other industry had such a tightly controlled and complicated quota system.[41] The MFA did slow down imports to the United States for many years, and it offered an interesting model for regulating global capital. Unlike purely protectionist measures, in theory it offered a framework by which representatives of government, industry, and workers from various nations could sit down together and rationally make decisions about a globalizing economy. In reality, power under the MFA remained tilted heavily in the direction of the developed nations.[42]

By 1978, the new textile parent union, the Amalgamated Clothing and Textile Workers Union (ACTWU), and textile employers deepened their alliance in the face of the Jimmy Carter administration's pressures to weaken the MFA regulations. Clothing and apparel unions joined a number of industry groups, including the American Textile Manufacturers Institute (ATMI), to form the Textile/Apparel Import Steering Group. Cannon Mills remained involved in the ATMI, and its president, Harold Hornaday, served on the ATMI's new political action committee.[43] In June, AFL-CIO president George Meany joined ATMI president Robert Small and other industry leaders at a steering group press conference on imports where the group called for passage of a bill that would completely exclude fiber, textile, and apparel imports from any duty reductions in ongoing multilateral trade negotiations in Geneva. Though the Senate and House passed the bill, Carter vetoed it, calling it inflationary.[44] Yet textile and apparel unions clearly held sway over the Carter administration's trade policy, and the U.S. special representative for trade negotiations was careful to meet with the union's leaders to inform them of the veto in advance. The labor-management alliance still had enough strength to persuade Carter to cut a separate agreement guaranteeing controls on imports in the textile and apparel industries. One leading journalist claimed it was as though Carter negotiated with a foreign power.[45] The textile companies were clearly delighted. "We win one," declared the *Southern Textile News*.[46]

Yet the industry was undermining its partner even as it stood next to labor on Capitol Hill. Like Cannon Mills, a number of textile employers continued to fight their workers' organizing efforts in the 1970s, such as J. P. Stevens and Burlington Mills, even as they united with the union on trade. In addition, the ATMI served as one of the key leaders in the fight against the 1978 labor law reform bill. The juxtaposition was stark. For example, the ATMI *Congressional Report*, on the very same pages that it celebrated the joint press conference with labor, warned that labor law reform was "down but not out" despite six failed cloture votes, and it urged members to contact senators to ensure the law remained dead.[47]

By the mid-1980s, this powerful labor-management alliance deepened its effort to rein in the nation's turn toward neoliberal trade policies. In 1985, the union and textile companies fought for the Textile and Apparel Trade Enforcement Act (also known as the Jenkins bill, after its sponsor, Congressman Edward Jenkins of Georgia). The law would have replaced the bilateral MFA system with unilateral quotas that were completely in U.S. control. The Jenkins bill had no real checks on capital's movement and investment and, unlike the MFA, it did not require negotiations with any other countries. It was a blunt tool with which to govern an increasingly complicated global economy. Nevertheless, the textile and apparel industry joined with labor unions to fight for its passage, forming the new Fiber, Fabric, and Apparel Coalition for Trade (FFACT).[48] Members of FFACT and its fourteen staff lobbyists met with senators and members of Congress, launched letter-writing drives among their members, and held joint press briefings. Cannon's president Doug Kingsmore served as an ATMI director, the group that was the source of half of FFACT's $2 million budget. Meanwhile, textile union staffers sat on FFACT's executive committee. The industry and unions together made up a powerful lobby, and they managed to get the bill through both houses before Ronald Reagan vetoed it within weeks of the second election at Cannon.[49]

Globalization and the 1985 Campaign

Despite its joint lobbying efforts with the union, Cannon Mills remained vigilantly antiunion as ACTWU kept a toe in the Kannapolis waters throughout the latter half of the 1970s. The union ran organizing efforts in 1976 and 1980, though it did not gather quite enough support from workers in these years to file for an election with the NLRB. Even though the workers did not have a union, their constant unionizing pressure helped push their company to improve wages and benefits. For instance, after the workers began signing cards in 1980, the company quickly announced an extra $2.2 million in benefits, including eliminating the requirement for employee contributions to the retirement plan and far better major medical coverage. Yet the company remained true to form, even as its leadership changed. "I pledge to you that [Cannon] . . . will do all we can to assure that we continue to operate in a union-free environment and avoid those obstructions and restrictions that go with unionism," wrote the new Cannon president Otto Stoltz in a 1980 letter to all workers.[50]

The early 1980s were rocky years for Cannon Mills as it struggled to weather the recession that wreaked particular havoc on the manufacturing sector. Whereas the company had seen the highest sales in its history in 1979 and earned over $40 million, by the third quarter of 1980 the company was showing nearly a million-dollar loss. The company began to lose market share, and consumers began to see its sheets and towels more as discount material than top-notch goods. Charles Cannon's cautiousness continued to shape the company culture, even years after his death in 1971. The company did little to invest in new machinery or to introduce new product lines, even as the textile industry was undergoing a wave of consolidation and mechanization. It continued to run a mill town, owning more than two thousand company houses until 1982, long after most textile companies had gotten out of that business. Yet that conservative culture made the company a juicy target for the sort of leveraged buyouts that were increasingly common in the early 1980s. Cannon products were still a household name, and the company had zero long-term debt, had more than

$180 million in working capital, and had just been relisted on the New York Stock Exchange. The stock was deliciously undervalued.[51]

David H. Murdock knew an opportunity when he saw it. The Los Angeles–based financier bought Cannon Mills for $413 million in 1982, finally taking the company out of the Cannon family by vacuuming up their stock. Murdock had made his millions through real estate and by buying up troubled companies. He operated in sixty countries, but Cannon was his first foray into manufacturing.[52] Murdock heavily invested in the struggling Cannon and spent $200 million to modernize the mills with imported Italian air jet looms. Such shuttleless looms were changing the industry as technology replaced workers. An old shuttle loom, for instance, required thirteen minutes to make the material for a man's shirt, while an air jet loom took only three minutes. Yet Murdock's reign coincided with a heavy slump in the textile industry driven by imports and overproduction. More than 350 textile plants closed between 1981 and 1986. Murdock slashed workers' pay, laid off 3,200 workers over three years—some with only a few hours' notice—and brought in industrial engineers to help squeeze more work out of the remaining employees.[53] Buddy Cannon, a longtime Cannon hourly worker, said Murdock cut his pay from $9.80 an hour to $6.44 and that his wife, Pinky, was down to working three days a week. Murdock sold off the company houses, giving workers ninety days in which to decide whether to buy their homes. The town of Kannapolis finally incorporated under Murdock's watch, its citizens suddenly governing themselves in the midst of the chaos.[54]

A month after Murdock bought Cannon, Robert Freeman began lobbying for another campaign. The union had high hopes that the new ownership and continued influx of African Americans and young workers into the mill would help it build support among a workforce that now numbered 10,500 workers, more than a quarter of whom were African American. Their "aspirations are far greater than the old textile mill hand," noted one ACTWU staffer in Kannapolis.[55] Union leaders proceeded cautiously and, not fully trusting organizers' positive reports, hired a Washington, D.C., polling firm to do a survey. That firm found that 42 percent of workers supported the union by August, compared to 36 percent who opposed it, with the rest undecided. Workers' top issues included wages and job security. Black workers remained far more likely than white workers to support the union—a full 69 percent of black workers were union backers, as opposed to only 34 percent of white workers. In 1982 Cannon had finally settled the 1970 racial discrimination suit, paying 3,700 workers a total of $1.65 million in back pay. Yet black workers still felt less secure in their jobs than did white workers, and 91 percent of black workers said that they wanted more protection from layoffs. Young workers were again at the forefront of support for the union in 1985, including 45 percent of white workers under the age of thirty-five.[56]

The union launched its new and improved effort in August 1984, passing out leaflets that targeted Murdock's changes. Slowly union activists gathered union cards. The tantalizingly close 1974 election remained on ACTWU's leaders' minds, and this time around they insisted on a more traditional, professionally run effort. Freeman only participated in the 1985 campaign from the sidelines as a retiree. The union leaders hired fifteen full-time staff members, contracted with advertising and polling outfits, spent $125,000 on television ads and billboards, hosted a phone bank to reach six thousand workers, and utilized a state-of-the-art computer system. All told, they spent somewhere just south of a million dollars, far more than the $100,000 Freeman had spent in 1974. The union petitioned for an election in August, claiming to have a substantial majority of workers signed up. "This time the response is better," concluded ACTWU southern regional director Bruce Raynor.[57]

This time around was different from 1974, but not in the way that the union had hoped. Even as Murdock remade the landscape of Kannapolis, he used the deeper earthquake of global economic changes to fight workers' unionization efforts. Cannon workers were already worried by Murdock's purchase of the company and anxious in the face of his many job cuts and changes. Murdock deepened this anxiety by blaming imports for the pay cuts and layoffs, and prevailed on the workers not to risk a union at a time when global competition was rampant. Days after union supporters petitioned the government to hold an election, Murdock sent out a letter to all workers that would make imports the central issue for the rest of the campaign. Saying Cannon was "in serious trouble," he argued that "our market base has been invaded by imports" and said he had been forced to pursue merger talks with other companies. He said he had put in an additional $12 million of his own funds to keep the company afloat and urged the workers to "not allow ACTWU to divide us at a time when, more than ever, we need to work together."[58] If that did not get the message through, the company also required workers to attend meetings to watch a video of the company president, Doug Kingsmore, declaring, "Cannon is not operating profitably" because of imports. Supervisors then followed up with workers

back in the mill, quizzing them with clipboards in hand. They ech
import message and made sure workers understood that Murdock w
continue to sink his money into a company that was not making a
a global economy. Kingsmore followed up the meetings with his ov....
in which he argued that if the company could not compete, it would have
to close its doors: "We are facing the worst obstacle (UNCONTROLLED
TEXTILE IMPORTS AND GREATLY INCREASED COMPETITION) in our company's
history. . . . Cannon's future is in the hands of the people who work at
Cannon."[59]

It was certainly true that Cannon Mills scrambled for footing in a globalizing economy. Though Murdock refused to make his earnings public,
he claimed to have lost money as the company's international sales fell by
more than half from 1981 to 1984 amid the downturn in the textile industry.[60] Yet when U.S. employers like Cannon faced a new global paradigm,
they were especially quick to try to limit labor costs by viciously fighting
workers' unionizing efforts. Manufacturers from many industries, not only
textiles, routinely capitalized on their workers' insecurities in a global economy and threatened to close the plant if the workers unionized. Political
scientist Kate Bronfenbrenner found that by the early 1990s half of all employers faced with a union organizing drive threatened plant closure and
12 percent actually followed through with the threat. In manufacturing, a
full 62 percent of employers threatened to shut down and move, compared
to 36 percent in less mobile sectors, like health care and retail. U.S. labor
law deemed such threats illegal, yet the penalties and enforcement were so
weak that employers continued to make the threats.[61] Though Cannon workers and other U.S. textile workers did face an uncertain future in a globalized economy, their nation's legal structure allowed employers to exacerbate
that insecurity.

The union staffers in 1985 thought that their operation was better than
the one in 1974, but they soon found themselves tilting at new windmills
within the global climate. "They outgunned us, outclassed us," remembered
ACTWU lead organizer Mark Fleischman. The company's campaign was
orchestrated by the management-side law firm Constangy, Brooks and
Smith, an Atlanta-based firm well known to the textile union for its harsh
campaigns. The firm trained supervisors to serve as messengers who to
Fleischman seemed "like an army of folks. . . . We were like kids with our
faces pressed up against the glass."[62] ACTWU tried to neutralize the company's import issue by pointing out that Murdock himself was a free trader:
"Murdock—king of the importers." One leaflet featured the local post office

with a headline that read, "Mortgaged," pointing out that Murdock had put up the town's land for collateral on loans for foreign machinery.[63] They held rallies and marches in Asheville, Raleigh, and Charlotte to position the union as an import fighter. They argued that the union could provide job security in the face of global competition and featured union members whose contracts included language on subcontracting globally. No one really believed them. In fact, the union's own polling firm found that while imports were one of the workers' most serious concerns, the vast majority of workers thought that the government was the only one who could rectify it. A mere 35 percent thought the union could "help make things better" on the import issue. The company kept up the offense. When union supporters presented Austrian-made yarn at a press conference, arguing that Cannon imported goods, the company sent a clear message by firing one of them.[64]

Cannon Mills even used its political activism around the Textile and Apparel Trade Enforcement Act (the Jenkins bill) as a way to sway votes in the union election, despite the fact that the union served as its lobbying partner on the bill. Under the headline "Which Will You Choose?" it circulated leaflets with photos of Murdock meeting with President Reagan on trade juxtaposed with photos of sparse union rallies. The company solicited letters from employees to Reagan to call for passage of the Jenkins bill, and a week before the election sponsored letter-writing tents at the main grandstand of the Charlotte Motor Speedway. An eight-hundred-member marching band, fireworks, a jet flyover, and a pre-race parade featuring Murdock rounded out the "Buy American" weekend of textile bill events. Richard Petty, the celebrity racer, toured Cannon's plants with a message tailored toward the upcoming union election: "Support Your Company—It Supports You."[65]

Meanwhile, Murdock continued to drive home the fear of imports in meetings with workers: "If I determine that Cannon cannot operate competitively, I can and I will cease to operate Cannon. This is my decision and mine alone, and no one can stop me—including this Union." Cannon workers got the message, and the company solidly defeated the union by a two-to-one margin, 63 to 37 percent. Workers cheered with cries of "We're Number One!" as the mill whistles sounded for what turned out to be a short-lived victory for union opponents. A mere seven weeks later, Murdock sold the mills to Fieldcrest for a quarter of a billion dollars.[66] 1985

Retail Topples the Smokestacks

The 1986 ACTWU Executive Board meeting in New York City was a grim one. The union's budget was off by a million dollars, a deficit it pinned in part on the loss at Cannon Mills and the failed Jenkins bill fight. The leaders passed a resolution to withhold any support from legislators who had voted against the Jenkins bill, but their power to weigh in as a political force in Washington was greatly diminished. The union had lost over a quarter of its membership in the last five years. Though it needed to organize at least twenty thousand workers a year just to keep membership even, it was averaging fewer than seven thousand.[67]

After the 1974 election, leaders at a similar executive board meeting had lauded the close Cannon election and thought that it could just be a matter of a few years before the mill would go union.[68] Yet they could not see from that vantage point that Cannon workers would have to wage their future unionizing fights on shifting terrain. Not only would their employer successfully use a globalizing economy to scuttle their unionizing efforts by 1985, but a more retail-driven economy overcame the power of the U.S. manufacturing sector. Though the apparel and textile sectors had long been interdependent, starting in the mid-1980s what had been separate operations were more tightly linked into global supply chains. Now large retailers, not manufacturers, would increasingly determine what products would be produced, what raw materials would be used, and how and when the goods would be transported. Retailers even learned to use point-of-sale information to trigger manufacturing when supplies ran low.[69]

Though logistical developments like large cargo ships and scanners facilitated this shift of power from producers to retailers, politics mattered too. Retail formed a powerful new lobbying group in 1984, the Retail Industry Trade Action Coalition, which led retailers in the fight against the Jenkins bill. Retailers found a strong ally in the Reagan administration. When textile companies and workers mounted a massive grassroots effort in 1986 to convince Congress to override Regan's veto of the Jenkins bill, the administration's records show it worked closely with its "friends" in retail on a last-minute lobbying frenzy.[70] The Reagan administration also gave retail greater access to the global rule-making process, sending its representatives to the MFA negotiations in Geneva for the first time in 1986. Retailers like the Gap, JCPenney, and Kmart actively lobbied against subsequent quota legislation. New textile and apparel bills passed Congress in 1988 and 1990, and they were ultimately vetoed by Presidents Reagan and

George H. W. Bush, respectively. After the 1990 defeat, the textile manufacturing coalition splintered as many companies accepted the new balance of power and began to move operations overseas rather than continue the political fight at home. By the time of the North American Free Trade Agreement in 1993, retail had effectively gotten its hands on the wheel that steered the textile industry's fate and was moving into the driver's seat of globalization.[71]

When textile employers fought their workers' efforts to form unions and prevented the unions from growing, they weakened the textile labor-management alliance, which had served as a counterweight to these retail interests. Over the decades, the textile and apparel unions depended too heavily on management-labor coalitions as tools to mitigate imports' impacts. In order for U.S. workers to win power within a globalizing capitalism, labor would have had to win effective curbs on capital's ability to move, such as through the failed 1972 Foreign Trade and Investment Act (the Burke-Hartke bill). This legislation would have ended tax breaks for transnational companies and given the executive branch power to restrict the export of capital if it believed too many jobs were at stake.[72] Labor also would have had to forge full partnerships with workers across the globe. ACTWU did begin to build some global alliances, such as by holding organizing training sessions with representatives from sewing shops in the Caribbean at the same time that the union was in the throes of the 1985 Cannon Mills election. Yet the efforts remained small and scattered, even after the union expanded such partnerships more broadly in the 1990s.[73] The union always emphasized that lobbying jointly with the employers was the most viable lever with which to soften the blow of global capital. Yet its ability to come to the table as a full partner in those efforts was quickly fading. Its membership dropped by half between the time of the 1974 Cannon election and the passage of NAFTA.[74] Though some of this membership loss was the result of layoffs in unionized plants, employers' refusal to allow a newly diversified working class to join textile unions mattered too, for they effectively blocked the union's ability to grow. In doing so, they enervated their own lobbying partner.

Cannon Mills changed hands several times over the next decades; textile giant Fieldcrest bought it after the 1985 election, and then Pillowtex took ownership in 1997. The company's workers tried three more times to win a union, in 1991, 1997, and 1999. Each time, the company fought the unionization effort by threatening workers' jobs in the face of imports. Kem Taylor remembered that her coworkers were frightened by management videos depicting "padlocks on gates, and grass all the way to the top (gates."[75] After the 1991 election, the NLRB found the company guilty of lating labor law 150 separate times and found its behavior so egregious it called for special remedies. On election day, for instance, the company fired a high-profile union leader, Elboyd Deal, and had security guards escort him out through work areas where other employees would be certain to see him. The NLRB ordered the company to allow union organizers in the plants and forced the president to read the NLRB remedy to all the workers, but it was not enough to support a union victory in a 1997 election.[76]

In 1999, a majority of the workforce finally voted by a narrow majority for the union (by then called the Union of Needletrades, Industrial, and Textile Employees, or UNITE) in a last-ditch effort to control the companies' forced speedups and to avoid layoffs. The workforce was now down to five thousand employees and included many more Hispanic workers, who, like the African American workers, tended to be supportive of the union. The workers won their first union contract in 2000, earning a 9 percent wage increase over two years and the first sick days in the textile industry.[77] They would not have the union contract for long, however. Just three years later, the company shut its doors due to global competition in North Carolina's largest mass layoff ever. Workers not only lost the gains they had made with the union but found many of their employer-provided social welfare protections, like health care, pulled out from under them. The new jobs they did find were often part time and poorly paid. When a Wal-Mart superstore opened in Kannapolis in 2003, for instance, more than half its new staff consisted of laid-off workers from the mill. Cannon workers' experience was a typical one in the textile industry. One study of the textile industry found that two-thirds of reemployed textile and apparel workers earned less in their new jobs than before. When the giant smokestacks of the old Cannon Mills' Plant 1 tumbled to the ground in 2006, the demolition was one of the largest in U.S. history.[78]

David Murdock bought the former mill site and invested $650 million in a gleaming new research facility dedicated to defeating leading causes of illness and death. A diet and longevity enthusiast, the billionaire told the *New York Times* he had a personal interest in the project; he hoped to live to see 125 years. Thousands of area residents became research subjects in the MURDOCK Study, giving blood samples to the project he funded for Duke University. It now employs renowned disease specialists who examine, no doubt, the muscles that once powered the mill's looms and the hearts that hungered for a brighter future.[79]

The Cannon Mills case suggests that we should look beyond complacent unions or an individualistic working class to explain labor's decline in the late twentieth century. At Cannon Mills, Southern textile workers wanted unions and tried hard to form them, even in the face of globalization. The civil rights movement bolstered the textile union's efforts by creating a diversified workforce at Cannon Mills, one that was more union-minded than preceding generations. Yet just as Cannon workers found a way out of the Southern frying pan, they found themselves tossed into the global fire. Globalization mattered deeply to these workers' fates, of course, and was bound to impact them, yet the Cannon Mills case reminds us that the terms on which U.S. workers would experience globalization were not inevitable but were rather determined by the larger legal and political context.

A globalizing economy did not necessarily have to mean weaker unions. In Germany, for instance, though textile and apparel employment dropped 60 percent between 1970 and 1990, the membership of the union representing these workers only dropped 20 percent. There, workers were more easily able to turn to unions to protect them from job losses and mediate globalization's effect. German workers can enter unions without having to fight with their employers and go through tumultuous union elections.[80] The Italian textile industry's workforce plummeted in the 1970s, but by the late 1980s that industry regrouped and workers' wages were above the European average. There, local labor movements supported the development of a network of smaller, specialized textile companies, giving workers a buffer against global forces. Throughout Europe, when textile workers did lose jobs, stronger labor movements were able to negotiate for income adjustment and assistance.[81] Within the U.S. political economy, in contrast, globalization severely undercut textile workers' unions. There, employers resisted workers' unionizing efforts, often using increased global labor competition as a weapon against organizing workers. At Cannon Mills, union organizing thus became a site not only for the unfolding of the cloth of globalization but for its very manufacture. When such U.S. textile workers lost the power to unionize, they also lost their platform from which to lobby and negotiate the terms under which their industry globalized and so were less able to counter the retail sector's growing push to deregulate trade policies.

We turn now to take a closer look at workers inside retail, the industry that was the clear winner over textiles in the trade struggles of the late twentieth century. The nation's turn toward a retail- and service-based economy was one of the driving factors behind labor's decline, since so few workers were traditionally unionized in this sector. Yet retail workers, too, tried to form unions during these early years of retail's ascendancy, attempting to turn the shifting tide in their favor. To explore such efforts, we will uncover a forgotten organizing campaign at a renowned department store and hear from the people who were in the thick of this remarkable workplace struggle.

6 Resistance in Retail

Organizing Woodward & Lothrop

· ·

Rosa Halsey helped build her union over lunch in the employee break room at Woodward & Lothrop's downtown store, strategizing with a posse of co-workers who never before had been personal friends. "Other people I met had the same spirit," she remembered. "We had a common goal." Halsey moved to the Washington, D.C., area in 1977 from Norfolk, Virginia, a town adjacent to Newport News. A young, African American mother, she quickly found a job in the accounts department of the Washington area's largest department store, widely known as "Woodies." In 1979, she joined her 5,300 coworkers in winning an NLRB union election that was the largest ever in Washington's history. As in the organizing efforts at Newport News and Cannon Mills, young workers, people of color, and women propelled the union drive. Three-quarters of the workers at Woodies were female, about half were under thirty-five, and more than a quarter were African American. What is different about the Woodies story, however, is that unlike shipbuilding and textiles, retail was an ascendant industry. Here was the future of the U.S. economy, and Halsey and her coworkers thought that future should include a union.[1]

Transformations in retailing were reshaping the nation's economy during the final quarter of the twentieth century. Giant, multinational retailers harnessed new technologies—like barcodes and enormous container ships—to shift the locus of power from manufacturing to retail. Retailers now determined what was manufactured and by whom, how it was transported, and how much it would cost. Retailing also changed American work. Ringing up customers became the new default working-class job; by 2015 the most common U.S. occupations were those of cashiers and salespersons. Yet the jobs were poorly paid, often part time or temporary, and came with paltry benefits, if any. Discounters like Wal-Mart led the way with low-road, antiunion labor practices, pulling down standards across the nation and weakening the social safety net as they refused to provide security for workers. Such tactics shifted social welfare costs to the public coffers and helped deepen the nation's economic divide.[2]

We know a new breed of retail companies first began to gain momentum in these years, but we have learned very little about the working people behind the cash registers. In fact, the new retail workforce was increasingly young, female, and African American. By 1970 a full half of sales clerks nationwide were under twenty-five and so had grown up in the wake of the civil rights movement. Nearly three-quarters of sales clerks and 88 percent of cashiers were women, including more African Americans than ever before.[3]

Many of these new retail workers, it turns out, did not back down easily when they faced deskilling and the gutting of wage and benefits standards. A fresh look at NLRB records reveals that the number of retail workers voting in elections in the 1970s increased by 28 percent compared to the previous decade, a rate not far behind the job growth in the industry, which increased by 39 percent. Workers at Caldor, Dillon Companies, Davison's, Hecht's, Gimbels, F. W. Woolworth, and Montgomery Ward all voted in union elections in the 1970s. These sales clerks and cashiers tried to organize, even while they remained less likely than other kinds of workers to have a union.[4]

The campaign at Woodward & Lothrop reveals how some members of America's transformed working class reacted to what some experts term the "retail revolution." These workers' hidden story reminds us that even in a world filled with worsening retail and service jobs, a different outcome for working people seemed possible. Halsey and her coworkers demanded security and respect for those who stocked shelves, swiped scanners, and served shoppers. Within their victory, we see some clues as to why and how retail workers across the United States lost control of their fate within twenty-first-century capitalism.[5]

Woodies and Its Workers: The History

Samuel Woodward and Alvin Lothrop opened the Boston Dry Good House in the nation's capital in 1880, changing the store's name to Woodward & Lothrop when they moved it to F Street in 1887. They made their names through the one-price marking system, eliminating salesperson haggling. The store became famous for its opulence, featuring live models, concerts, pony rides, and even a radio broadcasting station. It took off in the 1920s and 1930s, serving the growing army of government employees in Washington.[6]

Like the Newport News Shipbuilding and Dry Dock Company did, Woodies set up its own union in the 1930s as what one shipyard worker aptly termed a "union stopper." The independent union was born in a Woodward & Lothrop Board of Directors' meeting in 1937 soon after Sidney Hillman, the Amalgamated Clothing Workers of America president, announced that the CIO would launch an industry-wide drive in department stores. Luke Wilson, a member of the board of directors, suggested a company union when the directors fretted that the CIO was a "communistic" threat to the esteemed store. The first union to challenge Woodies in the fall of 1937, however, was an AFL Building Service Employees International Union local that sought to represent the majority-black unit of janitors. Soon after, a supervisor began to circulate a petition to start a company union. The petition came as a shock to employees. The new union collected initiation fees and dues and passed a constitution requiring everyone to join. The company allowed the group to sign up members at work and to hold meetings on the property. The NLRB found in 1938 that the Association of Woodlothian Employees was an illegal union, company directed, and ordered it disbanded. As in the Newport News case, however, the organization simply ducked and weaved. It changed its name and then won official NLRB sanction through an election in 1940 as the Union of Woodward & Lothrop Employees.[7]

The employee organization hung on for another thirty-nine years, beating out a 1947 challenge by the retail clerks' union by a two-to-one margin. Though workers sometimes expressed interest in organizing with a more potent union, the independent union continued to officially represent the workers, often signing one-year contracts with small increases. The company persisted in developing antiunion tactics, even while letting the in-house union do its job. For instance, it enlisted George Washington University psychology professors to survey workers in the 1950s as a means of ferreting out dissatisfaction, the kind of soft antiunion tactic once pioneered by Sears, Roebuck.[8]

Through the 1950s, African American workers had access to few jobs at Woodies. "If you are colored, you start here in uniform as a maid or porter. After twenty years, you're still in uniform," summed up one black worker in 1956.[9] Yet, by the late 1950s, the company found itself in the crosshairs of savvy civil rights leaders. These leaders served as de facto labor leaders for the black community, especially since some unions still excluded black workers. NAACP-led protests and boycotts convinced Woodies to employ eighty black women to wrap packages in the 1958 holiday season. They were the first black people to serve customers in any Washington-area department store, outside the tearooms, yet sales jobs remained strictly whites only. Not until after the Congress of Racial Equality got involved in negotiations with the company in 1961 did management finally hire four saleswomen for the holiday season. Woodies then expanded its black hiring in the mid-1960s following more CORE protests.[10] Leola Dixon was working as a housekeeper at the downtown store when Woodward & Lothrop tapped her to be one of the store's first black sales associates. "I was so nervous and I just stood behind the register" in the flowers and gifts department, remembered Dixon, until an older white supervisor kindly encouraged her to step forward and help the customers.[11]

Seeking Refuge amid the Retail Storm

In 1962, the same year Michael Harrington sparked a nationwide discussion of poverty amid an age of plenty with his book *The Other America*, he also published a lesser-known book that examined economic justice in a different way. In *The Retail Clerks*, Harrington profiled a single, growing union—the Retail Clerks International Association (RCIA). Though the union was still relatively small at four hundred thousand members, it had quadrupled in size over the preceding two decades. Harrington called it "labor's newest giant," for he believed that the RCIA represented labor's future, "a new type of industrial union" that was well on its way to organizing this expanding sector.[12]

It was not clear in the early 1960s, even to so prescient a scholar and activist as Harrington, that a rocky road lay ahead for workers in retail. The industry itself had grown along with the rise of a post–World War II consumerist economy built around a car-centered, suburban culture. When shoppers drove to those new suburban department stores, the people who waited on them were not likely to have a union; unionized department stores were mostly confined to downtown areas in cities like New York, Seattle, and San Francisco. However, when those consumers cruised down the suburban street to their local grocery store, chances were much better that a union clerk would ring up their Cheerios, especially if they lived in a northeastern or midwestern market. By the late 1970s, the Retail Clerks International Union—the same parent union that the Woodies workers would join—represented a quarter of the national grocery market and virtually all of it in Washington. Unionized retail workers had good wages and benefits, and guarantees of full-time work.[13]

The 1970s, however, brought profound changes to the retail industry that Harrington could not have foreseen. Discount stores like Wal-Mart, Kmart, and Target rose to prominence in this new economic structure over the next three decades and forced manufacturers and vendors to drive their prices down. For many years, New Deal–era federal fair-pricing laws had allowed manufacturers, not retailers, to set base prices. Discount department stores helped to persuade lawmakers to eliminate many of these laws in the 1970s, arguing that they were inflationary. There were forty-five such local and state laws in 1941, but by 1975 only thirteen survived. Now discounters could not only lower prices but also access brand-name merchandise that had been the purview of the conventional department stores. For the department store industry, this shift meant tremendous consolidation as firms sought to gain enough leverage to compete.[14]

Meanwhile, what had been decent jobs in retail quickly became very bad ones. Discounters made their profits, in part, by keeping labor costs to less than half those in department stores. Part-time work grew to be the norm and technological changes, like the rise of scanners, allowed for the mass deskilling of retail jobs. Retailers used to train working-class women to serve as salespeople, but by the late 1970s most workers received little, if any, training for what was considered a low-skill job. Wages fell much more quickly than before, and jobs became more contingent.[15] Whereas retail workers made three-quarters of what the average nonsupervisory worker made each week in 1949, by 1979 retail workers only earned 63 percent of the average worker's weekly wage; that figure dropped to 56 percent a decade later.[16]

By the time of the union election, Woodward & Lothrop stood just on the cusp of the retail revolution. It was still strong and profitable, but as one of the nation's last independent department stores, it sought new ways to compete within a rapidly consolidating industry. It owned fourteen stores in 1979 and two warehouses spread over the metropolitan area. Neither Wal-Mart nor upper-scale stores, like Nordstrom's and Macy's, had a presence yet in the Washington area, and Woodies occupied a kind of middle ground between upscale Garfinckel's and the lower-end Hecht's.[17] It had brought in a new president, Edwin K. Hoffman, in 1969, replacing family management. Hoffman revamped the stores, jettisoning departments like hardware and getting out of budget fashion entirely. This publicly owned store was soon doing well. The company boasted in its 1979 annual report of "the greatest increase in our market share in recent times." The company's net margin had nearly doubled in the previous six years to 4.6 percent, well above the median figure of 2.4 percent for the department store industry, making it the most profitable of the leading department store companies.[18]

Woodies did not pass this profit on to its workers. Woodies dealt with increased competition by following the discounters' lead and squeezing workers. Woodies' workers had few of the fringe benefits that filled in the gaps left by the patchwork U.S. social welfare state. Though full-time Woodies workers technically had access to health benefits and pensions, workers remember that mostly white-collar managers received these benefits, and part-timers were excluded. Only a quarter of Woodies' employees, including managers, were part of the group hospitalization plan, and less than a fifth were covered by Woodies' retirement plan. Top managers had contracts, including stock options and severance guarantees, but Woodward & Lothrop's rank and file were far more dependent on management's whims when it came to their economic security.[19] "Back then, they did not give good raises. They just did not. Your raises depended on your manager," remembered Leola Dixon, who continued to work in the flowers and gift department for many years.[20]

Job security was a recurrent theme among workers who wanted protection against unjust firings and favoritism. Two-fifths reported that they had been hassled by their supervisors or department heads. "If you made a mistake, it was like you killed somebody, but the other person, if they made a mistake, it's all well and good," recollected Barbara Cash, a merchandise receiver in the downtown warehouse. "If you didn't belong to a union the company could say, 'you're fired' if you did something they didn't think you should be doing."[21] Not everyone was dissatisfied. Frank Wright, a group leader in major appliances at the Lakeforest store, argued that "they treat their . . . employees fair. The pay is better than other operations and the benefits are much better. There is room for advancement for good people from within." Woodies workers, overall, reported that they liked their company and were proud to work for it. However, 86 percent thought the company could afford to pay them better.[22]

Winning a Union

As at Newport News, the workforce at Woodies included more women, people of color, and young workers than ever before, and this transformed workforce supplied the new union's grassroots momentum. Twenty-seven percent of Woodies' workforce was African American, and black workers were far more likely than whites to support the union. A full 77 percent of Woodies workers were women in 1979, reflecting a national trend.

Nationally, the percentage of female retail sales clerks rose from less than half in 1950 to more than 70 percent by 1979.[23] The older female department store workforce had been less willing to challenge the status quo. "The department stores for many years have had many widows and older people convinced that they are one big happy family," remembered one organizer. Yet at Woodies by the 1970s the scales were tipping in the other direction, and a new working class at Woodies viewed its rights with fresh eyes.[24] Young women were among the union drive's strongest supporters, especially those supporting a family, and many were inspired by the women's movement sweeping the nation. "Women were waking up in the seventies," according to Glenda Spencer-Marshall, a unionized discount store worker who served as a rank-and-file organizer on the campaign. Women who worked at Woodies "decided they wanted more and decided that they would have to be the ones to get more."[25]

Arthur Banks, an African American loading dock supervisor, noticed a change in the younger generation. The group members most energized about unionizing were those under the age of thirty-five, making up almost half of the workers. They were nearly twice as interested in joining a new union as the over-fifty crowd.[26] Even though Banks was a supervisor, he surreptitiously backed their union efforts. Banks remembered that the group pushing the union was different from his generation because they had grown up in an integrated world and had a different understanding of their rights following the civil and women's rights movements: "They were just more outspoken. They didn't really care about the repercussions of getting fired."[27]

One of the union drives' first instigators, however, was not young. Rather, Wilbur Reed was an African American man who, like Edward Coppedge at Newport News, had been active in the company union. A bus driver who shuttled workers between warehouses and stores, Reed seemed to know everyone, and he had once served as the company union's president. Reed, however, was dissatisfied with the paltry raises the company union had won, and with the fact that the workers had no right to outside arbitration to deal with grievances. He fed Local 400 (an RCIU affiliate) information about the workforce and worked behind the scenes to support it.[28]

Though many workers thought the company union weak and ineffective, it is likely that the Union of Woodward & Lothrop Employees laid the groundwork for Local 400's organizing efforts. As was the case at Newport News, the company union gave workers like Reed experience with the regular negotiations that were part of a union contract, even if they could never vote on it. Workers gained familiarity with a union, and many held office.

Thus, at both the shipyard and department store, company unions founded in the heyday of welfare capitalism smoothed the way for fresh union organizing among workers in the post–Civil Rights Act era.[29]

Local 400 first attempted to sign up Woodies workers in 1976. However, it could not convince the NLRB to allow it to hold separate elections among workers at individual stores and warehouses.[30] This was a typical dilemma in the new big chain stores and fast food joints. Would workers at one location be allowed to form their own union, or would they be forced to try to unite with workers at various stores spread across a vast urban area? In the early 1960s, the John F. Kennedy–appointed NLRB leaned toward the former, but employers hated this interpretation.[31] The Chamber of Commerce, for example, in 1966 called for the Labor Law Reform Group to prioritize policy favoring the larger voting units. The Richard Nixon–appointed NLRB gave the employers what they asked for and moved toward citywide elections.[32]

Thus, by 1976 Local 400 was forced to try to organize across all stores and warehouses at Woodies. It could not get enough workers to sign union cards to warrant a vote. The union next worked with activists to try to take over the Union of Woodward & Lothrop Employees' board and then to force a merger with Local 400. That did not work either. Instead, the company union's board elected a strong company supporter as president, Natalie Koeling. If Woodies workers were going to have a union with Local 400, they were going to have to do it the hard way—by taking on every corner of the area's largest private-sector employer.[33]

Thomas McNutt, the president of Local 400, was just crazy and ambitious enough to help them try. A young upstart within the RCIU, McNutt came out of the Michigan district council and quickly rose through the union's ranks. McNutt won the local's presidency in 1975 after having served as its trustee, and he made waves by prioritizing organizing and by negotiating top-notch contracts with full health benefits. "Our philosophy is never to be satisfied with what is," said McNutt.[34] McNutt knew that the Woodies union's contract would expire again in 1979, thus opening a window of time during which workers could legally switch unions. This time, he began amassing an army of organizers well in advance, calling on colleagues and allies throughout the union to send their own staff his way in 1978. The international union sent McNutt one of its top strategists, Jack Adams, to head the campaign. McNutt also recruited and trained union members from within the local to help on the drive.[35]

January 22, 1979, found two hundred staff members and rank-and-file volunteers spread out across Woodies' stores and warehouses in the

Washington area, including stores in suburban Maryland and Virginia. The organizers synchronized their watches and, at exactly 4:30 P.M., they started working their way from the top floor down through the department store levels, handing out handbills and passing out union cards. Managers scurried behind them collecting the papers.[36] Organizers met more enthusiasm than they had expected. "To me, it meant better benefits, better pay, better working hours, better working conditions. I didn't see any reason not to support it," recalled Adam Mathias, a young, white clerk at the Montgomery Mall store's luggage department.[37]

A survey commissioned by the union at the outset of the campaign revealed that top issues among workers were, in order, health and pension benefits, job security, and increased wages. Yet each of the Woodies stores and warehouses had different kinds of workers who had their own unique concerns and issues. Some of the suburban stores employed mostly older white workers who were more focused on retirement issues, for instance, whereas the workforce at the downtown warehouse on M Street was nearly all African American and mostly young. Pay and treatment were the biggest issues there.[38] The union approached this puzzle by building a balkanized organizing structure that gave each team a fair amount of autonomy. In effect, it chose to run sixteen different campaigns, assigning a team of organizers and volunteers to each store and distribution center and trying to match the staff demographics to those of each facility. Each team was free to create and distribute its own literature, drive its own message, and call frequent meetings, often in a hotel suite or the shopping mall's bar.[39]

The loose structure offered room for surprises, such as discovering a union hotbed in cosmetics. Though employees who work on commission are notorious for being the least supportive of a union, the teams at Prince George's and Montgomery Malls found that the commissioned women in the cosmetics departments were particularly interested in having a union because they wanted more control over rates of pay. "Pretty soon those girls were our shock troops," reported one organizer. When it became clear that the men working for commission in the suit department were "totally scared to death," the cosmetics union flotilla would float behind the racks to talk with them, and soon many signed up for the union.[40]

A thousand workers signed union cards in the first four days of the campaign. Hundreds more signed cards in the following weeks in meetings, in parking lots, in garages, and surreptitiously on the shop floor. "You hide behind the rack of clothes or you go in the store room" when told not to organize on the shop floor, remembered Mathias. Nearly a third of the workers who signed cards sent them through the mail. The union petitioned for an election with about 3,400 cards on April 3, 1979, the earliest date on which it could make a legal claim to challenge the independent union. Two days later the company and the company union filed nearly identical challenges to Local 400's petition, alleging that it had used improper methods to get signatures. The charges were weak and easily dismissed, according to the union's lawyer Carey Butsavage.[41]

The management of Woodies did not run a scorched-earth antiunion assault in the vein of the Cannon Mills campaigns. Rather, it walked a fine line between the union-busting tactics that were becoming de rigueur for employers at the time and a more paternalistic tone that matched the dignified public image Woodies carefully cultivated. "It's kind of like they went to a management library and got a notebook that has all the typical . . . boiler-plate stuff," recalled organizer Michael Earman. A letter from the company's president to workers was such a typical attempt to paint the union as an outside third party: "I personally feel that the treatment you and this Company are receiving from this union [Local 400] is offensive. . . . I encourage you to report to your personnel office when . . . you have been intimidated, harassed or in any way interfered with."[42] Management ran an inconsistent campaign, pleading with workers to trust the company to have the workers' best interests at heart. The company held mandatory antiunion meetings, but the tone was civil and nonthreatening. "It was politely put, that they wanted to make sure you knew what Woodies had to offer," remembered Halsey.[43]

Frontline supervisors turned out to be key to the company's campaign. Woodies relied on supervisors to carry a "neither union" message to their employees, urging them to let employees know that unions would hurt the company. Labor law did not permit them to support either union publicly. The company, however, knew that many supervisors supported Local 400 because if the rank-and-file workers got a raise, so would the supervisors. Banks, the loading dock supervisor, made quiet, positive comments about the union to some of his staff, though he knew his platform supervisor "might have balled me out."[44] At many other companies, supervisors would be unlikely to have even this sort of soft latitude. Most employers followed the advice laid out by one self-styled management guru in 1981 to fire promptly any supervisor who "is unable to grasp and comply with the union-free concepts."[45]

Woodies, however, still had one foot in the old way of doing things. If Woodies had run a more vigorous campaign, with the kinds of threats and intimidation that were so common by the 1980s and 1990s, it is much less likely that the workers would have won their union. Instead, Woodies did not even hire the Shawe & Rosenthal antiunion firm until six weeks before the election, and it chose not to run as intense a campaign as that same law firm ran at the Hecht's warehouse in the early 1980s, for instance. Woodward & Lothrop company records shed no light on the company's motivations for running a less threatening campaign. One union staffer speculated that unionized grocery stores may have advised against a fierce campaign, helping to sway Woodies' president, who also served as president of the Metropolitan Washington Board of Trade. "Ultimately, there were enough people . . . that were friends of Hoffman and they convinced him that Local 400 was not bad. . . . At that time it had a very good relationship with the owners of Giant Food," recalled Earman.[46] Whatever the immediate motivation, Woodies' decision to run a lighter campaign serves as a reminder that even by the late 1970s, corporations' antiunion stances were not yet so absolute as they would be a decade later. Unions still held great sway, and union busting was still considered unseemly for so prestigious an institution as Woodward & Lothrop. After all, the company carefully had cultivated a rarified reputation over many decades. Woodies proved itself to be on the more cautious end of the spectrum of corporate antiunion development in the late 1970s.

Local 400 organizers were thus relatively free to run a high-road campaign that capitalized on the momentum generated by this young and energetic workforce. They were surprised to learn from the survey they commissioned that a majority of workers generally liked working for Woodies, though they were dissatisfied with the pay and benefits. Organizers decided to run a campaign that stuck to a positive message. It was a strategy that resonated with Rosa Halsey, who looked forward to going across the street after work to the union's storefront union office, where she met with the organizers, whom she found to be "truthful and upfront."[47] Even Woodies' soft antiunion tactics, however, were enough to scare a number of the workers, and the union struggled with how to show that it was building support. One day organizers passed out glow-in-the-dark key chains shaped as "#1." The key chains were a hit, and the "#1" theme became a mechanism for workers to embrace the union without aggressive sloganeering. When Woodies banned organizers from leafleting at the Springfield Mall, the union handed shoppers bags emblazoned with "#1." Many union supporters wore golden "#1" lapel pins as they served customers.[48]

The union even rode the momentum generated by the 1979 smash box office hit *Norma Rae*. Organizers secured a Dupont Circle movie theater and hired shuttle buses to ferry workers to two private showings. Four buses went from the downtown store and warehouse alone. *Norma Rae* portrayed a strong female protagonist leading a Southern textile labor struggle, and her story resonated strongly with the heavily female Woodies crowd. Like Norma Rae, they yoked their challenges as working women to union activism.[49]

Because wages and benefits were key issues, union organizers featured the local's strong contracts at other retailers like men's clothing store Raleigh's, discount store Memco, and unionized grocery chains. There, the local had won full employer-paid health benefits, often including dental and eye care, and robust retirement plans and wage increases. Through leaflets, meetings, and conversations, they showed the Woodies workers what could be possible with a union. They even invited workers from Woodies to attend the union meetings of other unionized workers, like those at Giant and Safeway.[50]

Health insurance played a pivotal role in the campaign. Workers were already angry with the company for requiring high employee co-pays, and many part-timers resented not having access to the benefits. A few weeks before the date of the election, the union unearthed the forms that federal regulation required employers to file about employee benefits. These revealed that the company had not been rebating to workers remaining insurance funds at the end of the fiscal year. The union publicized the missing funds, and though the company called the union's claims "hogwash," it chose to rebate the money, cutting individual workers checks for as much as seventy-five dollars. The union claimed victory under the headline "Look What Local 400 Just Won for You!" "The best thing they could have said was nothing," remembered John Brown. "That was admitting . . . you got caught with your finger in the cookie jar."[51]

As the date of the union election approached in June 1979, the vote took on a special meaning for Local 400's parent union. The RCIU spent an unprecedented $2 million on the campaign. "This meant unlimited personnel, payroll. . . . We were able to max big money," remembered Samuel Meyers, a longtime vice president of the union.[52] The election would take place just a couple of weeks after the RCIU's merger with the Amalgamated Meat Cutters to form the new United Food and Commercial Workers union. The new union would have 1.3 million members, ranking this retail and food union as one of the nation's largest, comparable to those in auto and steel. The new president had high hopes of launching big campaigns in retail, banking, insurance, and finance. The Woodies election would be the first test.[53]

The day of the election dawned bright and hot, and it found Halsey brimming with hope. "I felt good, I felt like this was going to happen." Employees walked into the M Street warehouse, pointing number one with their fingers, and sales clerks wore their gold pins as a display of solidarity. Workers went into the election knowing that another large, local group of workers had recently ousted their own long-standing independent union at the Potomac Electric Power Company. Woodward & Lothrop sales clerks, order fillers, and others filed into employee break rooms to vote all day long.[54]

That afternoon, the NLRB agents comingled all the ballots and started to count them one by one. By evening, a crowd of workers and organizers gathered anxiously outside the NLRB headquarters. A couple hundred workers, meanwhile, came together at a rented hall in the Alexandria, Virginia, Ramada Inn, many sporting their "#1" union T-shirts. When the long-anticipated phone call came through, union supporters danced with word of their win, hugging one another in a huge mass and shouting, "We're Number One!" The workers had voted for Local 400 by a large margin: 2,407 votes for Local 400, 600 votes for the independent union, and 973 votes for no union. "I just can't wait for tomorrow," said one sales woman from cosmetics. "I just want to watch the look on my supervisor's face when I walk in wearing that pin."[55]

The First Contract: Securing Full Prosperity

Winning the election was a major step forward for the workers at Woodward & Lothrop, but all it really meant was that the federal government would now require the employer to bargain. Workers still had to fight to get their first contract. By the late 1980s, a full third of workers who won a union election never got one, in large part because employers increasingly gamed the system. Consultants counseled employers to drag their feet, pointing out that the law was so weak and the threat of penalties so negligible that employers should do all they could to stop the union from ever getting an agreement. Newport News had taken such advice and dragged out its first negotiations through a number of courts.[56]

In the end, Woodies chose to exploit a key Achilles' heel in the union movement: the "right to work" Sunbelt. Woodies was in a rather unique

Woodward & Lothrop workers celebrate upon learning that they won their union election. *Union Leader*, 1979. Courtesy of UFCW Local 400.

position of having workers spread out over Virginia, Maryland, and Washington, D.C. Virginia was what was commonly known as a "right to work" state, which meant that employers and unions were legally prohibited from negotiating a union security clause requiring all workers to either join the union or pay a fee equivalent to union dues. There, workers could get a free ride, benefiting from the contract without having to pay for it and making it much harder for unions to keep membership levels high. Maryland and Washington, D.C., however, allowed union security clauses, which were standard fare in labor contracts there.

Woodies refused to sign a union security clause for any of its workers, in any of the states, claiming to protect individual rights. It was a strategy that was typical of the National Right to Work Committee in the 1970s, which built on civil rights laws' defense of individual rights for its fight against collective bargaining. "My concern is the employee," claimed Hoffman in defending his decision. "It was this plantation mentality," remembered the union's lawyer. "The great protector of employees is not the union but the employer who is there to look out for his charges."[57] The National Right to Work Committee sought to bolster Woodies' efforts, sending out a letter to all area newspapers asserting, "We hope that braced by Virginia's Right to Work law, the company managers will not continue to surrender the rights of employees."[58]

Local 400 faced a real dilemma. The loss of a union security clause in all the stores would weaken the union for years to come, as it would have to constantly shepherd workers into the union, one by one. In many ways, this was the same dilemma that the union movement faced writ large in so-called right to work states. Local 400 could not afford to have the entire workforce follow the way of the Sunbelt.[59]

The union held fast in negotiations and used the contract fight as a way to further mobilize the workers. Whereas the old union had not even allowed workers to vote on the contract, the Local 400 members were very involved. Employees from each store met separately to discuss the issues that mattered most and elected a group to join the 150-person advisory board that supported the negotiating team. One worker from each store went into negotiations with the staff. By the time negotiations broke down over the union security issue on Halloween, the union had done enough rank-and-file education that hundreds gathered at the downtown Constitution Hall and voted to strike if they could not get an agreement. The following week, a federal mediator stepped in.[60]

The result was a compromise, a "modified" union security clause. Current workers in Maryland and Washington, D.C., would not have to join the union or pay the equivalent in dues, but new employees would. No Virginia workers would be required to join the union, per that state's laws. The agreement meant that while the workers got their contract, the local would always have a nonunion cadre in its midst and would never grow strong in Virginia.[61]

Yet the energy was still high in 1979, and 1,200 Woodies workers packed into an auditorium of the Shoreham Americana Hotel for the contract ratification meeting. They lined up at microphones to discuss the provisions, which included at least 8 percent wage increases each year for three years, with most workers receiving at least a dollar more an hour over the life of the contract. It broadened health care coverage and lowered co-pays, increased vacation days, and provided for free eye and dental care by the third year. The workers ratified their new contract with a nearly unanimous vote.[62]

Fifty Woodies workers stepped into leadership roles as stewards, a group fully representative of the racial and gender mix of the workforce. They went to workshops to learn how to enforce their new contract. Job security was key. For instance, they used their contract to help a silver polisher, Clarence Mills, who lost his job when Woodies closed its metal engraving department. The union pushed to get him a job in suits, and it also successfully helped John Thomas win his job back at the distribution center when he was fired for being fifteen minutes late. Local 400 had a health and welfare fund for unionized grocery store workers that provided actual health services, like dental and optical, at the union's building, and it built its own network of doctors. Although Woodies' workers were not part of that fund, union members and their families could now access its networks and go to the union building to get discounted health services.[63]

Women at Woodies used their contract to address issues that were shaped by gender. Though 66 percent of the company's commissioned salespeople were women—a job that paid more than cashier or clerk—women were less likely to sell high-ticket items like appliances. Their story was a typical one for women in sales; four-fifths of female retail workers were stuck in lower-ranked jobs.[64] In a high-profile case, the EEOC tried to rectify this retail glass ceiling in 1979 by suing Sears, Roebuck, the nation's largest retailer at the time. It alleged gender and racial discrimination in hiring and promotion in the more lucrative commissioned sales jobs. The EEOC eventually lost the case during the Reagan administration years.[65] At Woodies, however, workers found more success than did the Sears workers, and they did so using the older labor laws. Through the new union contract, workers won the right to move into any job outside their department; the company had to promote its own workers who were interested in the better-paying job before it hired from the outside. Thus women now had a clear and legally backed path into the higher-paying commissioned jobs. Even if women chose to remain in more stereotypically female departments, like cosmetics, the union improved wages and benefits there, too. In subsequent contracts workers even won access to benefits as part-timers, a real achievement for those women who chose to work part time for family reasons.[66]

Workers also used their contract to shore up their power on the shop floor. Many managers had grown accustomed to having free rein, and the company began to teach them how to honor workers' rights under a union contract. One new "complaint and grievance" checklist, for instance, instructed supervisors to "listen patiently. Don't interrupt. Consider the effect of your decision on the individual, your total group . . . don't pass the buck." Halsey served as a union steward and stepped in to help a young clerk when a supervisor yelled at her about not paying bills on time: "The young lady was crying, trying to explain to her that she'd just gotten the mail."

Halsey got upper management involved. "You don't get to do that anymore after the union," she asserted.[67]

Changes on the Workers' Terms

The Woodies workers won their union on the cusp of major changes in the retail industry and the U.S. economy. Over the next two decades, discount retail corporations like Wal-Mart began to outperform conventional department stores. They utilized the power of technology and globalization to drive up profits while forcing working standards down to a new low. Though retail employees were not directly pitted against overseas workers, as were the Cannon workers, they were all part of the new supply chains that designed, manufactured, shipped, and sold goods across nations and became the main drivers for much of the global economy. Department stores found themselves caught in a bind by the 1990s; they were too small to benefit from the scale-based efficiencies so effectively exploited by Wal-Mart, but were also too big to compete on flexibility. Two big waves of department store consolidation followed, in the mid-1990s and early 2000s.[68]

The storm of changes in the retail industry hit Woodward & Lothrop with great force. By the mid-1980s, the company found it increasingly difficult to maintain its market share. When management faced the possibility of a hostile takeover from a corporate raider, Hoffman pushed through a leveraged buyout by Al Taubman, a shopping center magnate from Detroit. He did so over the objections of the family shareholders, who fought back in a highly public shareholder vote battle.[69] Taubman then used Woodies to buy out Philadelphia's Wannamaker stores, which left Woodward & Lothrop too strapped for cash to be able to update merchandise continually. Meanwhile, Nordstrom's and Macy's entered the Washington area, joining Kmart and, eventually, Target and Wal-Mart in the outer suburbs. By 1995, Woodward & Lothrop could no longer compete and began looking for a buyer among the retail giants.[70]

Woodies workers thus joined the thousands of retail workers who faced department store consolidations in the 1990s. At Woodies, however, we can see how one unionized group of workers was able to bend the new changes in its direction and retain some powerful standing. When Federated Department Stores and May Company began a bidding war over Woodward & Lothrop in mid-1995, the union could have just scrambled for access to diminishing funds in bankruptcy court, doing battle with suppliers and buyers. Instead, the union declared that the workers wanted to be considered as a buyer. The union's lawyer remembered that the union never really had the funds to build a worker-owned corporation, but it gave the union negotiating power. "The buyout made us a player," said McNutt, the local's president. "It put us in the arena with the bidders and gave us access to all the financial information."[71] Though the union ultimately did not make an official bid to buy the company, it retained leverage by including in the most recent round of contract negotiations a clause that required any buyer to honor existing labor contracts. At first, the union forged an agreement with Federated under which all union workers would be retained, but then May Company asked for a meeting. McNutt sat down with May executives and came to an even better agreement two weeks later. May would also hire all workers covered by the Woodies contract, those workers would retain their union, and the company would even remain neutral in a card check process for its workers who were not unionized. May owned ten Hecht's facilities in Maryland and Washington, and none of these workers had a union. By September 1995, more than one thousand of these former Hecht's workers signed union cards, thus using the new negotiated process to form a union.[72]

Local 400 helped ease workers' transition in the 1995 buyout. Sue Bean was working in commissioned cosmetics sales at the time, and she remembers feeling very insecure about the sale. She turned to the union, which "made sure I was getting the same salary, the hourly wage. . . . I even got to work on the same cosmetics line." Mary Laflin was working at Hecht's, and "the first thing that happened to us, we all got raises . . . and they treated the people with a little more respect."[73] Meanwhile, the part of Hecht's workforce not included in the collective bargaining unit didn't fare so well; the company soon laid off seven hundred managers.[74]

In 2005, the workers retained their union in another major consolidation when Federated bought out May Company. By 2006, all the D.C.-area Hecht's stores were called Macy's. Workers at Macy's in the Washington area still have a union in 2017 and continue to use it to fight for fair access to scheduling, good wages, and benefits, including for part-timers.[75] Their union is the direct legacy of the one founded by the Woodies workers in 1979.

How the Nation's Biggest Job Became One of Its Worst

Retail work is a cornerstone of today's unequal economy. About one in ten workers in the United States works in retail; there are more people working as salespeople, cashiers, and stockers than in all production jobs combined.

Yet retail wages are among the nation's lowest, and employers often refuse to hire workers full time, give them benefits, or even give them a week's notice on their schedules. The result is that too many working families live in a cycle of poverty and crisis.[76] Most retail workers fared much worse in the 1980s and 1990s than did the Woodward & Lothrop workers. Woodies' median wage for sales clerks right before it sold to Hecht's was about $238 for a thirty-five-hour week. That was higher than the nation's average retail wage, and even more than that earned by department managers at Wal-Mart.[77] Woodies workers also had full health and retirement benefits, and they could use seniority in such issues as choosing the best shifts. None of this is available to most nonunion retail workers. If Woodies' workers were able to beat the retail odds with their union, then why couldn't more workers do the same? Why are retail jobs so bad today, and why are so few unionized?

Though globalization empowered massive retailers, creating a new locus of power within twenty-first-century capitalism, the terms of this change were determined by decisions made by employers, unions, and the state. Antiunionism was key to the big discounters' business model. Wal-Mart, for instance, forces employees to watch an antiunion "training" video on their very first day on the job. The company approaches unions as though they were a cancer, flying in a specialized team at the first appearance of union cards. When eighteen auto mechanics tried to form a union in Phoenix, the company parachuted in twenty outside managers. Kmart had a special security department to track union activity and report it to the board of directors. When retailers faced a newly energized workforce, most fought workers' unionizing efforts with tremendous vigor, and they did so with a freer hand as the government steadily weakened support for organizing. Workers thus entered a retail-based global economy on much weaker ground than they might have if the new, union-minded workforce had been able to organize.[78]

Though retail workers in the 1970s and early 1980s were trying to organize unions, most thus met far greater employer resistance than did Woodies workers and found such resistance unchecked by weak labor law. Consider the story at Hecht's in the years before its parent company bought Woodies. Soon after the Woodward & Lothrop workers won their union in 1979, workers at the Hecht's distribution center on New York Avenue filed for, but then lost, several NLRB elections.[79] Hecht's hired the same Baltimore-based "antiunion" consultant as had Woodward & Lothrop. Shawe & Rosenthal ran a no-holds-barred campaign at Hecht's in 1981;

the campaign included thirteen leaflets, twelve different posters, home mailings, paycheck stuffers, mandatory meetings, and constant supervisor one-on-one discussions.[80] A "campaign strategy" memo reveals that the union election was scheduled one week before the annual pay raise. Shawe explained to company management that they could not blatantly threaten to take away the annual raise if the workers voted for a union. Instead, Shawe instructed them how to legally seed uncertainty and fear: "If the Union wins the election, the Company could not lawfully implement a wage increase here unilaterally but would have to negotiate that matter with the Union."[81] A typical leaflet asked, "If the union calls a strike and I go out on strike, can I lose my job?" Answer: "YES! Under the law, if the union calls a strike to try to force the Company to agree to the union's economic demands the Company is free to permanently replace the strikers."[82] The firm drove home a threat of layoffs, a top concern of retail workers as the industry moved to more contingent employment models. A letter from the general manager of the warehouse read, "I have read Retail Clerks' contracts and I haven't seen one contract—not one—that doesn't provide for employee layoffs. Every single contract spells out the way to lay off employees. *That is what can happen in a union company.*"[83]

Finally, Hecht's feared that the Woodies workers' union victory could spread to their own company like a virus. They weren't alone in this fear. The head of the retail bureau of the Metropolitan Washington Board of Trade noted that the Woodies election inspired a "shock in the business community." Three days before the 1981 election, Hecht's management sent a letter to workers that highlighted the Woodies win: "We have committed to you in writing that Hecht's will provide you with wages and benefits equal to or better than competitive department stores—like Woodies. . . . With the United Food and Commercial Workers Union, Woodward & Lothrop employees have BOTH—the risk of a strike and the payment of union dues." In the face of such campaigning, Hecht's workers voted down the union, losing heart even after they had signed cards and triggered an election.[84]

Rampant resistance to organizing helped shaped the industry's unionization rate, but the union's decisions mattered, too. As was the case among the larger union movement, the UFCW pulled back from organizing starting in the mid-1980s. The giant Woodies election would be the last of its kind in retail. In the 1980s, when jobs in retail grew by a third, the number of union elections in retail sunk by half. By 1989, a mere 14,000 retail workers voted in NLRB elections annually. By 2000, that number was down to about 7,800, even as the industry itself grew by leaps and bounds.[85]

The UFCW was slow to organize among the newer generation of discount stores—like Wal-Mart—in part because it did not fully understand that these stores were a threat to its powerful position within the grocery store market. Over the previous decades, the union had won a strong footing within regional grocery chains, like Giant in Washington and Pathmark in New York. The union put much of its energy into winning agreements to expand unionization within these employers that were already under union contract. For many years, Wal-Mart seemed like a different kind of store entirely. Yet Wal-Mart's Supercenters, which now included groceries, exploded in growth in the 1990s, catapulting the company to the number one spot in the U.S. grocery market by 2001 and quickly undermining the UFCW's carefully cultivated contracts. Though the UFCW was able to forge community alliances that helped slow Wal-Mart's entry into urban areas, it found little success in unionizing the company's workers.[86]

There was also a cultural resistance within the union to the sort of no-holds-barred organizing techniques that the Woodies union staffers had used. Woodies organizers remember working ten- to twelve-hour days, and though many were from out of town, they rarely went home. Such commitment was not widespread in the UFCW, and much power in the union remained at the local level, where the "executive's primary concern is reelection, so he has to attend to members over organizing programs," remembered one organizing supervisor.[87] Few local leaders would put in the necessary resources. And while the UFCW did have some organizers who were women and people of color, the organizing staff was not fully representative of the industry's workforce, a key determinant for union success.[88]

Changes in interpretations of federal law also mattered. For instance, in the 1970s, shopping malls were quickly becoming America's de facto town squares, and the rules were still in flux as to who would have access and free speech in these quasi-public places. Retail organizers waged a fight for the right to speak to workers in the privately owned malls. The NLRB generally tried to find a balance between private property rights and the rights of employees to organize. For example, the NLRB ruled in favor of retail organizers who challenged Hutzler Brothers when it threw them off a parking lot in Towson, Maryland, in 1976.[89] Local 400 tested the law's bounds during the early weeks of the Woodies campaign. The local routinely sent organizers into the stores, even when they knew they risked arrest, in part to expose the company's true colors to its workforce. Twenty-two union organizers were arrested in the first two months of the campaign. They included Russell Wise, arrested for trespassing while passing out union cards in a parking lot, and Tony Gasson, whom security guards pulled from the stairs. While the union got many of the charges dismissed in the short term at Woodies, labor ultimately lost the battle for broad access to retail workers. "The law got built up at that time that was not good for us," remembered Local 400's lawyer. "Private property always trumps the rights of employees. At the time, that was not a given." A series of Supreme Court decisions in the 1980s and 1990s limited organizers' access to retail workers. The final blow was *Lechmere, Inc. v. NLRB*, which ruled that employer's property rights dominated over employees' freedom to organize. In that particular case, Lechmere had barred UFCW organizers from passing out leaflets in a company parking lot. After this case, organizers nationwide were largely confined to sidewalks out by the main thoroughfares.[90]

In addition, union leaders found that their time was increasingly focused on providing to members the kind of social provisions that workers in other countries got through the welfare state. James Lowthers, for instance, was elected Local 400 president in 1997. He remembered spending the majority of his time servicing the health and welfare trust, meeting with "eye people, dental people, panels of people," and even serving on the Maryland Health Services Cost Review Commission, which regulates state hospital rates. Saddled with this social provision role, unions often could devote less time and fewer staff resources to organizing.[91]

In the end, the fact that federal labor law increasingly failed to check employers' assaults on organizing did the most to seal the fate of unions in retail. Local 400's organizing effort at the Bi-Lo grocery chain in Norfolk, Virginia, in the late 1980s was typical. The local sank in resources and staff but lost two elections in the face of a brutal antiunion campaign, which included many of the threatening tactics that quickly became standard fare. Lowthers remembered that McNutt became disillusioned by the late 1990s and had stopped organizing. Lowthers was determined to recharge it. "When I first became president, I hired ten organizers. Then I beat my head against a wall for four or five years. I don't believe you can really organize in the United States anymore." Lowthers shut down the organizing department in the early 2000s and instead put $2 million into a community affairs department to shore up workers' waning power in contract negotiations. But he was never able to facilitate the planned jump into fresh organizing. "We could never get from there to there," mused Lowthers.[92]

No Natural Law

The Woodward & Lothrop workers' story reminds us that there is no natural law that retail work has to be bad work. Rather, employer behavior and state policy impacted the ways that globalization and technology affected workers. After all, if such forces had meant an inevitable decline in the quality of retail jobs, that would have held true around the world. In fact, the job quality in retail is a function of the legal paradigm in which the workers must operate. In Sweden and Denmark most retail workers have unions because the state strongly backs collective bargaining; workers there have not seen comparable levels of wage cuts. Though retail is less unionized in the United Kingdom and Australia than in other sectors, workers there have not seen the sweeping job degradation that U.S. workers have experienced. In the Netherlands and Germany, however, even though unions are strong, retailers have been able to circumvent minimum-wage laws by using legal exceptions for young workers, thereby worsening job conditions in retail.[93]

In the United States, retail companies used weak labor law to fight unionizing efforts, including those increasingly driven by young, female, and minority workers. Perhaps corporations only needed a small hammer to tamp down workers' efforts, but most thought they needed a massive sledgehammer, which they swung with abandon, pummeling the nation's system of economic levelers along the way. Retailers continued to wield this weapon long after the union threat weakened. Even as Amazon used e-commerce to disrupt Wal-Mart's business model, for example, it chose to adopt Wal-Mart's antiunion labor practices. Today's unequal economic divide rests, in part, on such corporations' fear of workers' class-based activism.[94]

Rosa Halsey, Adam Mathias, Barbara Cash, and their coworkers' fight succeeded, in part, because their employer did not attack their union with the kind of scorched-earth tactics that Wal-Mart and other discount retailers adopted. Woodies' relatively weak campaign meant that when young Woodies workers brought new consciousness about their rights into the workplace, they had a more open playing field than would workers who faced the full brunt of antiunion tactics. Having finally gotten the kinds of jobs from which they had long been excluded, they felt fairly free to organize. The absence of a full antiunion campaign at Woodies gives us a glimpse of the kind of future that might have met the newly forged working class in the 1970s if it had not faced such powerful employer resistance.

We turn now to a look at labor organizing among another primarily female service industry workforce: clerical workers. Like the Woodward &

Lothrop workforce, Boston's secretaries made new demands on the city's employers as they entered the workforce in the 1970s, seeking security and respect on the job. New ideas about their rights as women propelled their unionizing efforts. Unlike the working people of Woodward & Lothrop, Newport News, and Cannon, however, the women clerical workers in Boston experimented with an alternative avenue for worker power that circumvented the increasingly broken NLRB system: a worker association.

7 9to5

Framing a New Doorway

· ·

Young and ambitious, Fran Cicchetti took a secretarial job at a Boston insurance company and soon pushed her boss to make good on his promise
to train her as an underwriter. He instead groomed and promoted a male
clerical worker for the coveted slot. Her dark, Italian eyes flashed with outrage beneath a sweep of thick bangs: "That was when I started thinking
that, as a woman, I'd been lied to." In April 1974, she joined hundreds of
other Boston women in publicly calling on the city's employers to honor a
bill of rights for women office workers. "The companies do not see us in the
mainstream of the workforce. We are working for pin money they think and
aren't to be taken seriously. We've got to assert ourselves." As women like
Cicchetti entered America's workplaces in record numbers during the 1970s,
they carried new ideas about women's rights along with them. Cicchetti's
words neatly capture how respect and pay were inextricably linked in a
market-based society, and how mounting a challenge to gender norms on
the job was both a social and economic task for the nation's low-paid, coffee-
fetching "office wives."[1]

Cicchetti was an early activist in 9to5, one of the most well known of
the employment-based women's organizations that burst on the scene in the
1970s. Organizations like 9to5 represented a potent feminist strain within
that decade's working-class activism. The women office workers who
founded 9to5 in 1973 built what they called an "organization for women
office workers" in Boston—which was explicitly an association, not a union.
Through a combination of public pressure, savvy media outreach, and strategic affirmative action suits, 9to5 helped upend workplace gender norms
and challenge the terms under which millions of women entered the workplace in the 1970s. Cicchetti, for instance, went on to chair the group's finance
committee, which lobbied the state's insurance commissioner to issue new
standards on industry job postings and promotions. The women of 9to5,
however, also wanted to harness the power of collective bargaining, and
they built a bifurcated structure to do so. They maintained the association
9to5 while also launching their own union, Local 925 of the SEIU. They later

replicated this dual structure at the national level, with a separate association and union.[2]

Like the retail clerks, shipbuilders, and textile workers we met earlier in this book, the women who founded 9to5 were among the wave of young women and people of color who poured into a broad range of the nation's workforces, making new demands about their rights. What is different about the women of 9to5, however, is that they expanded the range of possibilities open to workers by simultaneously using strategies based both on and also beyond NLRB union elections. The group's founders pioneered a new form of labor organizing, one built on New Deal traditions and legal structures, as well as the tactics and legal strategies of the contemporaneous women's movement. The union, SEIU Local 925, won a few NLRB elections, but it found that most of the private-sector employers it challenged were able to block workers' organizing efforts by manipulating and breaking labor law. The association had more success. Boston's clericals managed to force some of the city's largest banks and insurance companies to post jobs, offer training, and even give raises—all without having to go through arduous NLRB elections or ever securing a union contract. Instead, they used affirmative action suits to expand workers' rights, and learned to make creative use of public opinion.

The 9to5 founders were essentially the foremothers of what today is known as "alt-labor," the wave of workers' centers, associations, and campaigns that seek to build power for workers outside the collective bargaining paradigm in the early twenty-first century. For a time, these women labor activists were able to use the new organizing forms of the women's movement, in combination with community organizing tactics, to build an entirely new doorway into economic security and greater equality for America's workers.[3]

Women's Rights Comes to the Office

It was no coincidence that some of the most forward-thinking labor organizing in the 1970s grew up among clerical workers. This group was primarily composed of women who found themselves at the epicenter of two major shifts: the mass entry of women into America's workforce and the cultural transformations rooted in the women's movement. By 1979 women made up a full 42 percent of all workers, up from 30 percent in 1960, and women were more likely to earn their paycheck in clerical work than in any other job. One in three women who worked for wages did so as an office worker.[4]

Meanwhile, secretarial work was undergoing a major shift of its own as technologies like photocopiers, memory typewriters, and, increasingly, computers furthered a century-long process of mechanizing office work.

Women ran the new office machines, and they did it cheaply. Early twentieth-century employers had learned that they could keep costs down by employing women as typists and stenographers, displacing the young aspiring businessmen who had once served as clerks. By the 1970s, a full 97 percent of typists were women. Yet female clericals earned less than men who worked as operatives, salesmen, or service workers—in fact, they earned less than all men except farm workers. "I replaced a man who was making $140 a week at $80," wrote one shipping clerk at A&P Tea Company in a 9to5 survey. "At my present raise rate, it will be eight years by the time I reach that pay."[5]

The office workers who organized wanted to upend unfair, gender-typed treatment in the office as much as they sought to address low pay, and the new ideologies of the women's movement gave their efforts momentum. The expectations that women clericals would get the coffee, buy the presents, and pamper their bosses collided with a growing sense of professionalism and entitlement. "My greatest gripe, besides the obvious problems of low pay and lack of respect, is that the men with whom we work refuse to recognize us as mature, adult women. . . . I am not a 'puss,' or a 'chick,' a 'broad' or a 'dear.' I am a WOMAN and I have a name, a full name of my own," insisted one Boston office worker, writing in response to an early 9to5 newsletter in 1973.[6]

Some 9to5ers embraced the new ideas of women's equality, even if they chose not to embrace its language. Judith McCollough, an office worker at Travelers Insurance in Boston, was typical of such working-class women attracted to the group. "I'd been interested in the women's movement," but was "slightly intimidated by it," remembered McCollough. Though she "identified with the idea that women should . . . do all the things that they wanted to do . . . The National Organization for Women . . . just didn't seem to connect to me." McCollough went on to join 9to5's staff and later became a national union organizer.[7]

Experimenting with New Forms of Worker Power

The founders of 9to5 did not set out to launch a new form of labor organizing. Karen Nussbaum and Ellen Cassedy were young, middle-class white women who met at the University of Chicago in 1969 when they were nineteen years old; both were active in the seismic social struggles of the late 1960s, including the antiwar movement and the women's movement. "I felt both the responsibility and the glory of fixing the world, and it was available to do, there was so much going on," remembered Nussbaum, who found political action within this zeitgeist far more interesting than college. She fled to Boston, where she organized with other women active in the effort to end the Vietnam War. But the rent soon came due and groceries were not free, so she got a job at Harvard as a secretary.[8]

Like many young activists in the New Left, Nussbaum found herself wary of organized labor but also intrigued by its transformative possibilities. Two events nudged her in the direction of labor work. First, during a massive antiwar mobilization in 1971, activists chanted, "What are the unions for? General strike to end the war!" Labor leaders' support for the war made unions anathema to peace activists like Nussbaum, yet something clicked as she watched the protesters. She began to think more deeply about unions as a tool for social change. Second, when she joined a picket line of working-class waitresses near Boston that same year, she witnessed the women's movement bubbling through: "I realized that there was this power in the ideas of women's liberation which could be exercised against the authority of the boss."[9]

Nussbaum brought these new ideas about labor organizing to her job at Harvard and organized a group of women in 1972 to "support each other and to act as a group to improve our situations as Services and Wages employees." They formed the Women Office Workers at Harvard, which was an organization made up of mostly young women who despised "wifely" duties like getting professors tea, and agitated for clearly defined job classifications and disclosed salaries. Though they didn't launch a union drive, they discussed unionization as one of the options for change.[10] Nussbaum soon expanded her labor activism among women in other workplaces. She helped organize a workshop for office workers at an antiwar Boston Women's Assembly in April 1972, out of which developed a discussion group of ten clericals from a hodgepodge of workplaces including a shoe factory, a hospital, universities, and insurance companies. The group ran a newspaper ad to attract new members and it caught the eye of women like Janet Selcer, a white, middle-class office worker who was more interested in issues of wealth inequality than "the cultural aspects of the women's movement." The group grew to about twenty-five people and soon formed the core of 9to5.[11]

Cassedy joined in the summer of 1972, moving to Boston after graduating from college. She also got a job as an office worker at Harvard. "I am

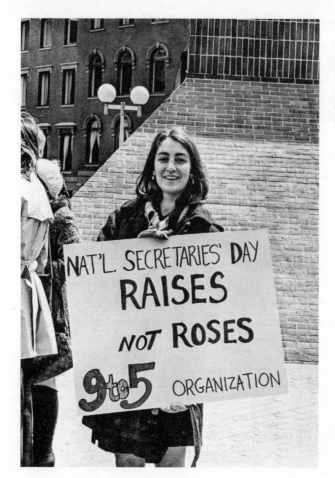

Karen Nussbaum at a 9to5 rally, Boston (1974). Karen Nussbaum, private photo collection. Courtesy of Karen Nussbaum.

writing as a newly recruited member of the labor movement," penned Cassedy to a favorite high school teacher who was active in his union. She understood her office worker activism as part of a larger wave of union organizing, explaining to her mentor that waitresses and hospital workers were organizing unions in Boston. Yet she also admitted to being wary of unions and the "corrupt and ambitious and reactionary labor leaders."[12]

The discussion group started handing out *9to5: Newsletter for Boston Area Office Workers* at subway stations and on the sidewalks outside major financial institutions in late 1972. Under such headlines as "We DO Have Rights" and "'Girls' till We Retire," they aimed to change the lens through which female clericals saw their own jobs. Meanwhile, they insisted that "we must get together as office workers, not only as women," and so kept readers updated on local union organizing at hospitals and insurance companies.[13] They saw themselves as part of a larger working women's movement. For example, one newsletter featured a map of the United States under the headline "What's Happening . . ." It highlighted the Farah slacks strike in El Paso and the Metropolitan Life Insurance Company unionizing effort in San Francisco alongside new groups like Chicago's Women Employed and Los Angeles's Working Women.[14]

The young women pooled their pennies to send Cassedy to Chicago for the Midwest Academy's first training in the summer of 1973. Founded by activist Heather Booth from the proceeds of a back pay award in an unfair labor practice suit, the Midwest Academy taught activists from a broad array of organizations the nuts and bolts of community organizing strategy and tactics. Booth had learned such tactics, in part, through the Industrial Areas Foundation, an organizing center founded in 1940 by Saul Alinsky. The center "provided good training," remembered Booth, "but they also did say they didn't think women could be organizers. We set up our own training session, and the first focus was on training women organizers." Cassedy returned from that session loaded with fresh ideas of how to build an organization that would apply community organizing tactics to build change among Boston's office workers.[15]

It was in turning their ad hoc newsletter group into a membership organization in 1973 that the women began to wrestle with the questions and issues that would propel them to build a fresh kind of labor organizing. In a foundational planning document, they made clear that long-term goals included "a labor movement comprised of democratic unions," yet they also valued an "independent women's movement" and bristled at a "labor bureaucracy" consisting of "a few men negotiating with corporations and government."[16] Nussbaum clarified in a subsequent memo that the goals should be transformational, including winning more "control of the workplace (the community and environment as well) by the people who work and live there."[17] They decided to build something in between the labor and women's movements, an association that would function as an "independent women office workers' organization." It would change an undemocratic labor movement by seeding it with the women workers. Cassedy thought the whole process should take about three to five years. In fact, the young women were pushed by both the limitations of the collective bargaining model and the rich possibilities of the women's movement to build something over the next decade that was much more significant and far more complex than their original concept.[18]

The organization took the newsletter's name, 9to5, and its first public event was a forum for office workers in November 1973, billed as "the beginning of an action-oriented organization, fighting for fair employment for the women in Boston's offices."[19] A hundred and fifty women attended. They were mostly young, white office workers, with a sprinkling of middle-aged and older women, a couple of African American women, and few whom Cassedy termed "Cambridge-area radicals."[20] "I am not the girl, the kid, dear or honeychile," testified Lillian Christmas, a legal secretary, during the meeting. "After nearly a quarter century of experience . . . why is my salary so low that I have to take in freelance typing to support my family?"[21]

Yet if the group was not focused on organizing employees at one workplace, as a union would be, whom should they target for change? The group's first official membership meeting answered that question by planning a meeting with the local chamber of commerce. They took twenty people and half a dozen reporters to meet with the chamber's executive vice president, and asked him to host a meeting for women office workers with local personnel managers. The chamber refused, arguing that "salaries and conditions of work are the responsibility of individual firms." That refusal "threw us for a loop," wrote 9to5 cochair Joan Tighe in early 1974, because it forced the group to figure out its own alternative steps.[22]

9to5 then began to develop an organizational model based on caucuses of workers within specific industries: insurance and finance, legal, universities, publishing, small businesses, temporary agencies, and health care. Members of each caucus would testify at their own hearings, to which they would invite representatives of government and business. In a sense, 9to5 recreated a miniature version of the industrial model that the unions of the CIO had forged when they abandoned craft unions in the 1930s, though the historical record does not indicate that 9to5 did so consciously. These industry-based committees, especially the publishing and insurance committees, would be the engines for the group's later development.

They also began to define more clearly their public goals through the Bill of Rights for Women Office Workers. They banged out their rights treatise in "two stormy meetings" in which the group lost a few African American members who left the group after they were unsuccessful in getting childcare included. African American women had long been more likely to work for wages than married white women, and black social reformers historically had a stronger tradition of prioritizing childcare than did their white counterparts. The black women at the 9to5 meeting may have had a better understanding of the thorny childcare dilemmas that would continue to bedevil all working women in a society that remained structured for single-breadwinner families. Yet 9to5's founders did not think they could win childcare, so they resisted including it among the demands. 9to5 would struggle throughout its years with issues of diversity, and this early defection by women of color turned out to be an important one. It helped set the early organization on a trajectory that limited its potential reach.[23]

Women from each industry testified at the April 1974 "Hearing on the Working Conditions of Women Office Workers." Three hundred office workers packed into the Boston YWCA for the meeting, including a very determined Fran Cicchetti. They signed the Bill of Rights for Women Office Workers, which included the rights to "respect as women and office workers," "comprehensive, written job descriptions," and "regular salary reviews and cost-of-living increases" among its thirteen demands. Interestingly, the group did not include higher pay or benefits among its original demands, only "benefits equal to those of men in similar job categories," despite the women's constant frustration with their low salaries. Their higher-pay campaigns would only develop toward the end of the decade as the group matured as an organization pushing for working-class economic power.[24]

9to5 chose a clear women's issue as the focus for their first public action: supporting maternity leave legislation. The groups' leaders experimented with three different varieties of power levers to advance their goals in spring 1974. Members picketed the state house twice; held a meeting with the chief lobbyist of the Associated Industries of Massachusetts, a trade group for industry that opposed the bill; and picketed the New England Merchants Bank for its opposition. From these activities, Nussbaum and the other leaders learned that their attempts to lobby government through the state house picket were far more popular among members, who found the "attacks on agencies and private companies an alien idea."[25]

Nussbaum and Cassedy thus followed their members' lead and steered away from confronting corporations directly, choosing instead to exercise power by pressuring and influencing government throughout 1974 and 1975. In this way, they searched for new ways for the state to support workers' organizing efforts outside collective bargaining. For instance, while the insurance committee passed out leaflets and surveys in front of Travelers Insurance, New England Mutual, and other major Boston insurers, they did not yet confront these companies directly about their employment practices and pay.[26] Rather, they used their surveys to build a report on the insurance industry, which then formed the basis for two public forums. Women in insurance were part of "an explosive situation," advertised a flyer for the

9to5 activists include a call for insurance regulations among their demands at a 1975 National Secretaries Day rally, Boston. *9to5 Newsletter*, May 1975. Schlesinger Library, Radcliffe Institute, Harvard University. Courtesy of Karen Nussbaum.

forum, featuring an image of dynamite stuck in a high-heel shoe.[27] Their report found that though 60 percent of the city's insurance workforce was female, a full 86 percent of those eighteen thousand women were in clerical positions. Though over half of the industry's men earned more than $10,000 a year, only 2 percent of women did so. Though 9to5 was not a union, Cicchetti chose words for reporters at the forum that hinted at a strike: "If we weren't there to answer the phones, make appointments, process claims, type the payrolls and file accounts, Boston's most lucrative business would lose its profits and come to a grinding halt."[28]

In July 1975, the new Massachusetts insurance commissioner accepted 9to5's proposal to issue new state regulations against sex discrimination in hiring, pay, and benefits and promotions within the insurance industry. The commissioner agreed to use his power to revoke individual companies' licenses if they discriminated against women and to refuse the entire industry a rate increase if too many companies did not change employment practices. The insurance regulations were the first of their kind in the nation.[29] Although the young activists of 9to5 had not challenged individual corporations directly, they nonetheless found themselves thwarted by corporate power. A group of twenty-five Massachusetts insurers challenged the new regulations in court, and the commissioner suspended the regulations "voluntarily."[30]

The temporary agencies committee of 9to5 also tried to use state regulation as a lever for worker power, and they ran into a similar roadblock when they championed a state senate bill governing temporary agencies. These agencies began to exercise enormous political power as the number of temporary workers doubled during the 1970s; temp work quickly became a favorite corporate strategy for managing profit in an era of global competition and for sidestepping social welfare obligations. The women of 9to5 tried to fight back. Their rather innocuous legislation would have required agencies to provide job descriptions, allowed temps to take permanent job offers from clients, and showed employees job evaluations. After the industry's lobbyists scuttled the bill, 9to5 met with the secretary of state to complain that many of the lobbyists weren't officially registered, but they never made real inroads in this growing industry.[31]

So if corporations could block legislation and effectively thwart government agencies from changing the rules that governed them, then what other levers of state power could a nonunion group of employees effectively pull? "If you look at the power structure of the office world in Boston, where do you go? How do you get near them?" remembered Cassedy of the group's dilemma.[32] Here, the Women in Publishing committee began to find the most fertile ground. Women in Publishing was 9to5's most active committee following the April 1974 forum, and it soon began distributing its own newsletter at publishing houses. The women of the publishing committee were the most middle-class group of all the 9to5 committees because nearly all publishing jobs required a college degree. This committee included Nancy Farrell, a production assistant at Allyn & Bacon who first got involved in Women in Publishing in 1974 because she was concerned that her employer did not post sales and management jobs. Farrell would later serve as 9to5's chairwoman and would help unionize Allyn & Bacon. Like Farrell, many of these women came into publishing expecting to rise quickly into editorial jobs but instead found themselves ghettoized in dead-end clerical positions. They paved a path on civil rights suits and direct corporate confrontation that would set the tone for the entire organization.[33]

Farrell and the other activists in the Women in Publishing subgroup began by claiming the high ground. They conducted a broad survey of the Boston publishing industry and released the report at a public forum detailing the rampant discrimination in the nation's second-largest publishing city. The report showed that though 66 percent of the Boston industry's workers were female, women only made up 6 percent of the management-level employees. They called for equal hiring and promotion across gender, for equal pay and benefits, and for companies to publicize affirmative action plans. They insisted that "stereotypical attitudes" about women "must be discredited." Interestingly, as with 9to5's bill of rights, this committee did not yet call for across-the-board higher pay.[34] They then worked with the new Massachusetts attorney general, Francis X. Bellotti, to file a joint suit against three of the city's largest publishers with the EEOC, the federal agency enforcing Title VII of the Civil Rights Act of 1964, as well as with its state-level equivalent, the Massachusetts Commission against Discrimination. The suits targeted Addison-Wesley Publishing, Allyn & Bacon, and Houghton Mifflin, alleging discrimination on the basis of sex and race. Five women editors in the Houghton Mifflin educational division meanwhile filed their own class action suit in federal court after discovering through the 9to5 survey that the company paid women an average of $3,400 less a year than men doing the same jobs.[35]

The women had found their answer as to how best to get corporate Boston's attention. The companies were shocked by the lawsuits, which seemed to come out of the blue in an industry that was not unionized and was not used to any sort of worker collective action. "We think a lot of women . . . we think they're very nice," asserted Addison-Wesley's apparently tone-deaf president Donald Jones in denying the charges to the *Wall Street Journal*. Addison-Wesley later counter-sued 9to5, unsuccessfully trying to force them to turn over all the group's records. Houghton Mifflin, meanwhile, hired a consulting firm to evaluate salaries and do interviews with employees, and it ended up giving workers a sizeable raise, some as much as $2,500. All the suits ended up being settled over the course of the next six years. First Houghton Mifflin settled the class action suit for $750,000. Then each of the three publishers agreed to settlements that amounted to $1.5 million in back pay, and agreed to create job ladders, post salaries, and offer new job training.[36]

9to5 was not alone among female workplace activists in using civil rights law to pry open doors in the 1970s that had long been closed to women. Women at the *New York Times* and *Newsweek*, New York City firefighters, steelworkers, and telephone operators were just some of the groups who successfully used class action suits to force equal access to a wide range of jobs.[37] What made 9to5's efforts different, however, was the extent to which the suits were embedded within the organization's many collective tactics for workplace change. 9to5 saw the cases as part of a strategy that involved personal empowerment, workplace coalition building, group confrontations with management, corporate public shaming, and alliances with women across industries. For example, though the early Women in Publishing group was originally loath to take on higher pay as an issue, it gained momentum and confidence through the suits, and soon launched a citywide wage survey in 1976. The 9to5 report of the survey of eighteen local publishing houses called publishing "a women's job ghetto" and found that the Boston-area employees made less than those in the national industry. They demanded higher wages—for all office workers in the industry—as well as equal pay and benefits for women.[38] They amplified their influence through savvy use of public opinion, awarding a "wasted womanpower award" to publishers with the worst maternity leave policies, salary reviews, and job posting plans. They leafleted not only workers but also shareholders at the Houghton Mifflin annual meeting. Within a year, they forced five publishers to institute new posting policies. This wide range of tactics, which 9to5 first tried in publishing, would serve as a toolbox for the group's later efforts to force change in other industries by the end of the decade.[39]

Local 925: A New Kind of Union

It was not long after founding 9to5 that the women went knocking on labor's door, meeting with ten unions active in the Boston area. "It was never . . . that we only wanted to have a women's work organization alone. We wanted to use it to prompt union organizing among office workers," remembered Selcer, one of the original group of twenty-five women. 9to5's founders saw the group as a precursor to unions, "a step in between," and had originally envisioned raising women's consciousness and then shepherding them into existing unions.[40]

Yet they encountered a mixed reception when they reached out to unions. "I don't want any Communist cunts around here," asserted Matt McGraw, the leader of SEIU Local 285 representing city workers.[41] Eddie Sullivan, a labor leader for university janitors and food servers, believed it was simply impossible to organize clerical workers.[42] District 65 was interested in a partnership with the clerical organization, and the national union representing office workers, the Office and Professional Employees International Union, seemed interested in hiring Nussbaum and Cassedy. A local labor educator, however, urged the women to rethink whether they should merge into a union, suggesting that the power they were building "was more precious than something to just give away," remembered Nussbaum.[43] The national-level SEIU was the only union willing to charter the group as an autonomous local and fund three people as organizers. 9to5 thus formed a union with SEIU in 1975 because it was important to the group that "we control how we use the money, where we organize, and how we organize."[44]

The new union chose as its name SEIU Local 925, a clear play on the 9to5 association's name. It had a close relationship with 9to5, and staff of both groups attended weekly meetings together. Nussbaum served as director of both organizations until 1978.[45] Nevertheless, Local 925 was its own separate membership organization. From the start, the group set out to be a different kind of union that harnessed the power of collective bargaining while also building on many of the women-focused organizing forms they had developed through their work with 9to5. "We started by making it personal, and that was different from the kind of organizing going on at the time," recalled Nussbaum. "The typical organizing was you stood at the plant gate and handed out leaflets. . . . Instead, we would use these surveys, talk to women individually. We assumed there would be five conversations with each individual before you could get them to sign a card."[46] They began to challenge clericals' assumptions about unions much in the same way they had challenged their ideas about gender roles. "Does a union mean time-clocks, limited wage scales and rigid working conditions? No, in fact it can mean the opposite," read one early organizing brochure. Though the union was open to male and female members, Local 925 positioned itself as a union addressing women workers' needs. "We are being taken advantage of because we are women and because we are unorganized," read recruitment literature.[47]

The young local launched its first campaign among forty librarians at Brandeis University. Local 925 found far more resistance from this liberal-minded university than it had anticipated. The librarians had already formed their own independent staff association in 1969 because, while they felt a "special kinship" to the institution, they also "felt increasingly ignored or even abused over the years." Their pay was lower than that of other librarians (some of them made only ninety-five dollars for a thirty-five-hour week), medical costs had increased, and they wanted more job security. Members of the association met with local unions and chose to launch a union organizing campaign with Local 925, which they found "sensitive to our cause."[48] Though publicly Brandeis said it "honors the right of its Library employees to choose freely to join or to refrain from joining a union," in fact it trained supervisors to warn employees about strikes, dues, and unions as "a third party." Supervisors were to make clear that "the law permits the hiring of a permanent replacement" in cases of economic strikes.[49] Once 89 percent of the librarians voted for the union in early 1976, the university dragged its feet in negotiations, refusing for six months to move on a single major item.[50] The women of Local 925 had to pull from many of the community campaign tactics developed by the 9to5 association in order to force the university's hand. Just as 9to5 had learned to leaflet downtown buildings, members of Local 925 began leafleting Brandeis alumni events in New York, Chicago, and Atlanta. They kept the Brandeis cause in front of reporters, activated Brandeis students in a group called Jewish Students for a Just Settlement, and pressured the National Women's Committee to stop raising funds for the library. "Union-busting isn't Kosher," read one solidarity leaflet. The university finally settled after nine months. Local 925 had tapped 9to5's broad array of nontraditional labor tactics and managed to bring home the first union contract covering university office staff in Boston.[51]

Though the going was slow and employer opposition was strong, the young local managed to win a few union elections among small units of clericals at private-sector employers like Allyn & Bacon, Educators Publishing Services (EPS), and Rounder Records. They developed their own unique organizing tactics and contract demands based on their experiences as working women. Consider the campaign at Allyn & Bacon, one of the three publishers named in the joint discrimination suit filed by the Massachusetts attorney general and 9to5. Even before the workers saw a settlement, the clericals started to explore unionizing. When it became clear that some employees thought of themselves as nonunion professionals, Farrell, the Women in Publishing activist, developed a distinctive tactic to build solidarity. During a union icebreaker, "the participants had to reveal their weight or their salary. The numbers came tumbling out . . . and they were low," Farrell remembered, noting that the women quickly opted to disclose their salaries.[52] Allyn & Bacon workers won an NLRB election and managed to get a legally binding contract with more flexible schedules, an average

18 percent salary increase, and a standing union-management committee on job training, three years before the civil rights suits settled.[53] The Local 925 contract at Rounder Records included issues uncommon in contemporaneous contracts, like parental leave and a no-discrimination clause that included sexual preference.[54] In other cases, Local 925 found the union paradigm limiting. When the union reached an impasse in negotiations with EPS, the women formed a conga line picket and held signs reading, "EPS— Every Person a Slave." The next Monday Nussbaum received a subpoena, as such public actions were in violation of labor law once the parties had reached an impasse. Eventually, Local 925 did sign a first contract with EPS, winning a 25 percent wage increase and improved medical insurance that was completely financed by the employer.[55] Yet Local 925 quickly ran up against the kind of increased private-sector employer resistance to unions that grew throughout the nation in the 1970s.

Activists found that the door through which workers could enter the union was far narrower than the entryway to the association. When they tried to organize a small radio station, for instance, they discovered that Alfred DeMaria, one of the nation's most notorious union busters, represented the company. The small Massachusetts College of Pharmacy called in the national Three M firm to successfully defeat a clerical unionizing effort there. Meanwhile, Allyn & Bacon never stopped resisting the local, dragging out negotiations at every turn. Eventually, that publisher moved to Newton and laid off many of the original staff, and the union was decertified. "We were trying to organize in . . . this private sector where the companies had this whole union-busting industry . . . but we didn't know anything about it. . . . It was really psychological warfare," remembered Local 925 organizer Dorine Levasseur. They found far more success organizing in the public and nonprofit sectors where employer resistance was lighter, such as among teachers' aides, librarians, and legal services employees. The local did not grow very large, reaching about a thousand members by 1981.[56]

Testing the New Organizing Model

Though Nussbaum and Cassedy had once thought that a union would negate the need for the association, they soon began to realize that there was enormous potential in the alternative organization. It was "clearly apparent that you hadn't exhausted the unbelievable opportunity that 9to5 the association created," remembered Nussbaum. "You could let anybody in and

hundreds of women would become activists and thousands would participate in one thing and . . . hundreds of thousands would hear about it and
be moved."[57] It turned out that in creating a separate, autonomous union in
1975, the organization had settled the question whether 9to5 was a union, a
point of confusion often raised by new recruits, the press, and the public.[58]
Clearly, 9to5 was not a union, because Local 925 was the union. Ironically,
this sharp separation freed up the association to move into deeper confrontations with corporate employers, including around "bread and butter" issues
like wages and benefits.

It was thus after the creation of Local 925, in the years between 1976 and
1980, that the association 9to5 began to most fully explore the potential of
its new model of labor organizing, and the first mechanism it used to organize Boston's bank and insurance company workers was a call for affirmative action enforcement. Like many workplace gender activists at the
time, 9to5 wanted to build on the idea that companies needed to take pro-
active steps to address past inequities through affirmative action, a phrase
that originated in a 1965 Executive Order issued by President Lyndon
Johnson that was then expanded in 1967 to include sex discrimination. Unlike many labor unions that were resistant to affirmative action remedies
that took precedence over union contracts' seniority provisions, the 9to5
activists embraced affirmative action as a labor organizing tool.[59] In early
1976, 9to5 voted to make affirmative action enforcement its signature campaign for the year, and it set out to target the banks and insurance companies it so far had found elusive. "Obviously, this is where 9to5 comes alive!"
one member urged, noting 9to5 found 842 Boston-area companies with
federal contracts exceeding $50,000, all of whom were legally required
to have an affirmative action plan.[60] They launched a campaign to teach
members about affirmative.action, first inviting women to a conference in
Boston with a mock-engraved "invitation to equal opportunity." They then
targeted various government agencies, pushing them to enforce affirmative action. Women from companies like Liberty Mutual and Aetna began to
gather after work to read their companies' affirmative action plans.[61]

Selcer played a lead role in the effort to target private-sector companies
through the affirmative action campaign. "We became very adept at making contacts on the inside," remembered Selcer, who passed out surveys in
front of Boston's banks and then held "endless numbers of lunches" with
the women office workers who responded. "I loved the one woman who
would say, sure you can come to lunch in the First National Bank of Liberty
Mutual. Then you felt like you were in the belly of the beast and all the

people you wanted to talk to were right there." Selcer and the other activists found ample evidence of discrimination by sex, race, and even age. After state officials and 9to5 held hearings on this issue, the U.S. Senate Banking Committee got involved, accusing the U.S. Treasury Department of not enforcing EEOC standards at financial institutions. 9to5 then filed a suit against New England Merchants Bank, citing it as a prime offender. 9to5's charges forced a Treasury Department suit, but the women found it more disappointing than the publishing suits. Though the Treasury Department found that the bank was not following affirmative action rules, it was slow to force this major financial institution into compliance. Yet the suit had far-reaching implications when other banks, like Boston Safe Deposit and Trust Company, voluntarily signed new affirmative action agreements.[62] 9to5's affirmative action campaign shifted into a defensive one when the new director of the national Office of Contract Compliance, Lawrence Lorber, announced plans in 1976 to release all but the largest firms from affirmative action requirements and to end compliance reviews in the precontract stage. 9to5 joined Women Employed and civil rights groups in a successful campaign to vigorously defend the existing affirmative action regulations.[63]

9to5's leaders found an affirmative action strategy fruitful, yet ultimately decided that its focus on government agencies rather than on corporations limited it as an organizing tool. "After we worked on government enforcement . . . we realized that we were teaching our members that government was the enemy," recalls Nussbaum. Instead, 9to5 began to run what it called "higher pay" campaigns, finally making a full-throated demand for increased wages and benefits across the board, as well as increased job training and promotions. Through these campaigns at large corporations, the organization found it was often able to raise wages and improve working conditions, all outside the collective bargaining paradigm. For instance, the group launched a campaign at First National Bank on Secretaries Day in April 1979. The group publicized the fact that the bank's own affirmative action report showed that women were underutilized in fifteen of thirty-six job categories, that it had no job posting system, and that a file clerk made a mere $6,800 a year. They began meeting with First National employees, started a newsletter for the group, set up an employee "hotline," launched a petition drive among depositors, reached out to community leaders, and held public demonstrations at stockholder meetings.[64]

The campaign worked. The bank announced a new job posting system immediately after the campaign launch, and within a year workers had won raises amounting up to 12 percent, a larger increase than in previous years.[65] 9to5 launched a similar campaign at the John Hancock Insurance Company, where women made up 60 percent of the workforce, including 85 percent of the lowest-level clericals. Nussbaum later served on a panel with a high-level executive from John Hancock who recalled that on the day 9to5 launched the campaign, he barricaded himself in his office and stayed there overnight, feeling under siege.[66] The John Hancock campaign resulted in a 10.5 percent average pay increase, the raising of the lowest pay grade, and the formation of an ad hoc committee to develop career paths for nonmanagement employees. These gains were comparable to what the Woodward & Lothrop workers won in their first union contract, though the Hancock workers never had a union. The company even contributed to local day care centers when the workers demanded assistance with childcare.[67]

As they ran these corporate-focused campaigns, the women of 9to5 redefined organizing by borrowing and adapting the forms that grew out of the women's movement. Gone were house calls and the card-signing routines of traditional union organizing. Instead they held what they called "recruitment" or "nurturing" lunches. These were like the consciousness-raising sessions popular among women's movement activists but, Cassedy recalled, were far less intimidating. Staff and leaders would sometimes have three such organizing lunches a day, as they had the goal of meeting with every member or potential member at least once a year. They prioritized leadership training and groomed members to take the lead in confronting power. "This was an organization that would take you as fast as you could go, even a little faster than you might be ready to go . . . to help change the world," recalled Debbie Schneider, who was recruited from a Boston-area publishing house and later went on to organize for SEIU.[68]

Taking the Dual Structure National

The women of 9to5 had hit on a novel structure for helping women office workers effect workplace change, especially since by the end of the decade employers had so narrowed possibilities for organizing unions. Activists balanced an association that combined public action and legal work with an official union that allowed workers to tap the most secure tier of the U.S. social welfare regime, legally backed collective bargaining. They were "constantly readjusting the balance between outreach and activism on one hand, and consolidating power on the other" union side, remembered Nussbaum.[69]

The group took this bifurcated structure national, replicating a nationwide association in 1977 and a national union in 1979. These remained independent, yet intertwined.

9to5, the association in Boston, was already integrated within a larger network of women office workers' organizations that were also experimenting with non-collective-bargaining solutions and that often learned from 9to5's model. Cleveland Women Working and San Francisco's Women Organized for Employment, for instance, also did surveys and reports on women in banks in order to force government action on discrimination. These groups shared ideas and tactics, but found that they often bumped up against one another in fundraising, and so looked for a way to consolidate and amplify their efforts. They first tried an informal joint organizing project and then officially launched a national organization, Working Women: A National Association for Office Workers. Nussbaum served as its executive director from her new base in Cleveland, where she moved in order to help expand the model to new communities. This new national association started with thirteen membership organizations in 1977 and grew to twenty-two chapters by 1983 when it changed its name to 9to5: National Association of Working Women.[70] Working Women quickly became a darling of progressive foundations like the Ford Foundation, the Stern Fund, and the New World Foundation, allowing it to raise in 1979 "more money than we dreamed possible." Such foundations soon provided well over half the group's budget, dwarfing income from membership dues. A canvass, grassroots fundraising, union support, and individual donations were among other funding sources.[71]

Boston's 9to5 continued as a separate organization and remained a chapter of this umbrella group. Its affiliation with Working Women broadened the Boston group's influence and helped it mature as part of a more racially diverse organization. All of the original 9to5 founders were white, as were most of the activists, and though the leaders asked each committee to build diversity into its plan, there was "some lack of consciousness on our part about what that task would look like and how to accomplish it," remembered Selcer.[72] As in the case of the African American women who wanted to include childcare in the bill of rights, the organization's priorities often reflected those of its majority white, young membership. As Working Women expanded in the 1980s to other cities that had a more diverse population, it was able to attract more women of color, who in turn influenced the direction of the organization. The Columbus, Ohio, chapter, for instance, pushed for Ohio State University to include clericals in its affirmative action discussions, which before had been confined to faculty and students. The Atlanta chapter included a sharp focus on minority workers in its surveys and reports, and African American leaders from the Baltimore chapter did minority outreach trainings for the group nationwide.[73]

Working Women chapters tested their wings as alternative labor organizations in the late 1970s, adopting Boston 9to5's "higher pay" campaign and focusing on discrimination at banks and insurance companies. Yet it was in the cultural realm that Working Women was able to make the most of its national-level platform. The group invited women office workers nationwide to join them in laying bare the contradictions between the emergent cultural shifts around gender and the stubborn reality of office sexism. Humor was often their weapon of choice. Consider, for instance, the group's petty office procedure contest. The boss who required his secretary to vacuum up his fingernail clippings after he scattered them all over the floor won the personal hygiene award. The women also "honored" the boss who required his secretary to sew up his split pants seam—while he was wearing them. Thirty-five women showed up at his office and presented him with an "executive sewing kit." Women nationwide read about the group under such headlines as "Have You Heard the One about the Boss Who . . . ?" Their Raises Not Roses campaign redefined the annual Secretaries Day rituals, as women turned out in rallies nationwide each year. Working Women was helping to drive a cultural shift, even before it inspired the *9 to 5* movie, which was the group's crowning achievement on the cultural front.[74]

Nussbaum had gotten to know the actress Jane Fonda in the antiwar movement, and when Fonda approached her about the idea of a movie, Nussbaum brought her to meet with forty women clericals in Cleveland. The women spent a long night talking with Fonda about problems on the job and how they had dreamed about standing up to the boss. Many details of the film grew out of Fonda's conversations with the Cleveland women. The film itself is a revenge fantasy in which three secretaries (played by Fonda, Lily Tomlin, and Dolly Parton) get even with a bigoted boss who is prone to yelling, lying, and "pinching and staring." After fantasizing about roping him like a steer, poisoning him, and executing him, they kidnap him and hold him captive. Some of the best moments of the film are farcical depictions of women dealing with errant copying machines and fraught memo-taking sessions, laying bare the ludicrous machinations of sexism on the job.[75]

The *9 to 5* film launched at Christmastime in 1980 and became a runaway hit, grossing more than $38 million in its first three weeks and later inspiring a spin-off television show and musical.[76] "Before that, we had had to argue carefully, make proof . . . and then Jane Fonda makes a movie that mocks discrimination in the workplace and the argument is over," remembered Nussbaum. The film made a deep imprint on the nation's understanding of gender at work. "The other day our lawyer saw the film," said Fonda in a promotion interview in 1980. "For the first time in all the years I've known him, when he wanted coffee, he went out and got it himself."[77] Working Women built on the film's popularity, launching the "Movement behind the Movie" tour in fifteen cities, where leaders and members did interviews with morning television shows and held recruitment meetings and rallies after work.[78]

Even as Working Women was helping to change cultural mores on gender, it found that it also needed the sharp teeth of collective bargaining in order to win lasting workplace gains in wages and benefits. By 1979, leaders decided it was time to take Boston's Local 925 national. Nussbaum and the members of Working Women approached and evaluated five unions as potential national partners—SEIU, UAW, UFCW, the Communications Workers of America, and the Office and Professional Employees International Union. The group wanted their partner union to commit resources to clerical organizing, establish a special structure in the union to address clericals' needs, and "make a commitment to several years of 'our' approach to organizing."[79] SEIU seemed the most willing. They bargained hard with SEIU's new national president, John Sweeney, and his male staff, insisting on salaries comparable to SEIU rates for other organizers. SEIU chartered the new union in 1981 as District 925, a stand-alone national local with its own officers, bylaws, and autonomy. Nussbaum would serve as its president while continuing to direct Working Women, thus linking the two organizations. Former Local 925 organizer Jackie Ruff would serve as the District 925 executive director.[80] "It was pretty revolutionary," remembered Ray Abernathy, a public relations consultant for unions who had a good sense of labor's attitudes. "The very idea of having a national union run by women was preposterous . . . women who were in positions of authority in the union were very often there as tokens."[81] District 925 launched with great fanfare, holding rallies and major press events in a bicoastal media launch in early 1981. Dabney Coleman, the actor who played the villainous boss in the 9 to 5 movie, helped publicize the group by answering its toll-free line, fielding calls from union-minded clericals. District 925 vowed to organize clericals nationwide, with a special focus on insurance and banking.[82]

In fact, while District 925 made headway in organizing public-sector workers, its private-sector efforts almost universally failed. The Equitable Insurance campaign, its earliest and largest such campaign, offers a glimpse at the deep corporate resistance the women faced in private-sector organizing. A few months after District 925's launch, a woman working as a claims adjuster at Equitable in Syracuse, New York, saw the new union mentioned on *60 Minutes*. She and others were upset by having no voice in the company's switch from paper claims to computers, and thought they were paid too little. Most were young, in their twenties and early thirties, and had a strong sense of both women's and class-based rights. "They were really smart working-class women from a working-class town which had a big union tradition," remembered Cheryl Schaffer, a District 925 organizer on the campaign. After meeting with organizers, nearly 70 percent of the ninety Syracuse workers signed a union card over a single weekend.[83] Equitable, meanwhile, hired Raymond Mickus Associates (a spin-off of Three M) to fight the unionization effort, and they began training the company's supervisors how to resist the union. Nevertheless, the workers voted forty-nine to forty for District 925 on February 4, 1982. When Equitable dragged its feet in contract negotiations, District 925 launched a national boycott, supported by the AFL-CIO and the National Organization for Women. A thousand demonstrators marched in New York City, including many construction workers, to protest Equitable's "corporate policy of anti-unionism." The group set up pickets in forty-one cities.[84] District 925 did finally win a contract, after twenty months of negotiations and after taking the corporation before the NLRB in Washington, but it could never make headway in the corporation's other national offices. Equitable closed the Syracuse claims office in 1987 and laid off all the unionized workers, effectively ridding itself of a union.[85]

District 925 ran into the same resistance that other bank, insurance, and financial workers faced when they tried to form unions. Employers were deeply alarmed by such clerical organizing, and they pushed back forcefully. Martin Payson, a partner in a law firm notorious for countering union organizing, dubbed organizing efforts among female office workers "the most significant trend in labor-management relations today."[86] Stephen J. Cabot, a well-known union avoidance lawyer, asserted that despite its lack of immediate NLRB election success, District 925 "is driving companies in the Northeast crazy . . . it's been very effective."[87] Employers flocked to seminars focused on rolling back clerical workers' organizing efforts, like the "Managing White Collar Women" seminar held by the Georgia Chamber of Commerce, and made liberal use of antiunion consultants' services.[88] District 925 did have greater success organizing in the public-sector, such as at the University of Washington in Seattle, at the University of Cincinnati, and among county workers in Ohio and Illinois.[89]

The mid-1980s proved to be rocky years for both District 925 and its sister, the national 9to5 association. The union found growth difficult in the face of corporations' escalating resistance to new organizing. Meanwhile, the 9to5 association's Achilles' heel was the same one that weakened so many nonunion labor organizations: funding. While the 9to5 association had a dues structure, in fact less than 5 percent of the organization's revenue came from membership dues. By far the greatest source of funding was grant money from foundations, followed by grassroots fund-raisers and canvassing. For a time under the Jimmy Carter administration, the organization had received some government funding, including for volunteers from Vista, a national program to alleviate poverty. However those public funds quickly dried up under the Reagan administration.[90] Foundations, meanwhile, began to lose interest as the women's movement succeeded at advancing many women's access to better jobs in the workplace. "By the eighties, we were not the shiny new object for foundations," remembered Cassedy. Many saw that there was "less of a need for an organization that screamed and yelled about women's rights in the office."[91] SEIU District 925 had a bigger cushion when it came to funding. While dues made up only about a third of its budget, the union headquarters was willing to subsidize the rest in order to support the union's organizing and servicing of contracts. However, because dues made up such a small part of the association's income, the loss of government and foundation grants was lethal. Unless chapters could raise their own funds, 9to5 was forced to turn them into all-volunteer chapters rather than staffed organizations, which blunted the organization's effectiveness. The Boston 9to5 chapter, for example, was forced to move into this all-volunteer model, and in 1985 closed its office.[92]

9to5 also weakened when many of the middle-class women who had bolstered its ranks, like those in Women in Publishing, discovered in the 1980s and 1990s that they had less need for an organization demanding job promotions and equal access. Middle-class, college-educated women found that the nation's workplaces were opening their doors. As they gained new access to professional jobs, they were no longer likely to work side by side with working-class women, and they became less likely to agitate for the rights of clericals. During the 1970s the lowest-paid women had seen the greatest increases in their wages among all women. During the 1980s and 1990s, however, the highest-paid women's incomes took off and working-class women remained stuck in low-paying, dead-end jobs. By 2003, wages had grown twice as fast among women in the top wage percentiles as among those at the median and bottom, helping drive the new inequality so pervasive by the early twenty-first century.[93]

Both the District 925 union and the association also suffered with the demise of the secretarial occupation. Computers changed the nation's offices in the 1990s, automating many of the tasks that 9to5's members had once fought to do with dignity. In 2015 there were half as many secretaries as there were in 1979, despite the fact that the workforce as a whole grew. After the 2008–09 recession alone, 1.7 million people shifted out of clerical and administrative positions as companies figured out new ways to make their own schedules or automate office tasks.[94]

9to5 continues to operate as an important voice for progressive employment policies for all women, not only office workers. The organization has played an especially key role in places where unions are traditionally weak, like in Atlanta, where it has helped win a minimum wage ordinance for workers paid with city funds. Yet the organization remains small, with four chapters, and does not have the same hold on the public's imagination that it once did. SEIU District 925 is no longer a nationwide local for office workers. Instead, its legacy organization is a large local in Seattle, Washington, representing mostly public workers, including in higher education.[95]

The New Door

The trajectory of the 9to5 activists reminds us that the gender revolution in late twentieth-century American workplaces was enormously powerful. Young women in the year 2000 had a world of opportunity open to them that was simply closed to young women in 1960. However, the economic reach of that revolution turned out to be greatly limited when weak labor law and corporate resistance enervated unions like SEIU District 925. Nussbaum, Cassedy, and the 9to5 founders had once believed that they could create an organization that would both build power for women at work and transform the gender dynamics of the labor movement. They had envisaged workplaces that would bend to the new women workers' needs, guaranteeing fair wages alongside equal access to jobs, offering working-class security alongside career ladders. What they could not see from the vantage point of the 1970s, however, were the seismic shifts that would undermine both unions and all workers' economic security, ushering in the kind of inequality and bad jobs that would plague working-class women by the close of the twentieth century.

In 2017, nearly twice as many women as men work in poverty-level jobs, sometimes in the nation's offices but more often in service jobs like as health care aides, cashiers, and food servers. Most remain burdened by the double duty of paid work and family caregiving; one recent AFL-CIO report found that women have less than forty minutes a day of personal time after fulfilling all their other responsibilities. The gender wage gap has been stubbornly slow to close, and women still make only eighty-three cents for every dollar earned by a man.[96] Women continue to work as secretaries, though fewer do so today. Tellingly, the occupation's gender dynamic has changed little; 95 percent of people holding the title of "secretary" or "administrative assistant" today are women. Very few of them have a union, however, especially in the private sector.[97]

Though 9to5 never boosted unions' membership rolls and did not close the gender wage gap, it did find a different kind of success; the experience of being a female office worker by the close of the century was far less demeaning and disempowering than in the early 1970s. As a result, the most important impact of 9to5 showed up in neither union membership tallies nor the Department of Labor's annual review of declining union membership statistics: women office workers experienced far less overt sexism on the job than they did in the years of 9to5's founding. 9to5 was a leader in expanding the national conversation on gender at work, and that conversation fundamentally changed the societal expectations for women working in an office.

In addition, 9to5 was the first service-sector organization to experiment with the sort of non-NLRB, community-based path for labor organizing that became increasingly important for workers by the twenty-first century. It preceded such groups as Jobs with Justice and Justice for Janitors, both founded in the late 1980s, which used non-NLRB tactics to gain new leverage over employers. 9to5 ran the kinds of campaigns against John Hancock Insurance and First National Bank that the labor movement would by the late 1980s come to call "corporate campaigns," campaigns enlisting the support of the community, shareholders, and other stakeholders to force corporate action for workers' rights. 9to5 was the first organization to run such corporate campaigns among service workers, though unions had used this tactic with blue-collar workers, such as the clothing workers' union at Farah, ACTWU at J. P. Stevens and the UMWA which brought striking Harlan County miners to Wall Street to picket against Duke Power. Such corporate campaigns became much more common by the late 1980s and 1990s.[98]

In the end, what was most unique about 9to5, however, was that the organization did not enlist these tactics only to bring women into unions. 9to5 used a host of nontraditional labor tactics to try to force change for women office clericals outside the collective bargaining structure, even as they held on to collective bargaining as one path to power through SEIU District 925. In balancing these approaches, Nussbaum and Cassedy represented a new breed of labor organizers who framed an entirely new doorway into the labor movement, a doorway employers could not block as easily as that into collective bargaining. Their approach could have been a revolutionary one for all of America's labor movement, but, as we will soon see, labor leaders considered and then rejected such a transformational change in the mid-1980s. They did so while facing tremendous pressures rooted in recession, continued weakening of labor law, and the Reagan administration's attacks on collective bargaining. The early to mid-1980s proved to be dark days for the union movement, and they marked the moment when the window of working-class promise in the 1970s began to close.

Conclusion

· ·

The 1970s union organizing push never reached its full promise. Nurses, clericals, shipwrights, textile workers, retail clerks, and other members of a newly diversified working class sought out unions for security in the face of enormous economic change throughout the decade. Yet too many of the workers' organizing efforts collided with panicked employers' reactions to the new globally and financially centered economy. Employers refused to tolerate unions any longer as profits grew scarce; they fought back and took greater advantage of weak U.S. labor law because they feared the impact of an active and diverse workforce on their bottom lines. The resulting contest had a far greater impact than the usual labor-management tug of war. Rather, it helped set the employment terms that would govern the nation's slow transition out of industrial capitalism—a progression that is still happening today.

Some of the workers did win their unions, of course, and they found a more secure economic footing as a result. Jan Hooks and Edward Coppedge went on to have long unionized careers at the shipyard, each retiring with a secure pension. Hooks remains active in the USWA Local 8888 retiree group, and Coppedge returned to his family's home in North Carolina. Barbara Cash and Rosa Halsey no longer work with a department store, though Macy's workers in Washington still have a union contract that is a legacy of the one at Woodies. Many Boston clerical workers at universities still have unions, though those at insurance and financial companies are far less likely to benefit from any sort of worker organization. The Cannon workers' story remains grim. Though they eventually won a union, the plant's closure devastated Kannapolis, and many have not recovered. Like most working people, they found themselves tossed without a life vest into a perilous economy in which wages remained virtually stagnant for decades, health care and pension coverage dropped, and part-time and contingent work became a new norm.[1]

As late as 1981, the blue-collar battle still raged on. Unions' sustained reach was clearly on view during the AFL-CIO's Solidarity Day in Washington on September 19, 1981. There, Hooks, Coppedge, and other Newport

Solidarity Day, the largest rally ever staged by the U.S. labor movement, Washington, D.C. (1981). AFL-CIO Photographic Prints Collection (RG96-001), Special Collections and University Archives, University of Maryland Libraries. Photograph © AFL-CIO, used with permission.

News shipyard workers marched alongside Karen Nussbaum and the clerical workers of SEIU District 925. Between a quarter of a million and 400,000 union members and supporters attended Solidarity Day, the largest labor rally ever staged by the American labor movement. "Behold your numbers, as far as the eyes can see," boomed AFL-CIO president Lane Kirkland's voice over a crowd that filled the streets from the Capitol building to the Washington Monument.[2]

Bearded mechanics, hard-hatted carpenters, secretaries in collared blouses, and actors in hip blue jeans made the pilgrimage to Washington to protest the Reagan administration's social spending cuts and attacks on labor and civil rights. Participants rode on three thousand chartered buses, a dozen specially chartered Amtrak trains, and the free subway trains

FL-CIO universally subsidized in the hours leading up to the rally. For , it was their first trip to the nation's capital. They wore paper hats and aps advertising their unions and toted signs with a dizzying array of messages: "Health Care for All," "Hands Off Social Security," "ERA Now," "A Clean and Healthful Environment," "Export Goods, Not Jobs." Had such a march taken place thirty years earlier, the union members would have made for a far less diverse crowd. In 1981, however, the working men and women gathered in Washington were a cross section of the nation's workforce and so embodied the changes wrought by the 1964 Civil Rights Act's opening of America's workplaces and unions. America's reshaped working class gathered together because it understood that it was under vicious attack. "We're tired of working people falling further and further behind while, it seems, the rich get richer," summed up Mary Jo Vavra, the first woman ever to work at the Hercules chemical plant in Jefferson, Pennsylvania.[3]

Labor invited elected leaders to attend Solidarity Day but did not give them access to the podium. Instead, union members heard from leaders of allied organizations such as Eleanor Smeal of the National Organization for Women, Benjamin Hooks of the NAACP, Rev. Jesse Jackson of People United to Serve Humanity, and Rev. Joseph Lowery of the Southern Christian Leadership Conference, among others. A disparate group of allies, including the Sierra Club and the United Methodist Church, joined the throngs of union members.[4] The broad support for the march signified a confluence, rather than a conflict, between the goals of civil and labor rights. Coretta Scott King drove home that point in her speech to the crowd: "In a very real sense, Solidarity Day is a continuation of the great march on Washington, the latest stop in our long journey toward fulfilling the American dream of freedom, justice and equality for all."[5]

Scholars rarely feature Solidarity Day in histories of labor's late twentieth-century decline. A surprising number of labor history textbooks and studies have no mention at all of labor's largest public gathering in history, a march comparable in size to the 1963 March on Washington. Yet Solidarity Day reminds us that even though working people did not triumph in their demands, they envisioned and fought for an outcome that was far different from the inequality and insecurity that would mark the next century's working-class experience.[6]

The tide soon turned, but not in the direction the Solidarity Day marchers had envisaged. The years from 1982 to 1985 turned out to be dark ones for the American labor movement and marked the period when workers'

Members of 1199, the National Hospital Union, marching as part of Solidarity Day (1981). AFL-CIO Photographic Prints Collection (RG96-001), Special Collections and University Archives, University of Maryland Libraries. Photograph © AFL-CIO, used with permission.

organizing efforts finally weakened. After more than a decade of increased employer resistance to organizing, unions were not prepared to meet the convergence of the 1981–82 recession, steep membership losses, the disastrous air traffic controllers strike, employers' demands for contract concessions, and the Reagan administration NLRB. It was a perfect storm, and union organizing never recovered.

The recession of 1981–82 brought on unemployment rates of 10 percent, the highest the nation had seen since the Great Depression. The job loss was not spread evenly across the nation's workplaces. Rather, many of the lost jobs were concentrated in the traditionally unionized manufacturing and construction sectors.[7] It was a bull's-eye hit on labor's source of strength. Membership in both the UAW and the USWA dropped by more than four hundred thousand between 1979 and 1984; UAW membership plunged by a full third. The carpenters, machinists, rubber workers, laborers, and ironworkers unions all showed similar steep membership declines.[8] Dereg-ulation in the trucking, airline, and transport sectors in the late 1970s and early 1980s also hit union membership hard when it allowed nonunion companies to enter the market more easily. Within three years of the Motor Carrier Act of 1980, for instance, the number of nonunion trucking compa-nies tripled and the number of long-haul truckers with a union card plunged. Unions suddenly had far fewer resources for organizing. They found them-selves unable to both invest in growth and fulfill the larger social welfare role on which the nation's economy had come to depend.[9]

Within this context of recession and membership loss, President Reagan's decision to fire the striking members of the Professional Air Traffic Control-lers Organization in 1981 had a chilling impact. The air traffic controllers, most of whom were white "suburban-dwelling military veterans," had turned their public-sector, professional organization into an aggressive union in the 1970s. Their decision to launch a massive, illegal strike reflected the same bold union-mindedness that powered the private-sector organ-izing wave in the 1970s. When Reagan abruptly fired the 11,345 strikers, he signaled the federal government's decision to step aboard the union-busting bandwagon that had become so common throughout the private sector in the previous decade. Though the use of strikebreakers had long been legal, and was common among Southern employers like Newport News, the strike helped create a new national standard on striker replacement.[10]

Employers began to demand and win massive contract concessions in nearly every industry—heavy metals, autos, newspapers, oil, meat cutting, rubber, and airlines. Employers perfected the union-breaking strate-gies, first pioneered by firms like Seyfarth Shaw in the mid-1970s, of bargaining to impasse, provoking a strike, and then replacing the striking union membership. Seyfarth Shaw counseled employers, for instance, to cross-train supervisors to break strikes and even hold strike drills. Bus drivers at Greyhound, hotel workers in Las Vegas, and copper miners in Arizona all waged massive strikes in these years to try to hold on to the gains they had won over previous decades, but to no avail. Making liberal use of strikebreakers, management gained major concessions across the board. In 1984, the Supreme Court even upheld the right of employers to use bankruptcy procedures to abrogate union contracts, a tactic used suc-cessfully by Frank Lorenzo at Continental Airlines.[11]

The Reagan administration, meanwhile, appointed conservative ideo-logue Donald Dotson to head the NLRB in 1983, and the agency began to issue a series of decisions rolling back workers' organizing rights even further. It gave employers more room to threaten plant closings, strikes, and layoffs if workers formed unions, deeming such threats an accurate portrayal of the "economic realities" of unionization. It even gave employers more latitude to change location and then operate without a union. The NLRB also slowed down the entire apparatus governing labor-management relations by decreasing its own activity. The Dotson NLRB issued decisions at a rate less than half of that at which the NLRB had issued decisions in 1976 and 1980 under President Jimmy Carter, for instance.[12] The effect of all these employer and government strategies, according to one prominent university leader, was to "redefine the current limits of acceptable behavior" for employers.[13]

In the face of this level of turmoil, unions began pulling back from organizing efforts in 1981. That year, fewer than 400,000 workers voted in union elections, the lowest level in more than two decades. The real turning point, however, came in 1982 when the number of workers voting in union elections plummeted. The number of workers lined up to vote in elections declined in 1982 by a full half, to 244,000 a year, compared to the average of half a million workers a year throughout the 1970s.[14] A monthly analysis confirms the quick fall in 1982. It shows a slow decline throughout 1981, down from an average of about 38,000 voters a month in the years 1977 to 1980. Then there was a rapid fall off in January 1982 when a mere 15,000 workers were set to vote in elections. By 1983, only about 14,000 voted in elections each month, and the annual number was down to a mere 165,000.[15]

Unions felt the full impact from the deep membership losses rooted in the recession and deregulation. Their budgets had taken a huge hit, and new organizing was expensive and difficult in the face of employers' lawbreaking tactics. Unions pulled back from new organizing and concentrated on defending their bases. The UAW, USWA, and Teamsters, for instance, each ran about half as many elections in 1982 as they had in the 1977 to 1979 period. The UFCW and SEIU both decreased their participation in NLRB elections in 1982 to about 60 percent of the late-1970s level. Construction unions, like the carpenters and laborers unions, also sharply slowed their organizing efforts. Union elections in the Southeast alone fell nearly 40 percent in just one year, from 1981 to 1982.[16]

A vicious cycle began to spin. As unions pulled back from organizing, workers had fewer chances to form unions. Workers, meanwhile, became less likely to press for unions. They understood very well the risks they would take in organizing through the broken NLRB election system, and were increasingly apprehensive. "Fear was probably the #1 reason for our decline," wrote UAW organizing director Ben Perkins in explaining the UAW's paltry 1982 organizing level. Employers' increased use of unfair labor practices, like threats and harassment, had a direct impact on workers' success in organizing. As unions' bargaining power weakened in the midst of the bevy of strikes, working people also began to be less sure that unions could still deliver access to the most secure tier of the social welfare state, and so they were less willing to join. Working people's interest in joining unions dropped in the early 1980s, and while union workers still firmly believed that unions raised wages and improved working conditions, workers without a union became less likely to believe this than they once had.[17]

Unions thought that the change in activity was temporary and that they would be able to transition back to higher organizing levels once they got past the Reagan administration and the recession. "Traditionally, since World War II, economic recessions have been accompanied, initially, by a decline in NLRB election activity," AFL-CIO organizing director Alan Kistler assured the executive council in 1982 as he explained the sharp drop in elections.[18] However, it turned out that the early 1980s saw a fracturing of the old organizing pattern, not an episodic interlude. Unions never jumped back in at the same level of NLRB elections in the private sector. In fact, the number of workers eligible to vote in NLRB elections never again topped a quarter of a million; that was true even after 1995 when John Sweeney won the first openly contested AFL-CIO presidential election on a much-heralded organizing platform. By 2005, the number of voters had fallen below 150,000 a year, and in 2016, the number was down to under 74,000, a mere fraction of the half million or so who had lined up to vote each year in the 1970s.[19]

Is there anything labor could have done to stem the losses? It likely would have taken a wholesale change of direction while the movement still had vestiges of strength in the private sector. Labor leaders did begin to wrestle with the magnitude of the challenge they faced, but they missed a pivotal opportunity in the 1980s to restructure the doorway through which America's working people could enter unions. The AFL-CIO's executive council founded a high-level Committee on the Evolution of Work in August 1982 to study the shifting economy and the shrinking union membership. The group of twenty-seven of the nation's most powerful union officers sought to "establish the degree of change, analyze its impact and develop possible solutions." The committee issued three reports, in 1983, 1985, and 1994.[20] While the 1983 report was mostly limited to a description of structural changes in the economy, the 1985 report was more expansive and reflected a series of intensive meetings with a wide range of academics, pollsters, and analysts. In that report, entitled "The Changing Situation of Workers and Their Unions," the labor leaders agreed to fundamentally reconsider "our notions of what it is that workers can do through their unions." Because employers had so effectively manipulated labor law to narrow workers' entryway to unions, "tinkering is futile," AFL-CIO secretary-treasurer Thomas Donahue told the leaders in a closed-door meeting. "We must consider whether radical change is possible."[21]

The leaders began to study an entirely new model for representing workers outside the increasingly fraught collective bargaining paradigm: associational membership. Under this model, workers would not have to go through the difficult NLRB election process to join a union—they could just sign up. However, under associational membership, workers would not be covered by a collective bargaining agreement and the union movement would have to find other ways to leaven workers' social welfare, as 9to5 had done in Boston. As a first step, the AFL-CIO began to negotiate a series of consumer-focused incentives with which to entice workers to join unions, such as a credit card with the nation's lowest interest rate, free legal services, and discounted disability insurance.[22]

Unions' interest in growing their own individual memberships, however, trumped their willingness to pool resources to launch such a movement-wide initiative for the broader public. A USWA officer worried that "open membership" would leave unions "banging into one another," and an IUE officer posited that the extra benefits for nonmembers would "milk unions" of precious resources. Though some of the leaders, like the American Federation of Teachers' Albert Shanker, were open to a "wide-open associate membership," others worried whether they could institute such changes under their organization's constitutions or were wary of giving the broad public voting rights. Above all, they wanted to make sure that their organization received revenue from any associational membership program.[23]

By 1986, the AFL-CIO had adopted the path of least resistance and left the decision whether to form new associate membership programs up to each affiliate union. Some unions did dive into experiments with this form. The American Federation of Teachers and AFSCME, for example, both used the associational status to recruit public-sector workers in states where collective bargaining was prohibited, such as in Texas. On the whole, however, leaders did very little to broaden workers' access to unions beyond the traditional collective bargaining model. The AFL-CIO's consumer-based "Union Privilege" program turned out to mainly be a perk of traditional union membership. Some unions used the credit cards and discounts to incentivize membership among workers who benefited from a union on their job but who chose not to join. Even as late as 1989, the AFL-CIO pushed for a union-movement-wide associational membership, but a number of affiliate unions scuttled the attempt.[24]

The 1994 report by the Committee on the Evolution of Work was far less ambitious than the 1985 report in matters of new organizing. Like the 1983 report, it was a high-level look at the changing economy with an added focus on "new labor-management partnerships," but with no mention of the thorny question of alternative membership structures.[25] The AFL-CIO did finally establish a community-based, associational model of membership— Working America—but it did not do so until 2003. Karen Nussbaum, the former 9to5 leader, was its founder and director. By then, however, union density in the private sector had dropped by half compared to the level in 1983 when the Committee on the Evolution of Work issued its first report. Today, private-sector union density is down to 6.4 percent, a mere quarter of its 1973 level.[26]

With no new doorways into unions, workers in the 1980s and beyond remained dependent on the old New Deal structures and weak labor law if they wanted to improve their situation at work. Yet employers remained free to exploit this law, and they continued to narrow workers' ability to win the higher wages and employer-based social welfare contained in union contracts. The eclipse of NLRB elections reached even beyond the workers who wanted unions. When fewer workers could organize, employers lost their fear of union drives and so became even less likely to match unionized wages and benefits. The threat once posed by union organizing virtually vanished. The result was that employers increasingly shirked the social welfare role for which collective bargaining had been the big stick. By the 1980s, even unionized workers lost bargaining power and struggled to maintain wage and benefits levels. Thus, not only did workers have a harder time getting a union, but even if they managed to win one, they found that collective bargaining itself increasingly held less sway. In blocking the threat of new organizing, employers had effectively closed off workers' gateway to the most secure tier of the nation's social welfare system. This hastened the nation toward increased economic inequality and helped make life precarious for the transformed working class.

The drop in union membership levels since the 1970s is a major contributor to today's inequality, alongside globalization and technological change. One-third of the income inequality among men, and one-fifth among women, was due to the drop in union density between 1973 and 2007, according to Bruce Western and Jake Rosenfeld. Their research controls for education levels and also examines the union effect on nonunion wages—such as through the threat of union organizing. They found that the decline of organized labor among men contributed as much to men's wage gap as did pay stratification by education. Lower across-the-board wage and benefits standards, in turn, further weakened unions' bargaining power.[27]

Unions' shrinkage especially hurt people of color. Racial wage gaps had begun to narrow by 1980, but then widened again in the ensuing decades, in part because unions no longer were able to blunt the divide.[28] Unions continue to lift wages for people of color. African American workers with a union made 18 percent more in hourly earnings than those who were not members in 2015, even after controlling for their level of education and type of job. Unionized Hispanic workers made 22 percent more. Yet too few ever get the chance to benefit from this union difference. Though black workers remain the most likely of all demographic groups to be members of unions, their unionization rate is less than half of what it was in 1983.[29]

The drop in union membership levels also narrowed workers' access to employer-provided health and retirement plans. The late 1970s was the peak level of such plans, but when union membership fell and unions became less of an organizing threat, employers were free to sever the link between union and nonunion benefits. In 1979, nearly 70 percent of workers had employer-provided health care, compared to just over half in 2010. Union members, however, remain far more likely to be covered by employer-provided health insurance and pensions than are workers without a union contract.[30]

Unions' decline reaches beyond the economic sphere into the political because it means that fewer members of the working class are engaged in workplace-level, ongoing discussion about politics. Unions devote tremendous energy and resources to education about candidates' stances on economic issues, and so serve as a key counterbalance to divisive cultural issues among union members. They have been especially influential among white union members, who tend to vote more conservatively than do union members as a whole.[31] Strong unions can be a key source of working-class progressivism, including in the South. Jan Hooks, the Newport News shipwright, was cut from the same cloth as other Southern, white working-class women—those "Wal-Mart Moms"—who helped to bring in a God- and employer-based conservatism in the 1970s. Hooks, however, was active in a black-led union that emphasized member education and political action.

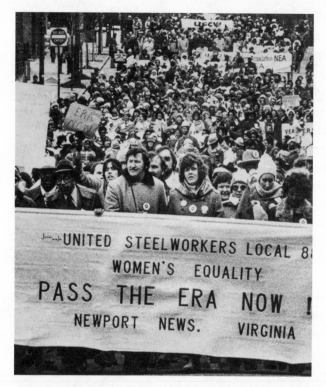

USWA Local 8888 members march for the Equal Rights Amendment in Richmond, Virginia (1980). AFL-CIO Photographic Prints Collection (RG96-001), Special Collections and University Archives, University of Maryland Libraries. AP Photo, used with permission.

Even though she had never voted before becoming active in the union, as a USWA member she helped push for progressive politics, such as by joining more than 7,000 participants in a labor-sponsored march for the Equal Rights Amendment in Virginia in 1980.[32]

Unions have long served as a load-bearing bulwark for the Democratic party. Members of union households have voted for the Democratic candidate in every presidential election for the last forty years, even in 1980 and 1984, supposedly the years of the "Reagan Democrats."[33] A majority of members of union households voted for Hillary Clinton over President Donald Trump in 2016, as did 56 percent of union members, though Clinton's union support was weaker than that of President Barack Obama.[34] Unions impact their members' votes. One study of the 1984 election compared voters according to their demographic profiles—teasing out statistics on white, working-class Northern males, for instance—and found that in 1984 someone who was a union member was far more likely to vote Democratic than someone similar to them who was not part of a union.[35] But a forty-year sustained attack on unions has hit its mark. Unions once made up a political powerhouse in the Midwest, in the very states that were key to

Trump's 2016 victory. Nearly one in four working people in Wisconsin, for instance, was a union member in the mid-1980s. By 2016, a mere 8 percent of Wisconsin workers had a union. In Michigan and Pennsylvania, union membership had dropped by half. As fewer people were able to enter unions, unions could turn out fewer people to the polls. The lower the membership, the less power they had to spread their political message, and no other Democratic-leaning organization filled this void.[36] Unions' erosion has helped tumble the Democrats' blue wall.

The years after 1985 marked a new historic phase in U.S. workers' union organizing efforts. Some of the more progressive unions increasingly put aside the New Deal tools of NLRB elections and began to explore new doorways through which workers could enter collective bargaining. They ran strategic campaigns that were more community based, like the groundbreaking Justice for Janitors campaign that kicked off in 1987. That effort used militant demonstrations, such as blocking bridges, and savvy public pressure to convince building owners to force their cleaning contractors to recognize the SEIU. Janitors could thus avoid having to go through the fire of an NLRB election.[37] Many unions focused on what they termed "comprehensive campaigns" or "corporate campaigns," which used multiple levers of power to persuade employers to recognize workers' collective bargaining rights, such as enlisting support from consumers, shareholders, and the general public.[38] The UFCW, for instance, claimed that by the mid-1980s, less than a sixth of its organizing wins came through the NLRB election process. More typical was its 1985 win at Magruder's supermarkets in Washington, where UFCW Local 400 threatened to picket stores, informing customers of the below-standard wages and benefits. Though this company agreed to come to the bargaining table, these tactics never worked with larger chains like Food Lion.[39] Unions began to use the successful shareholder-based tactics of the J. P. Stevens campaign more broadly in the service sector, filing shareholder proposals and holding annual meeting demonstrations to support the nursing home workers at the nationwide chain Beverly Homes, for instance.[40] Unions recruited and trained more young and college-educated organizing staff, pooling resources to form a new Organizing Institute in 1989. They also began to put less emphasis on single-shot elections and deepened long-term community ties, such as those established through Jobs with Justice, an organization founded in 1987 to build citywide community coalitions to support workers' rights. They began to be more savvy about leveraging governmental and community ties to establish new relationships with workers who had long been outside labor's ranks, such as among the seventy-four thousand public home health care workers in Los Angeles who formed a union with SEIU in 1999. Labor again attempted to reform labor law through the Employee Free Choice Act; this legislation would have increased employer penalties for labor law violations and allowed workers to choose a union by signing cards rather than through the fraught NLRB election process. Employers waged a fierce opposing battle, led by the national Chamber of Commerce. Supporters could not get enough votes to overcome an anticipated veto by President George W. Bush in 2007, or to build a filibuster-proof majority in the Senate in 2009, even with President Obama in the White House. The broken NLRB status quo remained in place.[41]

Most of these late twentieth-century campaigns and organizations, however, were still designed to bring workers into a traditional collective bargaining relationship. It has only been in the early twenty-first century that a broader array of workers' organizations has begun to experiment with alternative models of worker power outside the confines of traditional union contracts, models like those once rejected by the Committee on the Evolution of Work. Capitalism's latest transmutation demands it. Corporate structures in early twenty-first-century workplaces—in what one scholar titles the "fissured workplace"—are increasingly determined by the breakdown of the vertically integrated firm, which means workers often do not have clearly defined employers with whom to negotiate. In today's gig economy, employers have relinquished not only their social welfare role but often the employer-employee relationship itself. Workers find that they work for subcontractors, sometimes layers away from the parent corporation, or they discover they are legally independent contractors—even when they drive the same truck on the same route each day or sweep the same office floors. Labor law, meanwhile, has not kept up with the changing workforce, and millions of U.S. workers hold positions that exclude them from the Wagner Act's protections: they are part-time workers, low-level managers, international guest workers, temporary staff, or otherwise contingent. The result is that a new breed of worker organizations—"alt-labor" organizations—is struggling to shore up workers' economic security in new ways, such as through workers' centers, new occupational alliances, and public campaigns to raise wages.[42]

The future workers' rights movement will likely blend traditional labor unions and these new alt-labor forms, potentially on a global scale. As the twentieth-century version of industrial capitalism gives way to new forms, working people find themselves in need of a wholesale redefinition of collective bargaining. This institution may become less of a mediator between one employer and its employees, and more of a platform for "bargaining for the collective," serving as a mediator between centers of concentration of global capital (like e-commerce corporations or financial institutions) and entire swaths of working people who labor in similar occupations. As people no longer receive social welfare through employers, the role of the state may grow. Working people may be more likely to "bargain" with capital and the state by pooling power in political and community-based campaigns; they may no longer depend on specific employers for social welfare, but they will need to find new ways to force corporations to fund universal social welfare issues such as through a basic income, access to adequate and affordable health care, and reasonable family leave and child care.[43]

What it means to be a union member may thus change. Today, in order to be a union member, workers must be covered by a collective bargaining agreement; they either organize a union and win a contract, or they get a job that is already under contract. While this union membership form is likely to persist, future union members may join new occupational or geographically based working-class institutions that are not rooted in worksite contracts. These union members will strike, protest, campaign, and leverage new laws to improve their own working lives, and to ensure broader distribution of the nation's wealth.[44]

My hope is that as workers begin to explore new ways to build power, this book will complicate and enrich the conversation about how they lost that power in the first place. Future researchers will find a rich and unexplored trove of 1970s NLRB elections beyond what I was able to cover in these pages, including those among women, in the service sector, and in all geographic regions. Historians, so far, have largely ignored these workers' elections, perhaps believing they simply were not there. When we understand that America's newly diversified working class was actively organizing and held enormous possibility, the onus is then on historians to explain more fully why working people ended up in such a weak position. How did sustained class conflict impact the new political, legal, and economic structures that govern a transforming global capitalism? To what extent was neoliberalism an elite vessel to contain such conflict? What new tools do workers need in order to impact today's evolving system? By the 1980s and early 1990s, workers around the world faced a renewed attack, mirroring what happened to U.S. workers in the 1970s.[45] Does fresh knowledge of the 1970s U.S. workers' private-sector organizing offer new context for their global story? If historians are going to properly unpack neoliberalism and its legal and economic scaffolding, we must give working people and their organizations their honest due. Otherwise, we risk missing the full range of drivers behind workers' catastrophic economic insecurity.

As working people today try new strategies to rein in twenty-first-century corporations' outsized influence, they should carry with them full knowledge of what happened when their predecessors faced capitalism's latest shift. America's working men and women did not acquiesce. Their collective struggle did not fade away. Instead, a newly diversified workforce in the 1970s demanded full access to collective bargaining and tried to organize private-sector unions, making a massive push for broadly shared economic prosperity. Finally, it seemed, women and people of color would have full access to the New Deal's economic promise. These working women and men promised to reinvigorate the flagging union movement, bringing reinforcements just as labor faced radical structural changes at the workplace. Working people waged their fight, however, with what were revealed to be increasingly weak weapons—government-sanctioned NLRB union elections. The fact that employers were able to effectively shut down union organizing and close the door to workers' access to unions reverberates far beyond the labor movement. Employers have essentially blocked private-sector workers' entry into what functioned in the mid-twentieth century as the most secure tier of the nation's social welfare system. The state has not strengthened workers' access to unions, tapped another entity to pull citizens' social welfare provisions from employers, or robustly increased state-provided social welfare. Working people today thus must find a way to build power within an economy that is far more unequal and precarious than that once envisioned by the millions of workers who once went knocking on labor's door.

Acknowledgments

When I was a union organizer and labor communicator, every campaign was a collaborative effort. Even when I was the only organizer in a small Southern town, I knew that my work was part of a larger group's effort. Writing a book may be more of a solo endeavor, but I could never have done it alone. Woven into these pages are the ideas, encouragement, and hard work of many individuals. I am delighted to be able to give them my thanks.

I am grateful to have received generous support from numerous institutions. The University of Maryland Graduate School helped fund my work with both a Flagship Fellowship and the Dr. Mabel S. Spencer Award. The University of Maryland History Department provided dissertation, summer research, and travel support. Grants from the Walter P. Reuther Library, Schlesinger Library, Georgia State University Southern Labor Archives, and Hagley Museum and Library supported my research. A postdoctoral fellowship with Penn State University's Center for Global Rights offered the time and space to make revisions. I am thankful to have found a supportive intellectual home with Georgetown University's Kalmanovitz Initiative for Labor and the Working Poor; this is where I have brought the book through its final stages.

Historians benefit from entire teams of people who help us do our work. Numerous archivists were key, including Jen Eidson and Lynda Deloach, who were enormously helpful in accessing the George Meany Memorial Archives, as was Traci Drummond at the Southern Labor Archives. It has been an absolute privilege to work with my editor, Brandon Proia, and the entire University of North Carolina Press staff. Brandon's discerning edits polished this book and made it shine, and I've been buoyed by his steadfast belief in this project.

This book would not exist without the commitment and generosity of the working people, union members, and union staffers who took the time to dig out old union papers and talk with me about their experiences. Gary Hubbard got me going on the right track for the Newport News story. Karen Nussbaum and Ellen Cassedy offered wisdom that not only is fodder for the 9to5 chapter but also guides my ongoing work. I am especially grateful to the members, staff, and retirees of USWA Local 8888, UFCW Local 400, ACTWU, and the AFL-CIO.

A number of friends and colleagues offered priceless advice, guidance, and encouragement. Julie Greene has been with me every step of the way, always posing just the right questions to allow me to clarify and anchor my arguments. I have been enormously fortunate to have her as a mentor and friend. Robyn Muncy helped me work through my analysis of the relationship of union organizing to social welfare and sharpened the entire manuscript at several stages. Joe McCartin has been very generous, offering encouragement and sage advice throughout this entire process. His suggestions, along with those of Nancy MacLean and Nelson Lichtenstein, significantly improved the final product. Ira Berlin, Robert Bland, David Freund, Paul Gibson, Debbie Goldman, Sharon Harley, Jon Shelton, and David Sicilia all shaped my work while I was at the University of Maryland. I'd like to give a special thanks to Karen Ackerman, Mark Anner, Ron Blackwell, Jeremy Brecher, Heather and Paul Booth, Robin Broad, Kate Bronfenbrenner, John Cavanagh, Mike Cavanaugh, David Cecelski, Cathy Feingold, Fred Feinstein, Chris Garlock, Will Jones, Alex Keyssar, Virginia and Walter Knight, Robert Korstad, Thea Lee, Leslie Meyers-Joseph, Tim Minchin, Larry Mishel, Denise Mitchell, Chris Owens, Roz Pelles, Marilyn Sneiderman, Jacob Remes, David Richardson, Elin Slavik, and Naomi Williams. Although Judith Stein left us before this book's publication, readers will notice her influence throughout it. Larry Goodwyn always encouraged my organizing and scholarship, and I hope he would have taken pride in their synthesis here.

Lesley McCollough always believed that I could do this book thing, even when I was not so sure. I'm lucky to have had Kathy McDonald as my friend and coconspirator. Jay Driskell gets a huge thanks for digging in and giving the entire manuscript a solid edit. I am grateful to Jim McNeill who polished this book several times; he achieved martyr status with the final copy edit. Julie Farb shares my obsession with organizing and was a ready audience for new discoveries. Tim Tyson was always willing to kick around ideas and his steady affirmation and advice have been invaluable. Jennifer Hill, Liz O'Connor, and I have been a triad who shared similar life transformations, and they have helped anchor me. Justin Uehlein and I went through graduate school at the same time, and I've enjoyed the blossoming of our intellectual relationship. Taylor Windham buoyed me with pound cake and other goodies from his home cooking. This book would never have gotten written if Debbie Chang, Ed Feigen, Jill Jackson, Suzanne and Marion Mollegen McFadden, Reina Perdomo, and Darcy Sawatzki had not been generous friends, always willing to play host to my child. Rachel Mariano and Monica Ellingson are treasured friends who have stood with me ever since I first aspired to write.

My husband, Joe Uehlein, has been my most ardent supporter. If there are any worthy stories among these pages, his love and encouragement allowed them to be told. Thanks to my daughter, Anna Grace Uehlein, whose joy and playfulness sustain me. Judy Windham, my mother, has been nothing but encouraging at every stage in this project and in life, and I am a better person for it.

Appendix

NLRB Elections and Voters by Year

Table A.1 Number of NLRB Elections (RC), Number of Voters, and Percentage of
Private Production Workers Who Were NLRB Voters, 1949–1999

Year	Elections	Voters	Priv. prod. workers (in thousands)	% of priv. prod. workers who were NLRB voters
1949	5,282	541,283	33,159	1.63
1950	5,251	604,006	34,349	1.76
1951	6,271	651,651	36,225	1.80
1952	6,612	746,817	36,643	2.04
1953	5,886	✗ 726,620	37,694	1.93
1954	4,445	494,620	36,276	1.36
1955	4,003	471,709	37,500	1.26
1956	4,694	448,115	38,495	1.16
1957	4,499	441,542	38,384	1.15
1958	4,099	333,935	36,608	0.91
1959	5,022	395,635	38,080	1.04
1960	6,021	461,985	38,516	1.20
1961	6,042	436,181	37,989	1.15
1962	6,916	514,394	38,979	1.32
1963	6,512	468,116	39,553	1.18
1964	6,940	517,661	40,560	1.28
1965	7,176	512,159	42,278	1.21
1966	7,637	551,408	44,249	1.25
1967	7,496	592,309	45,137	1.31
1968	7,241	517,372	46,473	1.11
1969	7,319	552,037	48,208	1.15
1970	7,426	575,464	48,156	1.19
1971	7,543	546,632	48,148	1.14
1972	8,066	556,100	49,939	1.11
1973	8,526	506,387	52,201	0.97
1974	7,994	506,047	52,809	0.96
1975	7,729	533,576	50,991	1.05
1976	7,736	435,171	52,897	0.82
1977	8,308	519,102	55,179	0.94

Year	Elections	Voters	Priv. prod. workers (in thousands)	% of priv. prod. workers who were NLRB voters
1978	7,168	424,481	58,156	0.73
1979	7,026	528,798	60,367	0.88
1980	7,021	471,651	60,331	0.78
1981	6,439	395,573	60,923	0.65
1982	4,031	244,292	59,468	0.41
1983	3,241	164,925	60,028	0.27
1984	3,336	205,717	63,339	0.32
1985	3,545	211,161	65,475	0.32
1986	3,495	217,110	66,866	0.32
1987	3,149	198,865	68,771	0.29
1988	3,377	208,394	71,099	0.29
1989	3,670	243,045	73,017	0.33
1990	3,536	229,015	73,774	0.31
1991	3,089	192,257	72,631	0.26
1992	2,927	183,865	72,918	0.25
1993	2,991	203,674	74,761	0.27
1994	3,020	186,339	77,607	0.24
1995	2,860	191,825	80,125	0.24
1996	2,738	191,929	82,092	0.23
1997	3,029	215,562	84,541	0.25
1998	3,289	227,390	86,805	0.26
1999	3,120	221,210	88,997	0.25

Sources: Number of private production workforce (not seasonally adjusted) is from BLS, "Employment, Hours and Earnings from the Current Employment Statistics (National, SIC basis), 1949–1999," accessed September 9, 2016, http://www.bls.gov/data/archived.htm. Number of elections and eligible voters in RC elections is from NLRB Annual Reports, 1949–1999. See table 13 (1949–1950), table 10 (1951), table 9 (1952), and table 11 (1953–1999).

A Note on Data

This book uses as its key quantitative variable the number of eligible voters in NLRB elections in RC representation cases. Following the passage of the Taft-Hartley Act in 1947, the NLRB designated three types of representation cases for elections determining employees' union status: elections in RC cases are those triggered by the employees at a workplace who are trying to form a union; elections in RM cases are those triggered by management, and; elections in RD cases are those in which employees attempt to decertify their existing union. Before the Taft-Hartley Act, there were only "R" representation cases—there were no RC, RM, or RD categories. The year 1949 is the first for which full data is available for elections in RC cases.[1] A

Percentage of private production workers who were NLRB
eligible voters (RC) (1949–1999)

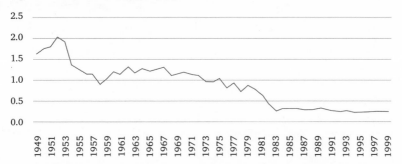

Source: Number of private production workforce (not seasonally adjusted) is from BLS,
"Employment, Hours and Earnings from the Current Employment Statistics (National,
SIC), 1949–1999," accessed September 9, 2016, http://www.bls.gov/data/archived.htm.
Number of eligible voters in NLRB RC election is from NLRB Annual Reports, 1949–1999.

study of the number of eligible voters in RC elections allows us to concentrate on
the cases in which employees themselves triggered a union election. The number
of "eligible voters" reflects the total number of workers in the voting units.

Figure I.1 reveals that the number of eligible voters in NLRB RC elections was
fairly steady throughout the 1950s, 1960s, and 1970s, though there were some ups
and downs. The numbers dropped sharply in 1982 and 1983, and never rebounded.
Figure A.1 shows the yearly percentage of the entire private production workforce
who were NLRB voters. "Production" workforce means the workforce that was nonsupervisory in all industries, including manufacturing, retail, service, and so on.
Figure A.1 reveals that while there was a slow decline in this ratio, it is clear that
the early 1980s is the period of sharp decline.[2]

Some scholars choose to measure workers' interest in unions through union density numbers or the percentage of NLRB elections won by unions, but both numbers are problematic.[3] Union density figures include only the people who already
have unions. Density numbers mask union organizing because they include not only
new members who organized a union but also the drop in union membership due
to plant closures and job loss. The union win rate (or the number of elections won
by unions) is also problematic. It measures worker interest at the end of the employer pressure campaign, after many employers threatened and fired workers. A
study of the number of workers eligible to vote in RC union elections allows a measure of worker organizing levels prior to the employer pressure campaign.

Notes

Abbreviations Used in the Notes

ACTWU — Amalgamated Clothing and Textile Workers Union (ACTWU) Papers, Kheel Center for Labor-Management Documentation and Archives, Catherwood Library, Cornell University, Ithaca, N.Y.

AFL-CIO ODR — AFL-CIO Organizing Department Records (1955–1975), RG28-002, George Meany Memorial AFL-CIO Archive, Special Collections and University Archives, University of Maryland, College Park, Md.

AKP — Alan Kistler Papers, 1954–2000, RG95-009, George Meany Memorial AFL-CIO Archive, Special Collections and University Archives, University of Maryland, College Park, Md.

BLS — U.S. Department of Labor, Bureau of Labor Statistics

Cannon — Cannon Mills Records, David M. Rubenstein Rare Book and Manuscript Library, Duke University, Durham, N.C.

EKS — Papers of Earle K. Shawe, University of Virginia School of Law Special Collections, Arthur J. Morris Law Library, Charlottesville, Va.

GSU — Southern Labor Archives, Special Collections and Archives, Georgia State University Library, Atlanta, Ga.

HHP — Herbert Hill Papers, 1869–2004, Library of Congress, Manuscript Division, Washington, D.C.

JCL — Jimmy Carter Presidential Library and Museum, Atlanta, Ga.

KCLMD — Kheel Center for Labor-Management Documentation & Archives, Catherwood Library, Cornell University, Ithaca, N.Y.

LAOCOC — Los Angeles, Orange Counties Organizing Committee

NAM — National Association of Manufacturers Records, Hagley Museum and Library, Wilmington, Del.

9to5 — 9 to 5, National Association of Working Women (U.S.) Records, Schlesinger Library on the History of Women in America, Radcliffe Institute for Advanced Study, Harvard University, Cambridge, Mass.

NLRB — Records of the National Labor Relations Board (Record Group 25), National Archives, College Park, Md.

PSU — Historical Collections and Labor Archives, Special Collections Library, Pennsylvania State University, State College, Pa.

SEIU 925 — Service Employees International Union (SEIU) District 925 Records, Walter P. Reuther Library, Archives of Labor and Urban Affairs, Wayne State University, Detroit, Mich.

TWUA	Textile Workers Union of America Papers, State Historical Society of Wisconsin, Madison, Wis.
UMD	George Meany Memorial AFL-CIO Archive, Special Collections and University Archives, University of Maryland, College Park, Md.
USDOL	U.S. Department of Labor
USWA Legal	United Steelworkers of America Legal Files, USWA Headquarters, Pittsburgh, Pa.
WPR	Walter P. Reuther Library, Archives of Labor and Urban Affairs, Wayne State University, Detroit, Mich.

Introduction

1. Hooks interview; Braden, "Shoulder to Shoulder"; Windham, "Signing Up in the Shipyard."

2. Hooks interview.

3. Ibid. On the relative size of the Newport News shipyard election, see AFL-CIO, "List of Large NLRB Elections, 1961 to 2010," which lists the Newport News election as the largest held in Southern workplaces since 1961. For the 1930s through the 1950s, see Marshall, *Labor in the South*, 182–245. There was an NLRB election held among Southern workers in the Bell System in 1949 with more than thirty thousand workers in nine states, but these workers were not all at one workplace. See CIO, *1949 Proceedings*, 81. See also *Steel Labor*, March 1978, 7.

4. Hooks interview.

5. Other scholarship on private-sector organizing in the 1970s includes Cobble, "'Spontaneous Loss of Enthusiasm'"; Nadasen, *Household Workers Unite*; Sacks, *Caring by the Hour*; Boris and Klein, *Caring for America*; Leon Fink and Brian Greenberg, *Upheaval in the Quiet Zone*; Minchin, *"Don't Sleep with Stevens!"*; Hoerr, *We Can't Eat Prestige*; and Joey Fink, "In Good Faith." For more on the impact of the 1964 Civil Rights Act, see MacLean, *Freedom Is Not Enough*; Cobble, *The Other Women's Movement*; Wright, *Sharing the Prize*; and Minchin, *Hiring the Black Worker*.

6. Cowie, *Stayin' Alive*. The phrase "last days of the working class" comes from the book's subtitle.

7. Class is not just a function of the workplace, but is determined by all levels of people's experiences, such as those relating to family, community, and the state. See Arnesen, Greene and Laurie, "Introduction," in Arnesen, Greene, and Laurie, *Labor Histories*, 1–15, and Katznelson, "Working-Class Formation: Constructing Cases and Comparisons." While studying workers who are struggling with the breakdown of the industrial system in the late twentieth century, I have found scholars' conceptions of class in the preindustrial era particularly helpful. For example, see Middleton and Smith, "Introduction," in Middleton and Smith, *Class Matters*, 11, which describes how recent scholarship has defined class as "neither simply a reflection of the productive relations of the objective world nor a subjec-

tively constructed identity fashioned from available linguistic and cultural resources. Instead, it comprises a constitutive element of social relationships emerging from inequalities in material conditions and social and cultural capital that serves as a primary way of signifying relationships of power." I use the term "working class" in this book to denote those people who share a state of relative material inequality as well as a lack of social power within the U.S. political economy.

8. Cowie, *Stayin' Alive*; Troy, "Twilight for Organized Labor"; Mike Davis, *Prisoners of the American Dream*; Goldfield, *Decline of Organized Labor*; Borstelmann, *The 1970s*; Schulman and Zelizer, *Rightward Bound*; Frum, *How We Got Here*.

9. See appendix. NLRB Annual Reports, table 13 (1949–1950), table 10 (1951), table 9 (1952), and table 11 (1953–1999). The increase in public-sector union membership is derived from table 1f, Union Membership, Coverage, Density, and Employment among Public Sector Workers, 1973–2007, in Hirsch and Macpherson, *Union Membership and Earnings*, 16.

10. For data on unfair labor practices, see NLRB Annual Reports, 1970–1980, table 2. These figures reflect the total number of 8(a) charges and 8(a)3 charges. The data on union win rate were found in Goldfield, *Decline of Organized Labor*, 90–91.

11. See appendix. NLRB Annual Reports, table 13 (1949–1950), table 10 (1951), table 9 (1952), and table 11 (1953–1999). For the number of private production workers (not seasonally adjusted), see U.S. Department of Labor, BLS, "Employment, Hours and Earnings from the Current Employment Statistics (National, SIC basis), 1949–1999," accessed September 13, 2016, http://www.bls.gov/data/archived.htm. Note that "production" workforce denotes the nonsupervisory workforce in all private-sector industries, including manufacturing, retail, service, and so on. NLRB, Election Report, FY 2016.

12. NLRB, Monthly Reports, 1970–1979, Election Reports: Cases Closed. The Pinkerton election was among 330 guards in Detroit in March 1977. Wright, *Sharing the Prize*.

13. Kalleberg, *Good Jobs, Bad Jobs*, 1–18; Standing, *Precariat*, 30–39; Mishel et al., *State of Working America*; Judith Stein, *Pivotal Decade*, xi–xiii; Schor, *Overworked American*, 1–15; Noah, *Great Divergence*, 23–27; Piketty, *Capital in the Twenty-First Century*, 24–25.

14. I am using the term "the long 1970s" to refer to the years from 1968 through 1981. Schulman, in *The Seventies*, also begins in 1968. Winslow, in "Overview: The Rebellion from Below, 1965–1981," uses the term "the long 1970s" to refer to the "mid-1960s" through 1981. Others begin in 1973, such as Borstelmann, *The 1970s*, 7, and Berkowitz, *Something Happened*.

15. Judith Stein, *Pivotal Decade*, xi–xii, 1–8; Stone et al., "Historical Trends in Income Inequality"; Root, *Fringe Benefits*, 185–96; Hirsch and Macpherson, *Union Membership and Earnings*, 11; Robert Brenner, *Economics of Global Turbulence*, 101; David Gordon, "Chickens Home to Roost"; McCartin, "Turnabout Years," 214.

16. Judith Stein, *Pivotal Decade*; Harris and Sammartino, "Distribution of Household Income"; Mishel, "Productivity and Median Compensation Growth"; Bivens

and Mishel, "Understanding the Historic Divergence"; Jacobson and Occhino, "Decline in Labor's Share of Income"; Mishel et al., *State of Working America*.

17. Hobsbawm, *Age of Extremes*, 277–80; Ferguson, *Shock of the Global*, 8–11; Judt, *Postwar*; Harvey, *Brief History of Neoliberalism*, 14–25; Judith Stein, *Pivotal Decade*; Standing, *Precariat*, 41–45; Rosenfeld, *What Unions No Longer Do*; Richard B. Freeman et al., "Declining Unionism"; Hirsch and Macpherson, "Union Membership and Coverage Database"; U.S. Department of Labor, BLS, "Union Members—2016," Economic News Release, January 26, 2017. The 1900 union membership figure is calculated from United States Bureau of the Census, *Statistical History*, 137, 178. Unions' impact on economic inequality is from Western and Rosenfeld, "Unions, Norms," 513; Rosenfeld, Denise, and Laird, "Union Decline Lowers Wages."

18. Meany quoted in "U.S. Needs '30,000 New Jobs a Week Just to Break Even,' " *U.S. News and World Report*, February 21, 1972, 27. Scholars who use this quote include Richard B. Freeman, *America Works*, 77; Fantasia and Voss, *Hard Work*, 125; and Lopez, *Reorganizing the Rust Belt*, 3. There were 8,526 union elections held in 1973. See appendix. For years prior to 1947, see Goldfield, *Decline of Organized Labor*, 90–91.

19. Lichtenstein, in his new introduction to *Labor's War at Home*, writes that the New Left generation saw trade unions as "positively anathema to many of us. The AFL-CIO remained a firm backer of the war in Vietnam; moreover, even the more progressive unions . . . appeared so strapped by bureaucracy, law, contracts and political allegiances that they hardly seemed an appropriate vehicle to advance the class struggle" (vii).

20. Moody, *Injury to All*; Mike Davis, *Prisoners of the American Dream*; Goldfield, *Decline of Organized Labor*. Geoghegan, *Which Side Are You On?*, also overlooks the magnitude of workers' organizing in the 1970s.

21. Textbook quote is from Nicholson, *Labor's Story in the United States*, 281. Cowie, *Stayin' Alive*, 12; Lichtenstein, *State of the Union*, 191–211, esp. 192. See Lichtenstein's new preface to *State of the Union* for a discussion of how historians have contested and expanded on the labor and civil rights dichotomy.

22. Cowie, *Stayin' Alive*; Sandbrook, *Mad as Hell*, 47–64; Edsall and Edsall, *Chain Reaction*; McGirr, *Suburban Warriors*; Lassiter, *Silent Majority*. For more on the construction workers attacking protesters, see Joshua Benjamin Freeman, *Working-Class New York*, 237–40. On busing, see Formisano, *Boston against Busing*, and Lukas, *Common Ground*.

23. On "silent majority," see Perlstein, *Nixonland*, 277–78; Brenner, Brenner, and Winslow, *Rebel Rank and File*; Nadasen, *Welfare Warriors*; Heather Ann Thompson, *Speaking Out*; McCartin, " 'Wagner Act for Public Employees' "; McCartin, " 'Fire the Hell Out of Them' "; U.S. Department of Commerce, United States Bureau of the Census, *Statistical Abstract of the United States: 2003*, "Nonfarm Establishments— Employees, Hours and Earnings by Industry: 1919 to 2002."

24. MacLean, *Freedom Is Not Enough*; Deslippe, *Rights, Not Roses*; Korstad, *Civil Rights Unionism*; Cobble, *The Other Women's Movement*; Honey, *Southern Labor*

and *Black Civil Rights*; Cobble, "'Spontaneous Loss of Enthusiasm'"; Na[ ]
Household Workers Unite; Barry, *Femininity in Flight*; Leon Fink and Brian [ ]
berg, *Upheaval in the Quiet Zone*.

25. See the introduction to Lichtenstein and Shermer, *The Right and Labor in America*, for a discussion of the limits and parameters of the midcentury labor accord. On the South and antiunionism, see Friedman, "Capital Flight, 'States' Rights.'" While Fones-Wolf's *Selling Free Enterprise* and Phillips-Fein's *Invisible* X
Hands remind us that business antiunionism was hardly new, a number of scholars argue that antiunionism held a particular sway in the 1970s: Hacker and Pierson, *Winner-Take-All-Politics*; Waterhouse, *Lobbying America*; Lee, "Whose Rights?"

26. Klein, *For All These Rights*; Hacker, *Divided Welfare State*; Gottschalk, *Shadow Welfare State*.

27. Richard B. Freeman and James L. Medoff, *What Do Unions Do?*, 230–39; Richard B. Freeman, *America Works*, 80–82; Fantasia and Voss, *Hard Work*, 75–76; Harrison and Bluestone, *Great U-Turn*; Hatton; *Temp Economy*; Weil, *Fissured Workplace*; Standing, *Precariat*; Logan, "'Union Free' Movement"; Robert Michael Smith, *From Blackjacks to Briefcases*.

28. Frymer, *Black and Blue*; Deslippe, *Rights, Not Roses*.

29. Western, *Between Class and Market*, 18–24; Jonathan C. Brown, *Workers' Control in Latin America*, 8–9; Martin, "Beginning of Labor's End?"; Salvati, "May 1968." For examples of scholars who argue that U.S. workers were more quiescent, see Goldfield, *Decline of Organized Labor*, 11–15; Lipset and Katchanovski, "Future of Private Sector Unions," 19–20; Mike Davis, *Prisoners of the American Dream*.

30. Carpenter quoted in Braden, "Shoulder to Shoulder," 93. On the number of workers voting in union elections, see table in appendix.

31. Goldfield, *Decline of Organized Labor*, 10; Hirsch and Macpherson, *Union Membership and Earnings*, 11. Note that Troy and Sheflin in *U.S. Union Sourcebook*, table 3.41, report a slightly higher union membership figure in 1975.

32. Hirsch and Macpherson, *Union Membership and Earnings*, 21–25. This union wage premium reflects mean hourly earnings and controls for years of schooling, potential years of experience, marital status, race and ethnicity, gender, part-time status, large metropolitan area, public sector, region, industry, and occupation. For more information, see note in Hirsch and Macpherson, *Union Membership and Earnings*, 6. Rosenfeld, *What Unions No Longer Do*; U.S. Department of Labor, BLS, *National Compensation Survey*.

33. Stein, *Running Steel, Running America*. On economic citizenship, see Kessler-Harris, *In Pursuit of Equity*, 5.

Chapter One

1. Cash interview; Form 5500, Annual Return/Report of Employee Benefit Plan, Woodward & Lothrop, August 30, 1978, and July 31, 1978, and Proxy Statement, Woodward & Lothrop, Inc., May 21, 1979, all in corporate files, W-V, c07/c/19, box

19, FAST Records, UMD; Kraft Opinion Research Center for Retail Clerks, Local 400, "A Survey of Opinion toward Unions among Woodward & Lothrop Employees in the Washington Metropolitan Area," March 1979, UFCW Headquarters Records; "It Costs $17,000 to Live Halfway Decently Today," *Retail Clerks Advocate*, June/July 1978.

2. Cash interview.

3. Ibid.; Collective Bargaining Agreement, Woodward & Lothrop, Inc. and Retail Store Employees Union, Local 400, November 18, 1979, to February 1, 1983, USDOL Historical Collective Bargaining Agreements Collection, KCLMD; *UFCW Action*, no. 1 (1980): 15.

4. Esping-Andersen, *Three Worlds of Welfare Capitalism*, 24, 36; Esping-Andersen, *Social Foundations of Postindustrial Economies*, 34–36; Hacker, *Divided Welfare State*, xi–xii, 5–27; Muncy, "Coal-Fired Reforms," 73; Linda Gordon, *Pitied but Not Entitled*, 1–13; Western, *Between Class and Market*, 29–49; Geoghegan, *Born on the Wrong Continent?*, 119–33; Richard B. Freeman, *America Works*. For "public-private welfare state," see Klein, *For All These Rights*.

5. Rosenfeld, *What Unions No Longer Do*, 1–9 (quote on 2); Western and Rosenfeld, "Unions, Norms"; Richard B. Freeman and James L. Medoff, *What Do Unions Do?*, 82–85. Unions have a more modest effect on wages and social welfare in other countries, such as those in Scandinavia, in part because unions are directly involved in setting state macroeconomic policies and so help lift all wages. See Richard B. Freeman, "What Do Unions Do?"

6. A number of scholars note collective bargaining's role within the social welfare state, but they tend to focus on unions that are already established. Here, I add a focus on union organizing as a gateway into collective bargaining, the most secure tier of U.S. social welfare. Klein, *For All These Rights*; Hacker, *Divided Welfare State*; Gottschalk, *Shadow Welfare State*; Stevens, "Blurring the Boundaries"; Michael K. Brown, *Race, Money*; Berkowitz and McQuaid, *Creating the Welfare State*; Linda Gordon, *Pitied but Not Entitled*.

7. There was state support for unionizing during World War I through the War Labor Board, but the federal government ceded this power in peacetime. See McCartin, *Labor's Great War*. Railroad workers secured the right to vote for collective bargaining in the Railway Labor Act of 1926, a law that still governs transportation workers such as those in airlines. The NLRA's immediate predecessor was the 1933 National Industrial Recovery Act, which brought together employers and unions on an industry-wide basis and essentially relied on employer voluntarism for much-needed wage hikes during the Great Depression. Employers widely broke their own agreements. Dubofsky, *State and Labor in Modern America*; National Labor Relations Act (Wagner Act), Pub. L. No. 74-198, 49 Stat. 449–50 (1935); Gross, *Making*. On the Wagner Act's limits, see Katznelson, *When Affirmative Action Was White*, and Katznelson, *Fear Itself*.

8. Brody, *Labor Embattled*, 105; Becker, "Democracy in the Workplace," 507–11; Gross, *Reshaping*, 106; Logan, "Representatives of Their Own Choosing"; quote

from "Report of the NLRB to the Senate Committee on Education and Labor under HR 9195," August 1940, 20, as quoted in Gross, *Reshaping*, 198.

9. Quote from "The Election," *Labor Trend*, July 9, 1946, as cited in Logan, "Representatives of Their Own Choosing," 556. The cases were *Virginia Electric & Power* and *American Tube Bending Co.* Goldfield, *Decline of Organized Labor*, 90–91; Griffith, *Crisis of American Labor*, 46–61; Lichtenstein, *Labor's War at Home*; Phillips-Fein, *Invisible Hands*, 20–25; Gross, *Reshaping*, 253.

10. Brody, *Labor Embattled*, 104–8; Becker, "Democracy in the Workplace," 545–46; Gross, *Broken Promise*, 1–4; Tomlins, *The State and the Unions*, 282–316.

11. Gottschalk, *Shadow Welfare State*, 42–44; Lichtenstein, *Most Dangerous Man in Detroit*, 282–83; Michael K. Brown, "Bargaining for Social Rights"; Roof, *American Labor*, 68–71.

12. Colin Gordon, *Dead on Arrival*, 57–59; Gottschalk, *Shadow Welfare State*, 41–48; Muncy, *Relentless Reformer*, 215–16; Michael K. Brown, "Bargaining for Social Rights," 647; Hacker, *Divided Welfare State*, 120–30.

13. Klein, *For All These Rights*, 116–61; Gottschalk, *Shadow Welfare State*, 48; Colin Gordon, *Dead on Arrival*, 66–67.

14. Michael K. Brown, "Bargaining for Social Rights," 669; Stevens, "Blurring the Boundaries," 140–41.

15. Michael K. Brown, "Bargaining for Social Rights," 653; Root, *Fringe Benefits*, 192; Hacker, *Divided Welfare State*, 132; Gottschalk, *Shadow Welfare State*, 46–47. Hirsch and MacPherson, *Union Membership and Earnings*, 21. On industrial jurisprudence, see Brody, "Workplace Contractualism in Comparative Perspective," 199–200.

16. "Policies for Unorganized Employees," *Personnel Policies Forum Survey*, no. 125 (1979): 13, as discussed in Richard B. Freeman and James L. Medoff, *What Do Unions Do?*, 150–53; Foulkes, *Personnel Policies*; Rosenfeld, *What Unions No Longer Do*, 74.

17. Jackson, *When Labor Trouble Strikes*, 36. On 1970 study, see E. R. Curtain, *White Collar Unionization*, 67, cited in Richard B. Freeman and James L. Medoff, *What Do Unions Do?*, 154–56; GE, "Final Captive Audience Speech," January 1978, folder 19, box 8, AKP.

18. George Perkel to Sol Stetin, January 6, 1978, Scott Hoyman to All Southern Textile Division Local Unions, February 10, 1978, and "Good Things Don't Just Happen," in 1978 Southern Wage Drive folder, box 60, 5619/007, ACTWU; Marion A. Ellis, "Cannon Mills, Union Prepare for Showdown in Kannapolis," *Charlotte Observer*, September 1, 1974, 1A; Jorgensen interview.

19. Linda Gordon, *Pitied but Not Entitled*, esp. 293–99; Kessler-Harris, *In Pursuit of Equity*, 88–106; Michael K. Brown, *Race, Money*, 63–96; Katznelson, *When Affirmative Action Was White*; Katznelson, *Fear Itself*; Poole, *Segregated Origins of Social Security*; Lichtenstein, *State of the Union*, 111.

20. Korstad and Lichtenstein, "Opportunities Found and Lost," 786. On unions excluding black workers, see Nelson, *Divided We Stand*; Griffith, *Crisis of American Labor*; Draper, *Conflict of Interests*; and Frymer, *Black and Blue*, 27–38, 64.

21. For scholarship focusing on the impact of Title VII of the 1964 Civil Rights Act, see MacLean, *Freedom Is Not Enough*; Cobble, *The Other Women's Movement*; Minchin, *Hiring the Black Worker*; Wright, *Sharing the Prize*; and Deslippe, *Rights, Not Roses*. On Hart-Celler's impact, see Ngai, *Impossible Subjects*. On Wagner's persistent limitations, see Nadasen, *Household Workers Unite*, 117–18; Boris and Klein, *Caring for America*; and Bardacke, *Trampling Out the Vintage*. For a good analysis of the increase of women in the workforce, see Borstelmann, *The 1970s*, 73–96. On black women and men in unions, see Rosenfeld, *What Unions No Longer Do*, 103–4, 128–29.

22. Chaison and Rose, "Canadian Perspective"; Roy J. Adams, "Union Certification"; Geoghegan, *Born on the Wrong Continent?*

23. "AFL-CIO Organizing Survey 1986–87 NLRB Elections," n.d. [ca. 1987], folder 9, box 10, AKP.

24. Gross, *Broken Promise*; Tomlins, *The State and the Unions*, 282–316.

25. Gross, *Broken Promise*, 35, 105–11; Brody, *Labor Embattled*, 107; Becker, "Democracy in the Workplace," 561–62. The 1946 case was *NLRB v. Clark Bros. Co.* The 1948 case was *NLRB v. Babcock & Wilson Co.*

26. Cynthia Haynes, interview by George Stoney and Judith Hefland, n.d. [ca. 1991], transcript, tape 8G, Uprising of '34 Collection, GSU.

27. The AFL-CIO estimated that 70 percent of employers held captive audience meetings in 1967. Statement of William L. Kircher to the Special Labor Subcommittee to the House Education and Labor Committee of HR 11725, a Bill to Amend the NLRA to Increase the Effectiveness of Remedies, August 7, 1967, box 2, AFL-CIO ODR. For the 1990s, see Bronfenbrenner, "Uneasy Terrain."

28. Brody, *Labor Embattled*; *Chicopee Mfg. Corp.*, 107 NLRB 106, 107 (1953), in Gross, *Broken Promise*, 109, 168.

29. *Birdsall Construction Co.*, 198 NLRB 163, 163 (1972), in Gross, *Broken Promise*, 228; *Leggett and Platt, Inc.*, 230 NLRB 463 (1977), as discussed in DeMaria, *How Management Wins*, 137; Bronfenbrenner, "Uneasy Terrain."

30. DeMaria, *How Management Wins*, xvii. For more on Alfred DeMaria as a noted antiunion consultant, see Robert Michael Smith, *From Blackjacks to Briefcases*.

31. NLRB Annual Report, 1950, table 3, and NLRB Annual Report, 1980, table 2. This is a comparison of 8(a)1 charges under the NLRA. There were 4,472 8(a)1 charges in 1950 and 31,281 such charges in 1980. See also Goldfield and Bromsen, "Changing Landscape of US Unions," 236; Townley, *Labor Law Reform*, 40. Long quote found in United States Congress, House of Representatives, *Pressures in Today's Workplace*, 1:213.

32. McCartin, "Wagner Act for Public Employees," 123; Richard B. Freeman and Casey Ichniowski, *When Public Sector Workers Unionize*, 1. The figure of four hundred thousand for annual public-sector unionization growth in the 1970s is derived from table 1f in Hirsch and Macpherson, *Union Membership and Earnings*, 16; Bronfenbrenner and Juravich, *Union Organizing in the Public Sector.*

33. Alan Kistler to Lane Kirkland, July 15, 1980, folder 30, box 11, AKP.

34. Notes at Future of Work Committee, April 19, 1984, memo to Charles Mc-Donald, box 4, AKP. Brown's quote is reflected in the memo writer's meeting notes. Though the document does not indicate the author, these are likely Alan Kistler's notes. NLRB Annual Reports, 1970–1989. See also appendix.

35. Fraser and Gerstle, *New Deal Order.*

36. Brown interview; Joost Polak, "Organizing Case Study: Woodward & Lothrop, Washington, D.C.," 1987, folder 23, box 9, AKP.

Chapter Two

1. Don Stillman, "Breaking GM's Southern Strategy," *Solidarity*, January 28, 1977, 9.

2. Ibid.; "UAW Wins $86 Raise in First Pact in Louisiana," *Organizer* 12, no. 1 (1977): 8; "UAW Wins Vote to Form Union at GM Plant in South," *Wall Street Journal*, December 24, 1976, 3.

3. Cowie, *Stayin' Alive*; Sandbrook, *Mad as Hell*; Borstelmann, *The 1970s*; Schulman, *The Seventies.*

4. For yearly data on the number of workers eligible to vote in union elections, see appendix. Examples were taken from NLRB, Monthly Reports, various months, 1970–1979, Election Reports: Cases Closed. Information on the national football players' election was found in the February 1971 report. "MSE vs. Union Campaign Expands," *Chicago Tribune*, May 1, 1979, C6; "Delivery Firm Gets Message as Union Bicyclists Picket," *Washington Post*, December 4, 1976, B1; "AS&T Union Drive Starts," *Washington Post*, September 10, 1974, D8; "Volkswagen Gets the UAW Label," *Solidarity*, June 1978, 3; "Yosemite Holds Labor Vote," *Los Angeles Times*, June 29, 1976, 3.

5. Kessler-Harris, *Out to Work*; Jacqueline Jones, *Labor of Love, Labor of Sorrow*; Ruiz, *From Out of the Shadows.*

6. Wright, *Sharing the Prize*; Department of Health, Education and Welfare, *Work in America*, 49; Lichtenstein, *State of the Union*, 196–200.

7. Moody, "Rank-and-File Rebellion," 133; Brecher, *Strike!*

8. Cowie, *Stayin' Alive*, 12, gives attention to the early strike years but incorrectly identifies only a "trickle" of strikes by the decade's close. USDOL, *Analysis of Work Stoppages, 1979*; USDOL, *Major Work Stoppages in 2015*; Hamilton, *Trucking Country*, 223; Moody, "Rank-and-File Rebellion," 141–42.

9. Moody, "Rank-and-File Rebellion," 135–41; Brecher, *Strike!*; Deslippe, *Rights, Not Roses*; Fonow, *Union Women*, 95–111; Cowie, *Stayin' Alive*, 251–54.

10. McCartin, "'Wagner Act for Public Employees'"; Leon Fink and Brian Greenberg, *Upheaval in the Quiet Zone*; Isaac and Christiansen, "Civil Rights Movement"; Hirsch and MacPherson, *Union Membership and Earnings*, table 1f, 16; "Membership Change," June 29, 1984, folder 10, box 4, AKP; Winslow, "Rebellion from Below," 16.

11. Department of Organization, Report to Executive Council Committee on Organizing, February 1971, folder 36, box 3, AFL-CIO ODR; Department of Health,

Education, and Welfare, *Work in America*, 54; Lichtenstein, *State of the Union*, 196–200.

12. Lerman and Schmidt, *Economic, Social, and Demographic Trends*; Schulman, *The Seventies*, 16–17; Moreton, "Make Payroll, Not War," 62–63.

13. Robert P. Quinn and Graham L. Staines, *1977 Quality of Employment Survey*; Richard B. Freeman and James L. Medoff, *What Do Unions Do?*, 29; James L. Medoff, "Study for AFL-CIO on Public's Image of Unions," *Daily Labor Report*, no. 247 (December 12, 1984): D-6; Gallup, "Labor Unions." Gallup made data for under-thirty union approvals in 1981 available to the author. Under-thirty approvals were 63 percent, compared to 55 percent in the general public. For another interpretation of polling in this period, see Richards, *Union-Free America*, 5. Richards argues that polling shows working people were rejecting unions, but does not examine the demographic and regional breakouts.

14. Kraft Opinion Research Center, "Survey of Opinion toward Unions"; Sidney Hollander Associates for TWUA, "Attitudes of Cannon Workers," box 27, M86-403, TWUA.

15. Cowie, *Stayin' Alive*, 42–49; Brecher, *Strike!*; A. C. Jones, "Rank and File Opposition," 298–306; "Rebellion and Reform," *Washington Post*, February 6, 1972; Glass interview.

16. Ganz et al., "Against the Tide"; Nussbaum interview, 2013; Cowie, *Stayin' Alive*, 68.

17. Minchin, *Hiring the Black Worker*, 246–47; "For Labor Law Victims: Time to Be Heard," *AFL-CIO American Federationist*, June 1978, 4.

18. "Rebellion and Reform," *Washington Post*, February 6, 1972; Cornelius Quinn, Thomas Hill, and James L. Nichols, *Maintaining Nonunion Status*, 17–19.

19. Crawford interview; "No 'Mob Action' Against Union, NLRB Orders," *Chicago Tribune*, October 22, 1963, C6.

20. Stillman, "Runaways," 50.

21. Crawford interview.

22. Stillman, "Runaways"; Lichtenstein, "Wal-Mart, John Tate."

23. Crawford interview.

24. Eury Nannie, Marion Crawford, and Tommie Crowe to Irving Bluestone, March 31, 1975, folder 28, box 53, Irving Bluestone Papers, WPR.

25. Stillman, "Runaways"; "UAW Continues Seeking Equity for Ga. Workers," *Organizer* 12, no. 1 (1977): 11.

26. "Victory at Monroe," *Solidarity*, March 12, 1978, 3; "Monroe Workers Speak Out on Their Historic Contract," *Solidarity*, March 12, 1978, 5, 12; Crawford interview.

27. BLS, *Perspectives on Working Women*, 3, 27.

28. Harley, Wilson, and Logan, "Black Women and Work," 7–8; Jacqueline Jones, *Labor of Love, Labor of Sorrow*, 1–10, 199–200.

29. Ruth Rosen, *World Split Open*; Evans, *Tidal Wave*; Borstelmann, *The 1970s*, 80.

30. Nussbaum, "Working Women's Insurgent Consciousness," 159.

31. Robert P. Quinn and Graham L. Staines, *1977 Quality of Employment Survey*; Richard B. Freeman and James L. Medoff, *What Do Unions Do?*, 29. A 1984 Louis Harris poll also showed that women were more interested than men. See Louis Harris and Associates, "A Study on the Outlook for Trade Union Organizing," November 1984, box 17, AKP.

32. "AFL-CIO Organizing Survey, 1986–87, NLRB Elections," n.d. [ca. 1987], folder 9, box 10, AKP.

33. Kistler, "Union Organizing"; BLS, *Perspectives on Working Women*, 94; BLS, *Women in the Labor Force: A Databook*, 96; "Labor Woos Women," *Dunn's Business Month*, September 1984, 83.

34. BLS, *Perspectives on Working Women*, 12; Executive Office of the President, Office of Management and Budget, *Standard Industrial Classification Manual, 1972*; Hatton, *Temp Economy*, 57.

35. NLRB Annual Reports, 1965–1985, table 16. See Windham, *Knocking on Labor's Door*, Ph.D. diss., for data tables. Note that starting in 1972, there were a small number of workers each year who voted in elections in the U.S. postal system, and starting in 1975 the NLRB added "public administration." These are counted here in the "services" category. These figures represent workers eligible to vote in RC, RM and RD representation case elections.

36. Susan A. Glenn, *Daughters of the Shtetl*; Orleck, *Common Sense and a Little Fire*.

37. BLS, *Perspectives on Working Women*, 10; Cobble, " 'Spontaneous Loss of Enthusiasm,' " 30–33; Tepperman, *Not Servants, Not Machines*, 79–93; Seifer and Wertheimer, "New Approaches to Collective Power," 156.

38. Turk, "Labor's Pink-Collar Aristocracy," 100.

39. Barbara Rahke, telephone interview by Stacy Heath, May 23, 2006, SEIU District 925 Legacy Project, Oral History Transcripts, WPR.

40. "Colleges Put Under NLRB Jurisdiction," *Chicago Tribune*, June 17, 1970, A6; Hurd, "Organizing and Representing Clerical Workers," 319; "U. of Chicago Loses Union Fight," *Chicago Tribune*, March 24, 1979, N7; Hoerr, *We Can't Eat Prestige*; Cobble, " 'Spontaneous Loss of Enthusiasm' "; Hurd, "Learning from Clerical Unions"; "Howard U. Union Bid is Rebuffed," *Washington Post*, June 16, 1974, B1; Local 925 Executive Board Meeting, October 6, 1980, folder 4, box 16, SEIU 925.

41. Virginia L. Tierney to Boston University Employees, May 4, 1978, folder 30, box 7, SEIU 925. See a series of letters in this folder for more examples of Boston and Brandeis Universities' tactics and messages to employees. "Yale's Labor Law Firm: A Report to the Community by Local 35, Federation of University Employees," ca. 1983, box 5, AKP; Gilpin et al., *On Strike for Respect*, 34; Bardacke, *Trampling Out the Vintage*, 512; Hurd and McElwain, "Organizing Clerical Workers"; Hoerr, *We Can't Eat Prestige*.

42. Cobble and Kessler-Harris, "Karen Nussbaum," 145.

43. BLS, *Perspectives on Working Women*, 12; Foner, *Women and the American Labor Movement*, 484; "Bank Unions Offer Women a Way Up," *Chicago Tribune*, April 8, 1976, A4.

44. "Bankers Flock to See Saga of 'Wilmar 8' Before Public Does," *Wall Street Journal*, January 30, 1981, 1; "Willman 8: Women Strike for Rights," *Los Angeles Times*, March 26, 1981; "The Willman 8 Featured by Atlanta Working Women," press release, July 23, 1981, Nussbaum Fundraiser folder, Atlanta 9to5 Working Women Records, GSU; Cobble, "'Spontaneous Loss of Enthusiasm.'"

45. Perras, "Effective Responses to Union Organizing," 92. NLRB, Monthly Reports, 1977, reveal that unions organizing bank workers included the SEIU, Office and Professional Employees International Union (OPEIU), UFCW, UAW, Amalgamated Clothing and Textile Workers Union (ACTWU), and IBEW.

46. "Largest Bank Workers Union in America Affiliates with Retail Clerks," *Retail Clerks Advocate*, June/July 1978, 10; "Union Tries 'Pension Power' of BofA," *Los Angeles Times*, January 9, 1990, D3; Foner, *Women and the American Labor Movement*, 484; C. C. Quarles to R. F. Harbrant and J. L. Fiedler, May 22, 1981, Corporate Files W-V, box 9, FAST Records, UMD; Perras, "Effective Responses to Union Organizing"; "AS&T Union Drive Starts"; "Banks Face New Drive to Unionize Employees," *Chicago Tribune*, January 10, 1977, D9.

47. "His Business Is Breaking Unions and Keeping Them Out," *Seattle Times*, November 28, 1982; "Bankers Flock to See Saga of 'Willmar 8' Before Public Does."

48. "9 to 5 Celebrates Five Years of Action," *Equal Times*, November 6, 1978, 9.

49. Nielsen, *From Sky Girl to Flight Attendant*, 112–15; "National Stewardesses Get Maternity Package," *S&S News*, March 1971, 1; "Women's Lib," S&S News, September 1970, 4; "Too Fat to Fly?" *FLIGHTLOG*, September 1973, 2; "OZA Attendants Protest Weight Code," *FLIGHTLOG*, September 1978, 11; "Does Sex Sell Airline Seats? Tail Slogan Hits Bottom," *FLIGHTLOG*, July 1974, 3.

50. Nielsen, *From Sky Girl to Flight Attendant*, 133. Note that flight attendants voted under the Railway Labor Act. Cobble, "'Spontaneous Loss of Enthusiasm,'" 27–30; Barry, *Femininity in Flight*.

51. Department of Organization, Report to Executive Council Committee on Organizing, February 1971, folder 36, box 3, AFL-CIO ODR.

52. Clete Daniel and Roger Keeran, "Labor Looks at Its Problems," *ILR Report*, Fall 1979.

53. "AFL-CIO Organizing Survey 1986–87, NLRB Elections," n.d. [ca. 1987], folder 9, box 10, AKP; Ben Perkins to Owen Bieber, April 28, 1983, folder 6, box 67, Douglas A. Fraser Papers, WPR.

54. Jackie Ruff, interview by Ann Froines, November 7, 2005, Washington, D.C., SEIU District 925 Legacy Project, Oral History Transcripts, WPR.

55. Deslippe, *Rights, Not Roses*, 116–24, Newman quote on 169; MacLean, *Freedom Is Not Enough*, 138.

56. "Women Unionists Form Coalition, Shape Goals," *AFL-CIO News*, March 30, 1974, 6; Judith Berek, interview by Kathleen Banks Nutter, transcript of video recording, January 3, 2004, 38, Voices of Feminism Oral History Project, Sophia Smith Collection, Smith College, Northampton, Mass.

57. The first survey is of union elections in California: "Survey of Voters in National Labor Relations Board Elections: Attitudes of Voters in Collective Bargaining Representation Elections and in Political Elections, Los Angeles and Orange Counties, California, 1966–67," prepared by San Fernando Valley State College Political Sciences Department Research Analysts for the LAOCOC, AFL-CIO, Spring 1968, box 53, AFL-CIO ODR. The second survey is covered in "Significant Conclusions from the AFL-CIO Organizing Survey," January 1984, folder 10, box 4, AKP.

58. Robert P. Quinn and Graham L. Staines, *1977 Quality of Employment Survey*; Richard B. Freeman and James L. Medoff, *What Do Unions Do?*, 29.

59. "AFL-CIO Organizing Survey, 1986–1987, NLRB Elections," n.d. [ca. 1987], folder 9, box 10, AKP.

60. Frymer, *Black and Blue*, 1; Rosenzweig et al., *Who Built America?*, 527; Korstad and Lichtenstein, "Opportunities Found and Lost," 793.

61. Officers' Report to the Convention, n.d. [ca. 1971], folder 31, box 3, AFL-CIO ODR.

62. Rosenfeld, *What Unions No Longer Do*, 100–130, esp. 103–4. Specific union density values for black men and for women were supplied to the author by Jake Rosenfeld; BLS, "Union Affiliation, 1983–2015."

63. Nelson, *Divided We Stand*; Griffith, *Crisis of American Labor*; Frymer, *Black and Blue*, 64.

64. Frymer, *Black and Blue*, 88–89.

65. Minchin, *"Don't Sleep with Stevens!,"* 69.

66. Frederick Simmons, video interview by Nicole Grant and Trevor Griffey, May 15, 2005, Seattle Civil Rights and Labor History Project, University of Washington, Seattle, Wash., http://depts.washington.edu/civilr/simmons.htm.

67. Todd Hawkins, video interview, United Construction Workers Association History Project, December 29 and 30, 2003, Seattle Civil Rights and Labor History Project, http://depts.washington.edu/civilr/ucwa_interviews.htm.

68. Frymer, *Black and Blue*, 93.

69. Moody, "Rank-and-File Rebellion," 116.

70. Hirsch and Macpherson, *Union Membership and Earnings*, 24. Hirsch and Macpherson's analysis reflects mean hourly earnings and controls for a number of factors. For more information, see this book's introduction, footnote 32.

71. "Newport News," *Steelabor*, March 1979, 8.

72. Coppedge interview, 2010.

73. Karen Anderson, "First Fired," 82–83; BLS, *Perspectives on Working Women*, 74; Rosenfeld, *What Unions No Longer Do*, 128; Harley, Rusan, and Logan, "Black Women and Work," 7–8; Foner, *Women and the American Labor Movement*, 392.

74. BLS, *Perspectives on Working Women*, 74; Glenn, "Racial Ethnic Women's Labor," 99–101; NLRB, Monthly Reports, 1970–1979.

75. Hirsch and Macpherson, *Union Membership and Earnings*, 25.

76. Rosenfeld, *What Unions No Longer Do*, 100–130, esp. 126–27.

77. "South Called 'Key' to Labor's Future," *Allied Industrial Worker* 22, no. 12 (September 1979): 4.

78. BLS, *Handbook of Labor Statistics*, 49–50; Leon Fink and Brian Greenberg, *Upheaval in the Quiet Zone*; "Bargaining Rights Awaken Hopes of Hospital Workers," *AFL-CIO News*, February 1, 1975, 7.

79. "Hospital Law Spurs Organizing Surge," *AFL-CIO News*, November 30, 1974, 1; Leon Fink and Brian Greenberg, *Upheaval in the Quiet Zone*, xii.

80. Nadasen, *Household Workers Unite*; Cobble, " 'Spontaneous Loss of Enthusiasm.' "

81. Griffith, *Crisis of American Labor*; Minchin, *Hiring the Black Worker*; Frederickson, *Looking South*, 168–71; MacLean, *Freedom Is Not Enough*, 78–90; Wright, *Sharing the Prize*, 107.

82. *Norma Rae*, directed by Martin Ritt, Los Angeles, Twentieth Century Fox, 1979; Leifermann, *Crystal Lee*. Quote from Fifth Circuit Court judge John Brown found in Minchin, *"Don't Sleep with Stevens!,"* 3.

83. Minchin, *Hiring the Black Worker*, 3; Conway, *Rise Gonna Rise*; Joey Fink, "In Good Faith."

84. J. P. Stevens to All Employees, April 25, 1973, quoted in Minchin, *Hiring the Black Worker*, 258.

85. Minchin, *"Don't Sleep with Stevens!"*; Cecily Deegan, "Rx for Rotten Conditions," *Southern Exposure* 9, no. 4 (Winter 1981): 67.

86. Paul Swaity to President Pollock, June 29, 1970, box 652, MSS 396, TWUA.

87. Sidney Hollander Associates, "Attitudes of Cannon Workers." See also Minchin, *Hiring the Black Worker*, 247–54, for a discussion of the positive role of black leadership in mixed-race union organizing campaigns in textiles.

88. Tim Honeycutt, video interview with the Honeycutt family, August 22, 1991, transcript, 29–32, Uprising of '34 Collection, GSU.

89. Sacks, *Caring by the Hour*, 56, 99–109.

90. Schulman, *From Cotton Belt to Sunbelt*, 135–66; Sugrue, *Origins of the Urban Crisis*, 125–77; Shermer, *Sunbelt Capitalism*, 226; Essletzbichler, "Job Creation and Destruction."

91. Cobb, *Selling of the South*; Schulman, *From Cotton Belt to Sunbelt*; Friedman, "Capital Flight, 'States' Rights' "; Cliff Sloan and Bob Hall, "Home in Greenville," *Southern Exposure* 8, no. 2 (Summer 1980): 91; Goldfield, *Decline of Organized Labor*, 118. A union security agreement is one in which an employee must either join the union or pay a regular financial contribution equal to services rendered by the union.

92. Analysis based on NLRB Annual Reports, 1960–1989, table 15 (1960–1971) and table 15A (1972–1989). See Windham, *Knocking on Labor's Door*, Ph.D. diss., for data tables. I define "Sunbelt" as all the states in the U.S. Bureau Census categories of the South Atlantic, East South Central, and West South Central, as well as New Mexico, Arizona, Nevada, and California. These figures for years 1960–1963

represent workers eligible to vote in RC and RM representation case elections. The figures for 1964–1989 represent workers eligible to vote in RC, RM, and RD representation case elections

93. Robert P. Quinn and Graham L. Staines, *1977 Quality of Employment Survey*; Richard B. Freeman and James L. Medoff, *What Do Unions Do?*, 29. Forty-six percent of blue-collar Southerners said they would vote yes for a union, compared to 37 percent in the Northeast, for instance.

94. "UAW Wins Apparent Major Concessions from GM in Battle to Organize the South," *Wall Street Journal*, September 12, 1978, 5.

95. Stillman, "Runaways," 50; Stillman, "Breaking GM's Southern Strategy," 9; "UAW Warns GM of Confrontation over Deep South Non-Union Plants," *Washington Post*, November 9, 1976, A4; "GM, UAW Reach Accord: 'Shortest Strike' is Over," *Chicago Tribune*, November 20, 1976, S1.

96. Stillman, "Breaking GM's Southern Strategy," 9; "UAW Wins $86 Raise in First Pact in Louisiana," *Organizer*, 12, no. 1 (1977): 8; "GM, UAW Fight in La. May Affect Northern Firms' Moves into South," *Washington Post*, December 21, 1976.

97. "UAW Spinning its Wheels in Organizing GM in South," *Chicago Tribune*, June 11, 1978, B9; "UAW's Failure to Organize GM Facility Leaves a Residue of Red Faces and Ill Will," *Wall Street Journal*, February 24, 1981, 56.

98. "GM, UAW Talks are Held Up By Dispute on Union Organizing Effort in the South," *Wall Street Journal*, July 17, 1979, 16; "Conspiracy Charge by Auto Workers Impedes GM Talks," *Washington Post*, July 17, 1979, A2; "Report on the UAW-General Motors 1979 Tentative Settlement," September 18, 1979, folder 11, box 5, Simon Alpert Papers, WPR; Ben Perkins to Owen Bieber, April 28, 1983, folder 6, box 67, Douglas A. Fraser papers, WPR; "UAW is Recognized by GM in Alabama," *Baltimore Sun*, September 7, 1982, C5.

99. Perkins to Bieber, April 28, 1983; Alan Kistler to Louis Ferman, August 31, 1983, folder 1, box 2, AKP; "Report of NLRB Board Elections Participated in by UAW, Year Ending 1975," n.d. [ca. 1976], folder 17, box 55, Douglas A. Fraser Papers, WPR; "Sights Set on Sunbelt," *Organizer* 13, no. 1 (1977): 12.

100. On Tupelo, see Joe Uehlein, interview by Joey Fink, March 24, 2012, in Fink, "In Good Faith"; "Unions Still Find a Tough Row to Hoe," *U.S. News and World Report*, June 21, 1982, 62–63; Alan Kistler to AFL-CIO Executive Council Committee on Organizing and Field Services, January 19, 1981, folder 14, box 4, AKP; David Moberg, "Hard Organizing in Sunbelt City," *Progressive*, August 1983, 34.

101. "AFL-CIO Drive Here Will Fail Hoffa Says," *Los Angeles Times*, March 27, 1963.

102. Walter P. Reuther, "Draft Proposal for a Comprehensive, Cooperative, Coordinated Organizational Drive," February 1961, folder 5, and Brendan Sexton to Walter P. Reuther, January 9, 1962, folder 6, both in box 319, Walter P. Reuther Papers, WPR.

103. The five original sectors were hard goods (lumber, steel, glass, and so on); soft goods (textiles, oil, chemicals, and so on); retail; government; and hotel and restaurant. "Organizational Structure: Coordinated Organizational Drive, Los Angeles and

Orange Counties," n.d. [ca. 1962], folder 29, box 52, AFL-CIO ODR; William L. Gilbert to John W. Livingston, January 19, 1965, and Marie Nixon to Charlie McDonald, January 29, 1981, both in folder 16, box 53, AFL-CIO ODR; Los Angeles Coordinated Organizing Campaign, "Projected Annual Cost of Staff," n.d. [ca. 1963], and President to Elmer Brown, February 15, 1963, both in folder 32, box 52, AFL-CIO ODR.

104. "The Organized and Unorganized in Los Angeles and Orange Counties," AFL-CIO Report, 1967, and Minutes, Combined Divisions Meeting, November 15, 1967, both in folder 2, box 53, AFL-CIO ODR; "Union Wins Election at Harvey Aluminum Firm," *Los Angeles Times*, December 3, 1964, 12; "1100 Packard-Bell Workers Go IUE," *IUE News*, September 21, 1967; Gilbert to Livingston, January 19, 1965; Minutes, Combined Divisions Meeting, June 28, 1978, folder 6, box 53, AFL-CIO ODR; "Combined Divisions Meetings," July 11, 1984, folder 2, box 12, AKP.

105. "Yes, We Can!" in Spanish and Mandarin (Chinese).

106. Ngai, *Impossible Subjects*, 227.

107. Fix and Passel, "U.S. Immigration"; Sabagh, "Los Angeles," 104.

108. Gibson and Lennon, "Foreign-Born Population"; Milkman, *L.A. Story*; Leon Fink, *Maya of Morganton*.

109. Milkman, "Undocumented Immigrant Workers," 35; Harry Bernstein, "Dispute Raises Illegal Alien Issue," *Los Angeles Times*, September 18, 1985, OC C1 as quoted in Delgado, *New Immigrants, Old Unions*, 10.

110. Delgado, *New Immigrants, Old Unions*, 1, 20–57.

111. "Illegal Aliens Union Targets," *Los Angeles Times*, January 30, 1975, 8A; "Garment Workers Turn Down Union," *Los Angeles Times*, March 8, 1975, A23.

112. "Valley Industry, Wealth Soak Up Illegal Aliens," *Los Angeles Times*, August 13, 1978, SF_c1; "Plant Closing Feared, but Strike Continues," *Los Angeles Times*, April 6, 1980, V1, and "Horikawa in Bitter Fight Over Union," *Los Angeles Times*, October 13, 1980, E1.

113. Bao, *More than Half the Sky*, 26.

114. Milkman, "Organizing Immigrant Women," 285; Bao, *More than Half the Sky*, 153, 67.

115. Milkman, "Organizing Immigrant Women," 291–94; Bao, *More than Half the Sky*, 211.

116. Lin, *Reconstructing Chinatown*, 68–70.

117. Rosenfeld, *What Unions No Longer Do*, 142; Louis Harris and Associates, "A Study on the Outlook for Trade Union Organizing," November 1984, box 17, AKP.

118. "Employees at Farah Accept New 3-Year Pact," *Washington Post*, March 8, 1974, A3; Cowie, *Stayin' Alive*, 54–57.

119. Bill Finger, "Victoria Sobre Farah," *Southern Exposure* 4, nos. 1–2, 1976, 47.

120. Quote is from "Farah Vows to Continue Struggle Against Union," *Los Angeles Times*, February 2, 1974, 19; "Farah Sign Pledge to Halt Some Unfair Labor Actions," *AFL-CIO News*, February 10, 1973, 2; "Council Presses Support for Farah Strike, Boycott," AFL-CIO News Service, July 20, 1972, box 3, AFL-CIO ODR.

121. "Employees at Farah Accept New 3-Year Pact."

122. Garcia, *From the Jaws of Victory*; Shaw, *Beyond the Fields,* 46; Bardacke, *Trampling Out the Vintage,* 2, 512, quote on 484.

123. "Labor Urges Amnesty for Illegal Immigrants," *New York Times*, February 17, 2000; AFL-CIO, "Resolution 5."

124. Both quotes are from Moberg, "Hard Organizing in Sunbelt City"; on the ILGWU, see "Illegal Aliens Union Target"; "Hospital Union 1199—Back Then and Now," *New York Amsterdam News*, June 2, 1979, 16; "Union Drive Effort Begins at Marriott," *New York Amsterdam News*, April 2, 1983, 14; "Horikawa in Bitter Fight Over Union"; "Mediator Speeds up Head-Start Union Talks," *Los Angeles Sentinel*, August 16, 1984, A2; Minutes, Combined Divisions Meeting, June 28, 1978, LAOCOC, folder 6, box 53, AFL-CIO ODR.

125. Richard B. Freeman, "Spurts in Union Growth."

126. Goldfield, *Decline of Organized Labor,* 90–91; Richard B. Freeman and James L. Medoff, *What Do Unions Do?,* 221–45.

127. Alan Kistler to Secretary-Treasurers' Meeting in St. Louis, Mo., March 1983, folder 8, box 2, AKP.

Chapter Three

1. Transcript of *The Last Word with Phil Donahue & Greg Jackson*, January 31, 1983, folder 8, box 5, SEIU 925.

2. Goldfield, *Decline of Organized Labor,* 18; Roof, *American Labor*; Rosenfeld, *What Unions No Longer Do.*

3. Lichtenstein, *State of the Union,* 212–15; Robert Brenner, *Economics of Global Turbulence,* 101; Robert Brenner, *Boom and the Bubble,* 17; Robert Brenner, "Political Economy of Rebellion," 51–62; Judith Stein, *Pivotal Decade,* xi, 8–12. On steel, see Tiffany, *Decline of American Steel.* On textiles, see Minchin, *Empty Mills.*

4. Judith Stein, *Pivotal Decade,* 102, 112; Westcott and Bednarzik, "Employment and Unemployment."

5. Ford quote in Robert M. Collins, *More,* 155; Cowie, *Stayin' Alive,* 221–27; Judith Stein, *Pivotal Decade,* 111–17; Robert Brenner, "Political Economy of Rebellion," 62; A. H. Raskin, "For Organized Labor, What Replaces 'More'?," *New York Times*, September 1, 1975, 15.

6. Robert Brenner, *Economics of Global Turbulence,* 99–106; Judith Stein, *Pivotal Decade,* 101–17; Vogel, *Fluctuating Fortunes,* 136; Lichtenstein, "Return of Merchant Capitalism"; Levinson, *Box,* 233; Bonacich and Wilson, *Getting the Goods*; Hamilton, *Trucking Country*; Harrison and Bluestone, *Great U-Turn.*

7. Judith Stein, *Pivotal Decade*; Eileen Appelbaum and Rosemary Batt, *Private Equity at Work*; Gerald F. Davis, *Managed by the Markets*; Dobbin and Zorn, "Corporate Malfeasance."

8. Hatton, *Temp Economy*; Weil, *Fissured Workplace*; Kalleberg, *Good Jobs, Bad Jobs*; Colin Gordon, *Dead on Arrival*; Standing, *Precariat*; Bivens and Mishel, "Understanding the Historic Divergence."

9. Phillips-Fein, *Invisible Hands*; McQuaid, *Uneasy Partners*, 125–71; Waterhouse, *Lobbying America*, 58; Vogel, *Fluctuating Fortunes*, 195–99; Hacker and Pierson, *Winner-Take-All Politics*, 121.

10. Lichtenstein and Shermer, *The Right and Labor in America*, 7.

11. Douglas Soutar, interview by Shelly Coppock, Litchfield, Arizona, November 16, 1990, transcript number 1175, 117, folder 30, box 1, transcripts #5843 OHT, NLRB Oral History Project II, KCLMD. On the Business Roundtable, see McQuaid, *Uneasy Partners*, 149–50, and Vogel, *Fluctuating Fortunes*, 198–99.

12. " 'Big' Labor and Big Strikes: Analysis and Recommendations," *NAM Reports* 12, no. 38 (September 18, 1967):10

13. "Target-GE!," n.d. [ca. 1970], folder 14, box 2, AFL-CIO ODR; "Here's How Terms Roll Up to $1.05," *UNITY* 2, no. 6 (1970): 2, box 2, AFL-CIO ODR; "End of the GE Siege . . . ," *New York Times*, January 31, 1970; "GE Strike Settlement Hailed as an 'End to Boulwarism,' " *AFL-CIO News*, February 7, 1970; Filippelli and McColloch, *Cold War in the Working Class*, 173–74.

14. Election data are based on the author's analysis of election tallies found in "IUD [Industrial Union Department] Data Center—NLRB Elections History: Elections Closed, Won and Lost, 07–61 thru 12–82," box 8, AKP, and "NLRB Elections History: Elections Closed, Won and Lost, 07–61 thru 12–71," folder 2, box 2, AFL-CIO ODR. The unions involved included the IUE, IBEW, United Electrical, Radio, and Machine Workers, UAW, and IAM. While in the 1960s workers won over half their elections at GE, the workers' win rate dropped to 39 percent in the 1970s.

15. Harrison and Bluestone, *Great U-Turn*, 21–52; Waterhouse, *Lobbying America*, 98–100; Richard B. Freeman, *America Works*; Colin Gordon, *Dead on Arrival*, 84–85.

16. Peter J. Pestillo, "Learning to Live without the Union," Industrial Relations Research Association Convention, August 30, 1978, folder 10, box 2, AKP. For more on the shift in large corporations' attitudes in this period, see Hacker and Pierson, *Winner-Take-All Politics*, 118–19; Waterhouse, *Lobbying America*, 19–28; Phillips-Fein, *Invisible Hands*, 166–212; Harrison and Bluestone, *Great U-Turn*, 3–20; and Vogel, *Fluctuating Fortunes*, 148–92.

17. Soutar, interview by Coppock. Soutar calls the group the "nothing committee" and then the Labor Law Reform Group. Other documents refer to it as the Labor Law Study Project. See, for instance, memorandum from R. T. Borth, "Responsibilities of Executive Director—Labor Law Study Project," April 5, 1967, box 62B, series 5, NAM, and "NAM-Chamber Inspired Labor Law Study Group to Continue Despite Election," *Daily Labor Report*, Bureau of National Affairs (BNA), November 15, 1968, A-10; Anthony P. Alfina to Robert T. Borth, January 5, 1967, box 62B, series 5, NAM. Gross, *Broken Promise*, offers a history of the formation and activities of the Labor Law Reform Group, 204–41.

18. The three were Guy Farmer, who chaired the NLRB under Dwight Eisenhower; Gerry Reilly, former NLRB member; and Theodore Iserman, a management-side lawyer. See Soutar, interview by Coppock, for the term "troika," as well as H. C. Lumb, T. C. Allen, and Lambert Miller, "NAM Executive Committee Report,"

February 15, 1971, folder Labor Law Reform, box 72, series 5, NAM. Gross, *Broken Promise*, 200–204.

19. For a description of the initial committee and its members, see Virgil B. Day, "Hot Spring Presentation on Labor Law Reform Project," May 14, 1966, folder LLRS/LLLSG, box 7, Douglas Soutar Papers, KCLMD. Companies represented on the LLRG steering committee in 1966, in addition to American Smelting and Refining (Soutar), GE (Day), and R. H. Macy (Atkinson), were AT&T, Ford Motor, Columbia Gas System Service, Union Carbide, General Dynamics, U.S. Steel, Sinclair Oil, and Sears Roebuck. An executive from BFGoodrich later joined the group. For more history of LLRG, see Lumb, Allen, and Miller, "NAM Executive Committee Report," and "NAM-Chamber Inspired Labor Law Study Group to Continue Despite Election," A-10.

20. For more on corporations moving to the south to avoid unions, see Cowie, *Capital Moves*, and Friedman, "Capital Flight."

21. Greene, *Pure and Simple Politics*, 88–93; Colin Gordon, *New Deals*; Philips-Fein, *Invisible Hands*.

22. Fones-Wolf, *Selling Free Enterprise*; Metzgar, *Striking Steel*; "Major Firms United to Limit Unions' Strength," *Los Angeles Times*, November 3, 1968, 1.

23. Gross, *Broken Promise*, 202–5; R. T. Borth, "Responsibilities of Executive Director," April 5, 1967, and Anthony P. Alfino to Robert T. Borth, January 5, 1967, box 62B, series 5, NAM.

24. "Labor Law Reform Study: Amendments to the Labor Management Relations Act," September 1969, box 72, series 5, NAM (hereafter "Labor Law Reform Study"). The Kennedy NLRB had revived the Harry S. Truman–era NLRB's *Joy Silk* doctrine in 1961, recognizing unions without an election in the cases of employer misfeasance, and then in 1964 the Johnson NLRB deepened its commitment by allowing unions to simultaneously petition for election and file refusal to bargain charges in the *Bernel Foam* case. See Joy Silk 85 NLRB 1263 (1949); Bernel Foam Products Co., 146 NLRB 1277, 56 LRRM 1039 (1964); Gross, *Broken Promise*, 167–71, 183–84. On J. P. Stevens, see "Labor Law Reform Study," xxxi–xxxii. On smaller units, see "Labor Law Reform Study," xxiii, and Sav-On Drugs 138 NLRB 1032 (1962).

25. "Labor Law Reform Study," U-1–U-5.

26. W. P. Gullander to William H. McGaughey, January 4, 1967, R. T. Borth, "Responsibilities of Executive Director," April 5, 1967, and Hill & Knowlton, "Communications Plan in Support of Labor Law Revision," May 1967, all in box 62B, series 5, NAM; Lumb, Allen, and Miller, "NAM Executive Committee Report"; Gross, *Broken Promise*, 205–9.

27. C. Devine to Mr. [Lambert] Miller, July 19, 1968, box 72, series 5, NAM; "NAM-Chamber Inspired Labor Law Study Group to Continue Despite Election," A-10. See George Denison and William Schulz, "Let's Enforce Our Labor Laws Fairly," *Reader's Digest Reprint*, 1968, box 190, Women's Department series, NAM; Gross, *Broken Promise*, 211.

28. "Congressional Review Needed," *Bridgeville News*, October 17, 1968. On identical editorials, see testimony by Senator Wayne Morse, August 2, 1968, Congressional Record, Senate, box 72, series 5, NAM.

29. Francis A. O'Connell, interview by Shelley Coppock, May 23, 1987, Aptos, California, box 1, transcripts #5843 OHT, NLRB Oral History Project II, KCLMD.

30. Gross, *Broken Promise*, 212; "Labor Law Reform Legislative Proposals Pending before Congress," February 1972, box 137, series 7, NAM.

31. Lumb, Allen, and Miller, "NAM Executive Committee Report."

32. Waterhouse, *Lobbying America*, 78–86; Labor Law Study Group, "Proposed Funding," January 28, 1972, and "Labor Law Study Group: General Membership," December 2, 1971, both in LLRS LLSG folder, box 7, Douglas Soutar Papers, KCLMD.

33. Phillips-Fein, *Invisible Hands*, 192; Linder, *Wars of Attrition*, 189–91; Waterhouse, *Lobbying America*, 83–88; Cowie, *Stayin' Alive*, 231; quote from "The Lobby with a Wallop," *Boston Globe*, September 14, 1975; Soutar, interview by Coppock; Linder, *Wars of Attrition*, 190, 207.

34. Waterhouse, *Lobbying America*, 78–86; Linder, *Wars of Attrition*, 182–230; Vogel, *Fluctuating Fortunes*, 160–63; Business Roundtable Labor Management Committee, Minutes, March 21, 1977, and Minutes of Labor-Management Meeting, November 9, 1977, both in box 8, Douglas Soutar Papers, KCLMD; Phillips-Fein, *Invisible Hands*, 190–200.

35. Douglas Soutar to R. F. Duemler, R. W. Reagles, J. W. Miller, F. A. O'Connell, J. Oliver, and R. C. Sonnemann, "Business Roundtable Labor-Management Committee 'Objectives,'" December 17, 1973, box 8, Douglas Soutar Papers, KCLMD.

36. Soutar, interview by Coppock, 103; Gross, *Broken Promises*, 219; "Blue Ribbon Committee of Lawyers for Labor Law Reform," n.d. [ca. 1966], folder 27, box 9, AKP; "Labor Opposes Appointment of Chicagoan to NLRB Post," *Chicago Tribune*, February 18, 1970, A3.

37. "The NLRB with GOP Majority Again, Is Seen Becoming More Pro-Business," *Wall Street Journal*, May 4, 1971, 38.

38. Gross, *Broken Promise*, 227–28. See Airporter Inn Hotel, 215 NLRB 824 (1974); Stumpf Motor Co., 208 NLRB 431, 432 (1974); and Birdsall Construction Company, 198 NLRB 163, 163 (1972).

39. Gross, *Broken Promise*, 230. See Green Briar Nursing Home, 201 NLRB 503 (1973).

40. Gross, *Broken Promise*, 242.

41. Goldfield, *Decline of Organized Labor*, 90–91.

42. For more scholarship on employers' historic resistance to unions and the rise of the antiunion industry, see Fones-Wolf, *Selling Free Enterprise*; Jacoby, *Modern Manors*; Phillips-Fein, "Business Conservatism on the Shop Floor"; Robert Michael Smith, *From Blackjacks to Briefcases*; Logan, "Union Avoidance Industry"; Logan, "Fine Art of Union Busting"; Logan, "'Union Free' Movement"; Norwood, *Strike-Breaking and Intimidation*; Richard B. Freeman and Morris M. Kleiner, "Employer Behavior"; and Lichtenstein, "Wal-Mart, John Tate."

43. Schlossberg and Scott, *Organizing and the Law.*

44. NLRB Annual Reports, 1950–1990. For the years 1951–90, see table 2. For 1950, see table 3. For full data, see Windham, *Knocking on Labor's Door*, Ph.D. diss. Section 8(a)1 of the NLRA "forbids an employer to interfere with, restrain, or coerce employees in the exercise of the rights" guaranteed by the NLRA. Examples may include threats, interrogation, or spying on union activity. Section 8(a)3 of the NLRA "makes it an unfair labor practice for an employer to discriminate against employees 'in regard to hire or tenure of employment or any term or condition of employment' for the purpose of encouraging or discouraging membership in a labor organization." Examples may include firing and demoting workers. All 8(a)3 violations are also counted as 8(a)1 violations. See NLRB, *Basic Guide*, 14–15. Unfair labor practice charges may be filed against either an employer or a union. Charges against unions are not included in these numbers. They are filed under Section 8(b) of the NLRA. The vast majority of charges are filed against employers.

45. Goldfield and Bromsen, "Changing Landscape of US Unions," 236, table 1.

46. Richard B. Freeman and James L. Medoff, *What Do Unions Do?*, 232.

47. Brody, *Labor Embattled*, 99–109; Bronfenbrenner and Juravich, "More than House Calls."

48. Pestillo, "Learning to Live without the Union."

49. Charles McDonald and Dick Wilson, "Peddling the Union-Free Guarantee," *AFL-CIO Federationist*, April 1979.

50. NLRB Annual Reports, 1950–1980, table 5. For data, see Windham, *Knocking on Labor's Door*, Ph.D. diss. This analysis is based on the number of CA cases, charges of unfair labor practices against an employer under section 8 (a) of the NLRA, and on the number of RC representation case petitions that were filed. For more explanation of RC representation cases, see appendix.

51. Hughes, *Making Unions Unnecessary*, 1.

52. Jacoby, *Modern Manors.*

53. Robert Michael Smith, *From Blackjacks to Briefcases*, 100–104; Levitt and Conrow, *Confessions of a Union Buster*, 39–50; Logan, "Union Avoidance Industry." Confusingly, the firm used another set of *M*s and was named Melnick, McKeown, and Mickus until 1975. It was also known as "Modern Management."

54. "Earle K. Shawe," biography, n.d., box 1, EKS; Lorraine Branham, "The Hired Gun: When Business Wants a Top Lawyer It Goes to Shawe," *Baltimore Sun*, November 12, 1981.

55. Lichtenstein, "Wal-Mart, John Tate."

56. Logan, "Union Avoidance Industry"; United States Congress, House of Representatives, *Pressures in Today's Workplace*, 3:112; "Significant Conclusions from the AFL-CIO Organizing Survey," n.d. [ca. 1984], folder 10, box 4, AKP.

57. Levitt and Conrow, *Confessions of a Union Buster*, 70.

58. Logan, "Union Avoidance Industry," 660; National Organizing Coordinating Committee, AFL-CIO, "Seyfarth, Shaw, Fairweather and Geraldson," *RUB*

Sheet: Report on Union Busters, no. 2 (March 1979); "The 'gang-of-four,' " *RUB Sheet*, no. 21 (October 1980).

59. Jackson, *When Labor Trouble Strikes*, 41.

60. "Weed Them Out," *RUB Sheet*, no.8 (September 1979), 8–9; "When the Boss Calls in This Expert, the Union May Be in Real Trouble," *Wall Street Journal*, November 19, 1979.

61. Levitt and Conrow, *Confessions of a Union Buster*, 72.

62. Robert Kai Whiting, "Announcing the Texas Labor Relations Review: An Executive Briefing," n.d. [ca. May 1984], folder 4, box 14, AKP.

63. Martin F. Payson, "How to Beat the Union Drive for Female Office Workers," *Nation's Business*, September 1983.

64. "Firms Learn Art of Keeping Unions Out," *Wall Street Journal*, April 19, 1977, 48.

65. John G. Kilgour, "Office Unions: Keeping the Threat Small," *Administrative Management*, November 1982.

66. MacLean, *Freedom Is Not Enough*, 109–10; Reed, "Title VII," 33.

67. "Significant Trends and Developments in Equal Employment Opportunity and Labor Law, 1979–1980," prepared by Shawe & Rosenthal for Thiokol Corporation, August 2, 1980, box 6, EKS; "United State Fidelity & Guaranty Company's Labor and Equal Employment Opportunity Challenges for the 1980's," August 14–17, 1980, box 1, EKS.

68. "EEO Corner," *AMR Reporter: Managing without Interference* 8, no. 8 (August 15, 1983): 1.

69. Robert R. Locke and J.-C. Spender, *Confronting Managerialism*.

70. "William E. Fulmer obituary," *Tuscaloosa Times*, October 6, 2010; Fulmer, *Union Organizing*, 76.

71. Kilgour, *Preventative Labor Relations*, 38–46.

72. Fulmer, *Union Organizing*, 43.

73. Kilgour, *Preventative Labor Relations*, 320.

74. McDonald and Wilson, "Peddling the Union-Free Guarantee."

75. Logan, "Union Avoidance Industry," 662; Hughes, *Making Unions Unnecessary*, 1, 5–19.

76. "When the Boss Calls in This Expert, the Union May Be in Real Trouble," *Wall Street Journal*, November 19, 1979; Richard B. Freeman and Morris M. Kleiner, "Employer Behavior," 351.

77. Schlossberg and Scott, *Organizing and the Law*, 67–101.

78. "Firms Learn Art of Keeping Unions Out"; DeMaria, *How Management Wins*, 57.

79. United States Congress, House of Representatives, *Pressures in Today's Workplace*, 1:208.

80. Schlossberg and Scott, *Organizing and the Law*, 192–93; Richard Prosten to AFL-CIO Organizing Committee, December 1977, box 9, unprocessed records, AFL-CIO ODR.

81. Kistler, "Union Organizing," 101.

82. United States Congress, House of Representatives, *Pressures in Today's Workplace*, 1:209; DeMaria, *How Management Wins*, 66.

83. DeMaria, *How Management Wins*, 98, 196.

84. Hecht's Campaign Calendar, April 24, 1981, master campaign file, and Hecht's Company, "Supervisors Discussion Guide," May 4, 1981, both in box 6, EKS.

85. "Instructions for Use of the Block 30 Sheet, Supervisory Training Session," 1982, box 111, Acc. 5619-017, ACTWU.

86. Anthony P. Dunbar and Bob Hall, "Union Busters: Who, Where, When, How and Why," *Southern Exposure* 8, no. 2 (Summer 1980): 30; Robert Michael Smith, *From Blackjacks to Briefcases*, 117.

87. Boardwalk Regency Hotel, "Questions and Answer Fact Sheet," September 1, 1980, master campaign file, box 6, EKS.

88. Brandeis University, "Guidelines for Supervisors and Managerial Employees during a Union Organizing Drive," January 12, 1976, folder 38, box 7, SEIU 925.

89. DeMaria, *How Management Wins*, 247.

90. Transcript of speech by E. D. Smith, GE, Goldsboro, N.C., November 8, 1978, folder 19, box 8, AKP.

91. Alan Kistler, Speech to Secretary-Treasurers Meeting, Saint Louis, Mo., March 1983, box 2, AKP. The survey was among units with over one hundred employees.

92. Kilgour, *Preventative Labor Relations*, 308.

93. "Decertification Activity," n.d. [ca. 1982], folder 10, box 4, AKP.

94. Earle K. Shawe, "The Move Towards De-Unionization," *Answer*, Fall 1979, 10; Earle K. Shawe, "Memorandum: The Labor Relations Implications of the Acquisition of All Portions, Inc. Indianapolis, Indiana Facility," August 23, 1976, box 4, EKS.

95. Statement of Charles McDonald to the Labor and Management Subcommittee of the House Education and Labor Committee oversight hearings on the Landrum-Griffin Act, Labor Management Consultants, February 7, 1984, folder 2, box 2, AKP.

96. Doreen Levasseur, interview by Ann Froines, February 23, 2005, Braintree, Massachusetts, SEIU District 925 Legacy Project, Oral History Transcripts, WPR.

97. "The Economy: AFL-CIO to Seek Far-Reaching Law Changes," *Boston Globe*, February 23, 1977, 31.

98. Judith Stein, *Pivotal Decade*, 181–83; Vogel, *Fluctuating Fortunes*, 138–40, 150–52.

99. Townley, *Labor Law Reform*, 124–26; Roof, *American Labor*, 157. Other scholarship on the labor law reform bill includes Judith Stein, *Pivotal Decade*, 180–90; Cowie, *Stayin' Alive*, 288–96; and Vogel, *Fluctuating Fortunes*, 148–59.

100. Stu Eizenstat to the President, June 30, 1977, folder Labor Law Reform, box 35, Office of the Chief of Staff, JCL.

101. Ibid.; Hamilton Jordan to President Carter, June 29, 1977, folder Labor Law Reform, box 35, Office of the Chief of Staff, JCL; F. Ray Marshall and Carin Ann Clauss, Press Briefing, July 18, 1977, folder Labor Law, box 112, Office of the Chief of Staff, JCL.

102. Townley, *Labor Law Reform*, 124–26.

103. Stu Eizenstat to the President, June 30, 1977; Quote from Stu Eizenstat to the President, August 1, 1977, folder Labor Law, box 112, Office of the Chief of Staff, JCL.

104. "Labor to Seek Business Help in Battle Over Reform Bill," *Baltimore Sun*, October 11, 1977, A8.

105. Thomas Ferguson and Joel Rogers, "Labor Law Reform and Its Enemies," *Nation*, January 6, 1979, 19; "Labor to Seek Business Help in Battle Over Reform Bill"; Waterhouse, *Lobbying America*, 128–29; Judith Stein, *Pivotal Decade*, 186–87; Vogel, *Fluctuating Fortunes*, 154–55.

106. Richard A. Riley to Members of Business Roundtable, August 2, 1977, as quoted in Judith Stein, *Pivotal Decade*, 187, 336n32. See also Ferguson and Rogers, "Labor Law Reform and Its Enemies," 19.

107. "Labor to Seek Business Help in Battle Over Reform Bill"; Judith Stein, *Pivotal Decade*, 187; Waterhouse, *Lobbying America*, 128–29; Ferguson and Rogers, "Labor Law Reform and Its Enemies," 18.

108. R. Heath Larry, "Introduction to Testimony by NAM on Amendments to the NLRA Presented to the Subcommittee on Labor-Management Relations of the Committee on Education and Labor, U.S. House of Representatives," July 26, 1977, box 177, series 9, NAM.

109. Virgil B. Day, "Hot Springs Presentation on Labor Law Reform Project," May 14, 1966, LLRS/LLRG, box 7, Douglas Soutar Papers, KCLMD.

110. R. Heath Larry, "Introduction to Testimony by NAM"; "Unions Push for Labor Law Reforms," *Los Angeles Times*, August 10, 1977, E12; AFL-CIO testimony before House committee, September 8, 1977, box 85, series 6, Office of the President, George Meany Files, UMD.

111. Waterhouse, *Lobbying America*; Vogel, *Fluctuating Fortunes*, 153–57; D. Quinn Mills, "Flawed Victory in Labor Law Reform," *Harvard Business Review*, May–June 1979, 92; Ferguson and Rogers, "Labor Law Reform and Its Enemies," 18; Chamber quote from "Special Edition: What You Can Do," Chamber of Commerce of the United States, *Congressional Action* 21, no. 32 (August 19, 1977): 8; Robert Palmer to NAM Members, December 5, 1977, and R. A. Riley to Firestone Shareowner, August 8, 1977, both in box 147C, series 7, NAM.

112. Townley, *Labor Law Reform*, 169.

113. "Labor Law Bill Advances, Faces Filibuster in Senate," *AFL-CIO News*, January 28, 1978, 1.

114. Townley, *Labor Law Reform*, 142–45, 174; "Special Edition: What You Can Do," Chamber of Commerce of the United States, *Congressional Action* 21, no. 32 (August 19, 1977): 8; Small Business Legislative Council, press release, May 16, 1978, and Steve Selig to Landon Butler, June 7, 1978, both in folder Labor Law, box 176, Office of the Chief of Staff, JCL.

115. "Stung by Loss on Situs Bill, Unions Plan Massive Campaign to Change Labor Laws," *Baltimore Sun*, April 13, 1977, A1.

116. "Unions Gear Up for Drive to Win Labor Reform Bill," *AFL-CIO News*, February 11, 1978, 1; Statement of Clarence Mitchell, Director, Washington Bureau of the NAACP, before the Senate Subcommittee on Labor, September 23, 1977, box 177, series 9, NAM; "Labor Law Reform," Statements Adopted by the AFL-CIO Executive Council, August 29–30, 1977, file 20/52, series 1, Support Services, AFL-CIO Publications, UMD; "What Labor Law Must Overcome," *AFL-CIO Federationist*, February 1978, 16–21; "Newport News 'Victims' Spark USWA Rally for Labor Law Reform," *Steel Labor*, July 1978, 5.

117. Bob Thompson and Frank Moore to the President, June 9, 1978, box 35, Moore—Office of Congressional Liaison, JCL; Roof, *American Labor*.

118. Marshall interview. See also Hower and McCartin, "Marshall's Principle," esp. 101, and "Backers of Labor Bill Give Up Filibuster Fight," *Los Angeles Times*, June 23, 1978, A5.

119. George Meany, "For Working Americans, Time for Justice," *AFL-CIO Federationist*, June 1978, 1.

120. George Meany, "An Open Letter to American Business Leaders," AFL-CIO News Release, May 4, 1978, box 85, series 6, Office of the President, George Meany Files, UMD.

121. Douglas A. Fraser to Labor-Management Group Members, July 17, 1978, folder Labor O/A, box 231, Eizenstat Papers, Domestic Policy Staff, JCL. Information on Reginald Jones found in "The Hot Battle Over Labor Law Reform," *Forbes*, September 1, 1977, 21, and Judith Stein, *Pivotal Decade*, 187.

Chapter Four

1. Coppedge interview, 2010; Coppedge interview, 2011.

2. The applicable law governing where the ships were built was the Buy American Act of 1933. See Frank, *Buy American*, 65.

3. Tazewell, *Newport News Shipbuilding*; Derdak, *International Directory of Company Histories*, 1:526–28; "A 'Make or Break' Strike in the South," *U.S. News and World Report*, February 12, 1979, 83–84; "New Unit Votes to Strike Giant Virginia Shipyard," *New York Times*, December 11, 1978, A-14.

4. Regional Director's Report, case no. V-C-82, June 13, 1937, Formal and Informal Unfair Labor Practices and Representation Case Files, 1935–1948, box 1580, NLRB; Northrup, *Organized Labor and the Negro*, 229–31; Halpern, "Iron Fist and Velvet Glove"; Jacoby, *Modern Manors*.

5. Brody, *Labor Embattled*, 100–102; Gross, *Making*; NLRB. v. Newport News Shipbuilding & Dry Dock, 308 U.S. 241 (1939); Northrup, *Organized Labor and the Negro*, 229–31; Brief for Newport News Shipbuilding and Dry Dock Company, case nos. 5-R-1557 and 5-R-1579, July 8, 1944, and Decision and Direction of Elections, NLRB, in the matter of Newport News Shipbuilding and Dry Dock Company and Industrial Union of Marine and Shipbuilding Workers of America, CIO, case nos.

5-R-1557 and 5-R-1579, August 4, 1944, Formal and Informal Unfair Labor Practices and Representation Case Files, 1935–1948, box 3904, NLRB.

6. "Shipyard Union Gets 4 Officers, 41 Delegates," *Baltimore Afro-American*, March 13, 1943, 20; Certification of Representatives, Newport News Shipbuilding and Dry Dock Company and Industrial Union of Marine and Shipbuilding Workers of America, CIO, case nos. 5-R-1557 and 5-R-1579, September 12, 1944, Formal and Informal Unfair Labor Practices and Representation Case Files, 1935–1948, box 3904, NLRB.

7. Moore interview; Thomas R. Bopeley to John A. Penello, February 17, 1959, Folder Re: Form 1085 (Financial Data), Records Relating to NLRB Involvement in the Industrial Security Program, 1957–1959, N3-25-87-1, NLRB; "Why You Should End the Tenneco-PSA 'Buddy System,'" in USWA election leaflet entitled "Vote USWA, Shipyard Organizing Committee," January 1978, folder 5, box 165, USWA Communications Department Records, PSU; "Shipyard Official Speaks," *Daily Press*, September 28, 1977, 30.

8. "PSA's Election Victories Reviewed," *Times-Herald*, June 24, 1979, 14; Lloyd McBride to President Carter, January 9, 1979, folder LA 5-10, box LA-9, White House Central File, JCL; "Va. Shipyard Workers Vote," *Washington Post*, May 10, 1972.

9. L. C. Ackerman, President and CEO, to Newport News Shipbuilders, March 2, 1972, box 2 of 2, Al Treherne Files, USWA Legal.

10. Jacoby, *Modern Manors*, 23, 205; Halpern, "Iron Fist and Velvet Glove"; Coppedge interview, 2010.

11. On "rights consciousness," see Lichtenstein, *State of the Union*, 191–211. On dichotomous relationship between labor and civil rights, see Frymer, *Black and Blue*. On labor and civil rights as interwoven, see Judith Stein, *Running Steel, Running America*, which covers the Newport News shipyard workers on pp. 192–93.

12. W. D. Wells to Herbert Hill, March 3, 1970, folder 15, box 140, HHP. One of the plaintiffs, Rev. J. C. Fauntleroy, was president of the local NAACP. See EEOC Conciliation Agreement, Thomas Mann, James Lassiter, Arthur Ford, and Reverend J. C. Fauntleroy, et al., and Newport News Shipbuilding and Dry Dock Company, March 25, 1966, folder 16, box 140, HHP; Northrup, *Organized Labor and the Negro*, 229–31; "Sweeping Fair Jobs Pact for Newport News Shipyard," *Norfolk Journal and Guide*, April 9, 1966, B2.

13. Hill, *Black Labor*, 206; "NAACP Files Job Bias Complaints Against Dixie Firms and Unions," *New York Amsterdam News*, August 7, 1965, 8; "Sweeping Fair Jobs Pact for Newport News Shipyard," *Norfolk Journal and Guide*, April 9, 1966, B2; "Milestones in the History of the U.S. Equal Employment Opportunity Commission," EEOC History: 35th Anniversary website, accessed July 1, 2016, http://www.eeoc.gov/eeoc/history/35th/milestones/1966.html; "Official Bias," *Congressional Record* 113, no. 146 (September 18, 1967), reprinted by National Industrial Council, box 64, series 5, NAM; "Concern over EEOC," *NAM Reports*, November 20, 1967, 6.

14. "Shipyard-U.S. Pact Protested," *Baltimore Sun*, April 26, 1966, C16.

15. "Union Denies Shipyard's Fair Employment Claim" *Norfolk Journal and Guide*, May 13, 1967, 2, and "Shipyard Controversy," *Norfolk Journal and Guide*, April 30, 1966, 27.

16. Wells to Hill, March 3, 1970.

17. Ibid.; Shirley Scheibla, "Barron's Reply to the Charge of Unjustified Criticism of the Role of the Equal Employment Opportunity Commission at the Newport News Shipbuilding and Dry Dock Co.," n.d. [ca. 1967], box 64, series 5, NAM.

18. "Mediators Urge Talks in Shipyard Dispute After Two-Hour Riot," *Wall Street Journal*, July 13, 1967, 11; "Strikers Riot at Shipyards in Virginia," *Chicago Tribune*, July 12, 1967, 3; an Associated Press photo in *Daily News-Record* (Harrisonburg, Va.), July 12, 1967, 1 reveals the mixed-race group of workers in the protest; Sherman Lafayette Demoss, letter, *Times-Herald*, February 26, 1979; "Union Approves Settlement Ending Shipyard Strike," *Washington Post*, July 17, 1967, A4.

19. Settlement Agreement, Hiawatha Darden et al. and Peninsula Shipbuilders Association v. Newport News Shipbuilding and Dry Dock Company, CA No. 95-69-NN (D.C. E. VA), August 3, 1971; "Motion to Dismiss the Complaint, Motion to Strike, and Motion for More Definite and Certain Statement," "Memorandum Opinion and Order," CA No. 95-69-NN, December 22, 1969; "Motion to Intervene Pursuant to Rule 24 of the Federal Rules of Civil Procedure," CA No. 95-69-NN, February 18, 1970, all in folder 15, box 140, HHP; "Ship Firm Talks Show Little Gain," *Baltimore Sun*, March 18, 1970, C7; "U.S. Accepts Job Program at Shipyard," *Baltimore Sun*, June 25, 1970, C9.

20. Braden, "Shoulder to Shoulder," 88; Hooks interview; Tazewell, *Newport News Shipbuilding*, 120–21, 173, 215; Reed, "Title VII," 33; Robinson, "Two Movements."

21. Coppedge interview, 2011; Coppedge interview, 2010.

22. A group of 1,200 professional and technical workers decided to leave the PSA in 1971. They formed a separate bargaining unit, called the Designers' Association of Newport News, which the company recognized for bargaining purposes. In 1976 they decided to affiliate with the USWA, and then voted for the USWA in a 1977 NLRB election. When the company refused to bargain seriously, the designers struck in April 1977. See "Chronology of Events Leading to Shipyard Strike," *Times-Herald*, January 21, 1979; McBride to President Carter, January 9, 1979; Sherman Lafayette Demoss, letter, *Times-Herald*, February 26, 1979; "Designers Reject Pact," *Washington Post*, November 28, 1971, A18; "Ship Designers Local Strikes Giant Yard at Newport News," *Baltimore Sun*, April 2, 1977, A9.

23. Chatak interview; Coppedge interview, 2011.

24. USWA, Local 8888, "Local 8888: Proud with a Purpose"; "An Editorial: All the Way with the PSA," *Journal and Guide*, January 25, 1978; Richard B. Freeman and James L. Medoff, *What Do Unions Do?*, 29.

25. Glass interview; Coppedge interview, 2010; "Union Organizers Savvy Strategists," *Industry Week*, August 7, 1978, 39.

26. "Steelworkers: The Family Union . . . Everyone Benefits," "PSA: The Give-Away 'Union,'" and "Vote for USWA Expected to Go above 60 Percent," January 1978,

folder 5, box 165, USWA Communications Department Records, PSU; "Union Organizers Savvy Strategists,"; "A Major Victory for Big Labor in Virginia," *Washington Post*, February 2, 1978, A1; "Tenneco Can Afford the Very Best," leaflet, n.d., Shipyard Organizing Committee (in the author's possession); Lewis quote from *PSA Shipbuilder*, special edition, January 28, 1978, box 2, Treherne files, USWA legal.

27. Hooks interview.

28. Coppedge interview, 2011.

29. Braden, "Shoulder to Shoulder," 88; Zucker, *To Increase Minority and Female Utilization*; Carpenter interview; Hooks interview.

30. Chatak interview; "Union Organizers Savvy Strategists,"; "Organizers Provided the Key Element for the 'Mission Impossible' Challenge at Huge Shipyard," *Steel Labor*, March 1978, 8.

31. Frankel interview; "Shipyard Official Speaks."

32. Newport News Shipbuilding and Dry Dock Company and Peninsula Shipbuilders' Association, 233 NLRB no. 207, ALJ at 16–25 (1977) 20, as quoted in "Brief on Behalf of the Intervenor USWA," Fourth Circuit Court of Appeals, No. 78-1900, NNS v. NLRB and USWA, p. 4, box LD-254, USWA Legal; William C. Humphrey [NLRB regional director] to E. D. David [PSA], September 13, 1978, and "Notice to Members Posted by Order of the National Labor Relations Board," n.d. [ca. 1978], folder 35, box LD-989, USWA Legal.

33. Carpenter interview; Moore interview.

34. McBride to President Carter, January 9, 1979; Keefer interview; David Beckwith, "Seyfarth, Shaw in DC," *Legal Times of Washington*, October 6, 1980, 32; National Organizing Coordinating Committee, AFL-CIO, "Seyfarth, Shaw, Fairweather and Geraldson," *RUB Sheet: Report on Union Busters*, no. 2 (March 1979), and "The 'gang-of-four,'" *RUB Sheet*, no. 21 (October 1980); Logan, "Union Avoidance Industry."

35. Carpenter interview; "An Editorial: All the Way with the PSA," *Journal and Guide*, January 25, 1978.

36. "Ministers Alliance Split Over Yard Union Battle," *Daily Press*, November 23, 1978; "Black Ministers Urge Shipyard to Negotiate," *Times-Herald*, November 17, 1978, 9; "Former State Senator, Newport News Pastor, W. Henry Maxwell Dies," *Daily Press*, November 13, 2010.

37. "Vote Tests Labor's Clout," *Times-Herald*, January 30, 1978, 9; "Union Organizers Savvy Strategists,"; Elmer Chatak to Al Treherne, March 1, 1978, folder 35, box LD-989, USWA Legal; "Health Blamed for King Absence," *Daily Press*, January 30, 1978; "Yard Tests Union Clout in South," *Times-Herald*, January 30, 1978, 9; "'Faceless, Nameless Numbers' Became Real People When Shipyard Workers Voted at Newport News," *Steel Labor*, February 1978, 8–9.

38. "Newport News," *Steel Labor*, February 1978, 3; Hooks interview.

39. "A Major Victory for Big Labor in Virginia,"; "How the News of USWA's Biggest Election Win Came," *Steel Labor*, March 1978, 10.

40. "Chronology of Events Leading to Shipyard Strike," *Times-Herald*, January 31, 1979; McBride to President Carter, January 9, 1979; "NLRB Overrules Objections,

Certifies Steelworkers in Newport News Shipbuilding Election," NLRB press release, November 1, 1978, box LD-257, USWA Legal.

41. Ralph W. Cousins to Dear Fellow Employees, November 10, 1978, box LD-257, USWA Legal.

42. "Newport News Finally Has Real Union as Shipyard Local Elects." *Steel Labor*, September 1978, 5, and "7500 Tell It as It Is to Lawbreaking Tenneco Bosses," *Steel Labor*, January 1979, 16; Carpenter interview.

43. "Yard Appeal Leaves Workers Without Pact," *Daily Press*, November 3, 1978, 1; BLS, *Analysis of Work Stoppages, 1978*, table 5.

44. Hooks interview; "7500 Tell It as It Is to Lawbreaking Tenneco Bosses"; "Yard Dispute Reaches Cabinet Level," *Times-Herald,* December 29, 1978, A1; D. T. Savas to Bruce Thraser, December 13, 1978, box LD-257, USWA Legal; Marshall interview.

45. "Federal Mediators Fail to Avert Yard Strike," *Daily Press*, January 30, 1979, A1; "Tenneco: Back to the 30s!," *Newport News Shipbuilding Strike Bulletin*, no. 1 (February 5, 1979).

46. According to the Virginia Right to Work Law, enacted in 1947 and revised in 1970, Article 3, Section 40.1-66, workers on strike were in violation of the law if they tried to prevent other workers from going to work. "Crosby Arrested at North Yard," *Times-Herald*, February 1, 1979, 3; "4 Steelworkers Arrested in Picket Line Dispute," *Times-Herald*, February 1, 1979, A1, and "8 Pickets Arrested Friday, Including Husband and Wife," February 3, 1979, 4; "Strikers at Newport News Urged to Return to Work," *Washington Post*, April 12, 1979, B1; Judith Stein, *Running Steel, Running America*, 193; Newport News Shipbuilding and Dry Dock Company v. National Labor Relations Board and United Steelworkers of America, 738 F.2d 1404 (U.S. Court of Appeals, 4th Cir. 1984); "Steelworker Fleet Braves Elements," *Newport News Shipbuilding Strike Bulletin*, no. 3 (February 19, 1979), 2.

47. Pike interview; "Potential for Chaos," *Times-Herald*, November 20, 1978; Lou Gioia, letter, *Daily Press*, November 18, 1979, 14; Jacob C. Vance, letter, *Times-Herald*, February 20, 1979; "Part of a Proud Union," *Steel Labor*, March 1979, 16. The workers' "Eighty-Eight! Close the Gate!" slogan referenced the Local 8888.

48. "High Stakes for Labor in a Shipyard Strike," *Business Week*, February 26, 1979, 49; "Local Firms Provide Discounts to Strikers," *Newport News Shipbuilding Strike Bulletin*, no. 4 (February 26, 1979): 3, and "Thrasher to Present USWA Check for $400,000," no. 3 (February 19, 1979): 1, and "Child Services Program Gears Up," no. 3 (February 19, 1979): 3.

49. Ad by Newport News Shipbuilding and Dry Dock Company from *Daily Press*, March 28, 1979; "Strikers at Newport News Urged to Return to Work."

50. Settlement Agreement, Case 5-CA-10616, Newport News Shipbuilding & Dry Dock Company, January 29, 1980, and "Notice to Employees," box LD-258, USWA Legal; "Strikers at Newport News Urged to Return to Work."

51. "A 'Make or Break' Strike in the South,"; "Strikers at Newport News Urged to Return to Work" ; Frankel interview; undated memo by Carl Frankel with notes for speech to AFL-CIO Legal Services Meeting, box LD-990, USWA Legal.

52. "Eyewitness from Newport News," *Steel Labor*, May 1979, 3; "Local 888 Members Postpone Strike Suspension," *Newport News Shipbuilding Strike Bulletin*, no. 11 (April 16, 1979): 1.

53. Hooks interview.

54. Newport News Shipbuilding and Dry Dock Company, Petitioner, v. National Labor Relations Board, Respondent and United Steelworkers of America, Intervenor, 738 F.2d 1404 (U.S. Court of Appeals, 4th Cir. 1984); Glass interview.

55. Hooks interview; "Local 8888 Striker," *Newport News Shipbuilding Strike Bulletin*, no. 13 (April 30, 1979): 4.

56. "Police Unleash Vicious, Unprovoked Attack," *Newport News Shipbuilding Strike Bulletin*, no. 12 (April 23, 1979): 1; Boyd-Williams interview; "Police Run Amok," *Steel Labor*, May, 1979, 3.

57. "2 Acquitted of Charges in Yard Strike," *Times-Herald*, January 12, 1980, 3.

58. "Strike Suspended," *Newport News Shipbuilding Strike Bulletin*, no. 13 (April 30, 1979): 1; Hooks interview.

59. Gross, *Broken Promise*, 242–46.

60. "Court Takes Middle Ground in Shipyard Election Appeal," *Daily Press*, March 3, 1979, 1; Frankel interview; "Torn Blank Ballots Found, NLRB Hearing Judge Told," *Daily Press*, March 29, 1979, A3; Carl Frankel notes, January 28, 1980, Speech File, box LD-257, USWA Legal; "A Chronology of Events that Led from Courtroom to Bargaining," *Steel Labor*, April 1980, 10.

61. "News Update for Tenneco Shipyard Workers from the USWA," no. 10 (September 27, 1979): box LD-257, USWA Legal.

62. "A Chronology of Events that Led from Courtroom to Bargaining"; Marshall interview; Frankel interview.

63. "Newport News Negotiators Report Progress in Shipyard Talks," *Steel Labor*, January 1980, 6; Newport News Shipbuilding and Dry Dock Company and United Steelworkers of America Local 8888, Collective Bargaining Agreement for the Term March 31, 1980, through Midnight October 31, 1983, 2971/14, USWA, District 35 Records, GSU.

64. "Labor Confrontation Ends as Yard, Union Sign Pact," *Daily Press*, April 1, 1980, 1; USWA, *Eighty-Eight Close the Gate*; Coppedge interview, 2010; Newport News Shipbuilding and Dry Dock Company and United Steelworkers of America Local 8888, Collective Bargaining Agreement for the Term March 31, 1980, through Midnight October 31, 1983, appendix D; USWA Local 8888, "Local 8888: Proud with a Purpose," 6.

65. Coppedge interview, 2011; USWA Local 8888, "Local 8888: Proud with a Purpose," 6–7.

66. "Legislative Committee Endorses John Dalton," *PSA Shipbuilder* 20, no. 11 (November 1977): box 2, Al Treherne's files, USWA legal; Moore interview; "Political Action," *Voyager: USWA Local 8888*, February 1983, 4 (in author's possession); Hooks interview.

67. "USWA Hails Victory at Newport News Shipyard," USWA Press Release, October 28, 1983, box 2, Al Treherne Files, USWA Legal.

68. Boyd-Williams interview.

69. "Big Test Nears on Benefits for Pregnancy," *Wall Street Journal*, January 3, 1983, 25; "Court Expands Pregnancy Law," *Los Angeles Times*, June 21, 1983, SD1; EEOC charge filed by Arnol Manning, USWA representative, October 19, 1979, in author's possession; Newport News Shipbuilding Co. V. EEOC 462 U.S. 669 (1983); Rowland, *Boundaries of Her Body*, 162–66; Goldstein, *Constitutional Rights of Women*, 488; Jacquelyn Dowd Hall, "Long Civil Rights Movement."

70. Pike interview; Hooks interview; Lichtenstein, *State of the Union*; Lichtenstein, *Most Dangerous Man in Detroit*; Fraser, " 'Labor Question.' "

71. AFL-CIO, "List of Large NLRB Elections"; Marshall, *Labor in the South*; "Largest Single NLRB Vote at Newport News," *Steel Labor*, March 1978, 7; steelworker figure from "Resolution Number 11: Organizing," *Proceedings, 19th Constitutional Convention, United Steelworkers of America*, September 18–22, 1978, Atlantic City, (Pittsburgh: United Steelworkers of America), 113.

72. Goldfield, *Decline of Organized Labor*, 90–91; Judith Stein, *Pivotal Decade*, xi–xii; Judith Stein, *Running Steel, Running America*, 192–271; Harrison and Bluestone, *Great U-Turn*, 21–52. See chapter 3 for discussion of manufacturing employers' deepening resistance to unions.

Chapter Five

1. Rowan and Barr, *Employee Relations Trends*, 82–83; Minchin, *Hiring the Black Worker*; MacLean, *Freedom Is Not Enough*, 76–90; Frederickson, *Looking South*, 137–79; Jacquelyn Dowd Hall et al., *Like a Family*, 66–67; Wright, *Sharing the Prize*, 107–14; "Cannon's Vote: A Signal to the Industry," *Charlotte Observer*, November 22, 1974; Lloyd Little, "Reasons behind Cannon Mills Union Defeat Examined," *Carolina Financial Times*, December 2, 1974.

2. Literature on globalization that seeks to identify its economic and political agents includes Stiglitz, *Globalization and Its Discontents*; Sassen, *Mobility of Labor and Capital*; Ellen Israel Rosen, *Making Sweatshops*; Greider, *One World, Ready or Not*; and Aaronson, *Taking Trade to the Streets*.

3. Wright, *Sharing the Prize*, 113–14; Minchin, *Empty Mills*, 4; BLS, *Handbook of Labor Statistics*, table 66. In 1963 there were 885,400 textile mill product employees, compared to 1,009,800 in 1973. Minchin, *Hiring the Black Worker*, 9; Lauren A. Murray, "Unraveling Employment Trends in Textiles and Apparel," *Monthly Labor Review*, August 1995, 62–71; Rowan and Barr, *Employee Relations Trends*, 11; Murray Finley, "Remarks," transcript of press conference at AFL-CIO headquarters in Washington, D.C., October 31, 1977, box 85, Office of the President, George Meany Files, UMD; Susan E. Shank and Patricia M. Getz, "Employment and Unemployment: Developments in 1985," *Monthly Labor Review*, February 1986, 6. For more on changes in textile and apparel, see Jane Lou Collins, *Threads*; Gereffi and

Korzeniewicz, *Commodity Chains and Global Capitalism*; Bonacich, *Global Production*; Minchin, *Empty Mills*; Ellen Israel Rosen, *Making Sweatshops*.

4. "The Passing of Mr. Charlie," *Forbes*, July 15, 1972, 22; Minchin, " 'It Knocked This City to Its Knees' "; "Businessman in the News," *North Carolina*, June 1971, 13; Vanderburg, *Cannon Mills and Kannapolis*; "Murdock's Rein Changes Life at Southern Mill Town," *Los Angeles Times*, August 25, 1985; "N.C. Mill Employees Bar Union," *Washington Post*, November 21, 1974, A14.

5. Vanderburg, *Cannon Mills and Kannapolis*, 50–57, 93–95; Hall et al., *Like a Family*, 187–95; Irons, *Testing the New Deal*, 123–32.

6. George Perkel to William Pollock, September 18, 1968, M86-403, box 27, TWUA; Daniel, *Culture of Misfortune*, 143; Minchin, *What Do We Need a Union For?*, 59; Griffith, *Crisis of American Labor*, 46–61.

7. Harold Daoust to William Pollock, April 16, 1957, MSS 396, box 490, TWUA; Lloyd P. Vaughn to John Livingston, June 24, 1957, box 56/32, AFL-CIO ODR; John D. Pedigo, "Report: Analysis and Recommendations, Cannon Situation," n.d. [ca. 1958], MSS 396, box 490, TWUA; H. S. Williams to William Pollock, November 14, 1957, MSS 396, box 126, TWUA; "Textile Mills in South Start Granting Pay Boosts," *Wall Street Journal*, February 2, 1959, 22.

8. "Cannon Mills Workers Bar the Union Again," *New York Times*, November 22, 1974, 19.

9. MacLean, *Freedom Is Not Enough*, 76–90; Minchin, *Hiring the Black Worker*; Wright, *Sharing the Prize*, 107–14.

10. Janet Patterson, interview by Alexandra Lescaze, part 1, February 5, 2002, transcript, *Where Do You Stand? Stories from an American Mill* (2004), collection held by Alexandra Lescaze, New York, N.Y. For more information on this film, see http://www.newsreel.org/nav/title.asp?tc=CN0169.

11. MacLean, *Freedom Is Not Enough*, 78; Minchin, *Hiring the Black Worker*, 31.

12. Minchin, *Hiring the Black Worker*, 240–45.

13. "Town Meeting Forum," June 1, 1954, box 5, M90-226, TWUA; "Segregation Controversy Thwarts Union Plans for Organizing Drive," *Wall Street Journal*, February 5, 1957, 1.

14. MacLean, "Redesigning Dixie with Affirmative Action"; "Memorandum in Support of Application for Issuance of Order to Show Cause Why Defendant Should Not Be Held in Contempt," EEOC v. Cannon Mills Company, Civil Action No. C-65-S-69, U.S. District Court for the Middle District of North Carolina, Salisbury Division, April 1, 1976, box 79, Cannon; Consent Decree, United States v. Cannon Mills Company, February 24, 1971, Civil Action No. C-65-S-69, box 79, Cannon; "U.S., Cannon Mills Settle Job Bias Suit," *Baltimore Afro-American*, March 6, 1971, 3.

15. Robert J. Denrow to Eugene T. Bost, May 10, 1977, box 79, Cannon; Minchin, *Hiring the Black Worker*, 113, 159; worker quote from *Hicks v. Cannon Mills*, found in Minchin, *Hiring the Black Worker*, 188.

16. Sidney Hollander Associates for TWUA, "Attitudes of Cannon Workers." The author's analysis shows that 57 percent of African American workers sup-

ported the union, compared to 31 percent of white workers. "Mr. Charlie's Ghost Lingers On," *Boston Globe*, December 29, 1974.

17. "Memorandum in Support of Application for Issuance of Order to Show Cause Why Defendant Should Not Be Held in Contempt," EEOC v. Cannon Mills Company; "Appeal of the Regional Director's Refusal to Issue a Complaint," Cannon Mills and TWUA, before the NLRB, Case Nos. 11-CA-6108 and 11-CA-6115, June 20, 1975, box 79, Cannon; Michin, *Hiring the Black Worker*, 61; "Cannon Settles Bias Suit," *Wall Street Journal*, January 15, 1982, 12; EEOC affidavit, Daisy R. Crawford, June 5, 1975, box 79, Cannon; EEOC charge of discrimination, Daisy R. Crawford, June 5, 1975, box 79, Cannon; Adgie O'Bryant Jr. to Cannon Mills Company, April 1, 1976, box 79, Cannon. See also MacLean, "Redesigning Dixie with Affirmative Action."

18. Bob Freeman and Raymond Melton, interview by George Stoney, August 24, 1991, transcript, tape 16G, 43–44, Uprising of '34 collection, GSU.

19. Ibid.; "Cannon Mills, Union Prepare for Showdown in Kannapolis," *Charlotte Observer*, August 29, 1974, 1A.

20. William Gordon, interview, July 19, 1978, TWUA Oral History Project, State Historical Society of Wisconsin, Madison, Wis.; Jorgensen interview.

21. Robert Freeman to Cannon People, n.d. [ca. 1974], box 83, M86-171, TWUA.

22. Robert Freeman to Nick Zonarich, March 5, 1975, M86-403, box 27, TWUA; Robert Freeman to Sol Stetin, July 31, 1974, M86-403, box 27, TWUA.

23. George Perkel to Sol Stetin, August 6, 1974, M86-403, box 27, TWUA; "Union Organizer Works Cannon Mills Facility," *Charlotte Observer*, October 13, 1973; Robert Freeman to Sol Stetin, July 10, 1974, M86-403, box 27, TWUA.

24. Sidney Hollander Associates for TWUA, "Attitudes of Cannon Workers"; A Cannon Employee for Almost 40 Years to Mr. Hornaday, November 7, 1974, and unsigned letter to Don Holt, November 19, 1974, both in box 80, Cannon; "N.C. Mill Employees Bar Union"; Robert Freeman to Sol Stetin, July 31, 1974, and George Perkel to Irving Kahan, September 27, 1974, both in M86-403, box 27, TWUA; "Compare Cannon and These Union Organized Textile Plants," Cannon leaflet, ca. August 20, 1974, box 81, Cannon.

25. Sidney Hollander Associates for TWUA, "Attitudes of Cannon Workers."

26. Ibid.; Delores Gambrell, interview by Alexandra Lescaze, interview 1, February 5, 2002, transcript, *Where Do You Stand?*

27. Sidney Hollander Associates for TWUA, "Attitudes of Cannon Workers"; Leonard Chapman, interview by Alexandra Lescaze, January 24, 2002, transcript, *Where Do You Stand?*

28. Sidney Hollander Associates for TWUA, "Attitudes of Cannon Workers," 26.

29. Ibid.; MacLean, *Freedom Is Not Enough*; MacLean, "Redesigning Dixie with Affirmative Action"; Estelle Spry to Dear Sir or Whoever This Consurns [*sic*], August 20, 1974, box 80, Cannon.

30. Scott Hoyman to Reed Johnston, August 13, 1974, M86-403, box 12, TWUA; Cannon Mills Co., Employer, and TWUA, Petitioner, Decision and Direction of

Election, October 29, 1974, box 81, Cannon; "Across the Lake in Kannapolis," *Textile Industries*, January 1975, 45; "Cannon Mills is Told to Hold Union Vote at Certain Facilities," *Wall Street Journal*, October 30, 1974, 17; "N.C. Mill Employees Bar Union."

31. Freeman to Stetin, July 10, 1974; "When Cannon Mills Drinks a Coca-Cola, the Politicians in Cabarrus County Burp," n.d. [ca. 1974], box 27, M86-403, TWUA; "Cannon Mills Suit Focuses Attention on Company Town," *Greensboro Daily News*, July 14, 1974, A1; "Cannon and Police Sued by TWUA," *Kannapolis (N.C.) Daily Independent*, July 7, 1974, 1A; Eugene T. Bost to Harold Hornaday, April 9, 1976, box 80, Cannon.

32. F. L. Wilson to All Cannon Mills Supervisors, October 31, 1974, and "Don't Let History Repeat Itself," n.d., both in box 80, Cannon; Freeman and Melton, interview by Stoney, tape 15G, 24–25; L. C. Wright and Mary Wright, interview by George Stoney, December 2, 1992, transcript, 1–3, Uprising of '34 Papers, GSU.

33. Cannon Mills Company to the Men and Women of Cannon, August 14, 1974, box 81, Cannon; Robert Freeman to Sol Stetin, November 27, 1974, M86-403, box 27, TWUA; cartoons in box 80, Cannon; training manual quote is from Raymond Brown, "A Quiz for Foremen," n.d. [ca. 1974], box 81, Cannon.

34. "Invitation List for Friday Meeting of Community," November 22, 1974, box 81, Cannon; L. D. Coltrane to Don S. Holt, November 15, 1974, box 80, Cannon.

35. "N.C. Mill Employees Bar Union"; Cannon Mills Co., Employer, and TWUA, Petitioner, Case No. 11-RC-3947, Tally of Ballots, November 20, 1974, box 81, Cannon; "Cannon Workers Assess Future After Historic Vote," *Charlotte Observer*, November 22, 1974, 2B.

36. Letters and telegrams found in box 80, Cannon. Yarn company CEO quote is from John L. Stickley to Don Holt, November 24, 1974, and J. P. Stevens quote is from Robert T. Stevens to Don Holt, November 22, 1974.

37. "Cannon Won, But TWUA Displayed Strength," *Charlotte Observer*, November 24, 1974, 12D; "Cannon's Vote: A Signal to the Industry," *Charlotte Observer*, November 22, 1974; "Reasons behind Cannon Mills Union Defeat Examined," *Carolina Financial Times*, December 2, 1974.

38. BLS, *Handbook of Labor Statistics*, table 66; BLS, All employees, thousands, textile mills, seasonally adjusted, Employment, Hours and Earnings, National, Current Employment Statistics.

39. Chorev, *Remaking U.S. Trade Policy*.

40. Vanderburg, *Cannon Mills and Kannapolis*, 161–67; Hickman Price to Solomon Barkin, November 17, 1961, M93-041, box 1, TWUA.

41. Solomon Barkin to Victor Canzano, July 13, 1962, M93-041, box 1, TWUA; John D. Morris, "Kennedy's Tactics Advance Trade Bill," *New York Times*, April 22, 1962, 12E; Chorev, *Remaking U.S. Trade Policy*, 71–101; Dickerson, *Textiles and Apparel*, 348–60, 376–80.

42. Choi et al., *Multi-Fibre Arrangement*, 86–119; Cline, *Future of World Trade*, 11.

43. The Textile Workers Union of America and the Amalgamated Clothing Workers Union merged to form the Amalgamated Clothing and Textile Workers

Union in 1976. Minchin, *Empty Mills*, 73; John Hamrick to Harold Hornaday, January 12, 1978, box 63, Cannon.

44. "Unions, Firms Urge Textile Import Curbs," *AFL-CIO News*, July 8, 1978, 1; "Remarks by AFL-CIO President George Meany at the Joint Labor-Industry News Briefing in the Caucus Room, Cannon House Office Building," June 29, 1978, box 85, series 6, Office of the President, George Meany Files, UMD; ATMI, press release, November 11, 1978, folder 464, box 33, Mildred Gwin Andrews Papers, Southern Historical Collection, Louis Round Wilson Library, University of North Carolina, Chapel Hill, N.C.; "3 Bills are Vetoed as Aiding Inflation," *New York Times*, November 12, 1978, 32; Destler, *American Trade Politics*, 61–62; Chorev, *Remaking U.S. Trade Policy*, 140.

45. Peter Murphy to Landon Butler and Laurie Lucey, White House Office, October 24, 1978, box 137, Landon Butler Papers, Office of the Chief of Staff, JCL; "Textile-Apparel Accord Sets Tighter Import Curb," *New York Times*, February 27, 1979, D6; Robert J. Samuelson, "Textile Trade: Bargaining from Weakness," *Los Angeles Times*, March 6, 1979, C5.

46. "We Win One," *Southern Textile News*, March 12, 1979, 4.

47. TWUA Executive Council Meeting Minutes, May 20–24, 1974, box 39, M86-403, TWUA; Minchin, *"Don't Sleep with Stevens!"*; Minchin, *Empty Mills*; Townley, *Labor Law Reform*, 148; ATMI Congressional Report, June 30, 1978, box 33, Mildred Gwin Andrews Papers.

48. Dickerson, *Textiles and Apparel*, 365; "Labor-Industry Coalition Formed to Support Fiber, Fabric and Apparel Import Control Program," press release, March 19, 1985, 5619-004, box 199, ACTWU. In addition to the ACTWU and the ILGWU the coalition included the ATMI, the American Apparel Manufacturing Association, and other industry groups such as those representing hosiery, uniforms, knitwear, and cotton and wool growers.

49. ATMI Annual Report, 1985, and FFACT Executive Committee Report, January 17, 1986, both in 5619-004, box 199, ACTWU; Destler, *American Trade Politics*; Dickerson, *Textiles and Apparel*, 365.

50. Robert Freeman to Scott Hoyman, May 18, 1976, and John Kissack to Paul Swaity, August 16, 1979, both in M86-403, box 27, TWUA; "Union Kicks Off Campaign," *Kannapolis (N.C.) Daily Independent*, September 18, 1980, 1; "Cannon Improves Employee Benefits," *Southern Textile News*, December 20, 1980; Otto Stolz to Cannon People, November 24, 1980, box 2, ACTWU vs. Cannon Mills Papers, GSU.

51. "A Rough Year for Cannon," *New York Times*, December 30, 1980, D1; Vanderburg, *Cannon Mills and Kannapolis*; "New Day at Cannon," *Charlotte Observer*, January 1, 1979.

52. "David Murdock Beats the Union," *New York Times*, October 20, 1985, F1; "At Textile Mills, New Owner Tactics Rip Good Will Woven of Paternalism," *Washington Post*, October 10, 1985, A3; "Cannon Mills Sold," *Kannapolis (N.C.) Daily Independent*, February 4, 1982, 1.

53. Abernathy, *Stitch in Time*, 189–90; Cynthia D. Anderson, *Social Conse-quences of Economic Restructuring*, 52; "Why David Murdock is So Afraid of a Union," *Business Week*, October 14, 1985, 43; "Firings at Cannon Mills Came With-out Warning," *Charlotte Observer*, June 29, 1982, B1; Henry Mann and Griff Morgan to Jim Walraven, May 12, 1982, 5619-038, box 11, ACTWU.

54. "A Test of Loyalty," *Winston-Salem Journal*, October 6, 1985, 1; "Murdock's Reign Changes Life at Southern Mill Town," *Los Angeles Times*, August 25, 1985, H1.

55. Robert Freeman to Sol Stetin, March 26, 1982, 5619-016, box 11, ACTWU; Pe-ter D. Hart Research Associates, "A Survey of Attitudes toward Union Representation among Cannon Mill Workers," August 1985, 5619-004, box 34, ACTWU; John Kissack to Paul Swaity, August 16, 1979, box 2, ACTWU vs. Cannon Mills Papers, GSU.

56. Minutes of Management Meeting Entitled "Cannon Mills," June 17, 1985, 5619-007, box 110, ACTWU; Peter D. Hart Research Associates to Amalgamated Clothing and Textile Workers Union, August 20, 1985, 5619-017, box 110, ACTWU; "Discrimination Suit Settled by Cannon," *Daily News Record*, January 13, 1982; "Cannon Settles Bias Suit," *Wall Street Journal*, January 15, 1982, 12; Peter D. Hart Research Associates, "Survey of Attitudes."

57. "David Murdock Says We Must Stand for Something," August 16, 1984, 5916-016, box 11, ACTWU; "Next Big Union Battle May Be Shaping Up at Cannon," *Charlotte Observer*, July 30, 1984, 2D; John Kissack to Sol Stetin, July 25, 1978, M86-403, box 27, TWUA; Freeman and Melton, interview by Stoney, tape 16G, 43–44; Bruce Raynor to Jack Sheinkman, Charles Sallee, and Jim Walraven, January 6, 1986, 5916-004, box 34, ACTWU; Memo re. Communications Campaign, May 9, 1985, 5619-016, box 11, ACTWU. The budget was extrapolated from the monthly budget found in Memo to George Solomons, re: Cannon, April 23, 1985, 5619-004, box 34, ACTWU, and Raynor to Sheinkman, Sallee, and Walraven, January 6, 1986. Free-man's budget is in Jack Goldstein to William DuChessi, January 14, 1975, M86-403, box 27, TWUA. "ACTW Files Petition with NLRB for Secret Ballot at Cannon," *Daily News Record*, August 7, 1985; "At Textile Mill, New Owner's Tactics Rip Good Will Woven of Paternalism."

58. "Union Continues to Try to Mislead You," April 11, 1985, 5610-016, box 11, ACTWU; "Murdock Letter Discloses Cannon Mills Merger Talks," *Los Angeles Times*, August 15, 1985, SC_C1; David M. Murdock to Cannon Employees, August 8, 1985, 5619-017, box 110, ACTWU.

59. ACTWU Legal Department, "Transcript of Captive Audience Video, Week of August 12, 1985," 5619-017, box 110, ACTWU; ACTWU Legal Department, "Can-non Mills," listing of fifty-eight Cannon employees describing supervisor actions, n.d., and Harold D. Kingsmore to Fellow Associates, September 5, 1985 (emphasis in original document), both in 5619-017, box 110, ACTWU.

60. "Merger Discussions Disclosed by Cannon Mills," *New York Times*, Au-gust 20, 1985, D5.

61. See chapter 3 for discussion of manufacturers. Bronfenbrenner, "We'll Close!"

62. Fleischman and Peckenham interview.

63. "Mortgaged! To Buy Foreign Imports," May 28, 1985, 5619-016, box 11, ACTWU.

64. Paul Filson and Mark Fleischman to Jack Sheinkman, May 7, 1985, 5619-004, box 34, ACTWU; Memo re. Communications Campaign, May 9, 1985, and "The Union Is Real Security," June 24, 1985, both in 5619-016, box 11, ACTWU; Peter D. Hart Research Associates, to ACTWU, August 20, 1985, and Release in Full and Covenant Not to Sue, Bobby J. Kemp, July 10, 1986, Affidavit, Bobby Joe Kemp, October 3, 1985, both in 5619-017, box 110, ACTWU.

65. "Which Will You Choose," leaflet, n.d. [ca. September 1985], 5619-017, box 111, ACTWU; "Speedway Activities Support 'Buy American',", 9, and "Letters Will Make a Difference," 2, *Cannon News* 15, no. 10 (October 2, 1985).

66. "Cannon Employee Questions Answered by Mr. Murdock," n.d., 5619-017, box 110, ACTWU. A typed note indicates that this document contains Murdock's answers to frequent employee questions, and a handwritten note indicates that it was passed out at Cannon's press conference on October 9, 1985. "Union Fails at Cannon by Wide Vote," *Washington Post*, October 12, 1985, A10; Cannon Mills Co., Inc. and ACTWU, Tally of Ballots, 11-RC-5314, October 10, 1985, 5619-017, box 110, ACTWU; "Cannon Workers Turn Back Union by an Overwhelming 2 to 1 Margin," *Kannapolis (N.C.) Daily Independent*, October 11, 1985, 1; "Fieldcrest Agrees to Buy Cannon Mills From David Murdock for $250 Million," *Wall Street Journal*, December 5, 1985, 22.

67. ACTWU General Executive Board Meeting, March 17, 1986, 5619-030, box 5, ACTWU; "Textile Union is Struggling to Organize Cannon Mills Workers as Ranks Shrink," *Wall Street Journal*, January 16, 1985, 12; Report to Executive Board from Organizing Committee, July 17, 1982, 5619-007, box 42, ACTWU.

68. TWUA Executive Council, January 27–31, 1975; Atlanta, Ga., M86-403, box 39, TWUA.

69. Richard Appelbaum and Nelson Lichtenstein, "New World of Retail Supremacy"; Lichtenstein, "Return of Merchant Capitalism"; Abernathy, *Stitch in Time*.

70. Bonacich and Wilson, *Getting the Goods*; Ellen Israel Rosen, *Making Sweatshops*, 191; "Where's the Beef?," Response to the Retail Industry Trade Action Coalition, July 31, 1984, 5619-004, box 194, ACTWU; Minchin, *Empty Mills*, 116.

71. Dickerson, *Textile and Apparel*, 480; Minchin, *Empty Mills*, esp. 136.

72. Judith Stein, *Running Steel, Running America*, 203–4; Judis, *Paradox of American Democracy*, 114–15. For examples of union efforts to pass this legislation, see "Almost 1,000,000 Lost," Industrial Union Department brochure, n.d. [ca. 1972], M86-019, box 57, TWUA; on the executive council of the AFL-CIO's taskforce to move a grassroots program to support Burke-Hartke, see Sol Stetin to Howard Chester, October 6, 1972, M86-019, box 57, TWUA.

73. Minutes, ACTWU General Executive Board, January 13–16, 1986, box 5, 5619-030, ACTWU; Jorgensen interview. For a critique of labor's unwillingness to forge such partnerships more broadly, see Frank, *Buy American*. See Minchin, *Empty Mills*, 235, on ACTWU global partnerships in the 1990s.

74. Minchin, *Empty Mills*, 186–190.

75. Cynthia D. Anderson, *Social Consequences of Economic Restructuring*, 73; "Background on Union Organizing at Cannon Mills," n.d. [ca. 2000], 6000-026, box 9, ACTWU; Kem Taylor, interview by Alexandra Lescaze, part 2, May 21, 2002, transcript, *Where Do You Stand?*

76. "Background on Union Organizing at Cannon Mills," n.d. [ca. 2000], 6000-026, box 9, ACTWU; Elboyd Deal and unnamed workers labeled "various / union," interview by Stoney and Associates, December 4, 1992, transcript, tape 286B, Uprising of '34 Papers, GSU; "NLRB Orders New Election at Fieldcrest," *Kannapolis (N.C.) Daily Independent*, September 5, 1995, 1; "NLRB Orders New Union Vote for Fieldcrest Cannon Inc. Plants," *Wall Street Journal*, September 6, 1995, eastern edition; "Union Apparent Loser in Election," *Charlotte Observer*, August 14, 1997, 1A.

77. "Victory for Union Plant in South is a Labor Milestone," *New York Times*, June 25, 1999, A16; "Union Claims Victory at Pillowtex Plants," *Wall Street Journal*, June 25, 1999, A2; "25-Year War Over: Historic Union Contract Ratified," *Kannapolis (N.C.) Independent Tribune*, February 11, 2000, 1.

78. Minchin, "'It Knocked This City to Its Knees,'" 295–96; Minchin, *Empty Mills*, 224; Catherine Carlock, "D. H. Griffin: You Know the Name. Now Meet the Man," *Triad Business Journal*, March 28, 2014.

79. Frank Bruni, "The Billionaire Who is Planning His 125th Birthday," *New York Times Magazine*, March 3, 2011; North Carolina Research Campus website, accessed October 4, 2016, https://transforming-science.com; MURDOCK Study website, http://www.murdock-study.com/.

80. Peter A. Hall and David W. Soskice, *Varieties of Capitalism*; Stiglitz, *Globalization and Its Discontents*. The German textile and apparel union was the Gewerkschaft Textil-Bekleidung. It later joined IG Metall. The statistics on German textiles were found in Campbell, *European Labor Unions*, 183.

81. Richard M. Locke, *Remaking the Italian Economy*, 140–47; Leslie Stein, "General Measures."

Chapter Six

1. Halsey interview; "NLRB Orders Union Election for Woodies," *Washington Post*, May 3, 1979, C1; Kraft Opinion Research Center, "Survey of Opinion toward Unions."

2. Lichtenstein, "Return of Merchant Capitalism"; Lichtenstein, *Retail Revolution*, 326–31; Moreton, *To Serve God and Wal-Mart*, 50–55; Greenhouse, *Big Squeeze*, 135–57; Lichtenstein, *Wal-Mart*; Ortega, *In Sam We Trust*; BLS, "Occupational Employment and Wages—May 2015," Economic News Release, March 30, 2016; "Wal-Mart Suggests Ways to Cut Employee Benefit Costs," *New York Times*, October 26, 2005, C1.

3. Bluestone, *Retail Revolution*; BLS, *Perspectives on Working Women*, 10, 74.

4. NLRB Annual Reports, 1960–1989; BLS, Employment, Hours and Earnings from the Current Employment Statistics, (National, SIC basis), Not Seasonally Adjusted, Retail Trade, SIC Codes 52–59, 1960–1989. An average of 32,197 retail workers annually voted in NLRB elections in the 1960s, compared to 41,167 in the

1970s. Full annual data is available in Windham, "Knocking on Labor's Door," Ph.D. diss., table 6; Barbara Cottman Job, "Employment and Pay Trends in the Retail Industry," *Monthly Labor Review,* March 1980, 40–43.

5. Lichtenstein, *Retail Revolution;* Bluestone, *Retail Revolution.*

6. "Our Past," *Woodlothian, 100 Years,* February 1980, folder 305, series V, subseries A, container 8, Woodward & Lothrop Records, Historical Society of Washington, D.C.; Lisicky, *Woodward & Lothrop,* 24–26.

7. Moore interview; Opler, *For All White-Collar Workers;* "Regional Director's Report in Matter of Woodward & Lothrop Corporation and Building Service Employees International Union, Local #82," Case No. V-C-371, n.d. [ca. 1938], and Certification on Counting and Tabulation of Ballots, October 29, 1940, both in box 1253, NLRB Formal and Informal Unfair Labor Practices and Representation Case Files, 1935–48, NLRB; Constitution of the Woodward & Lothrop Employees' Association, n.d. [ca. 1938], folder 65, series I, subseries B, container 2, Woodward & Lothrop Records.

8. "Store Workers Vote to Continue Own Union Setup," *Washington Post,* August 12, 1947, 9; Franz E. Daniel to Joseph F. Heath, April 19, 1956, box 55, AFL-CIO ODR; "Official Notice," August 1, 1955, Andrew Parker to Dear Store Member, May 26, 1952, and Memo to Andrew Parker from Thelma Hunt and Curtis E. Tuthill, May 5, 1952, all in folder 65, series I, subseries B, container 2, Woodward & Lothrop Records; Jacoby, *Modern Manors,* 95–142.

9. "Woodward and Lothrop Maintain Segregation," *Baltimore Afro-American,* November 24, 1956, 6.

10. "Negroes Boycott 5 Big Washingtonian Stores for a Day," *Wall Street Journal,* March 28, 1958, 12; "Labor Aide Hints Merit Hiring Near," *Baltimore Afro-American,* April 26, 1958, 5; "Group Demands Change," *Baltimore Afro-American,* May 31, 1961, 20; "Negro Job Progress is Seen Lagging in Government, Trade," *Washington Post,* October 23, 1965, B1; Lisicky, *Woodward & Lothrop,* 98.

11. Dixon interview.

12. Harrington, *The Other America;* Harrington, *Retail Clerks,* 2–7.

13. Cohen, *Consumers' Republic;* "Retail Clerks Union: High Hopes," *Retail Week,* July 15, 1979, 50–53; Lichtenstein, *Retail Revolution,* 178–79; "Unions' Organizing Push Could Alter D.C. Business," *Washington Post,* April 22, 1979, G1. In 1977 the Retail Clerks International Association changed its name to the Retail Clerks International Union. Job, "Employment and Pay Trends in the Retail Industry."

14. Petrovic and Hamilton, "Making Global Markets," 111, 136–37; Bluestone, *Retail Revolution,* 120–26; Lichtenstein, *Retail Revolution,* 46–69. Wal-Mart, Kmart, and Target chain stores all debuted in 1962.

15. Bluestone, *Retail Revolution,* 98–105, 108; Benson, *Counter Cultures,* 9–10; Mathias interview; Lichtenstein, *Retail Revolution,* 9–10.

16. Author's analysis of BLS, "Employment, Hours and Earnings from the Current Employment Statistics (National, SIC basis), Not Seasonally Adjusted, Retail Trade and All Private, Average Weekly Earnings of Production Workers, 1947–2002." In 1949, retail workers made an average $38.42 per week compared to average weekly

wage of $50.24 for all non-supervisory workers. In 1979, those figures were $138.62 and $219.91 per week, respectively. In 1989, the figures were $188.72 and $334.24, respectively. For comparable data for the years 1947 to 2002, see Windham, "Knocking on Labor's Door," Ph.D. diss., table 7.

17. "Our Future," *Woodlothian, 100 Years*, February 1980, folder 305, series V, subseries A, container 8, Woodward & Lothrop Records; 1979 annual report, folder 75, series III, subseries A, Woodward & Lothrop Records; Ellen Israel Rosen, *Making Sweatshops*, 178–81; Bluestone, *Retail Revolution*, 23; Lichtenstein, *Wal-Mart*, 14; "Woodies Slide into Extinction Began Decades Ago," *Washington Post*, June 25, 1995, B1.

18. "The Selling of Woodies," *Washingtonian*, November 1984; Message from Edwin Hoffman, *Woodlothian* Annual Report to Employees, February 1980, folder 305, series V, subseries A, container 8, Woodward & Lothrop Records; "Building Profit on a New Image," *Chain Store Age*, August 1978, 4; Woodward & Lothrop, Annual Report, 1979, folder 75, series III, subseries A, Woodward & Lothrop Records; "Woodward & Lothrop: Flourishing in the Face of Glossy Competition," *Business Week*, March 19, 1979, 156; "Woodies Approaches 100, Still Single," *Washington Post*, September 27, 1978, D8.

19. Cash interview; Mathias interview; "Woodie's Organizing Effort Rolling," *Union Leader*, February 1979, 1; Form 5500, Annual Return/Report of Employee Benefit Plan, August 20, 1978, and July 31, 1978, and Proxy Statement, Woodward & Lothrop, Inc., May 21, 1979, all in box 19, Corporate Files—W, FAST Records, UMD.

20. Dixon interview.

21. Kraft Opinion Research Center, "Survey of Opinion toward Unions"; Cash interview.

22. "Frank Wright," *Woodlothian, 100 Years*, February 1980, 13, folder 305, series V, subseries A, container 8, Woodard & Lothrop Records; Kraft Opinion Research Center, "Survey of Opinion toward Unions."

23. Kraft Opinion Research Center, "Survey of Opinion toward Unions"; Bluestone, *Retail Revolution*; BLS, *Perspectives on Working Women*, 10, 74.

24. Benson, *Counter Cultures*; Cohen, *Consumers' Republic*, 282–86; "Retail Union's Drive Stalls," *Baltimore Sun*, November 8, 1970, 27.

25. Spencer-Marshall interview.

26. Banks interview; Kraft Opinion Research Center, "Survey of Opinion toward Unions."

27. Banks interview.

28. Ibid.; Brown interview. The Retail Store Employees Union, AFL-CIO, Local 400 was a unit of first the RCIA, and then the RCIU when the parent union changed its name in 1977.

29. Kraft Opinion Research Center, "Survey of Opinion toward Unions"; Jacoby, *Modern Manors*, esp. 205.

30. "Woodie's Organizing Effort Rolling," *Union Leader*, February 1, 1979, 1; "Woodies Employees Vote Solidly for AFL-CIO Union," *Washington Post*, June 22,

1979, C8; Joost Polak, "Organizing Case Study: Woodward & Lothrop, Washington D.C.," 1987, folder 23, box 9, AKP.

31. Schlossberg and Scott, *Organizing and the Law*, 288; Gross, *Broken Promise*, 172; Sav-On Drugs, 138 NLRB 1032 (1962).

32. U.S. Chamber of Commerce, "The Need for Labor Law Reform," as reprinted in "Chamber Publicizes Panel Proposals for Amendments to Taft-Hartley Act," *Daily Labor Report*, December 23, 1966, A-1; NLRB Annual Report, 1972, 56–57; Gross, *Broken Promise*, 228–29; Twenty-First Century Restaurant, 192 NLRB 881 (1971).

33. "Woodies Only the First Step," *Washington Post*, April 4, 1979, D7; Brown interview; Earman interview; "Pepco Pact Set; Woodies Talks to Start Today," *Washington Post*, August 8, 1979, C1.

34. "The Nation's Capital Has an Outstanding Union: Local 400," *Retail Clerks Advocate*, April 1979, 12–15; Lowthers interview.

35. Lowthers interview; Earman interview; Brown interview.

36. "Woodie's Organizing Effort Rolling," *Union Leader*, February 1979, 1; Lowthers interview; "NLRB Orders Union Election for Woodies."

37. Mathias interview.

38. Brown interview; Earman interview; Kraft Opinion Research Center, "Survey of Opinion toward Unions."

39. Earman interview; Lowthers interview; "Woodward & Lothrop—Supplemental Notes," n.d. [ca. 1979], folder 23, box 9, AKP; Mathias interview.

40. Brown interview; Polak, "Organizing Case Study" (quotes from Mike Fusco).

41. Mathias interview; "Election at Woodies Coming Up," *Union Leader*, May 1979, 1; Thomas R. McNutt, "Dear Woodies Employees," May 8, 1979, box 19, Corporate Files—W, FAST Records, UMD; Butsavage interview.

42. Earman interview; letter quoted in "Woodies Drive in High Gear as Deadline Nears for Filing," *Union Leader*, April 1979, 1.

43. Halsey interview.

44. E. K. Hoffman to All Members of Management, May 1, 1979, reprinted in McNutt, "Dear Woodies Employees"; "Woodward & Lothrop—Supplemental Notes," folder 23, box 9, AKP; Banks interview.

45. Jackson, *When Labor Trouble Strikes*, 32–3.

46. "Hoffman Is Chosen BOT 'Man of Year,'" *Washington Star*, May 5, 1979; Earman interview.

47. Kraft Opinion Research Center, "Survey of Opinion toward Unions"; Lowthers interview; Earman interview; Halsey interview.

48. Earman interview; McNutt, "Dear Woodies Employees"; Polak, "Organizing Case Study."

49. "With the Movie Norma Rae in Town . . . ," *Union Leader*, May 1979, 1; Brown interview.

50. "Unions' Organizing Push Could Alter D.C. Business," *Washington Post*, April 22, 1979, G1; Memo to all Woodward & Lothrop Employees from RSEU Local

400, June 7, 1979, folder 23, box 9, AKP; Spencer-Marshall interview; Polak, "Organizing Case Study"; Halsey interview.

51. "Union: Woodies Makes a Profit on Insurance," *Washington Post*, June 15, 1979, E5; "Look What Local 400 Just Won for You!," leaflet from Woodward & Lothrop Organizing Committee, folder 23, box 9, AKP; Brown interview.

52. Samuel Meyers, interview, 1980, tape 5, UFCW Retired Leaders Oral History Project, State Historical Society of Wisconsin, Madison, Wis.

53. "The Big New Retailing Union Eyes the Services," *Business Week*, March 5, 1979, 73; "Retail Clerks Union, High Hopes."

54. Halsey interview; "Pepco Pact Set: Woodies Talks Start Today."

55. "Woodies Employees Vote Solidly for AFL-CIO Union"; "Woodies Win— Biggest Ever," 1, and "Woodward & Lothrop Footnotes," 3, *Union Leader*, July 1979.

56. Bronfenbrenner et al., *Organizing to Win*, 5; Logan, "'Union-Free' Movement," 197.

57. Lee, "Whose Rights?"; "Contract Talks Break Off," *Washington Post*, November 1, 1979, B3; "Federal Mediator Enters Stalled Talks at Woodies," *Washington Post*, November 6, 1979, D6; Butsavage interview.

58. "Free Advice Woodies Ignored," *Union Leader*, December 1979, 2. The letter was only picked up by the Reston, Virginia, paper.

59. Schulman, *From Cotton Belt to Sunbelt*; Cobb, *Selling of the South*.

60. "Woodies Contract Talks Coming Up," *Union Leader*, August 1979, 3; "Federal Mediator Enters Stalled Talks at Woodies"; "Contract Talks Break Off."

61. "Woodies Pact Ratified," *Union Leader*, December 1979, 1; Lowthers interview.

62. "Breakthrough Pact Won from DC Store Chain," *AFL-CIO News*, December 1, 1979, 2; Collective Bargaining Agreement by and between Woodward & Lothrop Inc. and Retail Store Employees Unions, Local 400, November 18, 1979, to February 1, 1983, USDOL Historical Collective Bargaining Agreements Collection, KCLMD; "6000 Woodies Members Ratify Local 400 Pact," *UFCW Action*, no. 1 (1980): 15.

63. "Local Holds 1st Seminar for Woodies' Stewards," *Union Leader*, September 1980, 3; "Woodie-O-Gram" and "Eye Care Center at Metro 400 Always Offers 'the Right Stuff,'" *Union Leader*, December 1980, 4; Lowthers interview.

64. Job, "Employment and Pay Tends in the Retail Industry."

65. Milkman, "Women's History and the Sears Case"; Kessler-Harris, "Equal Employment Opportunity Commission."

66. Bean interview; Collective Bargaining Agreement by and between Woodward & Lothrop Inc. and Retail Store Employees Unions, Local 400, November 18, 1979, to February 1, 1983; "New 3-Year Woodies Pact Brings Gain to 6000," *Union Leader*, March 1983, 1; "Food and Commercial Workers Ratify Contract with Woodward & Lothrop, Inc." *Retail/Services Labor Report*, March 1, 1983; Collective Bargaining Agreement by and between Woodward & Lothrop Inc. and United Food and Commercial Workers Union, Local 400, February 1, 1983, to February 1, 1986, USDOL Historical Collective Bargaining Agreements Collection, KCLMD.

67. "The Collective Bargaining Agreement: History and Background," n.d. [ca. 1980], box 19, Corporate Files—W, FAST Records, UMD; Halsey interview.

68. Gereffi and Korzeniewicz, *Commodity Chains and Global Capitalism*; Richard Appelbaum and Nelson Lichtenstein, "New World of Retail Supremacy"; Lichtenstein, "Return of Merchant Capitalism"; Wood and Wrigley, "Market Power and Regulation."

69. "The Selling of Woodies," *Washingtonian*, November 1984, 152; Woodward & Lothrop, "Why We Believe You Should Vote FOR the Proposed Merger of Your Company," *Washington Post* advertisement, July 24, 1984, A5.

70. "Another Discount Retail Giant Sets Sights on Area," *Washington Post*, January 10, 1995, A1; "Analysts See Woodies Sale Going Through," *Washington Post*, June 23, 1995, B1.

71. Butsavage interview; "Hecht's MD, District Workers Join Union," *Washington Post*, September 5, 1995, E1.

72. "Union to Forgo Bid on Woodies," *Washington Post*, April 21, 1995, F2; Butsavage interview; Dennis J. Roderick to Thomas McNutt, June 15, 1995, UFCW Local 400 Records, Landover, Md.; "May Co. Explores Possibility of New Bid for Woodies," *Washington Post*, July 11, 1995, D1; "Recognition and Neutrality Agreement," July 20, 1995, signed by representatives of Local 400 and May Department Stores, UFCW Local 400 Records; "Hecht's MD, District Workers Join Union"; Certification of Representative in the Case of the May Department Stores and UFCW Local 400 before Arbitrator Joseph Sickles, September 15, 1995, UFCW Local 400 Records.

73. Bean interview; Laflin interview.

74. "Farewell Woodies," *Washington Post*, November 17, 1995, A24.

75. "Era Ends with New Beginning," *Washington Post*, September 9, 2006, D1; Laflin interview.

76. Jordan, "Avoiding the 'Trap'"; Draut, *Sleeping Giant*, 61–70; Coulter, "Raising Retail."

77. Collective Bargaining Agreement by and between Woodward & Lothrop Inc., and United Food and Commercial Workers Union, Local 400, 1993, UFCW Local 400 Records; BLS, Employment, Hours and Earnings from the Current Employment Statistics (National, SIC basis), not Seasonally Adjusted, Retail Trade, Average Weekly Earnings of Production Workers, 1995; "Report Warned Wal-Mart of Risks Before Bias Suit," *New York Times*, June 3, 2010, B1.

78. Lichtenstein, *Retail Revolution*, 156–96; Lichtenstein, "Wal-Mart, John Tate"; Pier and Human Rights Watch, *Discounting Rights*; Thomas Jessen Adams, "Making the New Shop Floor," 225.

79. Brown interview; Brief on Behalf of the Hecht Company, the Hecht Co and UFCW, Case No. 5-RC-11515, before the NLRB, 5th Region, 1981, box 8, EKS.

80. "The Hecht Company Campaign Calendar," April 24 to June 1, 1981, box 6, EKS.

81. "Memorandum: Prepared for the Hecht Company," April 7, 1981, box 4, EKS.

82. "Dear Hechts Company Associates," n.d. [ca. 1981], folder 4d, box 4, EKS.

83. Jean Abbott to Dear Viola, May 15, 1981, folder 3d, box 6, EKS (emphasis in the original).

84. "$2 Million for Woodies Drive," *Washington Post*, June 23, 1979, D8; Irwin Zazulia and Edgar Mengafico to Dear Ms. Hill, May 18, 1981, folder 3e, box 6, EKS.

85. NLRB Annual Reports, 1980–1989; BLS, Employment, Hours and Earnings from the Current Employment Statistics (National, SIC basis), Not Seasonally Adjusted, Retail Trade, SIC Codes 52–59, 1980–1989; NLRB Annual Report, 2000, table 16.

86. Earman interview; Lichtenstein, *Retail Revolution*, 178–79; Lowthers interview.

87. Earman interview; Brown interview; quote from Dwayne Carman in Region 8 report, box 4, M93-009, RCIA Papers, State Historical Society of Wisconsin, Madison, Wis.

88. Spencer-Marshall interview; Bronfenbrenner and Juravich, "It Takes More than House Calls," 24–25.

89. "Retail Clerks Union: High Hopes"; Hutzler Bros. Co v. NLRB, 630 F.2d 1012 (U.S. Court of Appeals, 4th Cir. 1980).

90. Butsavage interview; "Election at Woodies Coming Up," *Union Leader*, May 1979, 1; Wise interview; "Organizer Has Big Beef," *Union Leader*, February 1979, 2; Lechmere, Inc. v. NLRB, 502 U.S. 527 (1992); Kelly and Seaquist, "NLRB v. Lechmere."

91. Lowthers interview.

92. Ibid.

93. Tilly and Carre, "Retail Work," 300–304.

94. Verne Kopytoff, "How Amazon Crushed the Union Movement," *TIME*, January 16, 2014; "Amazon Proves Infertile Soil for Unions, So Far," *New York Times*, May 17, 2016, B1.

Chapter Seven

1. Woman Alive!, *Nine to Five*; "9-to-5ers Press for Office Rights," *Boston Globe*, April 9, 1974; Nussbaum, "Working Women's Insurgent Consciousness"; Cobble, "'Spontaneous Loss of Enthusiasm.'"

2. Cobble, *The Other Women's Movement*, 214–16; Cobble, "'Spontaneous Loss of Enthusiasm'"; Cobble, *Sex of Class*; MacLean, "Hidden History of Affirmative Action"; Deslippe, *Rights, Not Roses*; Gabin, *Feminism in the Labor Movement*; Fonow, *Union Women*; Evans, *Tidal Wave*, 86–88; Ruth Rosen, *World Split Open*, 267–71; Cobble and Kessler-Harris, "Karen Nussbaum"; Windham, "'Sense of Possibility'"; Glick, "Bridging Feminism and Trade Unionism"; Tepperman, *Not Servants, Not Machines*; Nussbaum, "Working Women's Insurgent Consciousness"; Seifer and Wertheimer, "New Approaches to Collective Power"; Hoerr, *We Can't Eat Prestige*; Foner, *Women and the American Labor Movement*, 480–84.

3. For more on "alt-labor" see Eidelson, "Alt-Labor," and Windham, "Alt-Labor Groups."

4. BLS, *Perspectives on Working Women*, 1–3, 10–11.

5. Davies, *Woman's Place Is at the Typewriter*; Fine, *Souls of the Skyscraper*; Strom, *Beyond the Typewriter*; Turk, "Labor's Pink-Collar Aristocracy"; Tepperman, *Not Servants, Not Machines*; Greenbaum, *Windows on the Workplace*; Cobble, "'Spontaneous Loss of Enthusiasm,'" 30–33; BLS, *Perspectives on Working Women*, 9, 49; MacLean, "Hidden History of Affirmative Action"; 9to5 Job Survey, n.d. [ca. 1975], folder 74, box 2, 1972–1980 Records, 9to5.

6. Joyce Weston to Dear Sisters, May 22, 1973, folder 87, box 3, 1972–1980 Records, 9to5.

7. Judith McCollough, interview by Ann Froines, November 4, 2005, Washington, D.C., SEIU District 925 Legacy Project, Oral History Transcripts, WPR.

8. Cassedy interview; Nussbaum interview, 2013.

9. Nussbaum interview, 2013; Levy, *New Left and Labor*.

10. "Re: Alterations in the Job of Secretary," *Memorandum: Newsletter of Women Office Workers at Harvard*, no. 1 (April 1972): 1, and "Re: Job Re-Classifications," 1 and "Progress Report," 2, no. 2 (May 15, 1972) and "Re: Raises and Phases," no. 4 (August 1972): 1.

11. Ellen Cassedy, Karen Nussbaum, and Debbie Schneider, interview by Ann Froines, Washington, D.C., November 1, 2005, and Janet Selcer, interview by Ann Froines, Brookline, Mass., February 1, 2005, SEIU District 925 Legacy Project, Oral History Transcripts, WPR; Nussbaum, "Working Women's Insurgent Consciousness"; Nussbaum interview, 2013; Ellen Cassedy to Heather [Booth] and Day [Creamer], August 5, 1973, folder 126, box 3, 1972–1980 Records, 9to5.

12. Ellen Cassedy to Howard and Chris, September 19, 1972, folder 126, box 3, Additional Records, 1972–1985, 9to5; Cassedy interview.

13. "Every Morning . . ." *9to5: Newsletter for Boston Area Office Workers* 1, no. 1 (December 1972/January 1973): 1; "'girls' till we retire," *9to5 Newsletter* 1, no. 4 (Summer 1973): 1, and "We DO Have Rights," *9to5 Newsletter* 2, no. 1 (December 1973/January 1974): 1.

14. "What's Happening . . . ," *9to5 Newsletter* 1, no. 5 (October/November 1973): 4–5.

15. Cassedy interview; Nussbaum interview, 2013; Heather Booth, interview by Stacey Heath, May 17, 2006, SEIU District 925 Legacy Project, Oral History Transcripts, WPR.

16. Ellen Cassedy, Karen Nussbaum, and Joan Tighe, "The Future of 9to5: A Proposal for an Independent Women Office Workers' Organization," September 8, 1973, folder 1, box 1, Additional Records, 1972–1985, 9to5.

17. Karen Nussbaum, "The Long and the Short," ca. September 1973, in Nussbaum's possession, Washington, D.C.

18. Cassedy, Nussbaum, and Tighe, "Future of 9to5"; Cassedy interview; Ellen Cassedy to Heather [Booth], October 8, 1974, folder 127, box 3, 1972–1980 Records, 9to5.

19. Ellen Cassedy and Susan Fahlund to Dear Friend, October 27, 1973, folder 3, box 1, 1972–1980 Records, 9to5.

20. Ellen Cassedy to Heather [Booth], December 4, 1973, folder 126, box 3, Additional Records 1972–1985, 9to5; "9 to 5: An Organization for Office Workers," *Boston Phoenix*, November 27, 1973.

21. "We DO Have Rights," *9to5 Newsletter* 2, no. 1 (December 1973/January 1974): 1.

22. Cassedy to Booth, December 4, 1973; Karen Nussbaum, timeline and memo, n.d. [ca. 1974], in Nussbaum's possession, Washington, D.C.; Glick, "Bridging Feminism and Trade Unionism"; James Kelso to Ellen Cassedy, January 2, 1974, folder 3, box 1, 1972–1980 Records, 9to5; Joan Tighe, "Some Thoughts for 9to5: Medium Range/Joan," n.d. [ca. January 1974], folder 3, box 1, 1972–1980 Records, 9to5.

23. Nussbaum, timeline and memo; Linda Gordon, "Black and White Visions of Welfare," 584; Jacqueline Jones, *Labor of Love, Labor of Sorrow*; Nussbaum interview, 2013; Cassedy interview.

24. "Public Hearing Held on Conditions of Women Office Workers," press release, April 8, 1974, folder 626, box 11, Additional Records, 1972–1985, 9to5; "9-to-5ers Press for Office Rights," *Boston Globe*, April 9, 1974. In a later version of the Bill of Rights for Women Office Workers, the women called for "benefits and pay equal to those of men in similar job categories." See brochure entitled, "9to5," ca. 1978, folder 131, box 5, 1972–1980 Records, 9to5.

25. "9to5 Meets with Walter Meuther at the Associated Industries of Massachusetts about Maternity Leave Bill," May 22, 1974, folder 3, box 1, 1972–1980 Records, 9to5; "9to5 Confronts A.I.M.," *9to5 Newsletter* 2, no. 4 (June/July 1974): 5; Nussbaum, timeline and memo; "Pickets Urge Action on Maternity Benefits Bill," *Boston Globe*, July 3, 1974.

26. Steering Committee Meeting, October 29, 1974, folder 6, box 1, 1972–1980 Records, 9to5.

27. "Women in Insurance: An Explosive Situation," September 9, 1974, folder 128, box 5, 1972–1980 Records, 9to5.

28. "Claims against Boston's Insurance Industry," September 1974, folder 127, box 5, 1972–1980 Records, 9to5; "Women Office Workers Accuse Insurance Firms," *Christian Science Monitor*, September 10, 1974.

29. "Insurance Discrimination Revealed at Hearing." *9to5 Newsletter* 4, no, 2 (March 1975): 1, and "First in Nation," 4, no. 3 (May 1975): 1.

30. Glick, "Bridging Feminism and Trade Unionism," 70; "Insurance Firms Ordered to End Job Discrimination," *Boston Globe*, June 6, 1975, 3.

31. Hatton, *Temp Economy*, 22–23, 57; "Fact Sheet: State Senate Bill 303," folder 111, box 3, 1972–1980 Records, 9to5; "Temporaries—Low Women on the Totem Pole," *Boston Phoenix*, March 11, 1975, 12; "Temps File First 9to5 Legislation," *9to5 Newsletter* 4, no. 2 (March 1975): 2, and "Temps Bill," *9to5 Newsletter* 4, no. 3 (May 1975): 6, and "9to5 Temps Halt Illegal Lobbying," *9to5 Newsletter* 4, no. 4 (August 1975): 1; Glick, "Bridging Feminism and Trade Unionism."

32. Cassedy interview.

33. "Interview with Nancy Farrell," September 19, 1980, folder 915, box 14, Additional Records, 1972–1985, 9to5; Nancy Farrell, "My Entry into 925 History," February 6, 2004, folder 26, box 5, SEIU 925; "9to5 Election Results," *9to5 News* 5, no. 5 (December 1976/January 1977): 2.

34. "Women in the Boston Area Publishing Industry: A Status Report, March 1975," folder 906, box 14, Additional Records, 1972–1985, 9to5; "Publishers Just Eliminate Stereotypes in Books, Women Charge," *Boston Evening Globe*, March 26, 1975.

35. "Bias Charge is Filed," *Wall Street Journal*, December 4, 1975, 17; "Three Publishers Named in Discrimination Action," *Boston Evening Globe*, December 2, 1975; "9to5: A Success Story," *Boston Globe*, September 28, 1979, 17.

36. Jones quote in "Bias Charge is Filed"; "Boston Publishers See Organizing Bid Behind Sex Bias Suit," *Wall Street Journal*, April 11, 1977, 18; Women in Publishing, three-month plan, May 1977, folder 897, box 13, Additional Records, 1972–1985, 9to5; "9to5 Dealing—Successfully—with Problems for Women Office Workers," *Washington Star*, December 2, 1978; "Job Bias Settlements Costly for Publishers," *Boston Globe*, January 22, 1981, 49.

37. MacLean, "Hidden History of Affirmative Action."

38. Women in Publishing Wage Survey, December 1976, folder 75, and Press Statement, February 25, 1977, folder 78, box 2, 1972–1980 Records, 9to5.

39. "Women in Publishing Presents Dubious Distinction Awards to Boston Publishing Firms," June 26, 1975, folder 126, box 5, 1972–1980 Records, 9to5; "Boston Publishers See Organizing Bid Behind Sex Bias Suit," *Wall Street Journal*, April 11, 1977, 18; Minutes of the General Meeting Held May 22, 1976, folder 30, box 1, 1972–1980 Records, 9to5; "Women in Publishing Hails Job Posting Improvements," September 24, 1976, folder 126, box 5, 1972–1980 Records, 9to5.

40. Selcer, interview by Froines, SEIU District 925 Legacy Project, Oral History Transcripts, WPR; Cassedy, Nussbaum, and Tighe, "Future of 9to5"; Ellen Cassedy to Heather [Booth], October 8, 1974, folder 127, box 3, 1972–1980 Records, 9to5; Nussbaum interview, 2013.

41. Karen Nussbaum, "My Entry into 925 History," February 6, 2004, folder 25, box 5, SEIU 925. McGraw did, in fact, later give his approval to the young local.

42. Robert Welsh and Jon Hiatt, interview by Ann Froines, November 3, 2005, Washington, D.C., SEIU District 925 Legacy Project, Oral History Transcripts, WPR.

43. Ellen Cassedy to Heather [Booth], February 21, 1974, folder 127, box 3, 1972–1980 Records, 9to5; Nussbaum interview, 2013.

44. Karen Nussbaum to Vicki Legion, August 16, 1975, folder 291, box 5, Additional Records, 1972–1985, 9to5.

45. 9to5 Executive Board Meeting Minutes, July 19, 1976, folder 10, box 1, Additional Records, 1972–1985, 9to5; Nussbaum interview, 2013.

46. Karen Nussbaum, interview by Ann Froines, November 16, 2006, Washington, D.C., SEIU District 925 Legacy Project, Oral History Transcripts, WPR.

47. "Why Unionize and How to Do It: Local 925," n.d. [ca. 1977], folder 131, box 5, 1972–1980 Records, 9to5; "The Union for Office Workers: Local 925," ca. 1976, folder 292, box 5, Additional Records, 1972–1985, 9to5.

48. Library Staff Association to Brandeis Board of Trustees, December 8, 1975, and "Brandeis Library Staff Unionize," December 11, 1975, both in folder 37, and Open Letter to the Brandeis Community, September 19, 1975, folder 36, box 7, SEIU 925.

49. Helen Codare, Dean, to Members of the Brandeis University Library Staff, January 15, 1976, and "Guidelines for Supervisors and Managerial Employees during a Union Organizing Drive, January 12, 1976," both in folder 38, box 7, SEIU 925.

50. Planning Committee, February 9, 1976, folder 14, box 1, 1972–1980 Records, 9to5; Karen Nussbaum to John Geagan, October 12, 1976, folder 38, box 7, SEIU 925.

51. Brandeis/Pressure Campaign for a Fair Contract, ca. 1976, and Jackie to Karen Nussbaum, November 11, 1976, both in folder 39, "Union Busting Isn't Kosher," n.d. [ca. 1976], folder 38, and Karen Nussbaum to Julius Bernstein, January 11, 1977, folder 40, all in box 7, SEIU 925.

52. Farrell, "My Entry into 925 History."

53. "Victories: A Look at 1978," n.d. [ca. 1979], folder 290, box 5, Additional Records, 1972–1985, 9to5.

54. "Cash Payment for Sick Leave in First Rounder Records Contract," *News from Local 925*, January 1981, folder 25, box 7, SEIU 925.

55. Cobble and Kessler-Harris, "Karen Nussbaum," 143; "Local 925 Signs First Contract," *News from Local 925*, June 1976, box 4, Additional Records, 1972–1985, 9to5.

56. Nussbaum interview, 2014; "Election Victories," *News from Local 925*, April 1980, folder 25, box 7, SEIU 925; "Staying Local," *Local 925 News*, March 7, 1982, folder 25, box 7, SEIU 925; Proposal to SEIU to Support Expanded Organizing Program by Local 925 in the Boston Area, May 22, 1981, folder 18, box 7, SEIU 925; Dorine Levasseur, interview by Ann Froines, February 23, 2005, Braintree, Mass., SEIU District 925 Legacy Project, Oral History Transcripts, WPR; District 925 Executive Board Minutes, April 5, 1986, folder 34, box 4, SEIU 925; Dorine Levasseur to Janet Garabedian, December 9, 1982, folder 19, box 7, SEIU 925; "Service Employees Launch Drive for Women Workers," *AFL-CIO News*, March 7, 1981, 2.

57. Nussbaum interview, 2013.

58. Selcer, interview by Froines, SEIU District 925 Legacy Project, Oral History Transcripts, WPR.

59. Ruth Rosen, *World Split Open*, 304; MacLean, "Hidden History of Affirmative Action."

60. Enforcement Campaign Report, January 26, 1976, folder 14, box 1, 1972–1980 Records, 9to5.

61. Nussbaum, interview by Froines, SEIU District 925 Legacy Project, Oral History Transcripts, WPR; "An Invitation to Equal Opportunity," May 6, 1976, folder 128, box 5, 1972–1980 Records, 9to5; "Federal Govt. Target: Insurance," *Women Insurance News* 1, no. 2 (1976): folder 111, box 3, Additional Records, 1972–1986, 9to5.

62. Selcer, interview by Froines, SEIU District 925 Legacy Project, Oral History Transcripts, WPR; "Nine to 5 Blasts Banks and Bureaucrats," *Boston Phoenix*, October 5, 1976, 18; Ruth Olds to Weldon J. Rougeau, December 18, 1979, folder 12, box 1, 1972–1980 Records, 9to5; "9to5 Celebrates Five Years of Action," *Equal Times*, November 6, 1978.

63. "9to5 Targets Lorber," *9to5 News* 5, no. 5 (December 1976/January 1977): 1; "Affirmative Action Changes Opposed," *Boston Globe*, December 14, 1976; "Women, Civil Rights Groups Protest U.S. Hiring Revisions," *Boston Herald*, December 14, 1976.

64. Nussbaum interview, 2013; "9to5 Rally Announces First Victory in Campaign for Women at First National Bank," May 2, 1979, "9to5 Targets Stockholders," March 29, 1979, and "9to5 Announces Participation in Shadow Board of FNB," n.d., folder 742, and "9to5's Year at the First, Special Report," April 1980, and *First People First*, no. 1 (May 10, 1979): folder 769, all in box 12, Additional Records, 1972–1985, 9to5.

65. "Raises Won! First Responds to 9to5 Pressures," March 7, 1980, folder 769, box 12, Additional Records, 1972–1985, 9to5.

66. Susan O'Malley to Dorine Levasseur, June 16, 1981, folder 19, box 1, SEIU 925; "John Hancock Fact Sheet," folder 19, box 1, SEIU 925; Nussbaum interview, 2013.

67. "Raises Won!," *Hancock Observator*, no. 10 (September 29, 1981): folder 19, and "9to5 Focuses on Child Care at Hancock," *9to5 News* 11, no. 1 (February/March, 1982): 3, folder 20, both in box 1, SEIU 925.

68. Cassedy interview; Debbie Schneider, interview by Ann Froines, Washington, D.C., November 3, 2005, SEIU District 925 Legacy Project, Oral History Transcripts, WPR.

69. "Commonly Asked Questions about the Union and Suggested Answers," n.d. [ca. 1981], folder 292, box 4, Additional Records, 1972–1985, 9to5; Nussbaum interview, 2013.

70. Ellen Cassedy, Staff Reports to the Executive Board, November 28, 1978, January 22, 1979, and February 12, 1979, folder 27, box 1, Additional Records, 1972–1985, 9to5; "Working Women: National Association of Office Workers," 1978, folder 241, box 4, Additional Records, 1972–1985, 9to5; Revised 9to5 Chapter Listing, September 1983, folder 12, box 1, SEIU 925; "9to5 to Release 'Office Workers Speak Out,' and New 'Bill of Rights,'" February 22, 1983, folder 627, box 11, Additional Records, 1972–1985, 9to5.

71. "Working Women: Report from the National Office," November 19, 1979, and "Working Women, 1983–1984 Income," n.d. [ca. 1985], folder 203, box 4, Additional Records, 1972–1985, 9to5.

72. Sam, Maggie, and Joan to Executive Board, October 14, 1976, folder 7, and Executive Board Meeting, December 6, 1979, folder 9, both in box 1, 1972–1980 Records, 9to5; Selcer, interview by Froines, SEIU District 925 Legacy Project, Oral History Transcripts, WPR.

73. "Be a 9to5'er," *9to5 Newsletter* 4, no. 5 (January/February 1986): 1 and "Minority Outreach," *9to5 Newsletter* 4, No. 2 (March/April 1985): 3, both in box 26, "Fact Sheet on Working Women's Agenda Survey," February 1983, and "Office Workers Job Survey, Report, October–December, 1980," folder 1, box 101, all in Atlanta 9to5 Working Women Records, GSU.

74. Organizers Meeting, Detailed Agenda, Working Women, n.d. [ca. 1980], folder 111, box 3, Additional Records, 1972–1985, 9to5; "By the Seat of His Pants," *Boston Globe*, September 15, 1977; "Have You Heard the One about the Boss Who . . . ?," *Chicago Daily News*, September 13, 1977; "Rebellion behind the Typewriter," *Business Week*, April 26, 1980, 85; Nussbaum interview, 2013.

75. Karen Nussbaum, interview by Kathleen Banks Nutter, December 18–19, 2003, transcript, Voices of Feminism Oral History Project, Sophia Smith Collection, Smith College, Northampton, Mass.; Jane Fonda, telephone interview by Stacey Heath, SEIU District 925 Legacy Project, Oral History Transcripts, WPR; *9 to 5*, film, directed by Colin Higgins, Los Angeles, Twentieth Century Fox, 1980.

76. *9 to 5*, film; "Fox Studio's Woman Chief Smashes Mogul Stereotype," *Wall Street Journal*, January 13, 1981, 35; "Jane Fonda's Got a 9-to-5 Job in TV," *Baltimore Sun*, January 24, 1982, TVW6.

77. Nussbaum, interview by Nutter, Voices of Feminism Oral History Project; "Making it From 9 to 5," *Atlanta Journal and Constitution*, December 6, 1980, 28.

78. Nussbaum, "Working Women's Insurgent Consciousness," 165; Janice Blood to All Affiliates, August 29, 1980, folder 2, box 8, Atlanta 9to5 Working Women Records.

79. "Summary—Working Women, National Association for Women Office Workers Ponders Forging a Formal Relationship with a Major Union," n.d. [ca. 1979], folder 24, box 5, SEIU 925.

80. Karen Nussbaum to Bob Welsh, November 25, 1980, folder 24, box 5, SEIU 925; Memorandum of Understanding between Working Women and SEIU, February 1, 1981, folder 24, box 5, SEIU 925.

81. Ray Abernathy and Denise Mitchell, interview by Ann Froines, November 3, 2005, Washington, D.C., SEIU District 925 Legacy Project, Oral History Transcripts, WPR.

82. Ray Abernathy to Bob Welsh, January 29, 1981, folder 25, box 5, SEIU 925; "Bosses Watch Out: Office Workers Have Inside Line," n.d. [ca. 1981], folder 11, box 3, SEIU 925; News, AFL-CIO, press release, April 8, 1981, box 10, AFL-CIO ODR.

83. Cheryl Schaffer, interview by Ann Froines, January 19, 2006, SEIU District 915 Legacy Project, Oral History Transcripts, WPR.

84. David Moberg, "Clerks Outmaneuver Bosses," *In These Times*, March 30, 1983; Ruth Milkman, "Breakthrough at the Equitable," *Nation*, December 3, 1983; "District 925 and NOW Demonstrate at 41 Equitable Life Assurance Offices," *White Collar Report*, November 19, 1982; Abernathy and Mitchell, interview by Froines, SEIU District 925 Legacy Project, Oral History Transcripts, WPR.

85. Nussbaum, "Working Women's Insurgent Consciousness"; "Fact Sheet: The Equitable Life Assurance Society," n.d. [ca. 1982], folder 19, box 8, SEIU 925; "District 925 to Oppose Equitable's Plans to Close Syracuse Office," press release, March 27, 1987, folder 24, box 17, SEIU 925.

86. Martin F. Payson, "How to Beat the Union Drive for Female Office Workers," *Nation's Business*, September 1983.

87. "His Business Is Breaking Unions and Keeping Them Out," *Seattle Times*, November 28, 1982.

88. "Georgia Chamber Seminar Focuses on Managing White Collar Women," *White Collar Report*, September 24, 1982; "Anti-Union Seminar Held," *Times-Courier*, (Charleston, Ill.) January 20, 1982; Levitt and Conrow, *Confessions of a Union Buster*, 102–12. Levitt describes spending weeks at World Airways headquarters when secretaries and file clerks there tried to organize.

89. Bonnie Ladin to District 925 Executive Board, April 4, 1986, folder 34, and Executive Board Minutes, December 5, 1986, folder 35, both in box 4, SEIU 925; District 925, Union-Membership Statistics, July 1986, folder 28, box 5, SEIU 925; Schneider, interview by Froines, SEIU District 925 Legacy Project, Oral History Transcripts, WPR.

90. "Working Women: 1983–1984 Income," n.d. [ca. 1985], folder 203, box 4, Additional Records, 1972–1985, 9to5; Finance Report, January 1979, folder 8, box 1, 1972–1980 Records, 9to5; Karen Nussbaum to 9to5 Board Members, June 27, 1985, and Mike Sparks to the Board of 9to5, July 25, 1985, both in folder 8, box 1, SEIU 925; Pat Reeve to Dear [blank], December 28, 1984, folder 22, box 2, Additional Records, 1972–1986, 9to5.

91. Cassedy interview.

92. Ellen Cassedy and Karen Nussbaum, "Reports of Our Demise Were Premature," *Boston Globe*, November 16, 1985.

93. McCall, "Increasing Class Disparities among Women"; Lovell, Hartmann, and Werschkul, "More than Raising the Floor"; Nussbaum interview, 2013.

94. BLS, *Perspectives on Working Women*, 3, 10; BLS, "Employed Person by Detailed Occupation, Sex, Race and Hispanic Origin," 2015, http://www.bls.gov/cps/cpsaat11.pdf; "In Job Market Shift, Some Workers are Left Behind." *New York Times*, May 13, 2010, A1.

95. 9to5 website, accessed October 6, 2016, http://9to5.org/home; SEIU District 925 website, accessed October 6, 2016, http://www.seiu925.org/.

96. Draut, *Sleeping Giant*, 133–38; AFL-CIO, "Our Voices"; Gould, Schieder, Geier, "What Is the Gender Pay Gap and Is It Real?" The 83 cents figure is based on wages per hour for a median woman, working full-time.

97. BLS, "Employed Person by Detailed Occupation."

98. Tom Bethell, "1974: Contract at Brookside," *Southern Exposure* 4, nos. 1–2 (1976):114–24; Bill Finger, "Victory Sobre Farah," *Southern Exposure* 4, nos. 1–2 (1976): 45–49; Minchin, *"Don't Sleep with Stevens!"*; Juravich and Bronfenbrenner,

Ravenswood; Ashby and Hawking, *Staley*; "At Work: Different Tactics in Labor's Battles," *New York Times*, September 6, 1992, F23.

Conclusion

1. Hooks interview; Coppedge interview, 2011; Cash interview; Halsey interview; Bean interview; Laflin interview; Nussbaum interview, 2013; Minchin, "'It Knocked This City to Its Knees'"; Mishel et al., *State of Working America*; Kalleberg, *Good Jobs, Bad Jobs*.

2. "260,000 Protest Reagan Policies," *Los Angeles Times*, September 20, 1981, A1; "400,000 Hit Cutbacks in Programs," *AFL-CIO News*, September 26, 1981, 3; Photos of members of District 925 and 9to5 at the march can be found in folder 24, box 18, SEIU 925; Hooks interview; "Labor's Banner Day," *Steelabor*, October 1981, 7; "Today is Just a Start," *AFL-CIO American Federationist*, October 1981, 1; Minchin, "Together We Shall Be Heard."

3. "Solidarity Day! You Are Not Alone," *AFL-CIO News*, September 26, 1981, 1–16; "Solidarity Day: Behold Your Numbers," *AFL-CIO American Federationist*, October 1981, 1–22. Mary Jo Vavra quoted in "Pennsylvania: 'Tired of . . . the Rich Getting Richer,'" *Steelabor*, October 1981, 10.

4. "Massive Solidarity Day Protest," *AFL-CIO News*, September 26, 1981, 3; Eleanor Smeal, "The Unratified ERA States are Also Right-to-Work," *AFL-CIO American Federationist*, October, 1981, 6; Benjamin Hooks, "The Greatest Danger We Face is From Within," 9; Joseph Lowery, "This Robin Hood Robs Poor, Gives to Rich," 11; Jesse Jackson, " I am Somebody. I Want to Work," 16; "Labor Hoping for Massive Anti-Reagan March Today," *Los Angeles Times*, September 19, 1981, A1; "Labor Expects 100,000 for Solidarity Day," *Washington Post*, September 12, 1981, B1.

5. "Labor Marches on Washington," *Steelabor*, October 1981, 9; Coretta Scott King, "The Cynical Politics of Selfishness," *AFL-CIO American Federationist*, October 1981, 14.

6. Scholarship and textbooks that do not cover Solidarity Day include Rosenzweig et al., *Who Built America?*; Cowie, *Stayin' Alive*; Moody, *Injury to All*; and Nicholson, *Labor's Story in the United States*. On the 1963 March on Washington, see William Powell Jones, *March on Washington*, x. For more on Solidarity Day see Minchin, *Labor Under Fire*, 73–100.

7. Judith Stein, *Pivotal Decade*, 265–70; McCartin, *Collision Course*, 9–10; Westcott and Bednarzik, "Employment and Unemployment."

8. Membership Change, 1984, folder 10, box 4, AKP. The UAW showed a loss of 459,300 for 1979–1984. The USWA showed a loss of 416,500 for 1979–1984.

9. Hamilton, *Trucking Country*, 230; McCartin, *Collision Course*, 197–98; Levinson, *The Box*, 261.

10. McCartin, *Collision Course*, quote on 8. The 1938 *NLRB v. Mackay Radio and Telegraph* U.S. Supreme Court decision ruled that employers could hire striker replacements when union recognition or unfair labor practices were not at issue. On

strikebreakers at Newport News, see Ad for Newport News Shipbuilding and Dry Dock Company, *Daily Press*, March 28, 1979, USWA Legal.

11. Fantasia and Voss, *Hard Work*, 64–70; Harrison and Bluestone, *Great U-Turn*; Rosenblum, *Copper Crucible*; Brecher, *Strike!*, 247–49; Alan Kistler speech, 1984, folder 15, box 2, AKP; Moody, *Injury to All*; Kraft, *Vegas at Odds*; McCartin, *Collision Course*, 348–49. On Seyfarth Shaw, see "Seyfarth, Shaw, Fairweather and Geraldson," *Report on Union Busters: RUB Sheet*, no. 2 (1979) and "The Strike as a Management Weapon," no. 4 (1979): box 11, AKP. On Continental, see "A Make-or-Break Year for Nation's Unions," *U.S. News and World Report*, March 5, 1984, 75, and "Was Continental Action a Plot to Bust Unions or a Move to Survive?" *Los Angeles Times*, November 6, 1983, SG2.

12. Gross, *Broken Promise*, 257–59; Kenneth B. Noble, "N.L.R.B.: Thunder Against Thunder," *New York Times*, June 8, 1985, 6; Alan Kistler, untitled speech, 1984, folder 15, box 2, AKP.

13. Arnold Weber, speech at Washington University entitled "Lifeboat Labor Relations," May 1984, box 147A, series 7, Acc. 1411, NAM. Weber was president of the University of Colorado and later served as president of Northwestern University.

14. NLRB Annual Reports, 1959–1982. See appendix for data.

15. Author's analysis of NLRB, Monthly Reports, various months, 1977–1986, Election Reports: Cases Closed, table 1.

16. "NLRB, Single Union RC & RM Elections, 1977–1982, Top 20 AFL-CIO Unions in Activity, & IBT," folder 10, box 4, AKP; Alan Kistler, Address to AFL-CIO Executive Council, August 1982, folder 8, box 2, AKP.

17. Ben Perkins to Owen Bieber, April 28, 1983, folder 6, box 67, Douglas A. Fraser Papers, WPR; Charles McDonald to Thomas Donahue, February 16, 1983, folder 10, box 4, AKP; Farber, "Worker Demand for Union Representation." Note that more recent polling revealed that a majority of workers were once again interested in joining unions by the early 2000s. See Richard B. Freeman and Joel Rogers, *What Workers Want*.

18. Alan Kistler, Address to AFL-CIO Executive Council, August 1982, folder 8, box 2, AKP.

19. See appendix. NLRB Annual Reports, 1995–2005; Frank Swoboda, "AFL-CIO Elects New Leadership," *Washington Post*, October 26, 1995; NLRB, Election Report, FY 2016. This data covers RC elections.

20. Tom Donahue to All Members of the Committee on the Evolution of Work and Its Implications, October 21, 1982, and AFL-CIO Committee on the Evolution of Work, "The Future of Work," August 1983, both in folder 10, box 4, AKP; AFL-CIO Committee on the Evolution of Work, "The Changing Situation of Workers and Their Unions," February 1985, box 26, series 1, and AFL-CIO Committee on the Evolution of Work, "The New American Workplace: A Labor Perspective," February 1994, box 33, both in Support Services, AFL-CIO Publications, UMD.

21. AFL-CIO Committee on the Evolution of Work, "Changing Situation of Workers"; Notes at Future of Work Committee, April 19, 1984, folder 10, box 4, AKP.

22. "Union 'Associates': A Proposal for Action," n.d. [ca. 1985], folder 9, box 4, AKP. On development of the union benefits program, see David Silberman to Charles McDonald, March 5, 1985, folder 4, box 10, AKP; "Can Credit Cards and IRAs Rebuild the Labor Movement?," *Business Week*, November 4, 1985, 96; and Eric Starkman, "AFL-CIO in an Era of Change," *Detroit News*, November 8, 1987.

23. See Notes on Future of Work Committee Meeting, January 29, 1986, folder 9, box 4, AKP.

24. Charles McDonald, "The AFL-CIO's Blueprint for the Future—A Progress Report," Industrial Relations Research Association, 39th annual proceedings, 1987, box 65/17, George Meany Memorial Archive, Vertical Files, UMD; "AFL-CIO Considers Plan to Enlist Workers Outside Bargaining Context," *Washington Post*, February 19, 1989, A23.

25. AFL-CIO Committee on the Evolution of Work, "New American Workplace."

26. Windham, " 'Sense of Possibility' "; Hirsch and Macpherson, "Union Membership and Coverage Database"; BLS, Economic News Release, "Union Members—2016."

27. Hirsch and MacPherson, "Union Membership and Coverage Database"; Western and Rosenfeld, "Unions, Norms," 513–37; Mishel, "Faltering Middle-Class Wages"; Rosenfeld, Denise, and Laird, "Union Decline Lowers Wages."

28. Rosenfeld, *What Unions No Longer Do*, 126–27.

29. Economic Policy Institute, *State of Working America Data Library*, "Union Wage Premium," 2017. The union wage premium reflects the regression-adjusted hourly wage advantage of being in a union, controlling for experience, education, region, industry, occupation, race, ethnicity, and marital status. Being in a union is measured as being a union member or covered by a collective bargaining agreement. BLS, "Union Affiliation, 1983–2015." The African American unionization rate was 27.2 percent in 1983 and 13.6 percent in 2015.

30. Mishel et al., *State of Working America*, 175; Budd, "Effect of Unions," 178; Klein, *For All These Rights*, 5; Mishel, "Faltering Middle-Class Wages." Unionized workers are 28 percent more likely to have employer-provided health insurance and 54 percent more likely to have employer-provided pensions.

31. Francia, "Voting on Values or Bread-and-Butter?"; Francia, *Future of Organized Labor*.

32. On "Wal-Mart Moms," see Moreton, *To Serve God and Wal-Mart*, 4–5; Hooks interview; "Thousands March for ERA in Va. Capital," *Washington Post*, January 14, 1980, C1.

33. Francia, *Future of Organized Labor*; Best and Krueger, *Exit Polls*; "ABC News Poll, the 84 Vote, General Public Exit Poll," 1984, box 4, folder 6. Union households voted 49 percent for Carter and 41 percent for Reagan in 1980, according to this poll, and by 1984, the margin was 54 percent for Walter Mondale and 45 percent for Reagan. The CBS and *New York Times* polls show a 48 percent union household vote for Carter and 45 percent for Reagan in 1980, and 54 percent for Mondale and 46 percent for Reagan in 1984. Roper Center, Cornell University, "United States: Elections."

34. Harold Meyerson, "Trump Presidency Could Kill Labor Unions," *The American Prospect*, November 28, 2016. Union households voted 51 percent for Clinton over 43 percent for Trump. Union members voted 56 percent for Clinton and 37 percent for Trump.

35. Erikson, Lancaster, and Romero, "Group Components of the Presidential Vote."

36. Lane Windham, "Union Erosion Crumbled Hillary Clinton's Blue Wall," *The Hill*, November 22, 2016; Hirsch and Macpherson, "Union Membership and Coverage Database"; U.S. Department of Labor, BLS, "Union Members—2016," Economic News Release, January 26, 2017.

37. Rudy, " 'Justice for Janitors' "; Luff, "Justice for Janitors"; Waldinger et al., "Helots No More."

38. See, for instance, Resolution No. 85, "Comprehensive Organizing Campaigns," (1985) *Proceedings of the Sixteenth Constitutional Convention of the AFL-CIO*, 161; Fantasia and Voss, *Hard Work*, 128–29; Slaughter, "Corporate Campaigns."

39. "Organizing Activities," (1985) *Proceedings of the Sixteenth Constitutional Convention of the AFL-CIO*, 64; "Magruder Win Becomes a Labor Landmark," *Washington Post*, April 8, 1985, 1; "Unions Go for the Cut with Corporate Campaigns," *Atlanta Journal and Constitution*, February 12, 1993, G8; "Labor's Food Fight," *Washington Post*, March 1, 1993, F1.

40. Paul J. Baicich and Lance Compa, "Cooperate, Hell: Unions Get What They Fight For," *Washington Post*, December 1, 1985, C1; "NLRB Charges Beverly Enterprises Used Unfair Tactics to Block Union Activities," *Wall Street Journal*, September 8, 1987, 12; Craft and Exteit, "New Strategies in Union Organizing."

41. Foerster, "Labor's Youth Brigade"; "It's Hip to Be Union," *Newsweek*, July 8, 1996, 44–45; Brecher, *Strike!*, 253–55; Jeremy Brecher and Tim Costello, "Concluding Essay," in Brecher and Costello, *Building Bridges*; Boris and Klein, *Caring for America*, 189–200; Minchin, *Labor Under Fire*, 282–83, 292–95.

42. Weil, *Fissured Workplace*; Standing, *Precariat*; Eidelson, "Alt-Labor"; Windham, "Alt-Labor Groups"; Draut, *Sleeping Giant*, 179–212; Rolf, *Fight for Fifteen*.

43. Standing, *Precariat*; McCartin, "Bargaining for the Common Good"; Stern, *Raising the Floor*.

44. Andrias, "The New Labor Law."

45. Western, *Between Class and Market*, 145–54; Hobsbawm, *Age of Extremes*, 403–15.

Appendix

1. Taft-Hartley allowed management to trigger an election (an RM election) if (a) workers who did not already have a union demanded recognition without an election or (b) if it could produce substantial evidence that the existing union was no longer representative of the bargaining unit. Taft-Hartley allowed workers to decertify their existing union (an RD election). Lynch and Sandver, "Determinants of the Decertification Process," 85.

Note that in the 1949 to 1964 period, the NLRB annual reports contain a figure labeled "collective bargaining elections" that reflects the number of elections and eligible voters in both RC and RM elections. Goldfield, *Decline of Organized Labor*, 90–91, uses this amalgamated number for 1949 to 1964, so that book's data for those years differ from those presented here. This appendix reports data from RC representation case elections and so avoids this inconsistency in the NLRB's data reports. The NLRB's inclusion of the RM election numbers in the "collective bargaining elections" before 1965 serves to inflate the numbers of elections and workers eligible to vote in elections in the 1950s and early 1960s, as compared to the 1970s and later. The inclusion of the RM statistics especially skews the statistics for the 1950s because RM elections were much more common during the height of the Cold War than in later decades. For example, in 1950 nearly 250,000 workers at GE and Westinghouse voted in RM elections that were triggered by management seeking to assist the IUE in its effort to oust the more radical UE. Filippelli and Mc-Colloch, *Cold War in the Working Class*, 139–48. See also the 1950 NLRB Annual Report and the NLRB's discussion of its precedent-setting decision at Westinghouse that a union (the IUE) need not "make a showing if it is claiming to represent a unit substantially the same as that requested by a petitioning employer." NLRB Annual Report, 1950, 32.

2. Note that I use here the number of private production workers, rather than the entire nonagricultural workforce, which includes many supervisory workers who were not eligible to vote in union elections. Voos, in "Trends in Union Organizing Expenditures," also uses private production workers.

3. See, for example, Lipset and Katchanovski, "Future of Private Sector Unions," 9–13.

Bibliography

Primary Sources

Author's Interviews

Banks, Arthur L. Washington, D.C. August 20, 2013.

Bean, Sue. Telephone interview. July 31, 2013.

Boyd-Williams, Cynthia. Newport News, Virginia. October 28, 2010.

Brown, John D. Telephone interview. March 25, 2013.

Butsavage, Carey. Washington, D.C. June 17, 2013.

Carpenter, Peggy A. Telephone interview. September 30, 2010.

Cash, Barbara A. Upper Marlboro, Maryland. August 8, 2013.

Cassedy, Ellen. Takoma Park, Maryland. January 6, 2014.

Chatak, Elmer. Bethesda, Maryland. June 13, 2011.

Coppedge, Edward. Telephone interview. October 27, 2010.

———. Castalia, North Carolina. March 22, 2011.

Crawford, Marion. Telephone interview. June 13, 2014.

Dixon, Leola C. Takoma Park, Maryland. October 25, 2013.

Earman, Michael. Telephone interview. March 22, 2013.

Fleischman, Mark, and Nancy Peckenham. Takoma Park, Maryland. July 31, 2013.

Frankel, Carl B. Pittsburgh, Pennsylvania. August 17, 2010.

Glass, Alton H. Newport News, Virginia. October 27, 2010.

Halsey, Rosa M. Landover, Maryland. August 28, 2013.

Hooks, Carolyn Jan. Newport News, Virginia. October 27, 2010.

Jorgensen, Keir. Washington, D.C. April 16, 2013.

Keefer, Danny. Newport News, Virginia. October 28, 2010.

Laflin, Mary. Telephone interview. July 24, 2013.

Lowthers, James. Landover, Maryland. July 20, 2013.

Marshall, Ray. Telephone interview. August 4, 2011.

Mathias, John Adam. Kensington, Maryland. August 15, 2013.

Moore, Robert W. Telephone interview. October 14, 2010.

Nussbaum, Karen. Washington, D.C. December 18, 2013.

———. Washington, D.C. June 11, 2014.

Pike, Rickie L. Telephone interview. October 14, 2010.

Spencer-Marshall, Glenda. Telephone interview. September 23, 2013.

Wise, Russell. Telephone interview. March 21, 2013.

Collections

Atlanta, Georgia
    Jimmy Carter Presidential Library and Museum
        Domestic Policy Staff
        Office of Congressional Liaison
        Office of the Chief of Staff
        White House Central File
    Southern Labor Archives, Special Collections and Archives, Georgia State
        University Library
        ACTWU vs. Cannon Mills Papers
        Atlanta 9to5 Working Women Records
        United Steelworkers of America, District 35 Records
        Uprising of '34 Collection
Cambridge, Massachusetts
    Schlesinger Library on the History of Women in America, Radcliffe Institute
        for Advanced Study, Harvard University
        9 to 5, National Association of Working Women (U.S.) Records
Chapel Hill, North Carolina
    Southern Historical Collection, Louis Round Wilson Library, University of
        North Carolina
        John Harden Papers
        Mildred Gwin Andrews Papers
Charlottesville, Virginia
    University of Virginia School of Law Special Collections, Arthur J. Morris Law
        Library
        Papers of Earle K. Shawe
College Park, Maryland
    George Meany Memorial AFL-CIO Archive, Special Collections and University
        Archives, University of Maryland
        AFL-CIO Organizing Department Records (1955–1975)
        Alan Kistler Papers, 1954–2000
        Food, Allied, and Service Trades (FAST) Records, Mixed Correspondence,
          1970–1989
        George Meany Memorial Archive, Vertical Files, 1882–1990
        Industrial Union Department Records
          Organizing Department, Southern Office, International Unions and State
            Federations Correspondence, 1963–1985
          Subject Files, 1975–1984
        Office of the President, George Meany Files, 1940–1980
        Support Services, AFL-CIO Publications
    National Archives
        Records of the National Labor Relations Board (Record Group 25)

Detroit, Michigan
    Walter P. Reuther Library, Archives of Labor History and Urban Affairs, Wayne State University
        Douglas A. Fraser Papers
        Irving Bluestone Papers
        Service Employees International Union (SEIU) District 925 Records
        Service Employees International Union (SEIU) District 925 Legacy Project, Oral History Transcripts
        Simon Alpert Papers
        Walter P. Reuther Papers
Durham, North Carolina
    David M. Rubenstein Rare Book and Manuscript Library, Duke University
    Cannon Mills Records
Ithaca, New York
    Kheel Center for Labor-Management Documentation and Archives, Catherwood Library, Cornell University
        Amalgamated Clothing and Textile Workers Union (ACTWU) Papers
        Douglas Soutar Papers
        NLRB Oral History Project II
        U.S. Department of Labor Historical Collective Bargaining Agreements Collection
Landover, Maryland
    United Food and Commercial Workers (UFCW), Local 400 Records
Madison, Wisconsin
    State Historical Society of Wisconsin
        Retail Clerks International Association (RCIA) Papers
        Textile Workers Union of America (TWUA) Oral History Project
        Textile Workers Union of America (TWUA) Papers
        United Food and Commercial Workers (UFCW) Papers
        United Food and Commercial Workers (UFCW) Retired Leaders Oral History Project
New York, New York
    Where Do You Stand? Stories from an American Mill (2004), collection held by Alexandra Lescaze, transcripts of interviews
Northampton, Massachusetts
    Sophia Smith Collection, Smith College
        Voices of Feminism Oral History Project
Pittsburgh, Pennsylvania
    USWA Headquarters
        United Steelworkers of America Legal Files
Seattle, Washington
    University of Washington
        Seattle Civil Rights and Labor History Project

State College, Pennsylvania
> Historical Collections and Labor Archives, Special Collections Library,
>> Pennsylvania State University
>>> United Steelworkers of America (USWA) Communications Department
>>> Records
>>> United Steelworkers of America, *Newport News Shipbuilding Strike Bulletin*,
>>> HC-Serials

Washington, D.C.
> AFA/CWA Headquarters
>> Association of Flight Attendants (AFA) Records
> Historical Society of Washington, D.C.
>> Woodward & Lothrop Records
> Library of Congress, Manuscript Division
>> Herbert Hill Papers, 1869–2004
> United Food and Commercial Workers (UFCW) Headquarters Records

Wilmington, Delaware
> Hagley Museum and Library
>> National Association of Manufacturers (NAM) Records

Government Publications

Department of Health, Education, and Welfare. *Work in America: Report of a Special Task Force to the Secretary of Health, Education, and Welfare.* Cambridge, Mass.: MIT Press, 1973.

Executive Office of the President, Office of Management and Budget. *Standard Industrial Classification Manual, 1972.* Washington, D.C.: Government Printing Office.

National Labor Relations Act (Wagner Act), Pub. L. No. 74-198, 49 Stat. 449–50 (1935).

National Labor Relations Board. *Basic Guide to the National Labor Relations Act: General Principles of Law under Statute and Procedures of the National Labor Relations Board.* Washington, D.C.: U.S. Government Printing Office, 1997.

——. Election Report, FY 2016. Election Report for Cases Closed.

——. Monthly Reports, 1970–1986. Election Reports: Cases Closed.

National Labor Relations Board Annual Reports, 1949–2005.

United States Bureau of the Census. *The Statistical History of the United States from Colonial Times to the Present.* New York: Basic Books, 1976.

United States Congress, House of Representatives. *Pressures in Today's Workplace,* vols. 1–3. Oversight Hearings before the Subcommittee on Labor-Management Relations of the Committee on Education and Labor, 96th Congress, First and Second Sessions. Washington, D.C.: Government Printing Office, 1980.

U.S. Department of Commerce, United States Bureau of the Census. *Statistical Abstract of the United States: 1990.* Washington, D.C.: Government Printing Office, 1990.

——. *Statistical Abstract of the United States: 2003*. Washington, D.C.: Government Printing Office, 2003.

——. *Statistical Abstract of the United States: 2012*. Washington, D.C.: Government Printing Office, 2012.

U.S. Department of Labor, Bureau of Labor Statistics. *Analysis of Work Stoppages, 1978*, Bulletin 2066. Washington, D.C.: Government Printing Office, 1980.

——. *Analysis of Work Stoppages, 1979*, Bulletin 2092. Washington, D.C.: Government Printing Office, 1981.

——. Economic News Releases, 2010–2017.

——. "Employment, Hours, and Earnings from the Current Employment Statistics (National, SIC basis)." September 2016. http://www.bls.gov/data /archived.htm.

——. "Employment, Hours, and Earnings from the Current Employment Statistics (National)." February 2017. https://www.bls.gov/data/#employment.

——. *Handbook of Labor Statistics,* Bulletin 2217. Washington, D.C.: Government Printing Office, 1985.

——. *Major Work Stoppages in 2015*. February 10, 2016. http://www.bls.gov/news .release/pdf/wkstp.pdf.

——. *National Compensation Survey: Employee Benefits in the United States, March 2015*, Bulletin 2782. September 2016. http://www.bls.gov/ncs/ebs /benefits/2015/ebbl0057.pdf.

——. *Perspectives on Working Women: A Databook*, Bulletin 2080. Washington, D.C.: Government Printing Office, 1980.

——. "Union Affiliation by Employed Wage and Salary Workers by Sex, Race, and Hispanic or Latino Ethnicity, Annual Averages 1983–2015." Washington, D.C.: BLS, 2016.

——. *Women in the Labor Force: A Databook, December 2015*, Report 1059. February 2017. https://www.bls.gov/opub/reports/womens-databook/archive /women-in-the-labor-force-a-databook-2015.pdf.

Newspapers and Periodicals

Atlanta Journal and Constitution

Baltimore Afro-American

Baltimore Sun

Boston Globe

Business Week

Charlotte Observer

Chicago Tribune

Christian Science Monitor

Daily Independent (Kannapolis, N.C.)

Daily News-Record (Harrisonburg, Va.)

Daily Press (Newport News, Va.)

Detroit News

Equal Times

Forbes

Greensboro (N.C.) Daily News

Los Angeles Sentinel

Los Angeles Times

Nation

Newsweek

New York Amsterdam News

New York Times

Norfolk Journal and Guide

Progressive

Seattle Times

Southern Exposure
TIME
Times-Herald (Newport News, Va.)
Tuscaloosa (Ala.) Times
U.S. News and World Report

Wall Street Journal
Washingtonian
Washington Post
Washington Star
Winston-Salem (N.C.) Journal

Trade, Business, and Union Journals and Newsletters

9to5 Newsletter (National
  Association of Working
  Women)
9to5: Newsletter for Boston Area Office
  Workers (or 9to5 News)
AFL-CIO American Federationist
AFL-CIO News
Chain Store Age
Daily Labor Report
Daily News Record (DNR)
Dunn's Business Month
FLIGHTLOG
Harvard Business Review

Memorandum: Newsletter of Women
  Office Workers at Harvard
Monthly Labor Review
Retail Clerks Advocate
Retail Week
S&S News
Solidarity
Southern Textile News
Steelabor (or Steel Labor)
Textile Industries
UFCW Action
Union Leader (UFCW Local 400
  newsletter)

Other Primary Sources

AFL-CIO. "List of Large NLRB Elections, 1961 to 2010." November 1, 2010. Unpublished report in the author's possession.

——. "Our Voices: A Snapshot of Working Women, Results from a National Survey of Nearly 25,000 Working Women." Washington, D.C.: AFL-CIO, 2016.

——. Proceedings of the Sixteenth Constitutional Convention of the AFL-CIO, Anaheim, CA, October 28–31, 1985. Washington, D.C.: AFL-CIO, 1985.

——"Resolution 5: A Nation of Immigrants." AFL-CIO Convention Resolution, December 2001. http://www.aflcio.org/content/download/6951/75037/file /res5.pdf.

Congress of Industrial Organizations. 1949 Proceedings of the Eleventh Constitutional Convention of the Congress of Industrial Organizations, Cleveland, Ohio, October 31–November 4, 1949. Washington, D.C.: CIO, 1949.

Economic Policy Institute, State of Working America Data Library, 2017. http:// www.epi.org/data/

Gallup. Accessed April 29, 2016. "Labor Unions." http://www.gallup.com/poll /12751/labor-unions.aspx.

Kraft Opinion Research Center. "A Survey of Opinion toward Unions among Woodward & Lothrop Employees in the Washington Area." Washington, D.C.: UFCW Research Department, UFCW Headquarters Records, March 1979.

Sidney Hollander Associates for TWUA. "Attitudes of Cannon Workers in Kannapolis/Concord: The Job, the Employer, the Union. A Pilot Study." Baltimore: Sidney Hollander Associates, 1976.

United Steelworkers of America. *Eighty-Eight Close the Gate*. VHS. Pittsburgh: USWA, 1980.

United Steelworkers of America, Local 8888. "Local 8888: Proud with a Purpose." Brochure. June 26, 1985. In the author's possession.

Zucker, Norbert Y., Stella L. Hargett, and Irvin H. Bromall. *To Increase Minority and Female Utilization in the U.S. Maritime Industry. Final Report*. Washington, D.C.: Maritime Administration, U.S. Department of Transportation, 1985.

Secondary Sources

Aaronson, Susan A. *Taking Trade to the Streets: The Lost History of Public Efforts to Shape Globalization*. Ann Arbor: University of Michigan Press, 2001.

Abernathy, Frederick H. *A Stitch in Time: Lean Retailing and the Transformation of Manufacturing—Lessons from the Apparel and Textile Industries*. New York: Oxford University Press, 1999.

Adams, Roy J. "Union Certification as an Instrument of Labor Policy: A Comparative Perspective." In *Restoring the Promise of American Labor Law*, edited by Sheldon Friedman, Richard Hurd, Rudolph A. Oswald, and Ronald L. Seeber, 241–49. Ithaca, N.Y.: ILR Press, 1994.

Adams, Thomas Jessen. "Making the New Shop Floor: Wal-Mart, Labor Control, and the History of the Postwar Discount Retail Industry in America." In *Wal-Mart: The Face of Twenty-First-Century Capitalism*, edited by Nelson Lichtenstein, 213–29. New York: New Press, 2006.

Anderson, Cynthia D. *The Social Consequences of Economic Restructuring in the Textile Industry: Change in a Southern Mill Village*. New York: Garland, 2000.

Anderson, Karen. "First Fired: Black Women Workers during World War II." *Journal of American History* 69, no. 1 (June 1982): 82–97.

Andrias, Kate. "The New Labor Law." *The Yale Law Journal* 126: no.1 (Oct. 2016): 2–100.

Appelbaum, Eileen, and Rosemary Batt. *Private Equity at Work: When Wall Street Manages Main Street*. New York: Russell Sage Foundation, 2014.

Appelbaum, Richard, and Nelson Lichtenstein. "A New World of Retail Supremacy: Supply Chains and Workers' Chains in the Age of Wal-Mart." *International Labor and Working-Class History* 70 (Fall 2006): 106–25.

Arnesen, Eric, Julie Greene, and Bruce Laurie, eds. *Labor Histories: Class, Politics, and the Working-Class Experience*. Urbana: University of Illinois Press, 1998.

Ashby, Steven K., and C. J. Hawking. *Staley: The Fight for a New American Labor Movement*. Urbana: University of Illinois Press, 2009.

Bailey, Beth L., and David R. Farber. *America in the Seventies*. Lawrence: University Press of Kansas, 2004.

Bao, Xiaolan. *Holding Up More than Half the Sky: Chinese Women Garment Workers in New York City, 1948–92*. Urbana: University of Illinois Press, 2001.

Bardacke, Frank. *Trampling Out the Vintage: Cesar Chavez and the Two Souls of the United Farm Workers*. London: Verso, 2011.

Barry, Kathleen M. *Femininity in Flight: A History of Flight Attendants*. Durham, N.C.: Duke University Press, 2007.

Becker, Craig. "Democracy in the Workplace: Union Representation Elections and Federal Labor Law." *Minnesota Law Review* 77 (1991–1993): 495–603.

Bennett, James T., and Bruce E. Kaufman, eds. *The Future of Private Sector Unionism in the United States*. Armonk, N.Y.: M. E. Sharpe, 2002.

Benson, Susan Porter. *Counter Cultures: Saleswomen, Managers, and Customers in American Department Stores, 1890–1940*. Urbana: University of Illinois Press, 1986.

Berkowitz, Edward D. *Something Happened: A Political and Cultural Overview of the Seventies*. New York: Columbia University Press, 2006.

Berkowitz, Edward D., and Kim McQuaid. *Creating the Welfare State: The Political Economy of 20th-Century Reform*. 2nd ed. New York: Praeger, 1988.

Best, Samuel J., and Brian S. Krueger. *Exit Polls: Surveying the American Electorate, 1972–2010*. Washington, D.C.: CQ Press, 2014.

Bivens, Josh and Lawrence Mishel. "Understanding the Historic Divergence Between Productivity and a Typical Workers' Pay: Why It Matters and Why It's Real." Briefing Paper #406. Washington, D.C.: Economic Policy Institute, 2015.

Bluestone, Barry. *The Retail Revolution: Market Transformation, Investment, and Labor in the Modern Department Store*. Boston: Auburn House, 1981.

Bluestone, Barry, and Bennett Harrison. *The Deindustrialization of America: Plant Closings, Community Abandonment, and the Dismantling of Basic Industry*. New York: Basic Books, 1982.

Bonacich, Edna. *Global Production: The Apparel Industry in the Pacific Rim*. Philadelphia: Temple University Press, 1994.

Bonacich, Edna, and Jake B. Wilson. *Getting the Goods: Ports, Labor, and the Logistics Revolution*. Ithaca, N.Y.: Cornell University Press, 2008.

Boris, Eileen, and Jennifer Klein. *Caring for America: Home Health Workers in the Shadow of the Welfare State*. New York: Oxford University Press, 2012.

Borstelmann, Thomas. *The 1970s: A New Global History from Civil Rights to Economic Inequality*. Princeton, N.J.: Princeton University Press, 2012.

Boyle, Kevin. *The UAW and the Heyday of American Liberalism, 1945–1968*. Ithaca, N.Y.: Cornell University Press, 1995.

Braden, Anne. "Shoulder to Shoulder." *Southern Exposure* 9, no. 4 (Winter 1981): 88–93.

Brecher, Jeremy. *Strike!* Rev. ed. Oakland, Calif.: PM Press, 2014.

Brecher, Jeremy, and Tim Costello, eds. *Building Bridges: The Emerging Grassroots Coalition of Labor and Community*. New York: Monthly Review Press, 1990.

Brenner, Aaron, Robert Brenner, and Calvin Winslow, eds. *Rebel Rank and File: Labor Militancy and Revolt from Below in the Long 1970s*. London: Verso, 2010.

Brenner, Robert. *The Boom and the Bubble: The US in the World Economy*. London: Verso, 2002.

———. *The Economics of Global Turbulence: The Advanced Capitalist Economies from Long Boom to Long Downturn, 1945–2005*. London: Verso, 2006.

———. "The Political Economy of the Rank-and-File Rebellion." In *Rebel Rank and File: Labor Militancy and Revolt from Below in the Long 1970s*, edited by Aaron Brenner, Robert Brenner, and Calvin Winslow, 37–74. London: Verso, 2010.

Brody, David. *Labor Embattled: History, Power, Rights*. Urbana: University of Illinois Press, 2005.

———. "Workplace Contractualism in Comparative Perspective." In *Industrial Democracy in America: The Ambiguous Promise*, edited by Nelson Lichtenstein and Howell John Harris, 176–205. Washington, D.C.: Woodrow Wilson Center Press, 1993.

Bronfenbrenner, Kate. "Uneasy Terrain: The Impact of Capital Mobility on Workers, Wages, and Union Organizing." Cornell University, ILR School, 2000. http://digitalcommons.ilr.cornell.edu/reports/3/.

———. "We'll Close! Plant Closings, Plant-Closing Threats, Union Organizing and NAFTA." *Multinational Monitor* 18, no. 3 (1997): 8–14.

Bronfenbrenner, Kate, Sheldon Friedman, Richard W. Hurd, Rudolph A. Oswald, and Ronald L. Seeber, eds. *Organizing to Win: New Research on Union Strategies*. Ithaca, N.Y.: ILR Press, 1998.

Bronfenbrenner, Kate, and Tom Juravich. "It Takes More than House Calls: Organizing to Win with a Comprehensive Union-Building Strategy." In *Organizing to Win: New Research on Union Strategies*, edited by Kate Bronfenbrenner, Sheldon Friedman, Richard W. Hurd, Rudolph A. Oswald, and Ronald L. Seeber, 19–36. Ithaca, N.Y.: ILR Press, 1998.

———. *Union Organizing in the Public Sector: An Analysis of State and Local Elections*. Ithaca, N.Y.: ILR Press, 1995.

Brown, Jonathan C. *Workers' Control in Latin America, 1930–1979*. Chapel Hill: University of North Carolina Press, 1997.

Brown, Michael K. "Bargaining for Social Rights: Unions and the Reemergence of Welfare Capitalism, 1945–1952." *Political Science Quarterly* 112, no. 4 (Winter 1997): 645–74.

———. *Race, Money, and the American Welfare State*. Ithaca, N.Y.: Cornell University Press, 1999.

Budd, John W. "The Effects of Unions on Employee Benefits and Non-Wage Compensation: Monopoly Power, Collective Voice, and Facilitation." In *What Do Unions Do? A Twenty-Year Perspective*, edited by James T. Bennett and Bruce E. Kaufman, 160–92. Piscataway, N.J.: Transaction, 2007.

Campbell, Joan. *European Labor Unions*. Westport, Conn.: Greenwood, 1992.

Carroll, Peter N. *It Seemed like Nothing Happened: The Tragedy and Promise of America in the 1970s*. New York: Holt, Rinehart and Winston, 1982.

Cassedy, Ellen, and Karen Nussbaum. *9 to 5: The Working Woman's Guide to Office Survival*. New York: Penguin, 1983.

Chaison, Gary N., and Joseph B. Rose. "The Canadian Perspective on Workers' Right to Form a Union and Bargain Collectively." In *Restoring the Promise of American Labor Law*, edited by Sheldon Friedman, Richard Hurd, Rudolph A. Oswald, and Ronald L. Seeber, 241–49. Ithaca, N.Y.: ILR Press, 1994.

Choi, Ying-Pik, Hwa Soo Chung, Nicolas Marian, and Programme of Cooperation among Developing Countries, Exporters of Textiles and Clothing. *The Multi-Fibre Arrangement in Theory and Practice*. London: Frances Pinter, 1985.

Chorev, Nitsan. *Remaking U.S. Trade Policy: From Protectionism to Globalization*. Ithaca, N.Y.: Cornell University Press, 2007.

Cline, William R. *The Future of World Trade in Textiles and Apparel*. Washington, D.C.: Institute for International Economics, 1990.

Cobb, James C. *The Selling of the South: The Southern Crusade for Industrial Development, 1936–1980*. Baton Rouge: Louisiana State University Press, 1982.

Cobble, Dorothy Sue. *Dishing It Out: Waitresses and Their Unions in the Twentieth Century*. Urbana: University of Illinois Press, 1991.

———. *The Other Women's Movement: Workplace Justice and Social Rights in Modern America*. Princeton, N.J.: Princeton University Press, 2004.

———. *The Sex of Class: Women Transforming American Labor*. Ithaca, N.Y.: ILR Press, 2007.

———. "'A Spontaneous Loss of Enthusiasm': Workplace Feminism and the Transformation of Women's Service Jobs in the 1970s." *International Labor and Working Class History* 56 (October 1999): 23–44.

Cobble, Dorothy Sue, and Alice Kessler-Harris. "Karen Nussbaum: In Conversation with Dorothy Sue Cobble and Alice Kessler-Harris." In *Talking Leadership: Conversations with Powerful Women*, edited by Mary S. Hartman, 135–55. New Brunswick, N.J.: Rutgers University Press, 1999.

Cohen, Lizabeth. *A Consumers' Republic: The Politics of Mass Consumption in Postwar America*. New York: Alfred A. Knopf, 2003.

Collins, Jane Lou. *Threads: Gender, Labor, and Power in the Global Apparel Industry*. Chicago: University of Chicago Press, 2003.

Collins, Robert M. *More: The Politics of Economic Growth in Postwar America*. New York: Oxford University Press, 2000.

Conway, Mimi. *Rise Gonna Rise: A Portrait of Southern Textile Workers*. Garden City, N.Y.: Anchor, 1979.

Coulter, Kendra. "Raising Retail: Organizing Retail Workers in Canada and the United States." *Labor Studies Journal* 38, no. 1 (2013): 47–65.

Cowie, Jefferson. *Capital Moves: RCA's Seventy-Year Quest for Cheap Labor*. Ithaca, N.Y.: Cornell University Press, 1999.

———. *Stayin' Alive: The 1970s and the Last Days of the Working Class*. New York: New Press, 2010.

Cowie, Jefferson, and Nick Salvatore. "The Long Exception: Rethinking the Place of the New Deal in American History." *International Labor and Working-Class History* 74, no. 1 (2008): 3–32.

Craft, James A., and Marian M. Exteit. "New Strategies in Union Organizing." *Journal of Labor Research* 4, no. 1 (Winter 1983): 19–32.

Daniel, Cletus E. *Culture of Misfortune: An Interpretive History of Textile Unionism in the United States.* Ithaca, N.Y.: ILR Press, 2001.

Davies, Margery W. *Woman's Place Is at the Typewriter: Office Work and Office Workers, 1870–1930.* Philadelphia: Temple University Press, 1982.

Davis, Gerald F. *Managed by the Markets: How Finance Reshaped America.* New York: Oxford University Press, 2009.

Davis, Mike. *Prisoners of the American Dream: Politics and Economy in the History of the U.S. Working Class.* London: Verso, 1986.

Delgado, Hector. *New Immigrants, Old Unions: Organizing Undocumented Workers in Los Angeles.* Philadelphia: Temple University Press, 1993.

DeMaria, Alfred T. *How Management Wins Union Organizing Campaigns.* New York: Executive Enterprises, Prentice-Hall, 1982.

Derdak, Thomas. *International Directory of Company Histories.* Vol. 1. Chicago: St. James, 1988.

Derickson, Alan. *Health Security for All: Dreams of Universal Health Care in America.* Baltimore: Johns Hopkins University Press, 2005.

Deslippe, Dennis. *Rights, Not Roses: Unions and the Rise of Working-Class Feminism, 1945–80.* Urbana: University of Illinois Press, 2000.

Destler, I. M. *American Trade Politics.* Washington, D.C.: Institute for International Economics, 2005.

Dickerson, Kitty G. *Textiles and Apparel in the Global Economy.* Upper Saddle River, N.J.: Merrill, 1999.

Dobbin, Frank, and Dirk Zorn. "Corporate Malfeasance and the Myth of Shareholder Value." *Political Power and Social Theory* 17 (2005): 179–98.

Draper, Alan. *Conflict of Interests: Organized Labor and the Civil Rights Movement in the South, 1954–1968.* Ithaca, N.Y.: ILR Press, 1994.

Draut, Tamara. *Sleeping Giant: How the New Working Class Will Transform America.* New York: Doubleday, 2016.

Dubofsky, Melvyn. *The State and Labor in Modern America.* Chapel Hill: University of North Carolina Press, 1994.

Edsall, Thomas Byrne, and Mary D. Edsall. *Chain Reaction: The Impact of Race, Rights, and Taxes on American Politics.* New York: Norton, 1991.

Eidelson, Josh. "Alt-Labor." *American Prospect,* January 28, 2013. http://prospect.org/article/alt-labor.

Erikson, Robert S., Thomas D. Lancaster, and David W. Romero. "Group Components of the Presidential Vote, 1952–1984." *Journal of Politics* 51, no. 2 (1989): 337–46.

Esping-Andersen, Gøsta. *Social Foundations of Postindustrial Economies*. Oxford: Oxford University Press, 1999.

———. *The Three Worlds of Welfare Capitalism*. Princeton, N.J.: Princeton University Press, 1990.

Essletzbichler, Jurgen. "The Geography of Job Creation and Destruction in the U.S. Manufacturing Sector, 1967–1997." *Annals of the Association of American Geographers* 94, no. 3 (2004): 602–19.

Evans, Sara M. *Tidal Wave: How Women Changed America at Century's End*. New York: Free Press, 2003.

Fantasia, Rick, and Kim Voss. *Hard Work: Remaking the American Labor Movement*. Berkeley: University of California Press, 2004.

Farber, Henry S. "Trends in Worker Demand for Union Representation." *American Economic Review* 79, no. 2 (May 1989): 166–71.

Farber, Henry S., and Bruce Western. *Round Up the Usual Suspects: The Decline of Unions in the Private Sector, 1973–1998*. Princeton, N.J.: Industrial Relations Section, Princeton University, 2000.

Ferguson, Niall. *The Shock of the Global: The 1970s in Perspective*. Cambridge, Mass.: Belknap Press of Harvard University Press, 2010.

Filippelli, Ronald L., and Mark McColloch. *Cold War in the Working Class: The Rise and Decline of the United Electrical Workers*. Albany: State University of New York Press, 1995.

Fine, Lisa M. *The Souls of the Skyscraper: Female Clerical Workers in Chicago, 1870–1930*. Philadelphia: Temple University Press, 1990.

Fink, Joey. "In Good Faith: Working-Class Women, Feminism, and Religious Support in the Struggle to Organize J. P. Stevens Textile Workers in the Southern Piedmont, 1974–1980." *Southern Spaces*, July 15, 2014. https://southernspaces .org/2014/good-faith-working-class-women-feminism-and-religious-support -struggle-organize-j-p-stevens.

Fink, Leon. *The Maya of Morganton: Work and Community in the Nuevo New South*. With research assistance from Alvis E. Dunn. Chapel Hill: University of North Carolina Press, 2003.

Fink, Leon, and Brian Greenberg. *Upheaval in the Quiet Zone: 1199SEIU and the Politics of Health Care Unionism*. Urbana: University of Illinois Press, 2009.

Fix, Michael E., and Jeffrey S. Passel. "U.S. Immigration at the Beginning of the 21st Century: Testimony before the Subcommittee on Immigration and Claims Hearing, U.S. House of Representatives." Urban Institute, August 2, 2001. http://www.urban.org/sites/default/files/alfresco/publication-pdfs/900417-U -S-Immigration-at-the-Beginning-of-the-st-Century.pdf.

Foerster, Amy. "Labor's Youth Brigade: What Can the Organizing Institute and Its Graduates Tell Us about the Future of Organized Labor." *Labor Studies Journal* 28, no. 3 (Fall 2003): 1–32.

Foner, Philip Sheldon. *Women and the American Labor Movement*. New York: Free Press, 1979.

Fones-Wolf, Elizabeth A. *Selling Free Enterprise: The Business Assault on Labor and Liberalism, 1945–1960.* Urbana: University of Illinois Press, 1994.

Fonow, Mary Margaret. *Union Women: Forging Feminism in the United Steelworkers of America.* Minneapolis: University of Minnesota Press, 2003.

Formisano, Ronald P. *Boston against Busing: Race, Class, and Ethnicity in the 1960s and 1970s.* Chapel Hill: University of North Carolina Press, 1991.

Foulkes, Fred K. *Personnel Policies in Large Nonunion Companies.* Englewood Cliffs, N.J.: Prentice-Hall, 1980.

Francia, Peter L. *The Future of Organized Labor in American Politics.* New York: Columbia University Press, 2006.

——. "Voting on Values or Bread-and-Butter? Effects of Union Membership on the Politics of the White Working Class." *Perspectives on Work* 12, nos. 1–2 (Summer 2008/Winter 2009): 27–31.

Frank, Dana. *Buy American: The Untold Story of Economic Nationalism.* Boston: Beacon, 1999.

Fraser, Steve. "The 'Labor Question.'" In *The Rise and Fall of the New Deal Order, 1930–1980,* edited by Steve Fraser and Gary Gerstle, 55–84. Princeton, N.J.: Princeton University Press, 1989.

Fraser, Steve, and Gary Gerstle, eds. *The Rise and Fall of the New Deal Order, 1930–1980.* Princeton, N.J.: Princeton University Press, 1989.

Frederickson, Mary E. *Looking South: Race, Gender, and the Transformation of Labor from Reconstruction to Globalization.* Gainesville: University Press of Florida, 2011.

Freeman, Joshua Benjamin. *Working-Class New York: Life and Labor since World War II.* New York: New Press, 2000.

Freeman, Richard B. *America Works: The Exceptional U.S. Labor Market.* New York: Russell Sage Foundation, 2007.

——. "Spurts in Union Growth: Defining Moments and Social Processes." In *The Defining Moment: The Great Depression and the American Economy in the Twentieth Century,* edited by Michael D. Bordo, Claudia Golden, and Eugene N. White, 265–96. Chicago: University of Chicago Press, 1998.

——. "What Do Unions Do? The 2004 M-Brane Stringtwister Edition." In *The Future of Private Sector Unionism in the United States,* edited by James T. Bennett and Bruce E. Kaufman, 607–36. Armonk, N.Y.: M. E. Sharpe, 2002.

——. "Why Are Unions Faring Poorly in NLRB Elections?" In *Challenges and Choices Facing American Labor,* edited by Thomas A. Kochan, 45–64. Cambridge, Mass.: MIT Press, 1985.

Freeman, Richard B., Eunice Han, David Madland, and Brendan V. Duke. "How Does Declining Unionism Affect the American Middle Class and Intergenerational Mobility?" National Bureau of Economic Research, 2015. http://www.nber.org/papers/w21638

Freeman, Richard B., and Casey Ichniowski. *When Public Sector Workers Unionize.* Chicago: University of Chicago Press, 1988.

Freeman, Richard B., and Morris M. Kleiner. "Employer Behavior in the Face of Union Organizing Drives." *Industrial and Labor Relations Review* 43, no. 4 (April 1990): 351–65.

Freeman, Richard B., and James L. Medoff. *What Do Unions Do?* New York: Basic Books, 1984.

Freeman, Richard B., and Joel Rogers. *What Workers Want.* Ithaca, N.Y.: ILR Press, 2006.

Friedman, Tami J. "Capital Flight, 'States' Rights,' and the Anti-Labor Offensive after World War II." In *The Right and Labor in America: Politics, Ideology, and Imagination,* edited by Nelson Lichtenstein and Elizabeth Tandy Shermer, 79–97. Philadelphia: University of Pennsylvania Press, 2012.

Frum, David. *How We Got Here: The 70's, the Decade That Brought You Modern Life (for Better or Worse).* New York: Basic Books, 2000.

Frymer, Paul. *Black and Blue: African Americans, the Labor Movement, and the Decline of the Democratic Party.* Princeton, N.J.: Princeton University Press, 2008.

Fulmer, William E. *Union Organizing: Management and Labor Conflict.* New York: Praeger, 1982.

Gabin, Nancy Felice. *Feminism in the Labor Movement: Women and the United Auto Workers, 1935–1975.* Ithaca, N.Y.: Cornell University Press, 1990.

Ganz, Marshall, Kim Voss, Teresa Sharpe, Carl Somers, and George Strauss. "Against the Tide: Projects and Pathways of the New Generation of Union Leaders, 1984–2001." In *Rebuilding Labor: Organizing and Organizers in the New Union Movement,* edited by Ruth Milkman and Kim Voss, 150–94. Ithaca, N.Y.: Cornell University Press, 2004.

Garcia, Matt. *From the Jaws of Victory: The Triumph and Tragedy of Cesar Chavez and the Farm Worker Movement.* Berkeley: University of California Press, 2012.

Geoghegan, Thomas. *Were You Born on the Wrong Continent? How the European Model Can Help You Get a Life.* New York: New Press, 2010.

——. *Which Side Are You On? Trying to Be for Labor When It's Flat on Its Back.* New York: Plume, 1991.

Gereffi, Gary, and Miguel Korzeniewicz, eds. *Commodity Chains and Global Capitalism.* Westport, Conn.: Greenwood, 1994.

Gibson, Campbell J., and Emily Lennon. "Historical Census Statistics on the Foreign-Born Population of the United States, 1850–1990." Washington, D.C.: U.S. Bureau of the Census, 1999.

Gilpin, Toni, Gary Isaac, Dan Letwin, and Jack McKivigan. *On Strike for Respect: The Clerical and Technical Workers' Strike at Yale University, 1984–85.* Urbana: University of Illinois Press, 1995.

Glenn, Evelyn Nakano. "Racial Ethnic Women's Labor: The Intersection of Race, Gender, and Class Oppression." *Review of Radical Political Economies* 17, no. 3 (1985): 86–108.

Glenn, Susan A. *Daughters of the Shtetl: Life and Labor in the Immigrant Generation*. Ithaca, N.Y.: Cornell University Press, 1990.

Glick, Phyllis Sharon. "Bridging Feminism and Trade Unionism: A Study of Working Women's Organizing in the United States." Ph.D. diss., Graduate School for Advanced Studies in Social Welfare, Brandeis University, 1983.

Goldfield, Michael. *The Decline of Organized Labor in the United States*. Chicago: University of Chicago Press, 1987.

Goldfield, Michael, and Amy Bromsen, "The Changing Landscape of US Unions in Historical and Theoretical Perspective." *Annual Review of Political Science* 16 (2013): 231–57.

Goldstein, Leslie Friedman. *The Constitutional Rights of Women: Cases in Law and Social Change*. 2nd ed. Madison: University of Wisconsin Press, 1989.

Gordon, Colin. *Dead on Arrival: The Politics of Health Care in Twentieth-Century America*. Princeton, N.J.: Princeton University Press, 2004.

———. *New Deals: Business, Labor, and Politics in America, 1920–1935*. Cambridge: Cambridge University Press, 1994.

Gordon, David. "Chickens Home to Roost: From Prosperity to Stagnation in the Postwar U.S. Economy." In *Understanding American Economic Decline*, edited by Michael A. Bernstein and David E. Adler, 34–76. Cambridge: Cambridge University Press, 1994.

Gordon, Linda. "Black and White Visions of Welfare: Women's Welfare Activism, 1890–1945." *Journal of American History* 78, no. 2 (September 1991): 559–90.

———. *Pitied but Not Entitled: Single Mothers and the History of Welfare, 1890–1935*. New York: Free Press, 1994.

Gottschalk, Marie. *The Shadow Welfare State: Labor, Business, and the Politics of Health-Care in the United States*. Ithaca, N.Y.: ILR Press, 2000.

Gould, Elise, Jessica Schieder, and Kathleen Geier, "What Is the Gender Pay Gap and Is It Real?" Economic Policy Institute, October 20, 2016. http://www.epi .org/publication/what-is-the-gender-pay-gap-and-is-it-real/

Greenbaum, Joan M. *Windows on the Workplace: Technology, Jobs, and the Organization of Office Work*. New York: Monthly Review Press, 2004.

Greene, Julie. *Pure and Simple Politics: The American Federation of Labor and Political Activism, 1881–1917*. Cambridge: Cambridge University Press, 1998.

Greenhouse, Steven. *The Big Squeeze: Tough Times for the American Worker*. New York: Alfred A. Knopf, 2008.

Greider, William. *One World, Ready or Not: The Manic Logic of Global Capitalism*. New York: Simon and Schuster, 1997.

Griffith, Barbara S. *The Crisis of American Labor: Operation Dixie and the Defeat of the CIO*. Philadelphia: Temple University Press, 1988.

Gross, James A. *Broken Promise: The Subversion of U.S. Labor Relations Policy, 1947–1994*. Philadelphia: Temple University Press, 1995.

———. *The Making of the National Labor Relations Board: A Study in Economics, Politics, and the Law*. Albany: State University of New York Press, 1974.

——. *The Reshaping of the National Labor Relations Board: National Labor Policy in Transition, 1937–1947*. Albany: State University of New York Press, 1981.

Hacker, Jacob S. *The Divided Welfare State: The Battle over Public and Private Social Benefits in the United States*. New York: Cambridge University Press, 2002.

Hacker, Jacob S., and Paul Pierson. *Winner-Take-All Politics: How Washington Made the Rich Richer—and Turned Its Back on the Middle Class*. New York: Simon and Schuster, 2010.

Hall, Jacquelyn Dowd. "The Long Civil Rights Movement and the Political Uses of the Past." *Journal of American History* 91, no. 4 (2005): 1233–63.

Hall, Jacquelyn Dowd, James Leloudis, Robert Korstad, Mary Murphy, Lu Ann Jones, and Christopher B. Daly. *Like a Family: The Making of a Southern Cotton Mill World*. Chapel Hill: University of North Carolina Press, 1987.

Hall, Peter A., and David W. Soskice. *Varieties of Capitalism: The Institutional Foundations of Comparative Advantage*. Oxford: Oxford University Press, 2001.

Halpern, Rick. "The Iron Fist and the Velvet Glove: Welfare Capitalism in Chicago's Packinghouses, 1921–1933." *Journal of American Studies* 26, no. 2 (1992): 159–83.

Hamilton, Shane. *Trucking Country: The Road to America's Wal-Mart Economy*. Princeton, N.J.: Princeton University Press, 2008.

Harley, Sharon, Francille Rusan Wilson, and Shirley Wilson Logan. "Introduction: Historical Overview of Black Women and Work." In *Sister Circle: Black Women and Work*, edited by Sharon Harley and the Black Women and Work Collective, 1–12. New Brunswick, N.J.: Rutgers University Press, 2002.

Harrington, Michael. *The Other America: Poverty in the United States*. New York: Macmillan, 1962.

——. *The Retail Clerks*. New York: John Wiley and Sons, 1962.

Harris, Edward, and Frank Sammartino. "Trends in the Distribution of Household Income between 1979 and 2007." Pub. No. 4031. Washington, D.C.: Congressional Budget Office, 2011.

Harrison, Bennett, and Barry Bluestone. *The Great U-Turn: Corporate Restructuring and the Polarizing of America*. New York: Basic Books, 1990.

Harvey, David. *A Brief History of Neoliberalism*. Oxford: Oxford University Press, 2005.

Hatton, Erin Elizabeth. *The Temp Economy: From Kelly Girls to Permatemps in Postwar America*. Philadelphia: Temple University Press, 2011.

Hill, Herbert. *Black Labor and the American Legal System: Race, Work, and the Law*. Madison: University of Wisconsin Press, 1985.

Hirsch, Barry T., and David A. Macpherson. "Union Membership and Coverage Database from the CPS." Accessed September 8, 2016. http://www.unionstats.com.

——. *Union Membership and Earnings Data Book: Compilations from the Current Population Survey*. Arlington, Va.: Bureau of National Affairs, 2015.

Hobsbawm, Eric John. *Age of Extremes: The Short Twentieth Century, 1914–1991*. London: Abacus, 2003.

Hoerr, John P. *We Can't Eat Prestige: The Women Who Organized Harvard.* Philadelphia: Temple University Press, 1997.

Honey, Michael K. *Southern Labor and Black Civil Rights: Organizing Memphis Workers.* Urbana: University of Illinois Press, 1993.

Hower, Joseph E., and Joseph A. McCartin. "Marshall's Principle: A Former Labor Secretary Looks Back (and Ahead)." *Labor: Studies in Working-Class History of the Americas* 11, no. 4 (2014): 91–107.

Hughes, Charles L. *Making Unions Unnecessary.* New York: Executive Enterprises, 1976.

Hughes, Charles L., and Alfred T. DeMaria. *Managing to Stay Non-Union.* New York: Executive Enterprises, 1979.

Hurd, Richard W. "Learning from Clerical Unions: Two Cases of Organizing Success." *Labor Studies Journal* 14, no. 1 (1989): 30–51.

——. "Organizing and Representing Clerical Workers." In *Women and Unions: Forging a Partnership*, edited by Dorothy Sue Cobble, 316–36. Ithaca, N.Y.: ILR Press, 1993.

Hurd, Richard W., and Adrienne McElwain. "Organizing Clerical Workers: Determinants of Success." *Industrial and Labor Relations Review* 41, no. 3 (April 1988): 360–73.

Irons, Janet Christine. *Testing the New Deal: The General Textile Strike of 1934 in the American South.* Urbana: University of Illinois Press, 2000.

Isaac, Larry, and Lars Christiansen. "How the Civil Rights Movement Revitalized Labor Militancy." *American Sociological Review* 67, no. 5 (October 2002): 722–46.

Jackson, Gordon E. *When Labor Trouble Strikes: An Action Handbook.* Englewood Cliffs, N.J.: Prentice-Hall, 1981.

Jacobs, Meg. *Pocketbook Politics: Economic Citizenship in Twentieth-Century America.* Princeton, N.J.: Princeton University Press, 2005.

Jacobson, Margaret, and Filippo Occhino. "Behind the Decline in Labor's Share of Income." Federal Reserve Bank of Cleveland, February 3, 2012. https://www .clevelandfed.org/newsroom-and-events/publications/economic-trends/2012 -economic-trends/et-20120203-behind-the-decline-in-labors-share-of-income.aspx

Jacoby, Sanford M. *Modern Manors: Welfare Capitalism Since the New Deal.* Princeton, N.J.: Princeton University Press, 1997.

Jones, A. C. "Rank and File Opposition in the UAW in the Long 1970s." *Rebel Rank and File: Labor Militancy and Revolt from Below in the Long 1970s*, edited by Aaron Brenner, Robert Brenner, and Calvin Winslow, 281–308. London: Verso, 2010.

Jones, Jacqueline. *Labor of Love, Labor of Sorrow: Black Women, Work and the Family, from Slavery to the Present.* New York: Basic Books, 1985.

Jones, William Powell. *The March on Washington: Jobs, Freedom, and the Forgotten History of Civil Rights.* New York: W. W. Norton, 2013.

Jordan, Laura K. "Avoiding the 'Trap': Discursive Framing as a Means of Coping with Working Poverty." In *Retail Work*, edited by Irena Grugulis and Ödül Bozkurt, 149–71. Basingstoke, U.K.: Palgrave Macmillan, 2011.

Judis, John B. *The Paradox of American Democracy: Elites, Special Interests, and the Betrayal of Public Trust*. New York: Routledge, 2000.

Judt, Tony. *Postwar: A History of Europe since 1945*. New York: Penguin, 2005.

Juravich, Tom, and Kate Bronfenbrenner. *Ravenswood: The Steelworkers' Victory and the Revival of American Labor*. Ithaca, N.Y.: ILR Press, 1999.

Kalleberg, Arne L. *Good Jobs, Bad Jobs: The Rise of Polarized and Precarious Employment Systems in the United States, 1970s to 2000s*. New York: Russell Sage Foundation, 2011.

Katznelson, Ira. *Fear Itself: The New Deal and the Origins of Our Time*. New York: Liveright, 2013.

——. *When Affirmative Action Was White: An Untold History of Racial Inequality in Twentieth-Century America*. New York: W. W. Norton, 2005.

——. "Working-Class Formation: Constructing Cases and Comparisons." In *Working-Class Formation: Nineteenth-Century Patterns in Western Europe and the United States*, edited by Ira Katznelson and Aristide R. Zolberg, 3–41. Princeton, N.J.: Princeton University Press, 1986.

Kelly, Eileen P., and Gwen Seaquist. "NLRB v. Lechmere: Union Quest for Access." *Journal of Labor Research* 15, no. 2 (1994): 155–67.

Kessler-Harris, Alice. "Equal Employment Opportunity Commission v. Sears, Roebuck and Company: A Personal Account." *Feminist Review* 25 (1987): 46–69.

——. *In Pursuit of Equity: Women, Men, and the Quest for Economic Citizenship in 20th Century America*. New York: Oxford University Press, 2001.

——. *Out to Work: A History of Wage-Earning Women in the United States*. New York: Oxford University Press, 1982.

Kilgour, John G. *Preventative Labor Relations*. New York: Amacom, 1981.

Kistler, Alan. "Union Organizing: New Challenges and Prospects." *Annals of the American Academy of Political and Social Science* 473 (May 1984): 96–107.

Klein, Jennifer. *For All These Rights: Business, Labor, and the Shaping of America's Public-Private Welfare State*. Princeton, N.J.: Princeton University Press, 2003.

Kochan, Thomas A. *Challenges and Choices Facing American Labor*. Cambridge, Mass.: MIT Press, 1985.

Korstad, Robert Rodgers. *Civil Rights Unionism: Tobacco Workers and the Struggle for Democracy in the Mid-Twentieth-Century South*. Chapel Hill: University of North Carolina Press, 2003.

Korstad, Robert Rodgers, and Nelson Lichtenstein. "Opportunities Found and Lost: Labor, Radicals, and the Early Civil Rights Movement." *Journal of American History* 75, no. 3 (December 1988): 786–811.

Kraft, James P. *Vegas at Odds: Labor Conflict in a Leisure Economy, 1960–1985*. Baltimore: Johns Hopkins University Press, 2010.

Kruse, Kevin Michael. *White Flight: Atlanta and the Making of Modern Conservatism*. Princeton, N.J.: Princeton University Press, 2005.

Lassiter, Matthew D. *The Silent Majority: Suburban Politics in the Sunbelt South*. Princeton, N.J.: Princeton University Press, 2006.

Lee, Sophia A. "Whose Rights? Litigating the Right to Work." In *The Right and Labor in America: Politics, Ideology, and Imagination*, edited by Nelson Lichtenstein and Elizabeth Tandy Shermer, 160–80. Philadelphia: University of Pennsylvania Press, 2012.

Leicht, Kevin T. "On the Estimation of Union Threat Effects." *American Sociological Review* 54, no. 6 (December 1989): 1035–47.

Leifermann, Henry P. *Crystal Lee: A Woman of Inheritance*. New York: Macmillan, 1975.

Leiter, Jeffrey, Michael D. Schulman, and Rhonda Zingraff. *Hanging by a Thread: Social Change in Southern Textiles*. Ithaca, N.Y.: ILR Press, 1991.

Lerman, Robert I., and Stefanie R. Schmidt. *An Overview of Economic, Social, and Demographic Trends Affecting the US Labor Market*. Washington, D.C.: Urban Institute, August 1999.

Levinson, Marc. *The Box: How the Shipping Container Made the World Smaller and the World Economy Bigger*. Princeton, N.J.: Princeton University Press, 2008.

Levitt, Martin Jay, and Terry Conrow. *Confessions of a Union Buster*. New York: Crown, 1993.

Levy, Peter B. *The New Left and Labor in the 1960s*. Urbana: University of Illinois Press, 1994.

Lichtenstein, Nelson. *Labor's War at Home: The CIO in World War II*. With a new introduction by the author. Philadelphia: Temple University Press, 2003.

———. *The Most Dangerous Man in Detroit: Walter Reuther and the Fate of American Labor*. New York: Basic Books, 1995.

———. *The Retail Revolution: How Wal-Mart Created a Brave New World of Business*. New York: Metropolitan Books, 2009.

———. "The Return of Merchant Capitalism." *International Labor and Working Class History* 81 (Spring 2012): 8–27.

———. *State of the Union: A Century of American Labor*. Rev. ed. Princeton, N.J.: Princeton University Press, 2013.

———. "Wal-Mart, John Tate, and Their Anti-Union America." In *The Right and Labor in America: Politics, Ideology, and Imagination*, edited by Nelson Lichtenstein and Elizabeth Tandy Shermer, 252–75. Philadelphia: University of Pennsylvania Press, 2012.

———. *Wal-Mart: The Face of Twenty-First-Century Capitalism*. New York: New Press, 2006.

Lichtenstein, Nelson, and Elizabeth Tandy Shermer, eds. *The Right and Labor in America: Politics, Ideology, and Imagination*. Philadelphia: University of Pennsylvania Press, 2012.

Lin, Jan. *Reconstructing Chinatown: Ethnic Enclave, Global Change*. Minneapolis: University of Minnesota Press, 1998.

Linder, Marc. *Wars of Attrition: Vietnam, the Business Roundtable, and the Decline of Construction Unions*. Iowa City: Fanpihua, 1999.

Lipset, Seymour, and Ivan Katchanovski. "The Future of Private Sector Unions in the U.S." In *The Future of Private Sector Unionism in the United States*, edited by James T. Bennett and Bruce E. Kaufman, 9–27. Armonk, N.Y.: M. E. Sharpe, 2002.

Lisicky, Michael J. *Woodward & Lothrop: A Store Worthy of the Nation's Capital.* Charleston, S.C.: History Press, 2013.

Locke, Richard M. *Remaking the Italian Economy.* Ithaca, N.Y.: Cornell University Press, 1995.

Locke, Robert R., and J.-C. Spender. *Confronting Managerialism: How the Business Elite and Their Schools Threw Our Lives Out of Balance.* London: Zed Books, 2011.

Logan, John. "Consultants, Lawyers, and the 'Union Free' Movement in the USA since the 1970s." *Industrial Relations Journal* 33, no. 3 (2002): 197–214.

———. "The Fine Art of Union Busting." *New Labor Forum* 13, no. 2 (Summer 2004): 76–91.

———. "Representatives of Their Own Choosing: Certification, Elections, and Employer Free Speech, 1935–1959." *Seattle University Law Review* 23 (1999–2000): 549–68.

———. "The Union Avoidance Industry in the United States." *BJIR: British Journal of Industrial Relations* 44, no. 4 (2006): 651–75.

Lopez, Steven Henry. *Reorganizing the Rust Belt: An Inside Study of the American Labor Movement.* Berkeley: University of California Press, 2004.

Lovell, Vicky, Heidi Hartmann, and Mish Werschkul. "More than Raising the Floor." In *The Sex of Class: Women Transforming American Labor*, edited by Dorothy Sue Cobble, 35–57. Ithaca, N.Y.: ILR Press, 2007.

Luff, Jennifer. "Justice for Janitors." In *Encyclopedia of U.S. Labor and Working-Class History.* Vol. 2, *G–N, Index*, edited by Eric Arnesen, 729–31. New York: Routledge, 2007.

Lukas, J. Anthony. *Common Ground: A Turbulent Decade in the Lives of Three American Families.* New York: Knopf, 1985.

Lynch, Lisa M., and Marcus H. Sandver. "Determinants of the Decertification Process: Evidence from Employer-Initiated Elections." *Journal of Labor Research* 8, no. 1 (Winter 1987): 85–91.

Lynd, Staughton, and Alice Lynd. *The New Rank and File.* Ithaca, N.Y.: ILR Press, 2000.

MacLean, Nancy. *Freedom Is Not Enough: The Opening of the American Work Place.* New York: Russell Sage Foundation; Cambridge, Mass.: Harvard University Press, 2006.

———. "The Hidden History of Affirmative Action: Working Women's Struggles in the 1970s and the Gender of Class." *Feminist Studies* 25, no. 1 (Spring 1999): 42–78.

———. "Redesigning Dixie with Affirmative Action." In *Gender and the Southern Body Politic: Essays and Comments*, edited by Nancy Bercaw, 161–91. Jackson: University Press of Mississippi, 2000.

Mahon, Rianne, and Lynn Krieger Mytelka. "Industry, the State, and the New Protectionism: Textiles in Canada and France." *International Organization* 37, no. 4 (Autumn 1983): 551–81.

Marshall, F. Ray. *Labor in the South*. Cambridge, Mass.: Harvard University Press, 1967.

Martin, Tara. "The Beginning of Labor's End? Britain's 'Winter of Discontent' and Working-Class Women's Activism." *International Labor and Working-Class History* 75 (2009): 49–67.

McCall, Leslie. "Increasing Class Disparities among Women and the Politics of Gender Equity." In *The Sex of Class: Women Transforming American Labor*, edited by Dorothy Sue Cobble, 15–34. Ithaca, N.Y.: ILR Press, 2007.

McCartin, Joseph A. "Bargaining for the Common Good." *Dissent*, Spring 2016, 128–35.

——. *Collision Course: Ronald Reagan, the Air Traffic Controllers, and the Strike That Changed America*. New York: Oxford University Press, 2011.

——. "'Fire the Hell Out of Them': Sanitation Workers' Struggles and the Normalization of the Striker Replacement Strategy in the 1970s." *Labor: Studies in Working Class History of the Americas* 2, no. 3 (Fall 2005): 67–92.

——. *Labor's Great War: The Struggle for Industrial Democracy and the Origins of Modern American Labor Relations, 1912–1921*. Chapel Hill: University of North Carolina Press, 1997.

——. "Turnabout Years: Public Sector Unionism and the Fiscal Crisis." In *Rightward Bound: Making America Conservative in the 1970s*, edited by Bruce Schulman and Julian E. Zelizer, 210–26. Cambridge, Mass.: Harvard University Press, 2008.

——. "'A Wagner Act for Public Employees': Labor's Deferred Dream and the Rise of Conservatism, 1970–1976." *Journal of American History* 95, no. 1 (2008): 123–48.

McGirr, Lisa. *Suburban Warriors: The Origins of the New American Right*. Princeton, N.J.: Princeton University Press, 2001.

McQuaid, Kim. *Uneasy Partners: Big Business in American Politics, 1945–1990*. Baltimore: Johns Hopkins University Press, 1994.

Metzgar, Jack. *Striking Steel: Solidarity Remembered*. Philadelphia: Temple University Press, 2000.

Middleton, Simon, and Billy G. Smith, eds. *Class Matters: Early North America and the Atlantic World*. Philadelphia: University of Pennsylvania Press, 2008.

Milkman, Ruth. *L.A. Story: Immigrant Workers and the Future of the U.S. Labor Movement*. New York: Russell Sage Foundation, 2006.

——. "Organizing Immigrant Women in New York's Chinatown: An Interview with Katie Quan." In *Women and Unions: Forging a Partnership*, edited by Dorothy Sue Cobble, 281–98. Ithaca, N.Y.: ILR Press, 1993.

——. "Undocumented Immigrant Workers and the Labor Movement." In *Hidden Lives and Human Rights in the United States*, vol. 3, edited by Lois Ann Lorentzen, 35–53. Santa Barbara: Praeger, 2014.

——. "Women's History and the Sears Case." *Feminist Studies* 12, no. 2 (1986): 375–400.

Milkman, Ruth, and Kim Voss, eds. *Rebuilding Labor: Organizing and Organizers in the New Union Movement.* Ithaca, N.Y.: Cornell University Press, 2004.

Minchin, Timothy J. *"Don't Sleep with Stevens!" The J. P. Stevens Campaign and the Struggle to Organize the South, 1963–80.* Gainesville: University Press of Florida, 2005.

——. *Empty Mills: The Fight against Imports and the Decline of the U.S. Textile Industry.* Lanham, Md.: Rowman and Littlefield, 2013.

——. *Hiring the Black Worker: The Racial Integration of the Southern Textile Industry, 1960–1980.* Chapel Hill: University of North Carolina Press, 1999.

——. " 'It Knocked This City to Its Knees': The Closure of Pillowtex Mills in Kannapolis, North Carolina and the Decline of the US Textile Industry." *Labor History* 50, no. 3 (2009): 287–311.

——. *Labor Under Fire: A History of the AFL-CIO Since 1979.* Chapel Hill: University of North Carolina Press, 2017.

——. "Together We Shall Be Heard: Exploring the 1981 'Solidarity Day' Mass March." *Labor: Studies in Working Class History of the Americas* 12, no. 3 (September 2015): 75–96.

——. *What Do We Need a Union For? The TWUA in the South, 1945–1955.* Chapel Hill: University of North Carolina Press, 1997.

Mishel, Lawrence. "Unions, Inequality, and Faltering Middle-Class Wages." Issue Brief #342. Washington, D.C.: Economic Policy Institute, 2012.

——. "The Wedges between Productivity and Median Compensation Growth." Issue Brief #330. Washington, D.C.: Economic Policy Institute, 2012.

Mishel, Lawrence, Josh Bivens, Elise Gould, and Heidi Shierholz. *The State of Working America.* 12th ed. Ithaca, N.Y.: ILR Press, 2012.

Moody, Kim. *An Injury to All: The Decline of American Unionism.* London: Verso, 1988.

——. "Understanding the Rank-and-File Rebellion in the Long 1970s." In *Rebel Rank and File: Labor Militancy and Revolt from Below in the Long 1970s,* edited by Aaron Brenner, Robert Brenner, and Calvin Winslow, 105–46. London: Verso, 2010.

Moreton, Bethany. "Make Payroll, Not War: Business Culture as Youth Culture." In *Rightward Bound: Making America Conservative in the 1970s,* edited by Bruce Schulman and Julian E. Zelizer, 52–70. Cambridge, Mass.: Harvard University Press, 2008.

——. *To Serve God and Wal-Mart: The Making of Christian Free Enterprise.* Cambridge, Mass.: Harvard University Press, 2009.

Muncy, Robyn. "Coal-Fired Reforms: Social Citizenship, Dissident Miners, and the Great Society." *Journal of American History* 96, no. 1 (2009): 72–98.

——. *Relentless Reformer: Josephine Roche and Progressivism in Twentieth-Century America.* Princeton, N.J.: Princeton University Press, 2015.

Nadasen, Premilla. *Household Workers Unite: The Untold Story of African American Women Who Built a Movement.* Boston: Beacon, 2015.

——. *Welfare Warriors: The Welfare Rights Movement in the United States.* New York: Routledge, 2005.

Needleman, Ruth. *Black Freedom Fighters in Steel: The Struggle for Democratic Unionism*. Ithaca, N.Y.: ILR Press, 2003.

Nelson, Bruce. *Divided We Stand: American Workers and the Struggle for Black Equality*. Princeton, N.J.: Princeton University Press, 2001.

Ngai, Mae M. *Impossible Subjects: Illegal Aliens and the Making of Modern America*. Princeton, N.J.: Princeton University Press, 2004.

Nicholson, Philip Yale. *Labor's Story in the United States*. Philadelphia: Temple University Press, 2004.

Nielsen, Georgia Panter. *From Sky Girl to Flight Attendant: Women and the Making of a Union*. Ithaca, N.Y.: ILR Press, 1982.

Noah, Timothy. *The Great Divergence: America's Growing Inequality Crisis and What We Can Do about It*. New York: Bloomsbury, 2012.

Northrup, Herbert Roof. *Organized Labor and the Negro*. New York: Harper and Bros., 1944.

Norwood, Stephen H. *Strike-Breaking and Intimidation: Mercenaries and Masculinity in Twentieth-Century America*. Chapel Hill: University of North Carolina Press, 2002.

Nussbaum, Karen. "Working Women's Insurgent Consciousness." In *The Sex of Class: Women Transforming American Labor*, edited by Dorothy Sue Cobble, 159–76. Ithaca, N.Y.: ILR Press, 2007.

Opler, Daniel J. *For All White-Collar Workers: The Possibilities of Radicalism in New York City's Department Store Unions, 1934–1953*. Columbus: Ohio State University Press, 2007.

Orleck, Annelise. *Common Sense and a Little Fire: Women and Working-Class Politics in the United States, 1900–1965*. Chapel Hill: University of North Carolina Press, 1995.

Ortega, Bob. *In Sam We Trust: The Untold Story of Sam Walton, and How Wal-Mart Is Devouring America*. New York: Times Business, 1998.

Perlstein, Rick. *Nixonland: The Rise of a President and the Fracturing of America*. New York: Scribner, 2008.

Perras, Richard A. "Effective Responses to Union Organizing Attempts in the Banking Industry." *Labor Law Journal* 35, no. 2 (1984): 92–102.

Petrovic, Misha, and Gary G. Hamilton. "Making Global Markets: Wal-Mart and Its Suppliers." In *Wal-Mart: The Face of Twenty-First-Century Capitalism*, edited by Nelson Lichtenstein, 107–41. New York: New Press, 2006.

Phillips, Lisa A. W. *A Renegade Union: Interracial Organizing and Labor Radicalism*. Urbana: University of Illinois Press, 2013.

Phillips-Fein, Kim. "Business Conservatism on the Shop Floor: Anti-Union Campaigns in the 1950s." *Labor: Studies in Working-Class History of the Americas* 7, no. 2 (2010): 9–26.

——. *Invisible Hands: The Making of the Conservative Movement from the New Deal to Reagan*. New York: W. W. Norton, 2009.

Pier, Carol, and Human Rights Watch. *Discounting Rights: Wal-Mart's Violation of U.S. Workers' Right to Freedom of Association.* New York: Human Rights Watch, 2007.

Piketty, Thomas. *Capital in the Twenty-First Century.* Translated by Arthur Goldhammer. Cambridge, Mass.: Belknap Press of Harvard University Press, 2014.

Poole, Mary. *The Segregated Origins of Social Security.* Chapel Hill: University of North Carolina Press, 2006.

Portelli, Alessandro. *The Death of Luigi Trastulli, and Other Stories: Form and Meaning in Oral History.* Albany: State University of New York Press, 1990.

Quinn, Cornelius, Thomas Hill, and James L. Nichols. *Maintaining Nonunion Status.* Boston: CBI, 1982.

Quinn, Robert P., and Graham L. Staines. *The 1977 Quality of Employment Survey: Descriptive Statistics, with Comparison Data from the 1969–70 and the 1972–73 Surveys.* Ann Arbor: Survey Research Center, Institute for Social Research, University of Michigan, 1979.

Reed, Toure F. "Title VII, the Rise of Workplace Fairness, and the Decline of Economic Justice, 1964–2013." *Labor: Studies in Working-Class History of the Americas* 11, no. 3 (2014): 31–36.

Richards, Lawrence. *Union-Free America: Workers and Antiunion Culture.* Urbana: University of Illinois Press, 2008.

Robinson, Donald Allen. "Two Movements in Pursuit of Equal Employment Opportunity." *Signs* 4, no. 3 (Spring 1979): 413–33.

Rolf, David. *The Fight for Fifteen: The Right Wage for a Working America.* New York: New Press, 2016.

Roof, Tracy. *American Labor, Congress, and the Welfare State, 1935–2010.* Baltimore: Johns Hopkins University Press, 2011.

Root, Lawrence S. *Fringe Benefits: Social Insurance in the Steel Industry.* Beverly Hills: Sage, 1982.

Roper Center, Cornell University. "United States: Elections." Accessed September 13, 2016. http://ropercenter.cornell.edu/polls/us-elections /presidential-elections/.

Rosen, Ellen Israel. *Making Sweatshops: The Globalization of the U.S. Apparel Industry.* Berkeley: University of California Press, 2002.

Rosen, Ruth. *The World Split Open: How the Modern Women's Movement Changed America.* New York: Viking, 2000.

Rosenblum, Jonathan D. *Copper Crucible: How the Arizona Miners' Strike of 1983 Recast Labor-Management Relations in America.* Ithaca, N.Y.: ILR Press, 1995.

Rosenfeld, Jake. *What Unions No Longer Do.* Cambridge, Mass.: Harvard University Press, 2014.

Rosenfeld, Jake, Patrick Denise, and Jennifer Laird. "Union Decline Lowers Wages of Nonunion Workers." Washington, D.C.: Economic Policy Institute, 2016.

Rosenzweig, Roy, Nelson Lichtenstein, Joshua Brown, and David Jaffee. *Who Built America? Working People and the Nation's History.* Vol. 2. 3rd ed. Boston: Bedford/St. Martin's, 2008.

Rowan, Richard L., and Robert E. Barr. *Employee Relations Trends and Practices in the Textile Industry*. Philadelphia: Industrial Research Unit, Wharton School, University of Pennsylvania, 1987.

Rowland, Debra. *The Boundaries of Her Body: The Troubling History of Women's Rights in America*. Naperville, Ill.: Sphinx, 2004.

Rudy, Preston. "'Justice for Janitors,' Not 'Compensation for Custodians': The Political Context and Organizing in San Jose and Sacramento." In *Rebuilding Labor: Organizing and Organizers in the New Union Movement*, edited by Ruth Milkman and Kim Voss, 133–49. Ithaca, N.Y.: Cornell University Press, 2004.

Ruiz, Vicky. *From Out of the Shadows: Mexican Women in Twentieth Century America*. New York: Oxford University Press, 1998.

Sabagh, Georges. "Los Angeles, a Work of New Immigrants: An Image of Things to Come?" In *Migration Policies in Europe and the United States*, edited by Giacomo Luciani, 97–126. Norwell, Mass.: Kluwer Academic, 1993.

Sacks, Karen Brodkin. *Caring by the Hour: Women, Work and Organizing at Duke Medical Center*. Urbana: University of Illinois Press, 1988.

Salvati, Michele. "May 1968 and the Hot Autumn of 1969: The Response of Two Ruling Classes." In *Organizing Interests in Western Europe: Pluralism, Corporatism, and the Transformation of Politics*, edited by Suzanne Berger, Joint Committee on Western Europe, 331–36. Cambridge: Cambridge University Press, 1981.

Sandbrook, Dominic. *Mad as Hell: The Crisis of the 1970s and the Rise of the Populist Right*. New York: Alfred A. Knopf, 2011.

Sassen, Saskia. *The Mobility of Labor and Capital: A Study in International Investment and Labor Flow*. Cambridge: Cambridge University Press, 1988.

Schatz, Ronald W. *The Electrical Workers: A History of Labor at General Electric and Westinghouse, 1923–1960*. Urbana: University of Illinois Press, 1983.

Schlossberg, Stephen I., and Judith A. Scott. *Organizing and the Law*. 4th ed. Washington, D.C.: Bureau of National Affairs, 1991.

Schor, Juliet B. *The Overworked American: The Unexpected Decline of Leisure*. New York: Basic Books, 1992.

Schulman, Bruce J. *From Cotton Belt to Sunbelt: Federal Policy, Economic Development, and the Transformation of the South, 1938–1980*. New York: Oxford University Press, 1991.

———. *The Seventies: The Great Shift in American Culture, Society, and Politics*. New York: Free Press, 2001.

Schulman, Bruce J., and Julian E. Zelizer. *Rightward Bound: Making America Conservative in the 1970s*. Cambridge, Mass.: Harvard University Press, 2008.

Seifer, Nancy, and Barbara Wertheimer. "New Approaches to Collective Power: Four Working Women's Organizations." In *Women Organizing: An Anthology*, edited by Bernice Cummings and Victoria Schuck, 152–83. Metuchen, N.J.: Scarecrow, 1979.

Self, Robert O. *American Babylon: Race and the Struggle for Postwar Oakland*. Princeton, N.J.: Princeton University Press, 2003.

Shaw, Randy. *Beyond the Fields: Cesar Chavez, the UFW, and the Struggle for Justice in the 21st Century.* Berkeley: University of California Press, 2008.

Shermer, Elizabeth Tandy. *Sunbelt Capitalism: Phoenix and the Transformation of American Politics.* Philadelphia: University of Pennsylvania Press, 2013.

Silver, Beverly J. *Forces of Labor: Workers' Movements and Globalization since 1870.* Cambridge: Cambridge University Press, 2003.

Skocpol, Theda. *Protecting Soldiers and Mothers: The Political Origins of Social Policy in the United States.* Cambridge, Mass.: Belknap Press of Harvard University Press, 1992.

Slaughter, Jane. "Corporate Campaigns: Labor Enlists Community Support." In *Building Bridges: The Emerging Grassroots Coalition of Labor and Community,* edited by Jeremy Brecher and Tim Costello, 47–56. New York: Monthly Review Press, 1990.

Smith, Hedrick. *Who Stole the American Dream? Can We Get It Back?* New York: Random House, 2012.

Smith, Robert Michael. *From Blackjacks to Briefcases: A History of Commercialized Strikebreaking and Unionbusting in the United States.* Athens: Ohio University Press, 2003.

Standing, Guy. *The Precariat: The New Dangerous Class.* London: Bloomsbury Academic, 2011.

Stein, Judith. *Pivotal Decade: How the United States Traded Factories for Finance in the Seventies.* New Haven, Conn.: Yale University Press, 2010.

——. *Running Steel, Running America: Race, Economic Policy and the Decline of Liberalism.* Chapel Hill: University of North Carolina Press, 1998.

Stein, Leslie. "General Measures to Assist Workers and Firms in Adjusting to Injury from Freer Trade." *American Journal of Economics and Sociology* 42, no. 3 (July 1983): 315–27.

Stern, Andy. *Raising the Floor: How a Universal Basic Income Can Renew Our Economy and Rebuild the American Dream.* With Lee Kravitz. New York: Public Affairs, 2016.

Stevens, Beth. "Blurring the Boundaries: How the Federal Government Has Influenced Welfare Benefits in the Private Sector." In *The Politics of Social Policy in the United States,* edited by Margaret Weir, Ann Shola Orloff, and Theda Skocpol, 123–48. Princeton, N.J.: Princeton University Press, 1988.

Stiglitz, Joseph E. *Globalization and Its Discontents.* New York: W. W. Norton, 2002.

——. *The Price of Inequality.* New York: W. W. Norton, 2012.

Stillman, Don. "Runaways: A Call to Action." *Southern Exposure* 4 (Spring/Summer 1976): 50–59.

Stone, Chad, Danilo Trisi, Arloc Sherman, and Emily Horton. "A Guide to Statistics on Historical Trends in Income Inequality." Center on Budget and Policy Priorities. Last updated November 7, 2016. http://www.cbpp.org/cms/?fa=view&id=3629.

Strom, Sharon H. *Beyond the Typewriter: Gender, Class, and the Origins of Modern American Office Work, 1900–1930.* Urbana: University of Illinois Press, 1992.

Sugrue, Thomas J. " 'The Largest Civil Rights Organization Today': Title VII and the Transformation of the Public Sector." *Labor: Studies in Working-Class History of the Americas* 11, no. 3 (2014): 25–29.

——. *The Origins of the Urban Crisis: Race and Inequality in Postwar Detroit.* Princeton, N.J.: Princeton University Press, 1996.

Tazewell, William L. *Newport News Shipbuilding, the First Century.* Newport News: Mariners' Museum, 1986.

Tepperman, Jean. *Not Servants, Not Machines: Office Workers Speak Out!* Boston: Beacon, 1976.

Thompson, E. P. *The Making of the English Working Class.* New York: Pantheon Books, 1964.

Thompson, Heather Ann, ed. *Speaking Out: Activism and Protest in the 1960's and 1970's.* Englewood Cliffs, N.J.: Prentice-Hall, 2009.

Tiffany, Paul A. *The Decline of American Steel: How Management, Labor, and Government Went Wrong.* New York: Oxford University Press, 1988.

Tilly, Chris, and Francoise Carre. "Endnote: Retail Work—Perceptions and Reality." In *Retail Work*, edited by Irena Grugulis and Ödül Bozkurt, 297–306. Basingstoke, U.K.: Palgrave Macmillan, 2011.

Tomlins, Christopher L. *The State and the Unions: Labor Relations, Law, and the Organized Labor Movement in America, 1880–1960.* Cambridge: Cambridge University Press, 1985.

Townley, Barbara. *Labor Law Reform in US Industrial Relations.* Aldershot, England: Gower, 1986.

Troy, Leo. "Twilight for Organized Labor." In *The Future of Private Sector Unionism in the United States*, edited by James T. Bennett and Bruce E. Kaufman, 59–76. Armonk, N.Y.: M. E. Sharpe, 2002.

Troy, Leo, and Neil Sheflin. *U.S. Union Sourcebook: Membership, Finances, Structure, Directory.* West Orange, N.J.: Industrial Relations Data and Information Services, 1985.

Turk, Katherine. "Labor's Pink-Collar Aristocracy: The National Secretaries Association's Encounters with Feminism in the Age of Automation." *Labor: Studies in Working-Class History of the Americas* 11, no. 2 (2014): 85–109.

Vanderburg, Timothy W. *Cannon Mills and Kannapolis: Persistent Paternalism in a Textile Town.* Knoxville: University of Tennessee Press, 2013.

Vogel, David. *Fluctuating Fortunes: The Political Power of Business in America.* New York: Basic Books, 1989.

Voos, Paula B. "Trends in Union Organizing Expenditures, 1953–1977." *Industrial and Labor Relations Review* 38, no. 1 (1984): 52–63.

Waldinger, Roger, Chris Erickson, Ruth Milkman, Daniel J. B. Mitchell, Abel Valenzuela, Kent Wong, and Maurine Zeitlin. "Helots No More." In *Organizing* to Win: New Research on Union Strategies, edited by Kate Bronfenbrenner, Sheldon Friedman, Richard W. Hurd, Rudolph A. Oswald, and Ronald L. Seeber, 102–19. Ithaca, N.Y.: ILR Press, 1998.

Waterhouse, Benjamin C. *Lobbying America: The Politics of Business from Nixon to NAFTA*. Princeton, N.J.: Princeton University Press, 2013.

Weil, David. *The Fissured Workplace: Why Work Became So Bad for So Many and What Can Be Done to Improve It*. Cambridge, Mass.: Harvard University Press, 2014.

Weir, Margaret. *Politics and Jobs: The Boundaries of Employment Policy in the United States*. Princeton, N.J.: Princeton University Press, 1992.

Westcott, Diane N., and Robert W. Bednarzik. "Employment and Unemployment: A Report on 1980." *Monthly Labor Review* 104, no. 2 (February 1981): 4–14.

Western, Bruce. *Between Class and Market: Postwar Unionization in the Capitalist Democracies*. Princeton, N.J.: Princeton University Press, 1997.

Western, Bruce, and Jake Rosenfeld. "Unions, Norms, and the Rise in U.S. Wage Inequality." *American Sociological Review* 76, no. 4 (2011): 513–37.

Windham, Anna Lane. "Knocking on Labor's Door: Union Organizing and the Origins of the New Economic Divide (1968–1985)." Ph.D. diss., University of Maryland, College Park, 2015.

———. "'A Sense of Possibility and a Belief in Collective Power': A Labor Strategy Talk with Karen Nussbaum." *Labor: Studies in Working-Class History of the Americas* 12, no. 3 (2015): 35–51.

———. "Signing Up in the Shipyard: Organizing Newport News and Reinterpreting the 1970s." *Labor: Studies in Working-Class History of the Americas* 10, no. 2 (2013): 31–53.

———. "Why Alt-Labor Groups Are Making Employers Mighty Nervous." *American Prospect*, January 30, 2014. http://prospect.org/article/why-alt-Labor-groups -are-making-employers-mighty-nervous.

Winslow, Calvin. "Overview: The Rebellion from Below, 1965–1981." In *Rebel Rank and File: Labor Militancy and Revolt from Below in the Long 1970s*, edited by Aaron Brenner, Robert Brenner, and Calvin Winslow, 1–35. London: Verso, 2010.

Woman Alive! Nine to Five. VHS. Directed by Suzanne Jasper. New York: WNET and Ms. Magazine, 1975.

Wood, Steve, and Neil Wrigley. "Market Power and Regulation: The Last Great U.S. Department Store Consolidation?" *International Journal of Retail and Distribution Management* 35, no. 1 (2007): 20–37.

Wright, Gavin. *Sharing the Prize: The Economics of the Civil Rights Revolution in the American South*. Cambridge, Mass.: Belknap Press of Harvard University Press, 2013.

Zieger, Robert H. *The CIO, 1935–1955*. Chapel Hill: University of North Carolina Press, 1995.

———. "Textile Workers and Historians." In *Organized Labor in the Twentieth-Century South*, edited by Robert H. Zieger, 35–59. Knoxville: University of Tennessee Press, 1991.

Index

Note: Illustrations are indicated by page numbers in *italics*.

District 65, 164
District 925, 37, 38, 40, 172–75, 177, 179
District 1199, 45, 55, 70, *181*
Diversity in union membership, 7, 9, 22, 46, 93, 96, 142, 180; African-Americans, 29, 41–47; immigrants, 53–54; women, 31, 35–40
Dixon, Leola, 131, 133
Dodge Revolutionary Union Movement (DRUM), 30–31
Domestic workers, 44, 45
Donahue, Phil, 57
Donahue, Thomas, 185
Dotson, Donald, 182–83
Duke University: 47, 125

Earman, Michael, 137, 138
Economic divide, 5–6, 128, 150, 186, 192
Economic prosperity: broadly shared, 6, 11; collective bargaining and, 16–17, 141
Economic security, 15–16, 18–19, 30, 49, 81, 89, 92, 190
Eizenstat, Stuart, 77, 78
Elections, union. *See* Union elections
Employee Free Choice Act, 190
Employee representation plan (ERP), 87–88
Employers: antiunionism and, 8, 47, 56, 57–61; baby boomers and, 32–33; Civil Rights Act and, 33; collective bargaining and, 16, 20; fear of organizing by African-Americans and women, 70–71, 81; increased willingness to break labor law, 65–66; motivations of, in antiunionism, 58–61; political activity by, 59–60, 61–65; resistance of, to organizing, 3, 8, 20, 23–24, 52–53, 65–68, 73–76; social welfare and, 8, 16, 19, 26; Taft-Hartley Act and, 18–19; threats by, 75; unfair labor practices by, 65–66, *66*, *68*; union busting and; 57–81; union elections and, 17–18
Equal Credit Opportunity Act, 35
Equal Employment Opportunity Act (EEO), 71, 104
Equal Employment Opportunity Commission (EEOC), 8; African Americans and, 42, 44; Cannon Mills and, 111; flight attendants and, 39; gender and, 40, 104, 143; publishing and, 162; retail and, 143; shipyards and, 89–91; textiles and, 109; union busting and, 70, 71
Equal Rights Amendment, 41, *188*
Europe, 16, 150
Executive Order 10988, 25

Fair Labor Standards Act, 21, 45, 77
Fanning, John, 64–65
Farah Manufacturing Company, 54; union organizing and, 54, 157, 176
Farrell, Nancy, 161–62, 165
Feminism, 35, 152. *See also* Gender discrimination; Women
Fiber, Fabric, and Apparel Coalition for Trade (FFACT), 117–18
Finance: shift to, as locus of economic power, 5, 59; unionization in, 38; union voters in, *37*; women in, 36. *See also* Bank workers
Firings, by employers in union campaigns, 65–66, 94, 122, 147, 183
Fleischman, Mark, 121
Flight attendants, 7–8, 39–40
Fonda, Jane, 171, 172
Food Lion, 189
Ford, 28, 32, 61
Ford, Gerald, 58, 77
Ford, Harold, Sr., 95
Foreign Trade and Investment Act, 124
France, 16
Frankel, Carl, 94

and, 60; union organizing and, 4;
waning of, 58–59; in World War II,
44. *See also* Cannon Mills; Industrial
sector; Shipyards; Textile industry
March Group, 63
Marshall, Ray, 98
Maternity benefits, 41, 54, 104, 159, 163
Mathias, Adam, 136, 150
May Company, 144–45
McBride, Lloyd, 100
McNutt, Thomas, 135, 145, 149
Meany, George, 6, 40, 63, 80, 116–17
Melnick, Herbert G., 57, 69, 75
Midwestern Employers Council, 68
Miller, Edward, 64
Miners, 19, 30, 177, 182
Modern Management Methods (Three
M), 57, 68, 69, 70, 166, 173
Monroe Auto Equipment Company,
33–34
Moore, Robert, 88, 94
Multi-Fiber Arrangement (MFA), 116,
117, 123
Murdock, David H., 119–22, 125
Murphy, Thomas A., 78. *See also*
General Motors (GM).

National Action Committee for Labor
Law Reform, 79
National Association for the Advance-
ment of Colored People (NAACP), 80,
89, 95, 111, 130, 180, 224n12
National Association of Manufacturers
(NAM), 60, 63, 78–79, 90
National Association of Working
Women, 170–72
National Education Association (NEA),
31
National Federation of Independent
Business, 78
National Labor Relations Act (NLRA), 17,
18, 55, 204n7, 219n44; African
Americans and, 21; company unions

and, 87; exclusions in, 22, 54;
Taft-Hartley and, 18; union organizing
and, 23–24; weakening of, 65, 190
National Labor Relations Board
(NLRB), 1–3, *2*, 196–97; African-
Americans and, 41, 111; alternatives
to, 185, 189; captive audience
meetings and, 23; Carter administration and, 64, 78, 102; colleges and,
37; company unions and, 87, 130;
conservatives and, 18; eligible voters,
3, *4*, 36, *37*, 41, *49*, 183–84, *197*;
enforcement by, 17–18, 23–24, 34, 54,
66, 94, 96, 102, 111; finance and, 39;
George H. W. Bush administration
and, 102; hospitals and, 45; immigrants and, 52–53; Johnson administration, 62; Kennedy administration
and, 62, 135; Labor Law Reform
Group and, 62, 64–65; management
consultants and, 68, 72, 73–74; Nixon
administration and, 64, 135;
persistence of voters in 1970s, 3, 9,
10, 28, 35, 105; Reagan administration and, 102, 181, 182–83; retail and,
129, 135, 140–41, 146, 147–49;
slowness of processes, 54, 80, 97;
Sunbelt and, 48, *49*, 51; social
welfare and, 19; staff of, 96, 115, 140;
Taft-Hartley and, 18; unfair labor
practices and, 65, *66*, *68*, 125; union
organizing and, 23–24, 28, 93, 113,
148–49, 165, 173; union busting and,
66, 73–74; weakening of, 10–11, 23,
64, 153, 183, 186, 192
National Organization for Women, 80
National Right to Work Committee,
141–42
National Urban League, 80
National War Labor Board, 19
New Deal, 6, 17, 21, 61–62, 132, 153, 186,
192
New England Merchants Bank, 168

Working class, 1–3, 7; civil rights movement and, 3, 31, 180; defined, 201n7; diversification of, 4,7–9, 12, 29–30, 180; employers and, 8–9, 56, 70, 108, 150; global, 9; globalization and, 86, 108, 126; immigrants and, 51–55; politics and, 187–188; power; 6, 10, 85–86, 159; racial divisions in, 46–47; struggle and, 99, 129; unions and, 9, 11–12, 173; white, 7, 31, 46–47, 187–188; women in, 132, 152, 154, 173–175. *See also* Class.

World War II, 18, 19, 42, 44, 91, 109

Yale University, 38, 69
Yarrow, Mary Beth, 38

38 - resistance to clerical unions in universities

43 - civil rights = union rights

51 - immigrant organizing
59 - manufacturing ⇒ finance

68 - Modern/Management Methods

70 - RACE & GENDER

72 - capital flight

81 - union decline may not a natural process

87 - union victory Newport News

92 - what did they want
95 - complexities of Race PSA mid class blacks USNA work class dm
98 - 1978 strikes across various labor industries
102 - NLRB Boards vary under diff. presidents
103 - what a union can do
110 - Dairy Crawford → Cannon Mills civil rights & mom in tandem
111 - lack of gov support?
119 - out of local harns = newdoc
120 - Cannon mills blames imports & globalization
128 - Resistance in RETAIL → Woodward & Lothrop
135 - chain stores → impossible to organize all
145 - possibility of a worker owned company
152 - 9to5 workers assoc [women, clerians]
155 - women's lib ≥ power + authority of the boss
180 - solidarity Day
187 - unions decline, what is lost? decrease in political engagement
188 - "A forty-year sustained attack on unions has hit its mark
190 - problem w/ LW solution of employer social welfare role